TRAUMA AND THE ONTOLOGY OF THE MODERN SUBJECT

Recent scholarship has inquired into the socio-historical, discursive genesis of trauma. *Trauma and the Ontology of the Modern Subject*, however, seeks what has not been actualized in trauma studies – that is, how the necessity and unassailable intensity of trauma is fastened to its historical emergence. We must ask not only what trauma means for the individual person's biography, but also *what it means to be the historical subject of trauma*. In other words, how does being human in this current period of history implicate one's lived possibilities that are threatened, and perhaps framed, through trauma? Foucauldian sensibilities inform a critical and structural analysis that is hermeneutically grounded.

Drawing on the history of ideas and on Lacan's work in particular, John L. Roberts argues that what we mean by trauma has developed over time, and that it is intimately tied with an ontology of the subject; that is to say, what it is to be, and what it means to be human. He argues that modern subjectivity – as articulated by Heidegger, Levinas, and Lacan – is structurally traumatic, founded in its finitude as self-withdrawal in time, its temporal self-absence becoming the very condition for agency, truth, and knowledge. The book also argues that this fractured temporal horizon – as an effect of an interrupting Otherness or alterity – is obscured through the discourses and technologies of the psy-disciplines (psychiatry, psychology, and psychotherapy). Consideration is given to social, political, and economic consequences of this concealment.

Trauma and the Ontology of the Modern Subject will be of enduring interest to psychoanalysts and psychotherapists as well as scholars of philosophy and cultural studies.

John L. Roberts is Associate Professor in the Department of Psychology, University of West Georgia. His research interests include theoretical and philosophical approaches to psychology, histories of consciousness and subjectivity, and psychoanalysis.

TRAUMA AND THE ONTOLOGY OF THE MODERN SUBJECT

Historical Studies in Philosophy, Psychology, and Psychoanalysis

John L. Roberts
With an Afterword by Kareen R. Malone

Routledge
Taylor & Francis Group

LONDON AND NEW YORK

First published 2018
by Routledge
2 Park Square, Milton Park, Abingdon, Oxon OX14 4RN

and by Routledge
711 Third Avenue, New York, NY 10017

Routledge is an imprint of the Taylor & Francis Group, an informa business

© 2018 John L. Roberts

British Library Cataloguing-in-Publication Data
A catalogue record for this book is available from the British Library.

Library of Congress Cataloging-in-Publication Data
Names: Roberts, John L.
Title: Trauma and the ontology of the modern subject : historical studies
    in philosophy, psychology, and psychoanalysis / John L. Roberts.
Description: New York : Routledge, 2018. | Includes bibliographical
    references and index.
Identifiers: LCCN 2017016010 (print) | LCCN 2017034969 (ebook) |
    ISBN 9781315681931 (Master) | ISBN 9781317401650 (ePub) | ISBN
    9781317401667 (Web PDF) | ISBN 9781317401643 (Mobi/Kindle) |
    ISBN 9781138826724 (hardback : alk. paper) | ISBN 9781138826724
    (paperback : alk. paper) | ISBN 9781315681931 (ebk)
Subjects: LCSH: Psychic trauma—History. | Psychology. | Psychology. |
    Psychoanalysis.
Classification: LCC RC552.T7 (ebook) | LCC RC552.T7 R63 2018 (print) |
    DDC 616.85/21—dc23
LC record available at https://lccn.loc.gov/2017016010

ISBN: 978-1-138-82672-4 (hbk)
ISBN: 978-1-138-82673-1 (pbk)
ISBN: 978-1-315-68193-1 (ebk)

Typeset in Bembo
by Apex CoVantage, LLC

For Laura, Alexander, Zachary, Rachel, and Sophie

CONTENTS

ACKNOWLEDGEMENTS

I am deeply grateful to Kareen Malone, Christopher Aanstoos, and Hugh Craw-ford, as well as colleagues and students in the Psychology Department at the University of West Georgia, who have nurtured and encouraged this project. I also wish to extend my gratitude to colleagues outside of my department, who have been helpful all along the way. Without the support of my family, and my intimate circle of friends, this work would have not been possible.

Portions of Chapters 2 and 3 of this volume were first published in my article "Trauma, Technology and the Ontology of the Modern Subject," that appeared in *Subjectivity* (2013, 6.3, pp. 298–319), and in my chapter "Temporality, Alterity, and Traumatic Ethics," that appeared in *In the Wake of Trauma: Psychology and Philosophy for the Suffering Other* (Eds. E. Severson, B. Becker, and D. Goodman, Duquesne, 2016, pp. 155–173), reprinted by kind permission of Duquesne University Press. Portions of Chapter 4 are from my article in press "Obsessional Subjectivity in Societies of Discipline and Control," appearing in *Theory & Psychology*.

INTRODUCTION

Some time ago, I sat with a man dying of cancer. Sleepless in the days before his death, he sat on a couch in his modest home speaking with me of the most significant experiences of his life – his parents' divorce, father's death, and relationship with an estranged son. As his life dwindled, he became drawn to the receding horizon of those elusive questions: *Who am I? Who have I become? Who was I in the end?* I felt honored to be with my friend's struggle, to be allowed into this most precious of spaces, where his being could be actualized and memorialized. I am always deeply affected by these conversations, where we take hold of our own being in death and in life. Yet, I am also curious about this experience. Where did it come from, and what does it mean to ask oneself who one is? Strikingly, however, the pursuit of self-knowledge is far from an optional one, a luxury of our age. For us modern Western subjects, questions of identity – premised on biographical memory – inform our own sense of responsibility to others and ourselves. We may say, "I'm sorry to disappoint you, but *that's just who I am.*" Underlying conventional moral imperatives is the more foundational injunction to take possession of *who one is*. Therefore, we place an ethical value on knowing and speaking to our own idiosyncratic being, which we have the obligation to reconstruct through our own time.

One's reconstruction of biography, however, can break down, leaving gaps in memory. In other words, memory may be disrupted, or even diseased. Trauma is precisely that psychological and cultural architecture that allows us to understand how events of both formative and intervening intensity may dislocate our sense of who we are, and how pathogenic memories form. Certainly for contemporary life, the intensities of rape, torture, genocide, and accidents are thought of as traumatic. But this was not always the case. Suffering, as the contingent intervention of external events with searing intensity, did not always bear upon the biographical being of the subject, pressing into memory as unrepresentable, unmasterable. As Ian Hacking

Gaps reveal the structure.

(1995) remarks, "One feature of the modern sensibility is dazzling in its implausibility: the idea that what has been forgotten is what forms our character, our personality, our soul" (p. 209). Beginning in the nineteenth century, trauma first emerges in connection with railway accidents as "railway spine," connected as part of a wide web of knowledge around the doubling of consciousness, which included mesmerism, multiple personality, and hysteria – all involving an interruption in recollected experience. What follows from Charcot (1889), Freud (1920/1961), and Janet (1925) to van der Kolk (2014) and other clinical discourses is that trauma appears etched into the fabric of not only the way we think and speak, but also how we are affected and constituted. Such discourses embody the tension between repression and dissociation as ordering theoretical principles, which implicate the status of trauma as a discrete experience over against one more structural to the modern subject. Pursuant to differing theoretical strategies, and responding to differing socio-historical conditions, the shifting ground of psychiatric and psychological classification, thus, indicates important yet distinctive ways in which our struggles are encoded, recognized, and addressed. For instance, PTSD (post-traumatic stress disorder), as well-documented (Young, 1995), foregrounds acute, event-based trauma, whose prototypical instance is the wartime experience of the American Vietnam soldier, and more recently such narrowly constituted understandings have been challenged to include more developmentally chronic deprivations and violations (e.g., Herman, 1992). These formulations are central for the disease model understanding of trauma, and for its standardized, technological remediations in cognitive and behavioral therapies, among others. Alongside these developments, psychoanalytic thinking persists, trauma being the originary epicenter of a division of human being, and fundamentally formative of a subjectivity circulating around events in early life that displace memory. Trauma – especially for Lacanian perspectives – alters us in taking something from us, alienating us from ourselves, but giving us a different, an Other being in return. Moreover, these understandings of trauma as primordial would ostensibly include existential-phenomenological renderings such as that by Stolorow (2011) or Bracken (2002), where our being-in-the-world is unsettled as part of our condition as beings thrown into time.

Beyond the world of the clinic, trauma becomes not only a way of understanding individual being as a doubling of consciousness into what has been remembered and forgotten, but as the temporal rupture of identity trauma also appears as a wound to the social psyche and body; our culture marks time traumatically. It would be difficult to imagine the First World War as it has been represented without recourse to a theory of traumatic neurosis. The horrors of life in the trenches, the seemingly random yet mechanized slaughter, the putrid stench of death, the presence of rats "eating heartily" (Fussell, 2013) ruptured not only individual lives but also a Victorian worldview adhering to a rigidly exalted sense of human mastery, reason, and prudence. Likewise, the Holocaust is almost inconceivable without the framework of psychological trauma, as an event without witness, dividing its victim from what is human and outstripping its own status as atrocity or even as an archetypal expression of human evil and cruelty. As Dori Laub (1995) suggests, the Holocaust constitutes a singularly modern event problematizing individual and collective memory:

> What precisely made a Holocaust out of the event is the unique way in which, during its historical occurrence, *the event produced no witnesses* . . . the inherently incomprehensible *and* deceptive psychological structure of the event precluded its own witnessing, even by its very victims.
>
> *(p. 65)*

The nexus of traumatic suffering and Holocaust memory has given rise to a domain of psychosocial inquiry, multidimensional in scope, that not only seeks a zero-point in the abyss of genocide as a scar into modernity itself but charts across time its traumatic effects intergenerationally (Auerhahn & Laub, 1998; Rapoport, 2011). Moreover, recent scholarship has, similarly, demonstrated the intersection of biographical and cultural suffering in African-American experiences of shame, inner destitution, and double consciousness following years upon years of political, economic, and cultural oppression (Graff, 2011; Gump, 2010). Hence, modern subjectivity, as erased or altered in the void of trauma, mirrors historical and cultural trauma, where shared realities are both simultaneously eclipsed and born. In the field of cultural and literary studies, the nomadic movement of trauma out of purely psychiatric and psychological contexts is especially prominent in the work of Caruth (1996, 2002, 2013), who synthesizes psychoanalytic and post-structuralist understandings to postulate a traumatic basis for history itself. Moreover, trauma has conceptually and impressively served scholarship seeking to make sense of post-colonial oppression and suffering (Craps, 2015). In some parallel in the field of sociology, trauma has made its presence felt as "the acute discomfort entering into the core of the collectivity's sense of its own identity" (Alexander, 2012, p. 15), which has been productively applied in the context of African-American cultural identities, among others (Eyerman, 2001).

Unlike syndromes shifting in successive revisions of the *Diagnostic and Statistical Manual of Mental Disorders*, trauma is – thus – foremost among the excursions of the psy-disciplines to escape the narrow confines of psychopathology. Dissimilar to such diagnostic entities as attention deficit hyperactivity disorder (ADHD) or Dependent Personality as momentary accretions serving institutional normalization, the logic of trauma – as temporal dispossession – is deeply embedded in our psychological, cultural, and historical being. Yet, such imperial territorialization of the discourse of trauma by disparate disciplines (such as literary theory or sociology) – especially those serving to embed traumatic suffering within cultural memory – tends to render invisible its specifically historical genesis as a structural mode of subjectivity. Nonetheless, though a certain theoretical and conceptual fog obscures the appearance of trauma within psychiatric and psychological discourses of the nineteenth century as pertaining specifically to the birth of the modern subject within human sciences, over the past several decades critical approaches have appeared that locate such disciplinary knowledge within its particular socio-temporal clearing. For the history of ideas, Hacking (2002) adopts Foucauldian distance that grounds the *a priori* conditions of psychological notions of memory, multiple personality, and trauma – the latter as a way of "making up" a certain sort of person. Hacking's work is well known as historicist, but philosophically informed. For Foucault (1975/1995), institutions bearing power/ knowledge fashion human beings into subjects, producing moral, ethical, and economic effects. For many, Foucault's approaches may seemingly flatten a subjective position into a discursive or material effect. Yet, a subject position also retains a genesis – as the constellation of particular possibilities – within these disciplines.

Trauma, in its psy-formulations as a nexus of discourse and practice, becomes available to distribute resources, exculpate one from moral/legal liability, and for institutions to locate "traumatized" subjects recognizable in their brokenness. Many excavations and genealogies of trauma have been performed with care, and the work of Young (1995), Leys (2000), and Fassin and Rechtman (2009) demonstrate critical distance towards the concept of trauma, coupled with the admission that it is no less indispensable because of its socio-historical contingency. The necessity and unassailable intensity of trauma, strangely fastened to its emergence, demands that we deepen a simply historicist project. We must not only ask questions regarding the psychological templates of trauma, or its socio-historical location; we must begin to address the questions of its meaning for the modern subject. We must, thus, ask not only what trauma means for the individual person, but also *what it means to be the historical subject of trauma*. In other words, beyond the particular meaning of a specific person's trauma, what does it mean to be a modern subject whose possibilities are threatened, and perhaps even originally framed, through trauma? For the individual person and for knowledge itself (in philosophy, psychology, and psychoanalysis), beginning in the nineteenth century, memory and temporality are traumatically disrupted. Thus, another question emerges: *How is traumatic subjectivity implicated in problematic discourses on temporality and memory*? In other words, how does the victim's trauma mediate and mirror a certain temporal crisis in philosophical, psychological, and psychoanalytic discourses? Moreover, as the historical discourses forming trauma almost without exception correspond to clinical techniques for lessening suffering, a further question arises: *What is the significance to the modern subject for the technological remediation of traumatic effects*? What does it mean to therapeutically address the pathogenic memory borne by traumatic suffering? What structural regularities underlie these discourses? How do these technologies discipline or fashion a certain kind of subject? What forms of ethics – modes of self-relation in the Foucauldian sense – are implied in these practices, and what are the alternative possibilities for counter-ethics? Finally, *what are the socio-political ends to which technological repair of the subject's temporally rent being are deployed*? In its latent possibilities of negation, how does trauma – organized in normalizing practices and discourses – support the revealing of certain functional capacities for agency and biographical selfhood? How does traumatic subjectivity, and its disrupted being-in-time, both participate in and problematize post-industrial forms of governmentality, resting on biopolitical concerns with the welfare of populations?

In the main, these are ontological and hermeneutic questions, even if histori-cally emergent. Thus, in the appearance of trauma, the blending of Heideggerian sensibilities and Foucauldian criticality will deepen the analysis under consid-eration. In his final interview, Foucault remarked that Heidegger had been an "essential philosopher" for his work (Raynor, 2007). Within this overall arc, in an interview with Hubert Dreyfus and Paul Rabinow, Foucault (1983) outlines a "historical ontology" of the ways human beings constitute themselves as subjects. As juxtaposed with Heidegger's more universalist concern with Being, Foucaul-dian ontology is notably circumscribed in *pouvoir*, which means both "power" and also – a sense, lost in English – that of "making possible." For Heidegger (1927/1962), ontology notably relates to that which makes possible or "determines entities as entities, that on the basis of which [woraufin] entities are already under-stood" (pp. 25–26). Ontological investigations thus concern the *Being* (that is, the intelligibility) of beings, the ways in which beings historically and socially show up or are present *for us*; in Foucault's (1969/1972) idiom, the historical *a priori* and, for later Heidegger, the mode of revealing or disclosure. Moreover, both Foucault and later Heidegger find modern subjectivity beset with the impulse to technologically reduce phenomena to what can be discretely known and mas-tered, thereby concealing other possible ways of being. More pointedly, traumatic suffering in our epoch, however, relates to Foucault's (1984/1990) inquiry into "problematization," as it is "the proper task of a history of thought, as against a history of behaviors or representations: to define the conditions in which human beings 'problematize' what they are, what they do, and the world in which they live" (p. 10). Raynor (2007) observes that problematization, sketched out by Fou-cault in late interviews, concerns a triad of relations (truth/knowledge, rules/practices/power, and self-relation/ethics); however, it is the historical exigency at the intersection of these modes that parallels Heidegger's (1999) notion of *Ereignis* as the event of appropriation. What it means to be the historical subject of trauma, therefore, relates to a wider web of meanings, practices, discourses, and ethical mandates that would necessarily exceed the boundaries of the human sciences or the psy-disciplines, signifying that the heart of the matter is latent within many domains of knowledge and living. Another way to approach the issue is to inquire: *What is the question to which "trauma" is the answer?* In some ways, this reversal fore-grounds the field of trauma studies as problematized. Still, according to Raynor (2007), what situates Foucault within Heidegger's post-Kantian critical ontology is the attention to problematizing the present moment, in performing a "history of the present" (Foucault, 1975/1995). To this end, we would need to ask what pos-sibilities are both obscured and made possible in this, our own time, through our naming of the territory of trauma and its provinces, as identified with our own lives. As Foucault (1984/1990) writes, to respond to the *kairos* of our own epoch – the opportune moment of thought and praxis – is "to learn to what extent the efforts to think one's own history can free thought from what it silently thinks, and so enable it to think differently" (p. 9). One of the names of acting otherwise than the same thought, the same action, the same embodiment, the same relation

*Thesis:
unconceal-
ment.*

to others is an always transient, socially and historically situated freedom, with its attendant obligation of sober reflection.

References

Alexander, J. C. (2012). *Trauma: A social theory.* Cambridge, UK: Polity Press.

Auerhahn, N. C., & Laub, D. (1998). The primal scene of atrocity: The dynamic interplay between knowledge and fantasy of the Holocaust in children of survivors. *Psychoanalytic Psychology, 15*(3), 360–377.

Bracken, P. (2002). *Trauma: Culture, meaning, and philosophy.* London, UK: Whurr.

Caruth, C. (1996). *Unclaimed experience: Trauma, narrative, and history.* Baltimore, MD: Johns Hopkins University Press.

Caruth, C. (2002). An interview with Jean Laplanche. In L. Belau & P. Ramadanovic (Eds.), *Topologies of trauma: Essays on the limit of knowledge and memory* (pp. 101–125). New York, NY: The Other Press.

Caruth, C. (2013). *Literature in the ashes of history.* Baltimore, MD: Johns Hopkins University Press.

Charcot, J. (1889). *Clinical lectures on diseases of the nervous system delivered at the infirmary of la Salpêtrière* (Vol. 3, T. Savill, Trans.). London, UK: New Syndenham Society.

Craps, S. (2015). *Postcolonial witnessing: Trauma out of bounds.* London, UK: Palgrave.

Eyerman, R. (2001). *Cultural trauma: Slavery and the formation of African American identity.* Cambridge, UK: Cambridge University Press.

Fassin, D., & Rechtman, R. (2009). *The empire of trauma: An inquiry into the condition of victimhood* (R. Gomme, Trans.). Princeton, NJ: Princeton University Press.

Foucault, M. (1972). *The archaeology of knowledge, & the discourse on language* (A. M. Sheridan, Trans.). New York, NY: Pantheon Books. (Original work published 1969)

Foucault, M. (1983). On the genealogy of ethics: An overview of a work in progress. In H. Dreyfus & P. Rabinow (Eds.), *Michel Foucault: Beyond structuralism and hermeneutics* (pp. 229–252). Chicago, IL: University of Chicago Press.

Foucault, M. (1990). *The history of sexuality: Vol. 2. The use of pleasure* (R. Hurley, Trans.). New York, NY: Vintage. (Original work published 1984)

Foucault, M. (1995). *Discipline and punish: The birth of the prison* (A. Sheridan, Trans.). New York, NY: Vintage. (Original work published 1975)

Freud, S. (1961). *Beyond the pleasure principle* (J. Strachey, Trans.). New York, NY: Norton. (Original work published 1920)

Fussell, P. (2013). *The Great War and modern memory.* Oxford, UK: Oxford University Press.

Graff, G. (2011). The name of the game is shame: The effects of slavery and its aftermath. *The Journal of Psychohistory, 39*(2), 133–144.

Gump, J. P. (2010). Reality matters: The shadow of trauma on African American subjectivity. *Psychoanalytic Psychology, 27*(1), 42–54.

Hacking, I. (1995). *Rewriting the soul: Multiple personality and the sciences of memory.* Princeton, NJ: Princeton University Press.

Hacking, I. (2002). *Historical ontology.* Cambridge, MA: Harvard University Press.

Heidegger, M. (1962). *Being and time* (J. Macquarrie & E. Robinson, Trans.). San Francisco, CA: Harper. (Original work published 1927)

Heidegger, M. (1999). *Contributions to philosophy (from enowning)* (P. Enad & K. Maly, Trans.). Bloomington: Indiana University Press.

Herman, J. (1992). *Trauma and recovery.* New York, NY: Basic Books.

Janet, P. (1925). *Psychological healing: Vol. 1.* New York, NY: Macmillan.

Laub, D. (1995). Truth and testimony. In C. Caruth (Ed.), *Trauma: Explorations in memory* (pp. 61–75). Baltimore, MD: Johns Hopkins University Press.

Leys, R. (2000). *Trauma: A genealogy.* Chicago, IL: University of Chicago Press.

Rapoport, E. (2011). Growing up in the shadow of the Holocaust: A psychoanalyst addresses intergenerational transmission of trauma in her family. *Issues in Psychoanalytic Psychology, 33*, 43–49.

Raynor, T. (2007). *Foucault's Heidegger: Philosophy and transformative experience.* London, UK: Continuum.

Stolorow, R. (2011). *World, affectivity, trauma: Heidegger and post-Cartesian psychoanalysis.* New York, NY: Routledge.

van der Kolk, B. (2014). *The body keeps the score: Brain, mind, and body in the healing of trauma.* New York, NY: Penguin.

Young, A. (1995). *The harmony of illusions: Inventing post-traumatic stress disorder.* Princeton, NJ: Princeton University Press.

1

SUBJECTIVITY, FINITUDE, AND TEMPORALITY

Nihilism and modernity

Despite criticisms of Foucault's (1961/2009) *History of Madness*,[1] even mainstream historians find difficulty in ignoring the intersection of madness and "mental illness" with power. For instance, Wallace (2008) reservedly writes that "Foucault and company have performed valuable services in countering self-congratulatory Enlightenment-style progressivist historiographies of psychiatry" (p. 43). Formal respect, though, often means appropriation. Hence, for diagnostic purposes, theoretical hedging allows the sensitive clinician to make *post hoc* determinations of how cultural idioms of distress and explanations inform various patterns of symptoms, and even to acknowledge that "all forms of distress are locally shaped, including the DSM disorders" (American Psychiatric Association, 2013, p. 897). Briefly stated, currently dominant understandings of madness as mental illness implicitly continue the binary of natural category versus culturally located suffering. Furthermore, Wallace's (2008) acknowledgment that an "externalist," sociohistorically contextual account of psychiatric history would have merit preserves legitimacy of "internalist" histories, privileging causal development, continuity, and scientific progress. Whiggish history, promising mental hygiene and functionality, ensnares the subject's now-visible government and normalization through psychiatric discourse. Concerning efforts to escape Hegelian metanarratives, Foucault (1969/1972) writes that "we have to determine the extent to which our anti-Hegelianism is possibly one of his tricks directed against us, at the end of which he stands, motionless, waiting for us" (p. 235). Perhaps the same could be said to be true both of those reducing knowledge to institutional power and those extolling the timelessness of scientific progress as it pertains to the human sciences. As counterparts, these positions stand together, waiting for us, entangling our efforts of understanding in their reductions and liquidations.

Sociologically oriented external critiques of the psy-complex – including trauma – as proffered by Marxist critics, postmodernist historians, and others, strangely partake in a common maneuver as internalist confirmations of knowledge, albeit working towards different aims and under different assumptions (Gergen, 1997; Rose, 1996; Sampson, 1981; Young, 1995). Both internalist and externalist approaches could be said to arise under modern regimes of knowledge that aim at unmasking, towards exposing the vicissitudes of experience and intensities of trauma as "nothing but." In trauma studies, the internalist perspective often brings more optimism than positivistic rigor, projecting traumatic experience further and further into the past. For instance, Parry-Jones and Parry-Jones (1994) submit an eighteenth-century avalanche disaster to PTSD nosology. Additionally, Daly (1983) argues that evidence for PTSD is transcribed in the *Diary of Samuel Pepys*, arising out of the Great Fire of London in 1666, where Pepys writes of his terrible dreams. Trimble (1985) finds evidence of contemporary trauma in Shakespeare's *King Henry IV, Part One*, wherein Lady Percy describes Hotspur's nightmares and his dreams of war. These studies, and others,[2] contend that trauma is a universal, diagnostic classification – likely rooted in evolved physiological responses to overwhelming threat – transcending history. In contradistinction, as mentioned, the works of Young (1995), Leys (2000), Hacking (2002), Fassin and Rechtman (2009), and others, offer finely grained readings of trauma discourse as arising from particular social and historical contexts. Leys (2000) introduces her watershed analysis with an explicit reference to methodological angle and philosophical influence:

> I do not proceed as if trauma has a linear, if interrupted, historical development. Rather, I shall take a genealogical approach to the study of trauma, in an effort to understand what Michel Foucault has called "the singularity of events outside any monotonous finality."
>
> *(p. 8)*

In this passage, Leys signals her endorsement of Foucault's Nietzschean impulses. Indeed, as Foucault (1977) writes, "Genealogy . . . seeks to reestablish the various systems of subjection: not the anticipatory power of meaning, but the hazardous play of dominations" (p. 148). Still, histories rigorously charting discontinuity, even without constants and consoling self-recognition, bear their own vestigial, metaphysical burdens at least in practice if not in theory – i.e., "domination," "power," etc. as the endpoint for analysis. Though providing a useful high altitude view, historicist approaches far removed from their significance for present life may carry a suspicion that traumatic experience is merely epiphenomenal to psychiatric and psychological power/knowledge. Trauma is *nothing but* an impersonal, institutionally entrenched sociologically framed will-to-power. Though in seeming opposition, the internalist account of trauma, thus, also draws upon a kind of suspicion, of a different kind – that trauma is *nothing but* an intense stimulus overwhelming neurocognitive capacities to form narrative memory. The internalist and externalist accounts of trauma are, in this way, indebted to an epistemology that ostensibly locates the human subject and its empirical object in the same field of knowledge, with paradoxical consequences. Where subjectivity reigns as an arbitrary will-to-power, it will also reciprocally show up as a socio-historical principle of force in opposition to such agency. In a similar vein, the scientistic account spawns its own doppelgänger; the mechanical and material of neurobiological dysfunction requires an ideal subject who intentionally and accurately perceives such empirical reality of which it is composed. Either reductive possibility – "overmining" or "undermining" in Harman's (Kimball, 2013) terminology, respectively – results in detachment of the subject from itself as object, and an emptiness that separates the autonomous subject from its worldly tethering. Paralleling this mutual deferral is the "hermeneutics of suspicion" manifested through certain readings of Marx, Nietzsche, and Freud, where a critique of the contents of consciousness via historical materialism, will-to-power, or the unconscious only comes to light through an excess, a purification of consciousness (e.g., Leiter, 2004).

An approach to trauma falling back into, and immersed into, a world that it cannot escape must attend to residual metaphysical underpinnings in Nietzschean thought. Inasmuch, escaping the internalist/externalist polarity capturing recent histories requires an appreciation of its aspirations, and its current hold on our being as embodied in the problem of nihilism, Levin (1985) enigmatically notes that nihilism as a historical phenomenon is distinct from its concealed "essence." And, in separation from its symptomatic appearance as despair, spiritual destitution, pessimism, or paralysis, the most notable enunciation – perhaps – of a historically modern nihilism occurs in Nietzsche (1968), who writes that "the most extreme form of nihilism would be the view that every belief, every considering-something-true, is necessarily false because there is no true world" (p. 14).[3] Such a vacuum of meaning – touching both certain Christian understandings with onto-theological foundations and Enlightenment rationalities such as utilitarianism and scientism – emerges from the clutching of a metaphysical, yet absent, dimension of true knowledge and devaluing present becoming. In an overall sense, Nietzsche (1968) asserts that suffering borne out of nihilism involves a weakness, a failure to confront the unassailably subjective character of knowledge, which is fashioned out of a will to dominate life and death. This will-to-power, for Nietzsche, is an intertwining of willing creation, value, and truth that – importantly – must itself be embraced as an affirmation of life rather than its abject denial. In other words, an active nihilism, where human being affirms its own creative power to express its own subjective value through producing knowledge according to its own lights is set against a failure of nerve, a passively nihilistic disavowal of responsibility.

For Heidegger (1977a), Nietzsche's insight into nihilism becomes significant for modernity, but as a reconstitution of metaphysics through a form of subjectivity, whose will invokes perspectival knowledge according to its particular values. Revisioning the familiar scene of early Enlightenment Cartesian epistemology, where knowledge is attained through a kind of inner disengagement and self-confirmation, Nietzsche revives a subject *wanting to know*, yet in a different guise. Accordingly, Heidegger (1977a) argues that the Nietzschean subject – as opening the world and knowledge to its authoritative force of value/devaluing – recapitulates the Cartesian subject as a guarantor of its own path to knowledge: "Inasmuch as Descartes seeks this *subiectum* along the path previously marked out by metaphysics, he, thinking truth as certainty, finds the *ego cogito* to be that which presences as fixed and constant" (p. 83). As Levin (1987) suggests, nihilism – for Heidegger – does not involve our failure or weakness in taking up the creative expression left to us in the wake of the death of external absolutes; rather, nihilism relates to a negation of Being, to include its reduction to the phenomenon of will. Put differently, the nihilism continuing to manifest in our culture includes both a metaphysics of the subject whose will illuminates knowledge arbitrarily vis-à-vis truth, as well as the subject whose innate reason mirrors nature, knowledge of a world located elsewhere (e.g., Abrams, 1953). For the former, its own chosen values and commitments substitute for the absence of external guarantees (i.e., God and his moral inscriptions). For the latter, its own imperfectly imagined correspondence with nature promises knowledge. Enlightenment subjectivity – instantiated in Cartesian thought as well as its Romantic correction in Nietzsche – exists proximately within the same philosophical boundaries of narcissistic collapse.

For inquiry into the human sciences – psychology and psychiatry especially, and certainly for trauma – the epistemic groundwork of modern thought circumscribes Nietzsche's will-to-power, the monochromatic historicism that follows it, as well as the optimistic scientism that appears as its opposition. The notion of "modernity" for the present analysis will specifically relate to the disjuncture Foucault (1966/1973) describes in *The Order of Things*. In the largest sense, modernity relates, *inter alia*, to the historical process of the Enlightenment, involving the progressive mechanization of the natural world according to fixed natural laws, the procedural detachment of reason from particular moral or political ends, and the growing power of capital to regulate human affairs. Toulmin (1990) provides the image of the *cosmopolis*, a community ordered in parallel with a Newtonian universe, to describe the encircling of the social order and the natural world under an absolute gaze: "We are concerned, not with 'science' as the modern positivists understand it, but with a *cosmopolis* that gives a comprehensive account of the world, so as to bind things together in 'politico-theological,' as much as in scientific or explanatory, terms" (p. 128). For Foucault (1966/1973), the transparent point of reflection that would have allowed for a such an ideal epistemological relation between the social body and the cosmos characterizes the "classical" Enlightenment epoch, and eventually comes to crisis as being part of the very world it desires to free itself from, in order to survey. What results in the succeeding and more properly "modern" epoch is the return entry of the subject into a horizontal world, and – for knowledge – a flatland of objects, where within the human subject is incorporated the contours and qualities usually found in the empirical or objective world.[4] For Foucault (1966/1973), following a Heideggerian path, the Kantian premising of knowledge on its limit substitutes a different conundrum for the absentee guarantor of transparency. The failure of representation prompting the reciprocal deferral of subject over against its object becomes an "analytic of finitude," haunted by several related difficulties attending to the doubling of human being. As will be demonstrated later, different strategies exist for the grounding of human being that would address, yet also recapitulate, the void that separates the subject from itself as object; however, seeking both the emptiness of freedom and its own grounding, the modern subject finally searches for itself in time. Importantly, treatments of time under modern conditions differ markedly from that in pre-modern, and classical or early Enlightenment cultures.[5] Habermas (1996) enunciates a key theme in the formation of Enlightenment thinking – namely, that the subject may no longer tether itself in a living tradition, in time as cyclical. The classical substitution of an absolute gaze for lived proximity to an intelligible world only heightens the plunge of absolutist pretensions to knowledge, as space out of time, into the here and now. *Modernity is, therefore, the epoch that is erased of its ground in the past of tradition, but one that must attain its own grounding in its own horizontal plane of existence.* Our modern, and late (post) modern desire is to form our own ground, in our own time, and without relation to traditional ways of meaning-making and the guarantor of an absolute gaze, whether God or a point of ideal reflection.[6]

The "homogenous and empty time" of scientific inquiry, whose outward arc recaptures its past as *manipulanda*, gives way – in the human sciences, at least – to historicism where "the horizon open to the future, which is determined by expectations in the present, guides our access to the past" (Habermas, 1996, p. 13). Consequently, the foundation substituted for the past of tradition is the past of history. Time, as the heretofore engraving of the event into the fabric of reality – configured differently in pre-modernity and in the early Enlightenment – becomes historicality, radically regrounding the subject within its own limitations and possibilities as given over to it in its particular origin. As a result, the time of tradition, or the absolute time of Newtonian physics, is reconfigured under later modern conditions as an uneasy binary between a cognitive metric of time over against time that is subjectively meaningful.[7] Indeed, for the suffering subject, its transposition into temporality allows it to become located in a distinct origin, yet traumatically removed from its own genesis, ironically attaining its capacities for self-revision at the price of blindness. Because they tend to unwittingly partake in and absolutize the epistemic assumptions in the discourses in which they inquire, critical histories of trauma, as well as "self-congratulatory Enlightenment-style progressivist historiographies" (Wallace, 2008, p. 43), have been unable to more fully examine the ways that modern and traumatic subjectivities share in temporality.

In what follows, my overall aim will be to expand upon the nexus between finitude, temporality, and modern subjectivity. I will attend to the discontinuities between epistemic regimes (from pre-modern, to classical, to modern) that result in temporality for modernity as a kind of solution to epistemic crisis. First, drawing on the later Foucault's (2005) understanding of ancient Greek and early Christian ethics, I will principally examine the care of the self that existed before the modern episteme in the West, and briefly address this subject's suffering, in order to scaffold the ethical and discursive discontinuities that result in finitude structural for the modern subject. Second, drawing on Foucault's (1966/1973) conclusions from *The Order of Things*, I will describe fault lines of modern subjectivity – the crisis in representation (and what is excluded by this form of reason), the doubling of man, unthought, and temporality as the originary center of these fissures. Third, I will argue for restorative temporality as a discursive formation mobilized through modern philosophy (in Hegel, Schopenhauer, Nietzsche, Husserl, and Bergson) that would suture this subject's temporal wound simultaneously through its immersion and its transcendence. In main, I will suggest that these solutions cannot coherently provide both grounding and transcendence to the subject. Through the work of Derrida (1974), it will be argued that these approaches to temporality perpetually deconstruct themselves, and it will be suggested that our particularly modern hermeneutics of the subject necessitates a subjectivity bearing a kind of ontologically traumatic structure.

Pre-enlightenment subjectivity and truth

Unlike the early Foucault's (1969/1972, 1966/1973) concern with epistemic fields governing the subject's knowledge, and the middle Foucault's (1977, 1975/1995) shift to extrinsic power/knowledge (including both discursive and non-discursive means) producing individuals, the later Foucault (2005) articulates in *The Hermeneutics of the Subject* a co-constitution between the subject's modes of objectification and subjectification. Expanding on the ethical turn in Foucault's (1984/1988, 1984/1990) later work, including *The Use of Pleasure* and *The Care of the Self*, Han (2005) writes that "this mutual relativity of the subject of knowledge and what it knows is thus revealed as the only focal point from which a 'history of truth' can begin" (p. 177). Consequently, the eventual ontological elevation of the fully modern subject temporally alienated from itself, and psychopathology of trauma as an epistemic strategy for deploying its biographical functionality, invokes a retrospective positioning of subject in relation to knowledge and truth. The modern subject, whose being is open to the future and potentially erased of its past, stands at a distance from its ancestral forms. Though taking very different forms, and spanning considerable geography and historical periods, pre-modern subjectivity partakes in ways of being and relating whose horizons may be distinguished from that of modernity, and also the early Enlightenment or classical period.

In Greek antiquity, as chronicled in the later Foucault (2005), the injunction to care for oneself (*epimeleia heautou*) provides the "justificatory framework, ground, and foundation for the imperative 'know yourself'" (p. 8). This question arises prominently in *Alcibiades I*, where Plato's Socrates listens to the young Alcibiades' plans to be a wise ruler of the Athenian state. Naturally, Socrates does not let the moment pass, and seizes it for inquiry into the question of how one may govern wisely. For Socrates, governing wisely does not mean mastering specific skills (*technai*) – for instance, shipbuilding, speech-giving, or the art of negotiation.

Instead, Socrates invokes the Delphic inscription of *gnothi seauton* (to know thyself) as an aspiration that would allow through self-governance the manifestation of principles providing prudential governance of the city-state. What follows from Socrates' advice to Alcibiades concerning knowing oneself is that one does not attend to oneself as some*thing* to be known; the soul is not identified with anything like an object. Rather, to know oneself as having certain dispositions, habits, or qualities, one must first attend to oneself – care for oneself (*epimeleia heautou*). Caring for oneself, in this context, means actions – exercises (*gymnasia*) or meditations (*melete*) – by which the subject changes or transforms himself. For example, the later practice involves placing oneself in an imaginary situation and generating arguments and hypothetical courses of action, not unlike rhetorical techniques. Likewise, the self-forming activity (*askesis*) involved in the mastery of one's relation to embodied pleasures would require an engagement with one's own experience – in the formation of strategies of need, timeliness, and status (Foucault, 1984/1990). Such practices require and produce self-knowledge; however, the *how* of such transfigurations precedes the *what* or content of them. In other words, knowing oneself is subsumed under a care involving interested attention to one's comportment with others (especially in political matters), and hardly amounts to the seeking of interior being; it is part of a more expansive requirement that one become worthy of access to truth. Han (2005) argues that in relation to Enlightenment thinking, the antique structure of subjectivity involves a radically different understanding of truth – where truth is not adequation of knowledge to object but is, rather, spiritually, relationally, and communally defined in practice. The stance one takes in relation to oneself, thus, involves not technological intervention that manipulates in the service of external, putatively neutral, and objectified knowledge, but the properly Greek *techne* that reveals as *poiesis* – in the Heideggerian sense – as a bringing forth into light of the embodiment of one's truth that is made in the ethical moment, as it is in contact with others.

The elemental connection between truth and being implicates both *askesis* and *parrhesia*, the latter an ideal example of the embodiment of the speaker with the truth he/she speaks. Foucault (2011) notably argues that in Greek antiquity (and dispersed through the Roman period up until the fifth century AD in patristic texts), *parrhesia* is situated at the intersection of the injunction to speak truth, political governance, and the constitution of the subject – and, as such, virtue, duty, and technique. In other words, truth telling – which is to be distinguished from sagacious wisdom, professional expression of the rhetorician, and the technical arts of pedagogy – occupies territory at once epistemological, political, and ethical. As Foucault (2005) tells us, *parrhesia* is free in that it is released from rhetorical techniques and given over to the unsullied commitment, to the bond that unifies both the subject of enunciation and "at the very moment he says 'I speak the truth,' he commits himself to do what he says and to be the subject of conduct who conforms in every respect to the truth he expresses" (p. 406). In *parrhesia*, an identity of several elements – though signifying a certain authenticity – only superficially indicates a modern sensibility. First, such free speech possesses a frankness that avoids flattery, and – as cited previously – rhetorical stratagems aimed at falsely persuading. Second, the *parrhesiastes* orients his ("his" because the speaker must be a free citizen, and male) speech towards pointing out a flaw in the audience or majority to whom he speaks; it is a criticism. Third, the *parrhesiastes* must undertake some danger, such as a philosopher who speaks against tyranny, or an orator who knows that his unpopular speech may cause his downfall, or even a friend risking friendship with an utterance; courage is required for access to truth. Fourth, such speech is undertaken even as a form of duty that presses upon the *parrhesiastes* with considerable urgency, which involves an improvement of others' lives and that of the speaker as well. Fifth, and finally, the speech itself must touch truth – not an external truth "out there" in the world somewhere, or a confessional truth, but the coincidence of the speaker's belief, attributes, and action. Foucault (1983) remarks that truth – in this instance – differs markedly from Cartesian understandings because the speaker's moral qualities guarantee veracity rather than analytics of doubt and demonstration. Foucault (1983) demonstrates that *parrhesia* is hardly confined to any specific practice or domain, but rather diffuses itself across many fields of endeavor and activity – philosophical inquiry (i.e., Socrates' interrogation in *Laches*), communal life (*techne* comparable to piloting a boat or the practice of medicine), public life (whether in argumentation or in preparation for rulership, as in *Alcibiades I*), or in personal relationships (in friendship, or in the disinterested advice of an advisor). As Foucault (1983) reminds us, the qualification for truth-telling relates to its fundamentally political underpinnings – as related to the practice and problematization of democracy – and not as it would come to be transfigured in modern societies, in the institutional authority of the psychiatrist, psychologist, or psychotherapist. In these more contemporary practices, the relations of veridiction, governmentality, and subjectification would have altogether different outcomes under the aegis of biopower; however, for our purposes, what must be stressed is the unity of this triad. This places *parrhesia* within self-knowledge intertwined with one's worthiness to attain the truth, and its structural infusion throughout the *polis* and the cosmos; free speech involves the courageous discernment of the intelligible within the sensible.

Instantiated in Greek practice and truth-telling, the subject, therefore, seeks a kind of self-mastery through reason, but only through a notion of reason in conformity with the deep ordering of existence, one's soul, and one's pragmatic involvement with a community of listeners. Concerning the Platonic subject, Taylor (1989) writes that rationality is connected to the perception of a cosmic order, and a capacity for apprehension: "The correct vision is critical. There is no way to be ruled by reason and be *mistaken* or wrong about the order of reality" (pp. 121–122). Importantly, the intelligible order always involves its remembering reflected among other social subjects, and the proper government of human being in civic life. Thus, knowledge and subjectivity manifest a reciprocal or mutually constitutive affiliation around the articulation of a *substantive truth of being within which one inhabits and lives* personally, ethically, and dialogically rather than one held out from oneself in detachment. For Socratic inquiry, reaching its most visible form in *The Republic*, the capacity for apprehending truth appears intimately related to the subject's own preparation (and also political status), education, and will in perceiving the eternal form in the midst of decay, change, and contingency. Likewise, in Aristotelian terms, though obviously different in many respects, ethical life is lived as moderation (*sophrosyne*), which is related to a cultivation of an embodied rationality related to a final cause of living well: "Neither by nature, then, nor contrary to nature do the virtues arise in us; rather we are adapted by nature to receive them, and are made perfect by habit" (Aristotle, trans. 2009, p. 23). For Aristotle, in human affairs, free will facilitates an ethical entelechy situated in its specifically aristocratic, patriarchal cultural milieu (MacIntyre, 1984). Courage, therefore, is not the form of truth that can be known outside of its concrete practice, where finality of cause would implicate the willful cultivation of a truth of a citizenry in perpetual warfare: "First comes the courage of the citizen-soldier; for this is most like true courage" (Aristotle, trans. 2009, p. 51). It is, thus, possible – as Colebrook (1998) suggests – to locate Aristotelian virtue ethics within the context of Foucault's self-formative "games of truth" embedded in a specific hermeneutics stretching towards the *telos* of a *eudaimonia* situated in particular communities and their politics, which corresponds more deeply to fundamental structures of the natural world. For the Greek world (and successive worlds that took up their traditions), subjectivity would forge itself out of its own vision of its embeddedness in the natural and social orders – whether preexisting archetypal forms or the telic movements of beings and things. Foucault (1993) refers to this kind of self as the *gnomé* – finding expression as late as the first century AD in Greek, Hellenistic, and Roman thought – "where force of truth is one with the form of will" (p. 210). The living of intelligible truth – through the preparation of the soul, its recollection, its discernment in the sensible, and its telling according to the dictates of *parrhesia* to a community of others – requires self-transformation, a readiness and will of the subject to allow its presence.

For Christian thought, self-transformative ethics in relation to knowledge is bifurcated in different traditions. The ancient integration of caring for oneself and coming to truth/knowledge shows signs of coming apart. Of this widening division, Foucault (1993) observes that the two systems of obligation – that of the truth obligation concerned with access to a preexisting illumination of creation, and that of making or discovering truth inside the subject – have maintained a certain autonomy in Christian thought. Standing for the former are the obligations of faith, "the book," and Augustinian theology extending the Greek identity of self, truth, and knowledge, but containing a hint of modern reflective distance towards the subject's inner experience. The emergence of theology from the fifth to twelfth centuries – the anchoring point for an epistemically correct assertion being the subject of knowledge in relation to a God paradoxically immanent with, and transcendent to, his creation – would prefigure the Cartesian subject at rational distance with inner and outer reality. Han (2005) remarks that such a move begins the onward march of the dissolution of the bond between philosophy and spirituality (as a reciprocal capacity of truth and care of the self). Concerning the civic and pragmatic instantiation of the heavenly city, Augustine (trans. 2000) writes:

> In its pilgrim state the heavenly city possesses this peace by faith; and by this faith it lives righteously when it refers to the attainment of that peace every good action towards God and man; for the life of the city is a social life.
>
> *(p. 697)*

Though mindful of sociality, Augustinian interiority becomes guided by the singular light of an inner perfection beyond the soul, one illuminating the dispersed and sensible thoughts to be collated. A truthful and moral vision makes visible the concealed divinity inscribing parallel, worldly realities. For Augustine, this reflexive turn – having moral and social consequences – still involves self-transformation through perfection, attained through turning inward and upward to receive God's grace. The other tradition, chronicled more at length by Foucault (1993), involves the obligation of the Christian to express the truth about himself. This would be differentiated from the Greek and Roman practice of self-examination that would enjoin the subject to transform himself to attain a general truth that would be articulated forensically, or in common life oriented to public governance. Though this trajectory eventually crystallizes in confessional technology, penitential rites of the "ascetic-monastic" model in the third and fourth centuries consist of the *exomologesis* – the public recognition of one's sins through an acting out (not a nominalization or verbalization) that manifests the nature of the sin (such as wearing the hair shirt) (Foucault, 1993). Tertullian's (1979) own translation of the Greek *exomologesis* is *publicatio sui*, or self-publication, an act of self-revelation. To publish oneself as a sinner is to comport with the practice of voluntarily undergoing a kind of spiritual death, or of dying to one's bodily communion with the flesh of the world. Consequently, though highly modified from its pagan origins, the circularity between truth and self-transformation remains, though the way to truth made available via revelation and self-knowledge is attained through purification required to comprehend the Word (Foucault, 2005). Both the Augustinian turning to the inner light of God to discern truth inside of oneself and the *publicatio sui* relate to self-transformative procedures initiated in Greek and Roman traditions; however, the Christian injunction to ascertain how the *logos* somehow transfigures the inner body, the fallen soul who has become entangled with the flesh of life, forecasts later Cartesian detachment of oneself from one's passions. Nonetheless, for a subject preceding the advent of early Enlightenment and modern thought, the tapestry of the Word is enveloping, containing no end and no beginning, inexplicably torn only through the fallibility of the created.

The Word, as *logos*, bears creation, and provides – as it inscribes itself – contact between the uncreated and temporally eternal world, and what is run-down, decaying in the sensible world. For the eventual discernment of trauma as splitting open the subject into its own time, and according to the lights of its world, something, therefore, should be said regarding pre-modern notions of time. From the outset, it would seem that – while important, no doubt – time does not occupy the same figural position for the Western, pre-modern subject. With the exception, perhaps, of pre-Socratic thought, as interpreted by Heidegger (1975) *infra*, modern concerns with temporality do not for the most part appear for ancient conceptions of time that partake in the logocentric succession of Plato, Aristotle, et al. In the main, ancient and medieval thinking on time does not relate to the problem of the subject's means of access *to itself* through temporality, or the subject's dispersal of or tethering to itself in the flow of lived time. In contrast, the subject is usually figured as existing within a preordained, created world where time is given over by the eternal, whether manifested in an intelligible realm or in a telic world. Sherover (1975) summarizes well the common concern with the timeless:

> Plato grounded time in the work of the timeless Demiurge but insisted that time is the necessary principle of order in the world of nature. Aristotle grounded time in the unmoved (and, thereby, timeless) prime mover, Plotinus in the eternal One, and Augustine in the transcendent God. Each of them conceived of time as dependent upon a supervening timeless reality and sought out its meaning in some aspect of this transient world.
>
> *(p. 15)*

Platonic philosophy, thus, conceives of time as a kind of debased, sensible counterpart to eternity: "So time came into being with the heavens . . . and it was made as like as possible to eternity, which was its model" (Plato, trans. 1965, p. 52). Certainly, as is well noted, Aristotle's view of time follows his desire to understand phenomena in the natural world, which is subject to change. For Aristotle, time is countable, numerical change manifesting the physical world – a series of now-points – that impresses the soul; however, as Coope (2005) argues, in *Physics*, Aristotle makes change related to an arc of *entelecheia*, or actualization, wherein change (and motion, and time) become intertwined with his metaphysics of causation. Hence, though Aristotle departs from the Platonic notion that time issues forth from *another* timeless world, he relocates time within this external reality where things continually change without regress, precipitated by a prime mover and expanding through endless formal unfolding. Plotinus, though neo-Platonist, also draws somewhat on Aristotelian thought, holding as Plato that time is given to us by the eternal, not identical with it, but also arguing as Aristotle that time is related to the differentiation of life from itself (in a sensible world), as fallibly (rather than openly) lived to its futural completion: "Engendered things are in continuous process of acquisition; eliminate futurity, therefore, and at once they lose their being . . . for this reason it keeps hastening towards the future" (Plotinus, trans. 1969, p. 225). For Plotinus, time itself is not perceptible, but is the membrane that separates the eternal and earthly, providing both the ultimate cause and the impetus for the soul to attain communion with, and knowledge of, the One. Like Plotinus, Augustine (trans. 1963) also makes time a concern for the subject, in addition to the external world, famously arguing in a strikingly contemporary voice that time only comes from the future, and it can only pass through the present, on its way into the past. Augustine submits time to an inner ordering, in which memory and expectation play roles in a subjective orderability, paralleling the external world. Nonetheless, as noted by Sherover (1975), Augustine's realignment of time with motion (repudiated by Plotinus) results in a "final description of time as some kind of 'extension' of mind . . . time as some kind of concomitant of the divine creation of the 'heavens and the earth'" (p. 39). The pre-moderns, therefore, do indeed struggle with time; however, the difficulties presented involve a subject who must discern the mysteries of the existing world, replete with its celestial movements and hidden purposes, where its own incompleteness (as original sin, or as a being not fully actualized) is remedied through temporal communion with the Eternal, the One, or final cause. As such, the subject's transformative care of self, truth-telling, and moral action transpire within a world whose order and chaos is coiled within truths reflecting geometrically ordered and silently unfolding movements of beings and things comporting with their own cosmic imprints.

Pre-enlightenment subjectivity and suffering

A prehistory of trauma would necessarily address forms of suffering arising in Greek antiquity and thereafter. It appears relatively well known that Homeric conceptions of psyche (itself related to one's double destined for Hades) (Rohde, 1925) and mind are widely dispersed and relate to concrete expressions frequently connected to forms of embodiment – i.e., *phrenes* (associated with the lungs or diaphragm) and *kradie* (associated with the heart). Moreover, the Homeric subject manifests as permeable and immersed into an order of reality inhabited by divine entities – bearing the logic of this order – with inscrutable motives; irrationality and madness (mania and *lussa*), thus, are borne as a rift or intervention in the flow of events as usually lived. Thus, as Auerbach (1953/2003) suggests, Homeric reality is resolutely anti-psychological in any contemporary sense, but rather flush with a world whose divinities speak through its flesh. For instance, in the *Iliad*, Achilles' rage and grief at the death of Patroclus is mediated through the actions of Athena: "And Trojans hearing the brazen voice of Aeacides, all their spirits quaked . . . when they saw that fire, relentless, terrible, burst from proud-hearted Achilles' head, blazing as fiery-eyed Athena fueled the flames" (Homer, trans. 1990, p. 474). In much contrast, giving extra-human force less determination, though lacking the growing human agency present in Platonic or Aristotelian thought, the subject of Greek tragedy suffers from imbalance occurring when the harmony of existence is disturbed. Madness and suffering arise often in the form of seemingly irredeemable conflicts permeating reality itself. Consider, for instance, in Aeschylus' (trans. 1979) *Oresteia*, the position of Orestes himself who becomes overtaken by madness after avenging the death of his father, Agamemnon, by killing his mother, Clytemnestra, and her lover: "I am a charioteer – the reins are flying, look, the mares plunge off the track – my bolting heart, it beats me down and terror beats the drum, my dance-and-singing master pitched to fury" (p. 223).

The pursuit of Orestes by the Erinyes indicates an inviolable and naturalized law that blood must be paid with blood, even familial blood, should such a threshold be crossed. Critical to Orestes' quandary, however, is that the intersection he has entered is hardly his own, and that the working out of action pertains first and foremost to the traumatic aporia of justice in the social body. *When does justice ever arrive in a world of interminable retribution?* Simon (1978) writes that

> in Aeschylus these conflicts are located in the cosmos and in the society rather than in the individual. Orestes does not work through terrible conflict in order to reach some inner harmony. Rather relief comes by means of a juridical settlement of a battle over which he never had any control . . . It is as if madness is in the universe, in the order of things, or rather in the *disorder* of things.
>
> *(pp. 108, 136)*

In Greek tragedy, though never individualized in modern sense, the suffering subject – its conflicts, madness – increasingly falls under rational dominion; however, what connects more expressly political and philosophical pursuits with tragedy is that the fragmentation of life bears with it a certain problematic manifesting not only within the existence of particular people, families, clans, etc., but also relating fundamentally to a natural, temporal, cosmic order that is simultaneously ideal and out of joint with itself. Murder, as a form of human sacrifice to impossible demand, frequently bears the insanity of the culture itself, as free-floating guilt from a crime displaced through many acts, both human and divine (Burkert, 1966). Agamemnon murders his own daughter due to external, environmental exigencies that must be met with sacrifice, dislocating the possibility of justice, moderation, or soundness of mind (*sophrosyne*). Accordingly, as Simon (1978) observes, "The notion that the gods cause madness covers up the deep conflicts and guilt that must be at work somewhere in the life of the culture" (p. 102). Madness expresses an intensity of division between the demands of the ideal, the eternal over against the illusory or worldly, the phenomenal, what passes away, as well as the exclusion of an existing and necessary moral-legal act from its very position within justice (Lacan, 1986/1992; Sophocles, trans. 1984); meeting one's obligations becomes simultaneously necessary and forbidden. Padel (1995) argues, in some parallel, that madness in ancient Greek culture, and in tragedy in particular, owes to a confluence of darkness of mind (preponderance of black bile), wandering or alienation from communal life, and the damage done to self and others as a consequence. Especially agonizing are the intrusions of external and inscrutable experiences into the human world. In other words, the subject's own struggles must necessarily recapitulate the difficulties and temporal mistranslations of eternal forms and the exercise of non-human will upon a fragile and human world.

Though bearing the metaphysical inheritance of the aporetic spaces that would haunt the subject of Greek tragedy, philosophical understandings of madness or mental disturbance – from Platonic perspectives, at any rate – privilege an especially rational and active agency that would penetrate the tissues of illusion. Unlike the poetic reflection of imperfect human reality that is inscribed with a kind of divine madness – as proffered by Plato (trans. 1974, 1983) in *Ion* and *The Republic* – and aligned with the merely sensory capacities of the psyche, knowledge (*episteme*) is accessed through a sustained process of memorial unearthing (recollection or *anamnesis*). Significantly, for Plato, piercing the veil separating this world from its absolute but hidden guarantors requires a dialectic questioning (defining, distinguishing, ordering) within dialogical and embodied encounters with others. As Derrida (1981a) argues in connection with *Phaedrus*, for Platonic thought – and the metaphysical tradition in the West – writing itself attains a devalued status, being removed from knowledge or Being, and associated with the artifice of rhetoric and poetics: "Repetition is the very movement of nontruth: the presence of what is gets lost, disperses itself, multiplies itself through mimemes, icons, phantasms, simulacra, etc." (p. 447). Nonetheless, somewhat paradoxically, as Derrida (1981a) reminds us, it is the repetition of the dead marks of difference, of supplementarity, that must be uttered to usher in the presence of *logos*, but always within a determinate interpersonal and social engagement, where truth and speech converge for the *parrhesiastes*, and with certain forms of politics at stake. The pursuit of particularly rational and sane forms of life within the communal context warrants an attempted strict segregation of true knowledge, and true speech, from mere opinion (or *doxa*) but also what might be categorized as madness. In *Phaedrus*, perhaps not coincidentally, Plato (trans. 2005) unusually speaks to the gifts conferred by madness (prophecy, ritual, poetic inspiration, love); however, the deconstructive logic is not to be lost, as madness and sanity could be said to exchange positions of privilege, as could be said for the abstract capacities of writing over against the corporeal being of the speaking subject. Both inhabit a body warring against itself; sickness of the world. More distinctly, for Plato, the sickness of the psyche involves a disturbance in balance and harmony within the subject and pervading its correlates in that political state as well as reality itself. Justice is equated with health, and injustice is equated with sickness and, as Simon (1978) observes, it is true knowledge itself that is the moral good, and ignorance that is identified with the fading temporal world, the illusory appearances pertaining thereto, as well as the excesses of bodily passion, pride, and strivings for power – all forms of madness. Plato (trans. 1974), thus, writes that "the madman whose mind is unhinged imagines he can control gods and men . . . Then a precise definition of a tyrannical man is one who, either by birth or habit or both, combines the characteristics of drunkenness, lust, and madness" (p. 394). These diseases of the psyche, then, have as a fundamental condition a state of ignorance – that the highest forms of reason, arguably unchanging (ideas of justice, beauty, mathematical knowledge), have lost their hold in the vicissitudes of sensory experience. In *Timaeus*, Plato (trans. 2008) famously promulgates a teleological accounting of nature itself, against the atomistic understandings of Leucippus and Democritus, where the motions of the cosmos and its included bodies and entities are understood as following from their ensouled natures, in intelligent and synchronic movements. Before the demiurge, chaos reigns; however, the organizing creative act bears sameness, difference, and being. Gregory (2008) observes that *"Timaeus* develops an analogy between the nature of the world-soul and the nature of our own soul" (p. xlv). The animate nature of the cosmos, and human beings by extension, however, introduces an imperfection into regularities of motion – the regular workings of the mind are unsettled by experiences of being a created, worldly, material being:

> Housed within the body [is] another type of soul, a mortal kind, which is liable to terrible, but inevitable, experiences. Chief among these is pleasure, evil's most potent lure, then pain, fugitive from good; and then those mind-less advisers confidence and fear, and obdurate passion, and gullible hope.
>
> *(Plato, trans. 2008, p. 68)*

Madness, depicted here, amounts to a cosmological mistake and error that tracks the demiurge in its creation of the world over against an ideal and eternal realm that it must always already be separated from in its act.[8] In other words, creation itself – not unlike the dead signification of the writing – is always traumatically alienated from itself insofar as an eidetic nature is said to preexist or to inform the immanent act of bringing the world, psyche, and temporal being into existence. Consequently, madness is a kind of giving oneself over to the world as an act of profound abandonment of temperance or *sophrosyne*, or heeding the deep nature of things beyond appearance and passing away of phenomena.

In medieval contexts, the status of human being within *ens creatum* (creation by God, an infinite being) in some ways resituates the problem of madness as a misfortune, or flaw in the fabric of Being itself. It is well known among historians that madness as disease is linked in the medieval mind with guilt and sin (Porter, 2003). In other words, one's relationship to one's own fallen existence in the flesh would constitute the deepest premise underlying one's anguish. For early Christianity, the Augustinian view – which is relied upon by ecclesiastical authorities – constitutes madness as a form of demonic possession, treated by exorcism or whipping (Pietikäinen, 2015). Arguably, this positions consequent medieval understandings of madness within debates on theodicy, the Augustianian view being that evil (and, *prima facie*, madness) is set free as an error or imperfection in a perfectly created cosmos (Hick, 2010); the intractability of this issue speaks to the subject's fundamental alienation from divine logic. Significantly, then, madness would attain – as evidenced in Middle English texts – three somewhat contradictory functions within God's ultimately unintelligible plans for redressing the false being that announces through suffering: punishment (damnation), purgation (expiation), and testing (probation) (Doob, 1974). The variance of divine motive, necessarily obscure, would account for the liminal space occupied by the mad, as tortured souls stood side by side with "holy fools," who fused folly with revelation denied to others (Pietikäinen, 2015); however, madness is mostly excluded from architectures of salvation. As Doob (1974) argues, turning from final to efficient cause, many medieval authorities hold that original sin disturbed a prelapsarian humoral balance, which relates both an organic and moral reality to an underlying order governed by the mind of God. Hence, in the "Parson's Tale," Chaucer (trans. 2008) expresses a rather straightforward treatise on penitence, as well as the disorder affecting humankind through an upsetting of the soul's hierarchical relationship:

> God sholde have lordshipe over resoun, and resoun over sensualitee, and sensualitee over the body of man. But smoothly, whan man synneth, al this ordre or ordinaunce is turned up-so-doun . . . For sensualitee rebelleth thane agayns resoun, and by that way leseth resoun the lordshipe over sensualitee and over the body. For right as resoun is rebel to God, right so bothe sensualitee rebel to resoun and the body also.
>
> *(p. 294)*

The consequences of this upending, apart from the more general question of, as Burton (1621/1927) puts it, "what madness ghosts us all" (p. 36) as medieval subjects, concern the various maladies, hardly precise in any contemporary sense, such as frenzy (blood), senility (phlegm), wrath (choler or yellow bile), and melancholy (black bile) (Bartholomeus Anglicus, 1398), the latter related to fear, accidie, and grief. As Doob (1974) recounts, the manifestation of madness in its myriad forms, though involving this aforementioned fundamental unsettling of reason, occurs at its point of contact with the sufferer by way of different paths – direct intervention, intervention through angelic or diabolic intermediaries, environmental causation (i.e., seasons, stars), or the natural, physical condition and consequence of sinners who continually place their being in jeopardy. Many accounts of medieval perspectives on madness pay due attention to diabolic means of affliction; madness and demonic possession would frequently be depicted as having a causal relation, if not an identity in every case (Pietikäinen, 2015). In many respects, as related to intrusions of madness from *the world*, in its vast economic, religious, and psychosocial effects, the Black Death, perhaps, embodies – in our own historical imagination at the very least – an emblematic collective suffering of the medieval period. The experiences of those suffering are well chronicled by Boccaccio (1353/2003) in *The Decameron*, where reactions ranged from melancholic lamentation to laughing or jest. In some relation, historians have interpreted flagellantism as a particular and idiosyncratic form of religious madness associated with the Black Death, where the *disciplinati* would "travel from town to town, disseminating the call for personal and communal penitence" (Byrne, 2004, p. 78), and often attacking Jews and clergy (which resulted in charges of heresy). Indeed, pestilence and madness converge as the far-reaching consequences of the Fall, and of its reinscription into the world through the sinful acts of men. As William Langland (1378/2000) writes in *Piers Plowman*, "The recent plague . . . had been brought down on our heads solely on account of our sins" (p. 42). For the instant analysis, however, it bears mentioning that the mind of God remains inscrutable, yet – unlike the memorial abyss that would be characterized in twentieth-century Holocaust experience – the shortfall in understanding resides in the gap or aporia between creation and what surpasses Being in its creator. For the experience of what would later become trauma, it bears attending to Defoe's eighteenth-century retrospective historical novel about the 1665 Great Plague of London. Though situated within the modern period, Defoe's (1722/1986) depiction of the collective suffering having metaphysical scope captures both a pre-modern and transitionally early modern sensibility, as trauma appears to reside in the heavens. Amidst the unburied bodies, the publication of bills of mortality with increasing numbers of victims, and the mysterious appearance of a star or comet in the preceding months, Defoe's (1722/1986) narrator, H. F., speaks to the horrors that

> terrified the people to the last degree . . . even out of their wits. Some heard voices warning them to be gone . . . Others saw apparitions in the air . . . that they heard voices that never spake, and saw sights that never appeared . . . And no wonder, if they who were poring continually at the clouds saw shapes and figures, representations and appearances, which had nothing in them but air and vapour.
>
> *(pp. 42–43)*

Here, the breakdown in experienced reality vividly occurs, very appropriately, in the heavens, and what would be trauma is felt in the tissue of the world itself, which carries forward the wounds and tragic displacements of spirit as incarnated in mortal form and flesh.

Knowing and unreason

For Foucault (1993, 2005), the birth of Cartesianism signals the most decisive shift away from the requirement that the subject engage in a self-transformative practice or care of the self to come to knowledge. The *gnothi seauton* ascends, as epistemology, to its more contemporary understanding – knowledge of oneself, as distinguished from the preparation of oneself for the presence of truth. As a consequence, the "Cartesian moment," not exhausting varieties of Enlightenment thought, exemplifies the great divide that ethically separates the pre-modern and early Enlightenment periods, the latter comprising Foucault's classical episteme. This division exists along three related axes – that of representation over against the idea, the changing nature of mind, and the concomitant role of reason as procedural. First, as worked thoroughly in late modern philosophy (e.g., Heidegger, 1977b), Cartesian epistemology replaces the ancient notion that human beings inhabit a world that imperfectly instantiates ideas, requiring the subject to comport him or herself in accordance. Rather, apprehending reality involves having a correct image or picture that corresponds with the external world that *represents it*. Second, and relatedly, the Cartesian view of the mind begins to take its leave from the mind of God, or resemblance, or the scholastic infusion of God's rationality into the fabric of social existence. The subject comes to exist alongside God, its capacities for knowledge extended by analogy, thus disengaging the mind from embodied reality and disenchanting the world. As Descartes (1649/1989) proposes in *Passions of the Soul*, being given over to one's passions involves having one's rationality occluded by causalities investing the body. Third, Cartesian reason is also, accordingly, detached from particular worldly results, and – crucially, distinguishing it from other reason-centered philosophies such as Stoicism – from any specific substantive moral vision. Accordingly, Taylor (1989) argues that rationality becomes an internal characteristic of thinking itself, rather than embodying a certain vision of reality. Moreover, though Cartesian thinking would receive significant challenge from empiricist orientations, whether philosophical or scientific, the Cartesian outlook – as installing reason as procedural – has become the standard modern way of accounting for knowledge. For Taylor (1989), self-reflexivity as oriented towards self-sufficient certainty, and disengaged reason that is procedural as calculative instrumentality, may be applied to things in the world, or turned in on oneself. An epistemology patterned after Galilean and Baconian pursuits measuring the extensive qualities of the world may be turned inward, in Cartesian fashion, as a particular form of self-distancing. The inwardness that we moderns ("modern" in the largest sense) cherish, therefore, relates to the relative certainty that may be attained as thoughts, emotions, qualities, traits, etc. reflect the hard edges and distinctive contours of objects transparently perceived in space, and through time.

The objectivist reflexivity proffered in Cartesian thought partakes in the classical conception of time, as a hypostatization of ideal relations among beings, perceived from nowhere, from a fictional position outside the system itself, yet extrapolated from its inside. For subsequent scientific practice, the dominant perspective of Enlightenment thought connects the thought of Descartes, Newton, and Locke, involving an absolutization of time-space. For Descartes (trans. 1954), a distinction is to be made between what he calls "duration" and "time." Unlike more contemporary usage, the former (duration) refers to the atomistic splitting of now-moments from each other, distinguished from subjective perceptions of these moments (time). Spatial measurement, as abstraction, is torn away from its particular emplacement and comes to mediate between duration as objective or atomistic and the individualized time that arises in consciousness – i.e., the number ten, whether in space or time, embodies the same dissection: "The concept of the number ten is just the same whether it is referred to this *ten-foot* magnitude or to anything else" (Descartes, trans. 1954, p. 201). Of course, Newtonian physics – as theorized in this selection from the *Leibniz-Clarke Correspondence* – would make much of the continuous fabric of physical reality and the rule-like weave of its surface:

> Absolute, true, and mathematical time, of itself, and from its own nature, flows equably without relation to anything external, and by another name is called duration: relative, apparent, and common time, is some sensible and external (whether accurate or unequable) measure of duration by the means of motion, which is commonly used instead of true time; such as an hour, a day, a month, a year.
>
> *(Newton, 1956, p. 152)*

Newton, here, articulates the view that would support a standard of view of time for Enlightenment thought – time, like space, as an empty container in which different events could be substituted without reference to their particularity. Moreover, Locke, despite his emphasis on the *experience* in the succession of ideas, essentially internalizes Newtonian absolute time: "*Duration is but as it were the length of one streight* [sic] *Line*, extended *in infinitum* . . . one common measure of all Existence whatsoever, wherein all things whilst they exist, equally partake" (Locke, 1689/1975, p. 203). The Lockean flow of ideas, hence, perfectly corresponds with the tick-tock regularity of happenings of events in the physical world. The problem, of course, with this picture is that it is a picture, and would throw into question the subject being able to attain the point external to time/world, while remaining a part of it. Notwithstanding Hume's skeptical consignment of time as a secondary quality of mind (which positions him as foil for Descartes/ Newton), Leibniz would recall the scholastic understanding of time for support. Leibniz's dissent involves his desire to account for time as "well-founded" phenomenon, without establishing the dynamic interaction of substances (monads) upon an empty, purposeless ground of grid-like time and space. Instead, Leibniz offers a view of time that would – in a way – mediate the difference between pre-modern and Enlightenment theories, where time is understood as marked within relations among actual beings who inhabit an intrinsically harmonious world – indeed, the best of all worlds. Leibniz (1951) writes that "it cannot be said that (a certain) duration is eternal but (it can be said) that the things which continue always are eternal, (gaining always a new direction). Whatever exists of time and duration perishes continually" (p. 72). In other words, only actual things exist, and the product of their rational movement we know as time; however, in the absence of actual things and their change, there would be no time. Like Cartesian-Newtonian-Lockean identification of the subject with God-like perception, Leibniz relies on God himself as evidenced only through his creation as the absentee guarantor of what manifests as time. Thus, Leibniz, even with his refusal, takes part in the classical episteme, where relations in time, whether absolute or dependent on change in actuality, occur according to certain laws. The subject's gaze, whether oriented towards space, time, *or the contents of its consciousness*, strangely rests on its embeddedness in the world that it inhabits – its place among its regularities, its always already existent qualities – for its justification, even while presupposing its separation.

The classical episteme, bearing a broadly Cartesian reflexivity and *ethos* of self-relation, failed at the end of the eighteenth century. Foucault (1966/1973) holds that early Enlightenment or classical intelligibility is marked by manifestly unproblematic representation, by correspondence of the world with the set of identities and differences in an ideal conceptual space where "the manifestation and sign of truth are to be found in evident and distinct perception . . . Language has withdrawn from the midst of beings themselves and has entered a period of transparency and neutrality" (p. 56). The mental activity that distinguishes the classical period is that of discrimination, and Foucault excavates the analysis of wealth, natural history, and general grammar to demonstrate how classical knowledge represents reality as a table or grid, locating every being in its proper place through *mathesis* (algebraic and quantitative analysis) and *taxonomia* (qualitative but empirical ordering of complex natures). For instance, as to the latter method, authentically evolutionary theories for living beings are not thinkable under the rubric of natural history because such beings form a continuous expanse, not subject to the disjointing effects of time. Either method was in principle, if not in practice, exhaustive. Due to the frailties of this ideal schema, three related consequences follow that bear upon the emergence of the modern episteme, and the rise of the human sciences. First, representation comes to crisis in being grounded in something other than itself, losing the capacity to provide its own foundation. In other words, representation cannot justify its own processes in a manner that authentically corresponds to reality itself, to the ways that it would purport that its classifications would hang together. Furthermore, the subject of this epoch, possessing the technical fluency of classifying knowledge and holding correspondence out from itself, occupies an impossibly invisible position above knowledge, unable to account for itself in representation. Second, and relatedly, not only was the ideal subject out of play questioned in this crisis, the very act of representing reality was unable to be represented. In other words, though representations were themselves undoubtedly present in public, private, and in discourse, representation *as representation* was not possible as this would have threatened the grid-like reality that expanded in every direction as perceived by the ideal observer. Third, the ideal, almost God-like position of the classical subject ostensibly existing (*exsistere* – "to stand out") out of temporal reality becomes problematized. Recall that philosophies from Plato through Leibniz typically attempt to resolve the nature of time within a cosmic or metaphysical plane of argument. The embodiment of the subject *in time* – without the assumption of an eternal or atemporal vantage point – would supply a possible basis for the representation of representations, and a different basis for its ethical self-relation.

The blindness of self-reflection characterizing frailty of classical reason would intimately relate to the meaning of madness in this period. According to Foucault's (1961/2009) magisterial, if flawed, account of the history of madness in the age of reason, it is none other than Descartes (1641/2008) who signals the role of madness as a prototypical expression of the unreason that would constitute the inverse of reason. Indeed, as Foucault (1961/2009) argues, Descartes founds his method of skeptical inquiry on thinking that would overcome dreaming and error; however, madness is excluded at the outset from the thought experiment as incompatible with reason itself. Quite famously, such exclusion parallels the "Great Confinement," an institutional phenomenon in mid-seventeenth-century Europe – contested by some historians as to its geographical reach (Pietikäinen, 2015; Porter, 2003) – in which the mad were confined alongside the poor, rebellious youth, irresponsible parents, blasphemers, and the generally idle. Several consequences follow from the visible segregation of those evidencing the hold of unreason, particularly those believed to be mad. First, unreason as madness was disengaged from its dialogue with reason from the medieval period and Renaissance; its proximity to truth beyond rational convention, the "madness of the Cross" and wisdom of folly as ambiguously expressed in Erasmus or Shakespeare, was banished into silence as a possession by error about reality (Foucault, 1961/2009). Burton's (trans. 1927) *Anatomy of Melancholy* contains vestigial elements of the older order, where the suffering of melancholy continues the stain of original sin, making its appearance a uniquely human possibility. Nijenhuis (2015), arguing in favor of "traumatic melancholia," nonetheless, notes that, similar to Burton, other authorities on melancholia (i.e., Felix Plater) linked it not only to terrible events but to being damned and fearing punishment. The early modern perspective, however, would increasingly hold, as does Locke (1689/1975), that madmen wrongly associate certain ideas and reason improperly from them. Second, unreason does not become pervasively defined through discourse figuring it as deterministic mechanism as it would when theorized as mental illness in the nineteenth century; rather, unreason would not be a natural condition, having a psychological and physiological substrate, but would become nonhuman animality, characterized by an endless and nocturnal freedom (Foucault, 1961/2009). As Gutting (1989) notes, Foucault outlines many of the classification systems developed for madness in this period, but finds that none of these conceptual lenses (which include the emergent discourses on "nerves") persist for very long because they could not penetrate what, by definition, was excluded from them. Third, the early modern status of madness as a species of unreason would recapitulate, in a different form, a similar problem to the relation of madness and sin in the Middle Ages – that is, something foreign becomes necessary to the purity of a certain mode of existence:

> Madness was caught up and enveloped in the moral experience of an unreason that was proscribed by internment in the seventeenth century, but was also linked to the experience of an animal unreason that formed the absolute limit of the incarnation of reason . . . when seen as part of the animal world and its rampant unreason, it was its monstrous innocence that came to the fore. What resulted could be called a contradictory experience.
>
> *(Foucault, 1961/2009, p. 158)*

Representation, as the rational exercise of correlating the world itself with its perfectly contoured ideational surrogates, problematically excludes unreason as madness as a guarantor of its perfection. Someone could not be mad – possessed of error – and also have an accurate picture of the world, nor could one live a moral life that is distinctively human. Yet, in parallel with the demise of the classical episteme as a matter of paradox, such an absolutely and resolutely rational gaze would leave aside a range of experience that could not be made sense of as mad, and – thus – lose its exalted position. Madness, thus, becomes a trauma to reason as a superordinate position beyond the living beings forming the categories of reason themselves.

Modernity and knowledge

What is really striking about the modern age is not its fundamental reordering of epistemic structures – as previous shifts had always accomplished new beginnings – but the ways in which its discourses and institutions reconstituted pathways to knowledge amidst the very failure of classical systems of representation. There are several dimensions along which this collapse may be seen to become foundational. These fault lines emerge in relation to an ongoing crisis in representation, a turn towards structural over ideal classification, and an ultimate appeal to temporality and historicality over metaphysical conceptions of time. First, as suggested *supra*, representation is not sufficient unto itself, and must appeal to an "outside" in order to operate without contradiction. Kant (1781/2007) emblematically responds for a newer regime, arguing that the very cognitive filters that limit representation (including time) are positive conditions of the possibility for knowledge. The inauguration of the modern episteme is precisely the solution to this problem of where to locate the subject and its representations, for the reason that the limits of knowledge are structurally incorporated into a subject who may, in turn, empirically represent itself as an object of knowledge according to the lights of its own finitude. On the significance of the Kantian redrawing of human being, Foucault (1966/1973) notes that the Kantian perspective signals a new episteme, one beyond representation that proceeds from exhaustive classification to the condition of limit. This would have profound effects on the increasing splintering of disciplinary knowledge outside of the possibilities of pure representation. Indeed, the rise of certain disciplines – especially the human sciences – in the nineteenth century depends on the growing capacity of the subject to hold its representations at a distance from itself. Second, the capacity to apprehend the sedimentations of different fields of representation relates to a shift from locating realities by reference to identities and differences towards distinguishing the discrete structures of knowledge. Consequently, purely deductive sciences such as mathematics become distinguished from empirical pursuits (such as philology, economics, and biology), each containing its own functional account of its own domain of knowledge. Third, the court of last resort in upholding or striking down the rationality or coherence of projects of knowledge is generally not conceived of as a place of philosophical reflection, but appears as the furthest reaches of dispersion in that of origin or history.

The structural features governing the modern episteme are particularly manifest in Foucault's (1966/1973) analysis of the empirical sciences (i.e., philology, biology, and economics), and in the human sciences (i.e., literature, psychology, and sociology). In Foucault's view, the classical analysis of wealth bears a fundamental difference from the field of economics as it came to be constituted in the nineteenth century. For Adam Smith (1776/1970), a commodity held value because of its correspondence with the value of labor, which was statically represented as deriving from its exchange value in the marketplace. As Gutting (1989) notes, Smith's understanding, though pointing the way to the modern episteme, still remained captive in the previous epoch's concern with exchange. For Ricardo (1817/1973), however, value relates not according to an ideal analysis, but to its historical conditions of production:

> It will be seen then, that in the early stages of society, before much machinery or durable capital is used, the commodities produced by equal capitals will be nearly of equal value, and will rise and fall only relatively to each other on account of more or less labor being required for their production; but after the introduction of these expensive and durable instruments [machinery], the commodities produced by the employment of equal capitals will be of very unequal value; and . . . they will still be liable to rise or fall relatively to each other, as more or less labor becomes necessary to their production.
>
> *(p. 26)*

Similarly, the natural history of the classical age had been subsumed under different variables of description (i.e., form, number, arrangement, and magnitude), which could be simultaneously perceived by the eye and transparently represented (Foucault, 1966/1973). The rupture in this system of knowledge made biology possible, where a strictly non-perceptible, but theoretically posited, functionality of the organism within a historically changing environment becomes the touchstone for knowledge of life. Though philology of the nineteenth century developed at a slower rate than did biology, it follows the trajectory of abandoning representation for structural formalization, charting not the manner in which language would transparently form correspondence with the world, but its contours as rooted in the historical and cultural lives of its subjects. What manifests from this analysis of these seemingly disparate realms of knowledge is a persistent concern with structural principles that surmount representation by finding its ground elsewhere – not in the frozen field of space, but in movement, in change, in historical succession. Moreover, it turns out that – for Foucault (1966/1973) – the structural principles governing philology, biology, and economics, while embodying an underlying historical dynamism, submit the ongoing crisis of representation to different metaphors. As Gutting (1989) succinctly states, economics is premised on a model of knowledge wherein *conflict* is governed by a body of *rules*, biology on a model where *functions* are regulated by *norms*, and philology on human expression as having *meaning* within the context of a system of *signs*. Nonetheless, these structural principles are not themselves confined exclusively to the domains in which they most firmly reside. In any event, modern thought is defined by its anthropological reference, where the being of man as the human subject and his/her limitations and capacities for knowledge in time coincide.

The human sciences occupy a privileged position for modernity, embodying by virtue of their explicit concern with man the divergent possibilities of accessing the very finitude that defines knowledge in the epoch, but also the dangers of a profoundly forgetful regression. Notably, for Foucault (1966/1973), the human sciences are linked by analogy to these different domains of knowledge – sociology to economics (conflict), literary analysis to philology (meaning), and psychology to biology (function). For biology, as argued by Canguilhem (1989), norms, though potentially integrated into a legitimately scientific enterprise, are not themselves objective facts: "Strictly speaking then, there is no biological science of the normal. There is a science of biological situations and conditions *called* normal" (p. 228). The pathological or abnormal is coexistent with the normal, and constitutes health only in relation to a significant functionality for the organism. This does not result in an abject skepticism towards biological reality because the environmental and evolutionary contexts for the development of organisms over time are relatively stable in comparison to social or cultural conditions. While Canguilhem (1989) expresses skepticism that the norms of organisms may be applied to the norms of human beings in their social relations, Foucault (1966/1973) distinguishes a further danger for the human sciences that have patterned themselves after empirical sciences, causing the first term (function, conflict, signification) to become obscured under the ascendancy of the latter term (norm, rule, system), resulting in a tyranny of isolated pursuits losing their own original connection with the values governing their approaches to knowledge. Put differently, the human sciences – and for trauma, psychology, and psychiatry especially – leave their own grounding in the analytic of finitude, their association to the particular conditions (function, conflict, signification) embedded in the lives of suffering subjects. Foucault's (2003, 2008) work of the mid-1970s – including, *inter alia*, Collège de France lectures *Abnormal* and *Psychiatric Power* – began a large-scale unearthing of the regimes of knowledge underpinning the birth of psychiatric and psychological subjectivity. Following Foucault's investigations of deviancy in nineteenth-century psychiatry, which would trace the organization, coherence, and practices constituting certain objects of knowledge (such as infantile sexuality or childhood itself, or the neurological body), social constructionist approaches to the psy-disciplines would interrogate the institutional epistemologies that normalize behavior, thought, and affect (Burman, 1994; Gergen, 1997; Hook, 2007; Parker, 2014; Rose, 1996). As Gergen (1997) suggests, experimental methods in psychology tend to replicate the governing assumptions already embraced by the researcher, be they related to information processing or externally verified behavioral contingencies. In parallel, Danziger (1997) profitably examines how psychology's conceptual architecture (i.e., learning, personality, motivation, behavior, etc.) arises in certain modern, sociohistorical contexts for use – for instance, how "motivation" arises according to the functional dictates of industry to explain, predict, and control the productive achievements of workers, children, or consumers. In this way, psychology and sociology, among other disciplines, declare their autonomy from animating structural principles, which may betray their allegiance to certain assumptions regarding health or what a flourishing society would resemble. This seeming independence from claims of general knowledge authorizes their unique contributions, substituting valorized methodologies derived from the natural sciences within their social positioning.

Besides the human sciences, whose institutional boundaries tend to close ranks around their own shares of influence in the politics of knowledge, two other institutional practices, philosophy and the "counter-sciences" – with requisite attention to the ontological, epistemological, and historical – promise illumination of modern subjectivity in its failures (Foucault, 1966/1973). Philosophical inquiry instigates the search for the abstract conditions of possibility for representations of objects (whether those presented by sciences of life, labor, or language). The strand of philosophical discourse initiated by Kant frames a transcendental subject that would reconcile rationalistic and empirical thought. An opposing strand seeks understanding within the empirical mode, and Foucault places Marxist historicism, as well as positivism and phenomenological inquiry, in this category. Arguably, however, Foucault's project escapes the gravity of traditional philosophy, becoming allied – drawing on Bachelard (2002) – with a "psychoanalysis of knowledge." Indeed, the more ontologically attuned strands of psychoanalysis, set free from their scientistic appropriation in the human sciences (in psychology and psychiatry), form counter-sciences providing an especially penetrating analysis of the representations of the human sciences, attributed to a subject whose realities are ultimately regulated through principles of death, desire, and law. As Gutting (1989) notes, Foucault (1966/1973) clearly has Lacan in mind as he writes that psychoanalysis manages an advance over representation, surpassing its referential or signified knowledge in the forms of finitude that order the subject. As suggested, and as will be argued, Lacanian approaches to analysis may scaffold discursive possibilities for such representational depictions because psychoanalytic thought *traverses the epistemological space* through both an accounting of the unthought of the *cogito* that poses the limit for the subject's self-possession and a submission of subjectivity to diachronic rupture (Foucault, 1966/1973). Psychoanalytic expressions reveal defining points of a different sort of subjective structuration. From a Lacanian perspective, the presence of science as a formalizing and decentering orientation towards consciousness entails a linking of modernity and a certain epistemic constraint to reading this subject (Milner, 1991; Parker, 2011). Equally attuned to the break of modernity so fruitfully exploited by Foucault, Lacan's works newly conceptualize the diachronic and synchronic constitution of the subject, the effects being dependent on the inherent structure of language itself.

The analytic of finitude

The aporias ordering modern subjectivity, as epistemic conditions, occasion the emergence of man as a reluctant resident of the domains of knowledge previously consigned to a fallen world, or held out in detachment. Recall that the Western pre-modern subject before the Enlightenment inhabited worlds where one's inner or outer speech involved not detachment, but ethical immersion into an existence impossibly bound, for truth or suffering, to the intelligible. Early Enlightenment, Cartesian thought abandoned the requirement of self-transformational relation to knowledge, instantiating radical reflexivity of procedural reason as the point of access to a "punctual self" (Taylor, 1989). Importantly, this reflexivity that would allow the subject to represent the content of experience to itself would attain a further heightened capacity, as knowledge itself of what it means to be human came to be locally signified. This leads Foucault (1966/1973) to the somewhat astonishing conclusion that "before the end of the eighteenth century, *man* did not exist" (p. 308). The appearance of man, thus, coincides with the demise of the possibility for the attainment of an absolute knowledge from an ideal position of height, but the coming into possibility of representing representation. Modern thought is characterized by the emergence of man as a subject whose representations themselves become objects of empirical knowledge (i.e., statements about itself), as well as statements that index the external world vis-à-vis its capacities. For Foucault (1966/1973), who famously writes that man would be washed away by the tides as a face drawn in the sand, the structural conditions of the modern episteme would eventually give way to another order of "words and things" (*les mots et les choses*). This collapse, arguably underway, would involve transcendence of prevailing limitations and its succession in another order having altogether different frailties. As the immersion of pre-modern experience was surmounted in the detached rationality of classical representation, so modernity and its capacity to reflect upon representation would itself give way to further arrangements that become visible in the ruins of finitude. More pointedly, the analytic of finitude that discloses positive conditions for the modern subject, thus, also contains irreducible lacunae that problematize truth, knowledge, and subjectivity. Foucault identifies three structural conditions for the possibility of knowledge that follow from the analytic of finitude: the empirico-transcendental doublet, *cogito* and the unthought, and historicality/temporality.

The division of man into a kind of empirico-transcendental doublet appears in both philosophical discourse and in the intersection of the human sciences of psychiatry and psychology. For philosophy, this doubling follows from Kant's (1781/2007) famous answer to the challenge laid down by the Humean submission of experience, perception, and causality to sensation and sentiment. Kant wishes to preserve the contingent particularity of individual experience, while also arriving at the formal conditions for experiential knowledge; however, the residue of metaphysics shadows his efforts. Perpetual deferral between the transcendental *a priori* conditions of knowledge (i.e., the intuitions of space and time, and concepts of and principles of causality, substance, etc.) and the empirical determinations of man threatens to undermine the co-constitution of the doublet through immediate transposition of the transcendental into the empirical, and vice versa. In other words, the transcendental subject relies on the positive attributes of man for its being, while the sedimented findings of knowledge simultaneously require a transcendental subject. Han (1998) asserts of Foucault's critique of Kant that such a transposition of the transcendental within experience always occurs as if it were *already there* – that the *a priori* could only appear within experience even though experience only appears in the forms that the *a priori* would legislate as the conditions of experience. One seductive philosophical solution to this predicament is to ground thought in one or the other pole of analysis. In its transcendental form, what Foucault (1966/1973) calls the "eschatological" solution, empirical knowledge is captive to the heightened reflective capacities of philosophical inquiry, most evident as just seen in Kant. In its empirical form, this results in varieties of phenomenology and positivism (both those explicitly traveling under its guise and those unwittingly replicating such methods), whose contours must always methodologically mirror their ideal objects, and whose boundaries must rigidly exclude any Procrustean remainders. From Comte through the logical empiricism of the Berlin school, the aim has been for philosophical inquiry to adopt the methods of natural science, where functional description, explanation, and prediction replace transcendent knowledge. For positivism, however, the content of inquiry that would guarantee certainty would necessarily be bound to a metaphor of spatialized objects, retroactively forming its deductive-nomological method. Moreover, of Marx's dialectal materialism – arguably empirical in its historicism – Foucault argues that knowledge is found to have a historically formed yet socio-material substrate that would be amenable to empirical apprehension. Nonetheless, a historical metanarrative promising liberation and an unalienated transcendent subjectivity calling for class consciousness from the future occasion vacillation from empiricism (material conditions) to eschatology. For the most part, thus, Foucault (1966/1973) regards both positivistic and eschatological approaches as bound to reproduce the same quandary, the same doubled movement between subject and its predication as object.

The recalcitrant excess of non-knowledge that escapes understanding or transcription in the doubling of man is further articulated in the problem of the *cogito* and the unthought. Foucault (1966/1973) points out that if the modern subject is beset by the empirico-transcendental doublet, then he/she can neither occupy sovereignty of the *cogito* nor can he/she become identified with the deadened world of objects, which could never attain consciousness. Instead, what the modern subject *must* do is reimagine (i.e., theorize) itself as being accompanied by its own unthought – not hidden knowledge, but the outside, the Other of thought, the unconscious. Overall, this insight generates several related constraints for the engagement with the crisis of modernity. First, we must be wary of normalizing a certain transparency at the expense of its margin. This is most noticeable in the classical conception of the Cartesian *cogito*, but will be seen later for the normalizing clinical discourses around trauma. For Descartes (trans. 1954), it is always conceivable that the knowing subject is under illusion or madness, like those delusional sorts who "firmly assert they are kings, when really they are miserably poor" (p. 62); however, as argued previously, madness itself remains highly problematic. In Cartesian philosophy, the possibility of non-knowledge is primarily a foil for the scaffolding of reflection allied to God-like reflection, and the assumed beneficence of a God would never deceive the subject. Phrased differently, the outside of knowledge (including madness) is not questioned in classical thought and exists mostly as a way of establishing certainty; *it is unaccounted for.* Second, any philosophy of consciousness that ostensibly addresses knowledge evading the empirico-transcendental doublet cannot rely on the classical, Cartesian position. The modern *cogito*, as theorized in Husserl's (1991) phenomenology, thus contains impulses merely replicating the doublet – that is, the proliferation of experiential renderings, the position of the transcendental subjectivity of the *epoché*, and silence regarding the vanishing point leading from irreconcilable and parallel questioning. As to the direction that phenomenology shows us, Foucault (1966/1973) writes – implicitly evoking Heideggerian hermeneutics – that in regression to the *cogito* phenomenological inquiry has persistently led to questions of ontology. Third, such an ontology must reimagine finitude as part of its rendering of the subject, lest it merely recapitulate the struggles of the subject at the level of epistemology. Overall, ontologies of the subject making finitude structural to the subject's very being (such as certain readings of Freud) cannot depend upon the reassertion or refashioning of an integral subjectivity. Consequently, unthought, as incorporated into modern subjectivity, is not coincident with knowledge, and does not rely – like the ever diminishing size of Russian nesting dolls – on the concealed homunculus for its being. Fourth, unthought recapitulates the historical subject's relation to time, and its existence in time, because the transcendental subject brings an impermissible extra-temporal perspective to the empirical subject's historical involvement.

Modernity and temporality

Recall that for the pre-moderns, time in the world – as manifested in the thought of Plato, Aristotle, Plotinus, and Augustine – relates to a timeless order that, in principle, could be imperfectly discerned by the subject. It was the world that took up the burden of fastening the subject to meaning, to its own life, and part of the subject's relation to itself through time emanating from a nearby elsewhere, giving purpose to the fallen, decaying, run-down world of creation, and its madness. In a sense, the subject's return to itself through this other world involved piercing the mystery parallel to the existing world, as if accessing one's origin in an intelligible realm or in one's historical unfolding was simply a matter of peeling back an occluding layer of film that separates one from deep infusion into the cosmos. For the early Enlightenment or classical subject, the raising of the subject to an ideal position facilitated a transparent rendering of the subject's knowledge of itself. Whether through the analysis of wealth or general grammar, its representations are not yet problematized, and the subject finds itself intact within a grid of knowledge resembling a table and in which "its starting-point is at the same time outside real time and inside it: it is the first fold that enables all historical events to take place" (Foucault, 1966/1973, p. 329). Its relationship to itself through time remains essentially synchronic, as it had been for pre-modernity, assuming as it does a transcendental stance towards its knowledge as a spatialized extension from itself – *space out of time.* For classical thought, bearing notions of time as a reification of the beings and entities within its absolutization as an empty container, or real and dynamic relations guaranteed by an immanent rationality among them, the knowing subject is not identified in time itself, or even in its own history. For this subject, due to the vast distance that it puts between itself alongside God and its knowledge, a third term, or excess, escapes the subject – that is, its structuration through time.

Standing at the threshold of the epistemic fault line defining modernity, and initiating the inquiry into the limits of knowledge in the *Critique of Pure Reason*, Kant (1781/2007) provides the previously unseen foundation for classical thought by grounding representation of the external object in a human relation with the world. For Kant, and for Foucault, what becomes clear is that the apparent difference between rationalist and empiricist philosophies collapses under a shared philosophical horizon of the adequation of idea with object. Consequently, the Kantian and modern "epistemological turn" sublates both the Newtonian absolutist conceptions of time and the Leibnizian conception of space/time as a hypostatization of ideal relations among objects. Rather, time, for Kant, becomes neither empirical nor conceptual but a form of *a priori* intuition. Hoy (2009) writes,

> For Kant, the main reason time cannot be perceived is because although perception is constantly changing, time itself does not change. Time is the framework for all perception . . . This argument represents a revolutionary perspective on time. Instead of talking about the nature of time as it is in itself, Kant focuses attention on time as a function of our minds.
>
> *(p. 7)*

Though time for Kant is formative of sensible forms of experience, he does not theorize time in a way that would explicitly account for the subject's own immersive relation within, which would amount to a more psychologically descriptive rendering of his epistemological solution to the classical problem of time as ideal relation. The Kantian project of removing time from its exclusion in the exterior world has the effect of positing the subjective interiority of time consciousness as an analogue to the consciousness of physical events and objects in the outer world. Kant (1781/2007) writes that "even our inner experience, which Descartes considers undoubted, is possible only on the supposition of outer experience" (p. 238).

Kant's cognitivist stance towards time, as a synthetic joining of ideal time and external event, opens the theoretical possibility for a return to historical origin as a promising solution to the crisis of finitude, yet the doubling of man and the unthought continues to track these efforts. The modern subject must differently address the difficulty posed by the loss of its exalted position and its temporal interpolation among beings and entities themselves; a deeper reconciliation calls. In some ways, nihilism, having hounded logocentric thought from Plato through the late eighteenth century, poses a greater threat than ever to the subject's anchoring to its life. With the skyhooks of God, and transcendental subjectivity, no longer offering their otherworldly aid, it now falls to the subject to find itself within its own eye-level vision. The subject must find a way to ground itself in a kind of historical time that will solidify itself, to cross the chasm of reciprocal deferral from subject to object. As suggested earlier in the disciplines of biology, economics, and philology, and in the human sciences, modern thought, thus, searches for itself in its history. However, as the reader may suspect, the paralogisms seemingly surmounted will press themselves yet again into the Kantian order. Two related consequences ensue from intervention into the succession of past events, to which the knowing subject of the present does not belong (Foucault, 1966/1973). First, an event posited as the subject's true origin will always be found not to be actually true because of its relative position between what occurs before and after. In other words, any putatively determined origin (past) will depend on the passage of history into a projection towards some end (future); *the retreat to origin always recedes* (Foucault, 1966/1973). Second, any event that is offered as the subject's origin will always turn out to be *other than, exterior to* the subject itself (Foucault, 1966/1973). Consequently, the modern subject's origin always retreats as more unthought. This will, according to Foucault (1966/1973), submit the subject to the finite expression of its temporal dispersal – that life, history, and language now participate in an extricable relation with time. The subject's own being, thus, becomes an Otherness that is simultaneously remote and constitutive of the present. Historical inquiry and grounding, hence, are inextricably related to a different temporality, neither a metaphysical relation of the subject with time nor a purely Kantian or epistemological exercise. Rather, the *modern subject's being-in-time* supplants any consideration of its being located elsewhere, the possibility that it may merely extend or reference its being or entities in a neutral or objective spatial grid, or that these co-ordinates mirror its cognitive faculties.

Philosophical discourse would, in bridging the Cartesian divide between subject and object through integrative temporality, memorially reconstruct pre-modern forms of self-relation in a more self-reflexive mode. Throughout antiquity, as Foucault (2005) reminds us, the subject must always ask himself what work must be carried out on oneself – "What is the price I have to pay for access to the truth?" (p. 189). As a result, unlike Cartesian reflexivity, the subject of Greek and Roman antiquity does not seek a detached relationship with itself in forms of decontextualized knowledge. This subject, whose thoughts do not reside within its encapsulated mind, itself resides within the expanded field of psyche and its unfoldings. The subject is always already related to the enveloping Mind, which is revealed – as suggested previously – in a circular relation with the timelessness that emanates into it from the intelligible. The time of speaking, *parrhesia*, and the coincidence of will and knowledge (*gnomé*) require self-transformation (i.e., ascetic practices) for the subject to become worthy of truth. Christianity continues to associate self-transformation and truth; however, a profound historical change occurs, wherein the subject becomes compelled to speak his/her own truth – related to sin or wound – as the placeholder of his/her position in the temporal (i.e., fallen, decaying) world. In stark contrast, Cartesianism raises the *gnothi seauton* as a modern exclusion of the requirement of self-transformation in coming to disinterested knowledge.[9] Reflexivity becomes loosened from its explicitly ethical position, giving way to an *a priori* rationality that seeks to get further and further behind its worldliness, extricating itself through its atemporal identification of time and space. Crucially, however, the self-transformative impulse returns in modern thought. Though Kant, through his position of man as an empirico-transcendental doublet, ignores the necessary transformation of the subject as prerequisite for coming to knowledge, other forms of modern philosophical discourse take up subjectivity within temporality as a means of refashioning the ancient practice of self-transformation in a modern idiom.

Within the "continental tradition" of philosophical inquiry, constellating certain thought and discourse around temporality will allow us to see more clearly what needs to be accounted for in order to avoid the impossibilities befalling the subject within the analytic of finitude. Though he does not explicitly relate them to temporality, the later Foucault (2005) appears particularly interested in the thought of Hegel, Schopenhauer, Nietzsche, and Heidegger as attempts to reintroduce self-transformation into the subject's access to truth and knowledge, and would reinstate the nexus between spirituality and knowledge; however, in what appears below, I will alter this arrangement to suggest that temporality as a potentially transformative suturing of the temporal crisis of modernity appears most prominently in the thought of Hegel, Schopenhauer, Nietzsche, Husserl, and Bergson. Heidegger, it will be argued, belongs to a different and more nuanced rendering of finitude (along with Levinas and Lacan) that will come to be seen as traumatic. Importantly, under the later Foucault's reflective categorization of the various interconnected emphases of his work – veridiction (knowledge), governmentality (power), and subjectification (ethics) – the following could conceivably be approached by any one of these axes. For instance, Han (2005) refers to certain philosophical movements (such as in Hegel et al.) that would escape the analytic of finitude as modes of ethical self-transformation. Nonetheless, in order to demonstrate that these movements ultimately fail – as philosophical inquiry – to escape the analytic of finitude under the threat of deconstruction, it will serve to adhere to a discursive analysis and reserve for Heidegger, Lacan, and Levinas a discussion of ethics. In addition, the latter forms of thinking have gone much further in contemporary life in creating derivative, and more overtly, ethical practices such as existential psychotherapy and Lacanian psychoanalysis. More directly, the instant analysis of discourse on temporality involves that which meets specific qualifications as a discursive formation. As Foucault (1969/1972) contends,

> Whenever one can describe, between a number of statements, such a system of dispersion, whenever, between objects, types of statement, concepts, or thematic choices, one can define a regularity (an order, correlations, positions and functionings, transformations), we will say, for the sake of convenience, that we are dealing with a *discursive formation*.
>
> *(p. 38)*

Several important insights follow from this passage, as well as Foucault's archaeology, more generally. First, the rules of discursive formations exist at the level of *savoir* and, hence, are not reduced to the status of grammatical rules or logical strictures; they are more akin to the ways more explicit or formalized knowledge "hangs together" at an implicit or unconscious level. Second, a discursive formation does not exist due to strict unity of its elements. In other words, there is bound to be significant dispersion of statements within a discursive formation. Third, discursive formations exist along several dimensions – objects (what entities the statements concern), enunciative modalities (institutional sites), concepts (relations of ordering), and themes (theoretical viewpoints) (Foucault, 1969/1972). The instant discussion will involve the latter two axes – concept and theme – for which Foucault (1969/1972) delineates rules. For the former, positivities are governed by logic concerning the succession of statements, rules of formation (fields of presence, concomitance, and memory), and procedures for intervention; for the latter, statements occurring within specific themes or strategies occupying the pattern of concept are structured through points of diffraction and economies of constellation (Foucault, 1969/1972). For the analysis of fragmented time *as said to be* or *signified as* experienced, the discursive formation of restorative temporality is regulated through the following conceptual logic, each containing points of diffraction: 1) the problem of access; 2) the project of the subject's infusion; 3) the task of transformative transcendence; and 4) the remainder of excess. Overall, it will be argued that these discursive features govern the subject's potential for entering into the flow of experienced time while maintaining its possibilities for self-knowledge, the restorative temporality that would address the fissure or gap in being that occasions the analytic of finitude. Other forms of discourse around time or temporality are not included because they do not address subjectivity, and merely recapitulate Enlightenment rationality (Reichenbach, 1971; Russell, 1915), assume a human condition without finitude (Dewey, 1998; Peirce, 1905; Royce, 1904; Whitehead, 1964) or point to a condition of "post-finitude" (Deleuze, 1966/1988, 1994). In other words, these alternative discourses, for these differing reasons, exceed the fields of presence – the range of acceptable statements – that would form the boundaries of discourses returning the subject to its immersion in the temporality of its own self-overcoming.

Restorative temporality and the problem of access

The first discursive feature structuring restorative temporality relates to a kind of seamless access, an ideal descent into time from a consciousness hovering above it. It serves to remember that for the subject of antiquity and Christianity there is little struggle with the question of how the subject itself appears within time; the created world is metaphysically imbued with its own temporal processes. Likewise, for the classical subject, who identifies with an absolute vision that homogenizes time and space, access is of no concern. In contrast, for thought seeking to locate the subject *within* duration, the experience of temporality, or as being-in-time, required is the graceful entrance into the flow of time without giving away its status as a philosophical intruder. Aside from Kant's disenchanting and cognitive structuring of time, Hegel (1830/1970) posits temporal being as the becoming of externality, time presupposing place in the here and now of duration (i.e., as flowing from changes in the world) – where spirit actualizes itself by constantly differentiating itself:

> It is not *in* time that everything comes to be and passes away, rather time itself is the *becoming*, this coming-to-be and passing away, the *actually existent abstraction*, *Chronos*, from whom everything is born and by whom its offspring is destroyed. The real is certainly distinct from time, but is also essentially identical with it.
>
> *(p. 35)*

For Hegel, the present is a result of an actual and externalized past, and is pregnant with the future of a teleologically oriented and dialectical series of overcomings towards absolute spirit. As a result, the Hegelian subject is identified with a moment that is radically contingent, yet dormant with a future that promises to unite subject and substance and bestow freedom, always in the guise of concrete negation, and most radically as the negation of negation. But, the question remains for a rational being inscribed in the world and its shifting personal, interpersonal, and social relations: How does one discern, or enter into, its current historical position from the perspective of a future that has not transpired? Heidegger (1988) critiques Hegel on this very issue, that of presupposing an endpoint from the beginning. Unlike Hegel, Schopenhauer (1958a) – with distaste for systematic philosophy – imagines a subject suffering in its moment-by-moment dying, where every present is constantly destroyed. The essence of time, in a vein more psychologistic than Kant, involves a succession of willed representations as "everything that in any way belongs and can belong to the world is inevitably associated with this being-conditioned by the subject, and it exists only for the subject" (p. 3). Schopenhauer, thus, notably submits the Kantian enterprise to the dictates of sufficient reason, arguing that human cognition forms the representations presencing in the spatio-temporal world, even if aspects of representations – such as the origin of blind or non-rational will in-itself – are obscured in our view. Similar to Hegel, Schopenhauer finds an island amidst time, not in the future, but the eternal aesthetic, which shelters the subject from the transience breaking against and washing away present experience. In other words, persons possessed of adequate intellect may in some sense bypass the principle of sufficient reason in apprehending ideas of the beautiful. For Bergson (1896/1988), the almost magical arrival of the subject in durational time occurs in a gap between the constraints of memory and perception. One may recall that for Bergsonian temporality, a Proustian movement of perpetual differentiation occurs as one state qualitatively passes into the next (i.e., "the smell of my coffee, with the light from the window, became a particular sadness"). This differentiation, bearing freedom of will, occurs as perception (serving action rather than knowledge) presses forward into memory (as image and idea). Though Bergson eschews representation in favor of perception, and embodied action, the problem arises that Bergson's subject – who, strikingly, is living into memory – always finds itself positioned within a virtual world of ideas, through memory. The Bergsonian subject must *represent itself* as one of perception, and seems to suddenly appear into language, while really he/she has been there all along. Husserl (1991), who, against Kant, also thoroughly sketches a theory of duration or internal time consciousness, confronts an inverse issue in privileging a transcendental subject. Notably, Husserl (1991) argues that though sensations have no temporal extension, they give rise to impressions that begin in the present and extend forward (in anticipation) and sink into the past (retention), and further into secondary memory. Husserl's famous example, of course, involves a melody, where each note experienced can only be grasped in its fullness as the flow from past to future; there is no series of "now" points in a song. Ironically, perhaps, because of his keen attention to the bright light of consciousness, time itself as being registered by unexperienced sensations seems to appear out of nowhere. The grounding of temporality for Husserl (1991), as pointed out by Heidegger (1927/1962, 1985), is not experienced time at all but is a place where there is no time, a location of pure presence. Dragging their metaphysical ancestry behind them, these fictions give the subject access to its temporal being through a sort of nowhere point, a secret entryway that defies the logic of the thought itself – the future in the present, the aesthetic encounter, perception as representation, or the absent sensory impression. This leaves Nietzsche (1974), as a transitional figure, to explicitly and presciently formulate his notion of temporality as fiction, that of eternal return – the idea that everything that has ever occurred, or is occurring, will occur again. Though seemingly absurd, this thought experiment very nearly embodies – as a kind of closed circuit – a temporal world that cannot be accessed, ideally, from the outside. Thus, Nietzsche's doctrine of eternal recurrence, as a metafictional description of the problem, allows us to see what the other perspectives do not quite accomplish. There is no way in or out of being-in-time – not through reflection, perception, or contemplation; we are always already immersed in it, and any authentic account of temporality must begin there.

The project of the subject's infusion

Under the analytic of finitude, the subject finds itself oscillating between the transcendental position (whether of knowledge or will) reminiscent of the classical episteme and being frozen into objects of knowledge – whether the disciplinary knowledge of the human sciences (for instance, psychological theories of perception, or cognition), or as represented (or held out) to oneself in experience (i.e., "These are merely my emotions"). One project, differently configured across the discursive formation espousing restorative temporality, concerns that of infusing the subject and his/her experiences and being within the flow of time. The potential exists, thus, for a holistic merger that would reestablish an anchor to meaning, a re-enchantment of a more secular world. Following William James' (1890) notion of "specious present," a duration of present consciousness containing our awareness of time as a qualitative process, Husserl (1991) writes that

> since temporality always becomes constituted phenomenologically and stands before us in appearance as an objectivity or as a moment of an objectivity only through this constitution, a phenomenological analysis of time cannot clarify the constitution of time without considering the constitution of temporal objects. By *temporal objects in the specific sense* we understand objects that are not only unities in time but that also contain temporal extension in themselves.
>
> *(p. 24)*

Husserl, here, speaks not of "objects" of representation (of knowledge), but of intentionality. In the specious present, experiencings of whatever kind always involve a vectored and intentional connection to past and future manifestations. Indeed, experience is only possible at all because of the retention of specific experiences of objects, thoughts, feelings, people, etc. and their protention into the future. Time, for Husserl, is ostensibly a *living present*, rather than a depicted one. Like Husserl, and against the Newtonian impulse, Hegel also contends that the present cannot exist independently of the past and future. In some ways, however, Hegel (1830/1970) attempts a kind of reverse of the phenomenological project of intentionality, instead grounding temporality within events and relations external to, rather than identical with, each other: "Negativity, as point, relates itself to space, in which it develops its determinations as line and plane; but in the sphere of self-externality, negativity is equally *for itself* . . . Negativity, thus posited for itself, is Time" (pp. 33–34). For Hegel (1830/1970), the modern subject has been incorrectly imagined as an empty structure for knowing an outside world, whereas its being is historically contingent upon its progressive dialectical social relations. Contingency emerges, as well, for the Bergsonian subject, who perceptively moves through the world by encountering its memories, as they are coming towards the subject: "It is from the present that the appeal to which memory responds . . . It should descend from the heights of pure memory down to the precise point where action is taking place" (Bergson, 1896/1988, p. 153). The instantiation of the subject in time follows from its location in unconscious memory; its entire past may be drawn from novel ways of sensing, perceiving, and acting. In some parallel with Hegelian and Bergsonian differentiation, Nietzsche's subject, though fastened to the past, finds in its materials a more authentic and self-defining involvement. The Nietzschean subject's temporal being bestows meaning polemically. Rejecting traditional authorities of reason and morality, Nietzsche finds in temporal experience the possibilities of inspiration, dignity, and critique. For instance, in what he calls "monumental" relation to history, one may draw courage to heroically and existentially live one's own life in one's own terms. One's life, and one's history, is an ongoing affirmation, rather than passive reception. In anticipating the more fully developed existential thought of Heidegger (1927/1962) and Sartre

(1956), Schopenhauer (1958b) equates infusion into lived time as the process of dying: "The human individual finds himself . . . as a vanishing quantity . . . His real existence is only in the present, whose unimpeded flight into the past is a constant transition into death, a constant dying" (p. 311). The subject's being-in-time, therefore, relates to its suffering; temporality infuses one into life because of its purchase on negation over against the integrity of one's experience, sense of embodiment, and selfhood – as also will be seen in Heidegger, Levinas, and Lacan.

The task of transformative transcendence

As Han (2005) argues, Foucault's interest in Hegel, Schopenhauer, and Nietzsche relates to their recontextualization of epistemology, and their submission of knowledge to the task of self-transformation as truth. I would also suggest that Bergson and Husserl, albeit in different ways, take part in the modern recreation of the ancient and/or Christian requirement that to approach truth, one must undergo a kind of change in subjectivity. Hegel, as stated, subscribes to the notion that consciousness must transform itself through successive dialectical relation in discrete social and historical situations. In the Marxist iteration of Hegelian thought, for instance, the feudal subject presses his master for more autonomy in the uncertain hope for a freer exchange of capital. The end result of Hegel's historical and phenomenological purification may be a profoundly modern, absolute reflexivity; however, the journey there is worked out through time, and is soiled with sacrifice, even bloodshed. Schopenhauer (1958b) also points the way to an effacement – that of the will for transcendence of the phenomenal experience of suffering:

> If, therefore, the object has to such an extent passed out of all relation to something outside it, and the subject has passed out of all relation to the will, what is thus known is no longer the individual thing as such, but the *Idea*, the eternal form, the immediate objectivity of the will at this grade . . . he is *pure*, will-less, painless, timeless *subject of knowledge.*
>
> *(p. 179)*

Schopenhauer, in this passage and more explicitly, appears to return to a Platonic stance towards knowledge. Nonetheless, its more contemporary, and Eastern, form of self-renunciation – in both aesthetic and moral terms – transcends the passing away of experience aimed not at an intelligible world beyond this world but in a respite from the non-purposive, conflicting will at the center of everything. As a point of thematic diffraction, Nietzsche (1974), though similarly concerned with will, advocates for the heroic self-willing of the overman, who will be able to bear the weight of existence – that of affirming a life lived over and over again, according to his or her own lights. Truth, in his conception, is seized as a renunciation, but not of will or the energetic impulses to create or destroy; rather, Nietzsche desires to shed the deception and illusion allied to a slavish *ressentiment* towards power, and the construction of passive/aggressive systems of morality and rationality that conceal their aims. Husserl and Bergson, though lacking an explicitly defined sense of spiritual transformation, offer theories of temporality that necessitate and/ or culminate in transcendence. For Husserl (1991), apprehending the flow of the living present calls forth a double intentionality. On the one hand, a horizontal intentionality tracks protention and retention, or duration. On the other hand, a transverse intentionality tracks objects across their successive manifestations. The unity of time results in the subject's capacity to stand out from the flow, a non-temporal temporalizing. However, this absolute, transcendental subject arises out of its discernment of noetic structure from the lived noematic qualities of particular experiences themselves. In contrast, Bergson (1896/1988) proceeds somewhat synchronically, holding that temporality stems from a pure becoming in the form of a coexistence of perception and memory; the past is not distinct from the present, but part of the perceptive acquisition of shards or strands of a pure memory, a virtual repository of ideas. In a Proustian and somewhat Nietzschean vein, the subject achieves transcendence through actualizing a particular past according to its current exigencies. The Bergsonian subject is able to achieve freedom through calling into being its possible pasts.

The remainder of excess

For the discursive formation of restorative temporality, the subject's fictional access to itself in time, arising from impossible aims of transformative transcendence and infusion into contingency, results in an excess of what cannot be thought. While the arrival of the subject's temporal being ostensibly rescues its position from historically stultifying ontotheological systems, the empirico-transcendent doublet and its accompanying unthought are not surmounted in theoretical attempts to suture temporality from the outside. In different ways, Hegel, Schopenhauer, Nietzsche, Husserl, and Bergson rely on a metaphysical elsewhere, a point external to their various understandings, to make their theories work. According to Foucault's (1969/1972) archaeological method, this would, in part, characterize a particular referential point in their discursive regularities. For our postmodern condition, Hegelian metaphysics, critiqued by many over the past thirty years, produces

> a metanarrative, for the story's narrator must not be a people mired in a particular positivity of its traditional knowledge . . . The narrator must be a metasubject in the process of formulating both the legitimacy of the discourses of the empirical sciences and that of the direct institutions of popular cultures. This metasubject, in giving voice to their common grounding, realizes their implicit goal.
>
> *(Lyotard, 1984, p. 34)*

As suggested, the Hegelian address of finitude is to defer to a metaphysical futurity that is silently and implicitly embedded in personal, interpersonal, or social dialectical paths through self-externalization. This futurity – both as metanarrative and the presumed coming of a metasubject – is both there and not there; its presence as eventual historical fulfillment is required for a vectored unfolding through time, yet it is also always absent and cannot be found anywhere. The Hegelian reliance on an external future shares a structural feature with a Bergsonian metaphysics of exteriority. For Bergson, duration is grounded on the double and fictional coordinates of pure memory and pure perception. As Bergson (1896/1988) writes, "Ideas – pure recollections summoned from the depths of memory – develop into memory-images" (p. 125), whereas pure perception hypothesizes that a subject unburdened by the inscriptions of memory into its world would attain "a vision of matter both immediate and instantaneous" (p. 34). Consequently, Bergson's metaphysics appears to require two separate locations of nowhere, each to offset its other as a concrete operation. For instance, pure perception undergirds the phenomenon of living into an actualized past because perception is only engraved in the particular by the exigencies of the past; it must start out as "pure," which it never is. Schopenhauer's metaphysical orientation, of course, involves less of an explanation of how subjectivity is structured, and more of a fevered search for relief from its fastening to its own conflicting impulses and desires. Schopenhauer's (1958b) philosophical discourse, therefore, bleeds into that of mysticism, where his asceticism offers escape into a place beyond time where his distinction between will and representation, paralleling subject and object, collapses: "Nothing will be left but to refer to that state which is experienced by all who have attained to complete denial of the will, and which is denoted by the names ecstasy, rapture, illumination, union with God" (p. 410). Though Schopenhauer posits that will underlies all appearance (and representation), both tendencies defer to this other term for its reality. For example, will may only be understood through appearance, which, as such, only exists in relation to something underneath. Nietzsche's will-to-power is governed by a similar sense of elsewhere, though his thought clearly comes down on the side of sanctioning the subject's will to affirm life, to create knowledge according to its own values, desires, etc. Hence, Nietzschean thought is inversely related to the excess that authorizes it, the nihilism that it opposes at every turn, manifesting within the human subject as inauthentic denial, repression, non-knowledge – and temporality as a vaporous passing into nothing, rather than recurrent possibility of affirmation. In Nietzschean thought, it is nihilism itself strangely begging to be affirmed as one's own, as one's historical being could be disaffirmed at any moment. This deconstructive path through the discourse of restorative temporality culminates with Derrida's critique of the internal time consciousness of Husserl. Notably, Derrida (1973) questions Husserl's non-temporalizing temporality as an unblinking eye, privileging a metaphysics of presence where an irreducible "now" draws its retentions and protentions into itself for comprehension. In fact, argues Derrida (1973), the absent moment – one that must be represented to consciousness – is a condition for this living presence, "Nonpresence and nonevidence are admitted into the *blink of an instant*. There is a duration to the blink, and it closes the eye. This alterity is in fact the condition for presence, presentation, and thus for *Vorstellung* [representation] in general" (p. 65). Derrida's deconstruction of presence regarding Husserlian time consciousness, in some way, appears to be a mere prop for the practice of reading texts to unravel their logic via their lacunae or paradoxes (i.e., that the present moment is embedded with absence); however, a closer look not only at Derrida's critique of Husserl but at the above binaries reveals not only theoretical or textual dismantling. Rather, the fissure or gap that arises in theories that attempt to suture temporality also invade the very subject whose being exists in time. From Hegel's metasubject through Husserl's subject of presence, the discourse of restorative temporality always involves a struggle with an absence that makes possible the present of duration or contingently lived time.

The trauma of philosophy

Philosophical discourse on fractured temporality manifests the *savoir* in which discourses on psychological trauma (*connaissance*) will partake. In other words, trauma – though its status in philosophy is not the same as in the human sciences – arises in the structural crisis of the analytic of finitude. On the plane of discourse or textuality, Derrida (1974) profitably inquires into the trauma of philosophical thought, of the subject's disrupted transparent temporal possession of itself, and its missives to itself and others. Pre-modern and classical projects of attaining mastery over time through communion with the eternal, or projecting absolute time, respectively, are given over to more modest epistemological aims: "So careful to place cosmic time within brackets [they] must, as consciousness and internal time consciousness, live a time that is an accomplice of the time of the world" (Derrida, 1974, p. 67). Yet, the consciousness sought in these more earthly, modern pursuits begets knowledge resting on its origin in exteriority – in others, in history, in language, in sociality, in "the time of the world." In deconstructive terminology, consciousness requires a differing and supplemental term, non-identical to itself. In other words, the bracketing of Husserlian phenomenology – its transcendent function of attaining non-temporalizing temporality – is itself dependent on something other than itself, if not on Newtonian time, then on the succession of other happenings. As implied previously, the same could be said for Hegel's juxtaposition of absolute consciousness and negation, Bergson's binary of a pure past and pure perception, Nietzsche's will-to-power over against denial or emptiness, or Schopenhauer's ascetic escape from transient suffering. In each case, consciousness would lose its transcendental status were it not separate from its grounding, yet also dependently part of the contingencies that govern its emergence. As in psychological theories of trauma – where the possibilities of representation necessitate a space between antimimetic representation and the other scene – spectatorial depiction relies on a slicing of the originary temporal immersion and event through signification. Derrida famously relates temporality to signification, holding the spacing of language articulates – forming joints, and a series of differences – the spoken, phonic stream of temporality. The hinge, or break, or joint (*brisure*), that marks the articulation or fracture of the unity of signifier and signified paradoxically gives rise to the homogeneity of temporality. Nonetheless, the original fullness of the past, the current plenitude of the now, or the fulfillment of what will come, as it is in Husserl et al., can only be spoken of in difference as a non-identity, written of as other than now; it exists within the spacing of the mark.

For Derrida (1973), temporalization is not possible without another related sense of difference – that of the *différance* of signification. Central to Derridean deconstructive practice, *différance* – not quite a word or a concept – embodies and joins two dimensions of signification prior to representation. First, as mentioned, it is to "differ" and signifies a non-identity, a disjuncture in sameness that manifests in the visible joint or articulation (*brisure*) in the elements spacing what, for us, "makes sense." Second, it is also "to defer," to force a detour. Under Anglo-Saxon conceptions of law, it may be associated with the defense to a claim, the demurrer, which is derived from the Latin *morari*, or delay. Like the demurrer, deferral simultaneously refutes a claim of presence and puts it off to another time. For Derrida, the concern with "presence" takes its lead from Heidegger's critique of the metaphysics of presence; however, he enlarges Heidegger's analysis beyond the being (ontic reality of traits, qualities, facts, etc.) of beings into one that takes on meaning itself – the will, desire, to come into the fullness of conscious presence. As deconstructed, which discloses the trauma of philosophy, the failure of the discursive formation of restorative temporality under Husserl et al. to address the fissure in the subject's being-in-time rests not on some oversight or lack of theoretical rigor. Rather, signification itself gives the subject its being-in-time, which makes a theoretical representation of integrative temporality impossible. Not surprisingly, Derrida (1973) draws on the language of psychoanalysis in fleshing out *différance*:

> The structure of delay (*retardement: Nachträglichkeit*) that Freud talks about indeed prohibits our taking temporalization (temporalizing) to be a simple dialectical complication of the present . . . With the alterity of the "unconscious," we have to deal not with the horizons of modified presents – past or future – but with a "past" that has never been nor will ever be present, whose "future" will never be produced or reproduced in the form of presence.
>
> *(p. 152)*

For Freud (1900/1953), *Nachträglichkeit*, often translated as "deferred action" or "afterwardness," refers to the phenomenon whereby an earlier event is retroactively interpreted as traumatic after a later event. For instance, under classical psychoanalytic theory, a small child chances to observe her parents in the act of love-making. At the time, its impression is unfinished so to speak, and later in her life – in the midst of her own more developed, sexual experience – she experiences trauma relating to the first event. While a theory (most likely one with scientific pretentions) allied to a linear notion of time may conceptualize the first experience as "dormant" or "latent" in the child, the one offered by Derrida (and later discussed for Lacan) would hold that the past never really preexists the present (or alternatively, the present does not retain the past) but bears its trace through deferral and repetitive difference – *différance*. The past as it appears does not contain a fullness that is lost, but is only retrieved under certain conditions, and – like Proust's Combray – it appears as it was never lived, and has been received as a trace of signification, a message from an immemorial past, routed through the future.

What this means, of course, is that signification as an act of representation tends to structurally revolve around an absent presence, a lacuna in what many take to be ordinary temporal reality. In literary studies and for critical theory, over the past thirty years, this deconstructive tenet has been feverishly applied to texts of aesthetic importance, as well as others from a wide range of disciplines. As Derrida (1978) writes, "This is why classical thought concerning structure could say that the center is, paradoxically, *within* the structure and *outside* it" (p. 279). This insight involves a submission of their claims to presence, to coherence, to the logic of *Nachträglichkeit* via the destabilizing temporal play of the signifier, and its recalcitrant need for a supplement that always threatens to undo a text from its margins, from the future as an expression of will or desire. For the discourse of restorative temporality, and discourses of psychological trauma, the conflict between coherence and destabilization attains an agonistic crescendo. As argued *supra*, emblematic of temporal integration, Husserlian and Bergsonian time – as forms of representation – must obey the law of deferred action or afterwardness (in French, *après coup*), as must antimimesis for psychological trauma. Put differently, understandings of time cannot themselves account for a more originary or ontological trauma in theoretical metaphors lugging the heavy baggage of completeness and integrity. Consequently, a historicist perspective on subjectivity as a symptom of modernity indicates a temporality that cannot hermeneutically suture the wounding of the encounter with exteriority, with the systematic play of differences, with the incapacity to limit the proliferation of traces that disappear into an immemorial past. Derrida (1981b) writes that

> there is no subject who is its agent, its author, and master of *différance* . . .
> Subjectivity – like objectivity – is an effect of *différance*. . . . This is why the
> *a* of *différance* also recalls that spacing is temporization, the detour and post-
> ponement by means of which intuition, perception, consummation – in a
> word, the relationship to the present, the reference to a present reality, to a
> *being* – are always *deferred*.
>
> *(pp. 28–29)*

The condition of the subject not being present to itself in a persistent deferral irrevocably transforms the Cartesian *cogito* from the potential of sovereign transparency to consciousness whose basis is always other than itself (Foucault, 1966/1973). The unthought of consciousness temporally deferred arises as a historical remainder of the transcendental, unified subject, whose empirical being exists among the linguistic traces of specific institutional, disciplinary, everyday practices. The disjuncture between the subject capable of making representations (the classical Cartesian subject) corresponding to an external reality, and the modern subject who is capable *of representing those very representations to itself* requires a space of reflexivity to obtain distance from its knowledge. The sacrifice for this reflexivity is the abandonment of adequation, and the recurrent aporia between the constituting consciousness and a historically receding origin. By necessity, an apparent arrival at the subject's historical origin will be distantly empirical and interpreted in light of the present and future (one of an infinite number of histories), but simultaneously any true origin would exclude the present and future (an absolute history eradicating the efficacy of the presently undecidable moment). Consequently, Kant's (1781/2007) First Antinomy of Reason (the world has a beginning in space/time, or the world has no beginning in space/time), solved by the leap from realism to epistemology, returns to inform an ontology of the subject.

The archaeological excavation and deconstructive analysis of restorative temporality profitably expose a number of related paralogisms regarding ecstases of time – the absence of presence, the immemorial past, the transcendent apprehension of time from a point that is nowhere, etc., but the question remains as to how far these approaches may be taken as inquiries into trauma, whether psychological or philosophical. To further clarify the current direction, it may be helpful to recall Foucault's (1998) rebuttal to Derrida's (1978) critique of *Madness and Civilization*, wherein Derrida argues that Foucault's attempt to "write a history of madness *itself. Itself.* Of madness itself" (p. 33) is incomprehensible because it conducts itself as an archaeological enterprise. As a result, any putative expression of the truth of madness occurs within a structuralist analysis – what Derrida would call "meta-metaphorics," the language of Reason *par excellence*. Foucault notes in his response that Derrida, though wanting to expose rationalist, monological aspirations, himself performs a sort of generalization of doubt derived from his own epistemic privileging – not of the binary of madness/reason but of dreaming/thinking, or uncertainty and certainty. For my purposes, it is Foucault's (1998) vitriolic conclusion that puts the issue in high relief because he speaks of the classical "system of which Derrida is the most decisive modern representative, in its final glory: the reduction of discursive practices to textual traces; the elision of the events produced therein and the retention only of marks for reading" (p. 416). Derrida, it can be maintained, for all his theoretical destructiveness, is – like a rabid atheist caught still in the entangling arguments against God – held in the orbit of representation. Deconstructive practice, then, frequently appears as a cogently pursued breakdown of representation under the aegis of its hyper-Cartesian reversal – radicalized doubt. In this way, the practice of attending to the signification that accompanies and disrupts – while producing – temporalization is burdened by a parasitic relation to the metaphysics of presence. This is not coincidently similar to Derrida's own critique of Heidegger's destruction of metaphysics, as metaphysics becomes a tar baby for us all; any attack gets the attacker stuck in. For Derrida, the aporia between the transcendental and empirical enables metaphysics, and Heidegger's difference between Being and being amounts to textual differences that require endless supplementation, and vary meaning in the play across endless contexts. More specifically, Derrida holds that Heidegger collapses the difference (the trace) between signifiers, privileging a unitary notion of presence over absence. It is the interval between Being and beings, presence and absence that creates metaphysics; Heidegger is, thus, unconsciously recapitulating metaphysical claims. Nonetheless, if Heidegger's trajectory stands on the side of presence against absence – bearing the invisible claims of entities to exist in the world – Derrida's own course stands on the side of problematized and overturned classical representation where the marks, the textual differences, traces, themselves bear their own disembodied and deathless losses of correspondence with something like reality.

Though the discursive formation of restorative temporality, as an archaeological monument formed through a deconstructive *savoir*, points the way beyond representation, and the signification of temporality, its own supplement – that of the subject – must make its reappearance. As Heidegger (2000) puts the issue, "Because humanity is itself historical, the question about its own Being must change from the form 'What is humanity?' into the form '*Who* is humanity?'" (p. 153). The subject of trauma is, therefore, one who is an effect of *différance*, a subject bearing a lack of presence in his/her being-in-time. But, this subject appears at a particular historical moment, and crucially as one whose knowledge and/or truth manifests in relation to his or her finitude. The subject's position within the analytic of finitude, which manifests the crisis of representation and the founding of human being on its limit as an emptiness, must be resituated. Epistemological dimensions of the analytic must be surpassed, and the subject, and its fragmentation, must be located on deeper, more ontological ground. Moreover, to surmount the nihilism that accompanies the reduction of trauma to the transcendental sociology of archaeology or deconstruction, the question of the Nothing, the space that inhabits the subject's being, must be engaged differently. This Nothing that haunts the subject's relation to time as temporality, rather than merely denoting a logical fallacy, Kantian paralogism, will be repositioned within the subject's very being as a withdrawal from itself. As will be argued, several related but distinct approaches to contemporary subjectivity (i.e., that of Heidegger, Levinas, and Lacan) question the possibility of a transcendental subject by founding human being on varying forms of non-Being (for Heidegger, the *Abgrund*). These approaches avoid the atemporal vantage point on temporalized knowledge that plagues epistemological reduction through a fundamental reordering of the subject's unthought within the outside of diachrony as a matter of its Being and its ethical relation to alterity.

Notes

1 Some historians (e.g., Mora, 2008) take issue, *inter alia*, with Foucault's claim that tolerant medieval attitudes towards madness were replaced by rationalistic seventeenth-century antipathy. For the practice of history, it usually is the case that evidence can be found on many sides of an issue; Foucault simply refuses to foreground positions culminating in

comfortable and confirmatory knowledge and his histories rely on counter-memories, foregrounding the position of the historian as one of advocacy.

2 See Boehnlein and Kinzie (1992); Gersons and Carlier (1992); and van der Kolk, Weisaeth, and van der Hart (1996). Taylor (2006), advocating cognitive-behavioral treatment for PTSD, writes that "there is evidence of PTSD in antiquity, such as in the Epic of Gilgamesh . . . because the fundamental features of PTSD symptoms – such as acquisition of trauma-related fear and avoidance, and increased vigilance for threat – likely arise from basic survival mechanisms" (p. 21).

3 Levin (1987) observes that for Nietzsche, the patterns of nihilism in human experience appear in part as inertia, apathy, weakness of will, numbness, envy, emptiness, rage, self-contempt, and general spiritual desolation. Regarding the latter, Nietzsche (1968) himself writes that "A certain spiritual weariness . . . [reaching] the most hopeless skepticism regarding all philosophy, is another sign of the by no means low position of these nihilists" (p. 38).

4 These determinations as to what characterizes or defines any particular epoch are notably difficult and, of course, dependent on how such definitions work in any particular context. It may make sense to define modernity as synonymous with the Enlightenment in one context, and to define it much more narrowly in another – i.e., "modernist" literature as eschewing omniscient narration, etc. In recent years, modernity has been questioned as a kind of myth. As Latour (1993) argues, the modern distinctions between nature/society and human/thing have never been entirely workable; however, his analysis ultimately does not question the existence of modernity as a project, but its viability as a project.

5 It may be noted that I am using the terms "pre-modern" and "pre-Enlightenment" synonymously, even while preserving "modern" for later Enlightenment thought.

6 MacIntyre (1984) argues that, for ethics or morality, the Enlightenment project was bound to fail because "of an ineradicable discrepancy between their shared conception of moral rules and precepts on the one hand and what was shared – despite much larger divergences – in their conceptions of human nature on the other" (p. 52). In brief, MacIntyre contends that the Enlightenment project has been hounded by a persistent skepticism regarding any teleological understanding of morality, which would presumably ground moral conduct and a collective vision for a just society.

7 I am not asserting that Newtonian physics, as emblematic of Enlightenment scientific thought in general, does not exert considerable influence after the classical period. Rather, as consonant with positivism, it loses much of its absolutist pretensions.

8 The attention here to imbalance and metaphysical disorder, to some extent, tracks the Hippocratic theory of humors that would run parallel to more external explanations for madness until the early modern period (Pietikäinen, 2015; Simon, 1978).

9 This explains, in part, the intrinsic suspicion that the contemporary person often directs at secular practices that require transformation for the attainment of truth. For instance, psychotherapy is often derided as interminable, and psychoanalytic institutes are often described as "cultish" because they demand something other than the production of knowledge.

References

Abrams, M. H. (1953). *The mirror and the lamp: Romantic theory and the critical tradition.* Oxford, UK: Oxford University Press.

Aeschylus. (1979). *The oresteia* (R. Fagles, Trans.). New York, NY: Penguin.

American Psychiatric Association. (2013). *Diagnostic and statistical manual of mental disorders* (5th ed.). Washington, DC: Author.

Aristotle. (2009). *Nicomachean ethics* (W. D. Ross, Trans.). Oxford, UK: Oxford University Press.

Auerbach, E. (2003). *Mimesis: The representation of reality in Western literature* (W. R. Trask, Trans.). Princeton, NJ: Princeton University Press. (Original work published 1953)

Augustine. (1963). *Confessions* (R. Warner, Trans.). New York, NY: Mentor-Omega.

Augustine. (2000). *The city of god: Basic writings of Augustine* (Vol. 2, M. Dods, Trans.). New York, NY: Random House.

Bachelard, G. (2002). *The formation of the scientific mind: A contribution to a psychoanalysis of objective knowledge* (M. M. Jones, Trans.). Manchester, UK: Clinamen.

Bartholomeus Anglicus. (1398). *De proprietatibus rerum* (J. Trevisa, Trans.). Westminster, UK: Wynkyn de Worde.

Bergson, H. (1988). *Matter and memory* (N. M. Paul & W. S Palmer, Trans.). New York, NY: Zone books. (Original work published 1896)

Boccaccio, G. (2003). *The decameron* (G. H. McWilliam, Trans.). London, UK: Penguin. (Original work published 1353)

Boehnlein, J. K., & Kinzie, J. D. (1992). Commentary. DSM diagnosis of post-traumatic stress disorder and cultural sensitivity: A response. *Journal of Nervous and Mental Disease*, *180*, 597–599.

Burkert, W. (1966). Greek tragedy and sacrificial ritual. *GRBS*, *7*(2), 87–122.

Burman, E. (1994). *Deconstructing developmental psychology*. London, UK: Routledge.

Burton, R. (1927). *The anatomy of melancholy* (F. Dell & P. Jordan-Smith, Eds.). New York, NY: Farrar and Rhinehart. (Original work published 1621)

Byrne, J. P. (2004). *The black death*. Westport, CT: Greenwood.

Canguilhem, G. (1989). *The normal and the pathological* (C. Fawcett, Trans.). New York, NY: Zone Books.

Chaucer, G. (2008). The parson's tale. In L. D. Benson (Ed.), *The riverside Chaucer* (pp. 287–328). Boston, MA: Houghton Mifflin.

Colebrook, C. (1998). Ethics, positivity, and gender: Foucault, Aristotle, and the care of the self. *Philosophy Today*, *42*(1), 40–52.

Coope, U. (2005). *Time for Aristotle: Physics IV. 10–14*. Oxford, UK: Oxford University Press.

Daly, R. J. (1983). Samuel Pepys and post-traumatic stress disorder. *The British Journal of Psychiatry*, *143*, 64–68.

Danziger, K. (1997). *Naming the mind: How psychology found its language*. London, UK: Sage.

Defoe, D. (1986). *A journal of the plague year*. London, UK: Penguin. (Original work published 1722)

Deleuze, G. (1988). *Bergsonism* (H. Tomlinson & B. Habberjam, Trans.). New York, NY: Zone. (Original work published 1966)

Deleuze, G. (1994). *Difference and repetition* (P. Patton, Trans.). New York, NY: Grove Press.

Derrida, J. (1973). *Speech and phenomena* (D. B. Allison, Trans.). Evanston, IL: Northwestern University Press.

Derrida, J. (1974). *Of grammatology* (G. Spivak, Trans.). Baltimore, MD: Johns Hopkins University Press.

Derrida, J. (1978). *Writing and difference* (A. Bass, Trans.). Chicago, IL: University of Chicago Press.

Derrida, J. (1981a). *Dissemination* (B. Johnson, Trans.). Chicago, IL: University of Chicago Press.

Derrida, J. (1981b). *Positions* (A. Bass, Trans.). Chicago, IL: University of Chicago Press.

Descartes, R. (1954). *Philosophical writings, a selection* (E. Anscombe & P. T. Geach, Trans.). Indianapolis, IN: Bobbs-Merrill.

Descartes, R. (1989). *Passions of the soul* (S. Voss, Trans.). Indianapolis, IN: Hackett. (Original work published 1649)

Descartes, R. (2008). *Meditations on first philosophy* (M. Moriarty, Trans.). Oxford, UK: Oxford University Press. (Original work published 1641)

Dewey, J. (1998). Time and individuality. In L. A. Hickman & T. M. Alexander (Eds.), *The Essential Dewey: Vol. 1. Pragmatism, education, democracy* (pp. 217–226). Bloomington: Indiana University Press.

Doob, P. B. R. (1974). *Nebuchadnezzar's children: Conventions of madness in Middle English literature*. New Haven, CT: Yale University Press.

Fassin, D., & Rechtman, R. (2009). *The empire of trauma: An inquiry into the condition of victimhood* (R. Gomme, Trans.). Princeton, NJ: Princeton University Press.

Foucault, M. (1972). *The archaeology of knowledge & the discourse on language* (A. M. Sheridan, Trans.). New York, NY: Pantheon Books. (Original work published 1969)

Foucault, M. (1973). *The order of things: An archaeology of the human sciences* (A. Sheridan, Trans.). New York, NY: Vintage. (Original work published 1966)

Foucault, M. (1977). Nietzsche, genealogy, history (D. F. Bouchard & S. Simon, Trans.). In D. F. Bouchard (Ed.), *Language, counter-memory, practice* (pp. 139–164). Ithaca, NY: Cornell University Press.

Foucault, M. (1983, October-November). *Discourse and truth: The problematization of parrhesia. Lectures delivered at the University of California, Berkeley.* Retrieved from http://www.lib.berkeley.edu/MRC/foucault/parrhesia.html

Foucault, M. (1988). *The history of sexuality: Vol. 3. The care of the self* (R. Hurley, Trans.). New York, NY: Vintage. (Original work published 1984)

Foucault, M. (1990). *The history of sexuality: Vol. 2. The use of pleasure* (R. Hurley, Trans.). New York, NY: Vintage. (Original work published 1984)

Foucault, M. (1993). About the beginning of the hermeneutics of the self: Two lectures at Dartmouth. *Political Theory, 21*(2), 198–227.

Foucault, M. (1995). *Discipline and punish: The birth of the prison* (A. Sheridan, Trans.). New York, NY: Vintage. (Original work published 1975)

Foucault, M. (1998). My body, this paper, this fire (G. Bennington, Trans.). In J. D. Faubian (Ed.), *Aesthetics, method, and epistemology* (pp. 393–417). New York, NY: New Press.

Foucault, M. (2003). *Abnormal: Lectures at the Collège de France 1974–1975* (G. Burchell, Trans.). New York, NY: Picador.

Foucault, M. (2005). *The hermeneutics of the subject: Lectures at the Collège de France 1981–1982* (G. Burchell, Trans.). New York, NY: Picador.

Foucault, M. (2008). *Psychiatric power: Lectures at the Collège de France 1973–1974* (G. Burchell, Trans.). New York, NY: Picador.

Foucault, M. (2009). *History of madness* (J. Murphy & J. Khalfa, Trans.). London, UK: Routledge. (Original work published 1961)

Foucault, M. (2011). *The government of self and others: Lectures at the Collège de France 1982–1983* (G. Burchell, Trans.). New York, NY: Picador.

Freud, S. (1953). The interpretation of dreams. In J. Strachey (Ed. & Trans.), *The standard edition of the complete psychological works of Sigmund Freud* (Vols. 4–5). London, UK: Hogarth Press. (Original work published 1900)

Gergen, K. (1997). *Realities and relationships: Soundings in social construction.* Cambridge, MA: Harvard University Press.

Gersons, B., & Carlier, I. (1992). PTSD: The history of a recent concept. *British Journal of Psychiatry, 161*, 742–749.

Gregory, A. (2008). Introduction. In *Plato, Timaeus and critias* (pp. ix–lvii). Oxford, UK: Oxford University Press.

Gutting, G. (1989). *Michel Foucault's archaeology of scientific reason.* Cambridge, UK: Cambridge University Press.

Habermas, J. (1996). *The philosophical discourse of modernity* (F. G. Lawrence, Trans.). Cambridge, MA: MIT Press.

Hacking, I. (2002). *Historical ontology.* Cambridge, MA: Harvard University Press.

Han, B. (1998). *Foucault's critical project: Between the transcendental and the historical* (E. Pile, Trans.). Stanford, CA: Stanford University Press.

Han, B. (2005). The analytic of finitude and the history of subjectivity. In G. Gutting (Ed.), *The Cambridge companion to Foucault* (2nd ed., pp. 176–209). Cambridge, UK: Cambridge University Press.

Hegel, G. W. F. (1970). *The philosophy of nature* (A. V. Miller, Trans.). Oxford, UK: Oxford University Press. (Original work published 1830)

Heidegger, M. (1962). *Being and time* (J. Macquarrie & E. Robinson, Trans.). San Francisco, CA: Harper. (Original work published 1927)

Heidegger, M. (1975). *Early Greek thinking: The dawn of Western philosophy* (D. F. Krell & F. A. Capuzzi, Trans.). San Francisco, CA: Harper.

Heidegger, M. (1977a). The word of Nietzsche: "God is dead" (W. Lovitt, Trans.). In *The question concerning technology, and other essays* (pp. 53–112). New York, NY: Harper.

Heidegger, M. (1977b). The age of the world picture (W. Lovitt, Trans.). In *The question concerning technology, and other essays* (pp. 115–154). New York, NY: Harper.

Heidegger, M. (1985). *History of the concept of time* (T. Kisiel, Trans.). Bloomington: Indiana University Press.

Heidegger, M. (1988). *Hegel's phenomenology of spirit* (P. Emad & K. Maly, Trans.). Bloomington: Indiana University Press.

Heidegger, M. (2000). *Introduction to metaphysics* (G. Fried & R. Polt, Trans.). New Haven, CT: Yale University Press.

Hick, J. (2010). *Evil and the god of love.* New York, NY: Palgrave.

Homer. (1990). *The illiad* (R. Fagles, Trans.). New York, NY: Penguin.

Hook, D. (2007). *Foucault, psychology, and the analytics of power.* London, UK: Palgrave.

Hoy, D. C. (2009). *The time of our lives: A critical history of temporality.* Cambridge, MA: MIT Press.

Husserl, E. (1991). *On the phenomenology of internal time consciousness* (J. B. Bough, Trans). Dordrecht, the Netherlands: Kluwer.

James, W. (1890). *The principles of psychology* (Vols. 1–2). New York, NY: Henry Holt.

Kant, I. (2007). *Critique of pure reason* (M. Weigelt, Trans.). New York, NY: Penguin. (Original work published 1781)

Kimball, L. (2013). The object strikes back: An interview with Graham Harman. *Design and Culture, 5*(1), 103–117.

Lacan, J. (1992). *The seminar of Jacques Lacan: Book VII. The ethics of psychoanalysis, 1959–1960* (D. Porter, Trans.). New York, NY: Norton. (Original work published 1986)

Langland, W. (2000). *Piers Plowman* (A. V. C. Schmidt, Trans.). Oxford, UK: Oxford University Press. (Original work published 1378)

Latour, B. (1993). *We have never been modern* (C. Porter, Trans.). Cambridge, MA: Harvard University Press.

Leibniz, G. (1951). *Leibniz: Selections* (P. P. Weiner, Ed.). New York, NY: Charles Scribner's Sons.

Leiter, B. (2004). The hermeneutics of suspicion: Recovering Marx, Nietzsche, and Freud. In B. Leiter (Ed.), *The future for philosophy* (pp. 74–105). Oxford, UK: Oxford University Press.

Levin, D. M. (1985). *The body's recollection of being: Phenomenological psychology and the deconstruction of nihilism.* London, UK: Routledge.

Levin, D. M. (1987). Psychopathology in the age of nihilism. In D. M. Levin (Ed.), *Pathologies of the modern self* (pp. 21–83). New York, NY: NYU Press.

Leys, R. (2000). *Trauma: A genealogy*. Chicago, IL: University of Chicago Press.

Locke, J. (1975). *An essay concerning human understanding*. Oxford, UK: Clarendon. (Original work published 1689)

Lyotard, J.-F. (1984). *The postmodern condition: A report on knowledge* (G. Bennington & B. Massumi, Trans.). Minneapolis: University of Minnesota Press.

MacIntyre, A. (1984). *After virtue*. Notre Dame, IN: Notre Dame University Press.

Milner, J.-C. (1991). Lacan and the ideal of science. In A. Leupin (Ed.), *Lacan & the human sciences* (pp. 27–42). Lincoln: University of Nebraska Press.

Mora, G. (2008). Mental disturbances, unusual mental states, and their interpretation during the middle ages. In E. R. Wallace & J. Gach (Eds.), *History of psychiatry and medical psychology* (pp. 199–226). New York, NY: Springer.

Newton, I. (1956). Principia. In H. G. Alexander (Ed.), *The Leibniz-Clarke correspondence, together with extracts from Newton's principia and opticks* (pp. 142–183). Manchester, UK: Manchester University Press.

Nietzsche, F. (1968). *The will to power* (W. Kaufman & R. J. Hollindale, Trans.). New York, NY: Vintage.

Nietzsche, F. (1974). *The gay science* (W. Kaufman, Trans.). New York, NY: Vintage.

Nijenhuis, E. (2015). *The trinity of trauma: Ignorance, fragility, and control*. Göttingen, Germany: Vandenhoeck & Ruprecht.

Padel, R. (1995). *Whom gods destroy: Elements of Greek and tragic madness*. Princeton, NJ: Princeton University Press.

Parker, I. (2011). *Lacanian psychoanalysis: Revolutions in subjectivity*. London, UK: Routledge.

Parker, I. (2014). *Discourse dynamics: Critical analysis for social and individual psychology*. London, UK: Routledge.

Parry-Jones, B., & Parry-Jones, W. L. (1994). Post-traumatic stress disorder: Supportive evidence from an eighteenth century natural disaster. *Psychological Medicine, 24*, 15–27.

Peirce, C. S. (1905). What pragmatism is. *The Monist, 15*(2), 161–181.

Pietikäinen, P. (2015). *Madness: A history*. London, UK: Routledge.

Plato. (1965). *Timaeus and critias* (D. Lee, Trans.). New York, NY: Penguin.

Plato. (1974). *The republic* (D. Lee, Trans.). New York, NY: Penguin.

Plato. (1983). *Ion and Hippias major* (P. Woodruff, Trans.). Indianapolis, IN: Hackett.

Plato. (2005). *Phaedrus* (C. Rowe, Trans.). London, UK: Penguin.

Plato. (2008). *Timaeus and critias* (R. Waterfield, Trans.). Oxford, UK: Oxford University Press.

Plotinus. (1969). *Enneads* (S. Mackenna, Trans.). New York, NY: Random House.

Porter, R. (2003). *Madness: A brief history*. Oxford, UK: Oxford University Press.

Reichenbach, H. (1971). *The direction of time*. Berkeley: University of California Press.

Ricardo, D. (1973). *The principles of political economy and taxation*. London, UK: Dent and Sons. (Original work published 1817)

Rohde, E. (1925). *Psyche: The cult of souls and belief in immortality among the Greeks* (W. B. Hillis, Trans.). London, UK: Routledge & Kegan.

Rose, N. (1996). *Inventing ourselves: Psychology, power, and personhood*. Cambridge, UK: Cambridge University Press.

Royce, J. (1904). *The world and the individual*. New York, NY: Macmillan.

Russell, B. (1915). On the experience of time. *The Monist, 25*(2), 212–233.

Sampson, E. E. (1981). Cognitive psychology as ideology. *American Psychologist, 36*(7), 730–743.

Sartre, J.-P. (1956). *Being and nothingness* (H. E. Barnes, Trans.). New York, NY: Simon and Schuster.

Schopenhauer, A. (1958a). *The world as will and as representation: Vol. 1* (E. F. J. Payne, Trans.). New York, NY: Dover.

Schopenhauer, A. (1958b). *The world as will and as representation: Vol. 2* (E. F. J. Payne, Trans.). New York, NY: Dover.

Sherover, C. M. (1975). *The human experience of time: The development of its philosophic meaning*. Evanston, IL: Northwestern University Press.

Simon, B. (1978). *Mind and madness in ancient Greece: The classical roots of modern psychiatry*. Ithaca, NY: Cornell University Press.

Smith, A. (1970). *The wealth of nations. Books I-III*. Middlesex, UK: Penguin. (Original work published 1776)

Sophocles. (1984). *Antigone* (R. Fagles, Trans.). New York, NY: Penguin.

Taylor, C. (1989). *Sources of the self: The making of the modern identity*. Cambridge, MA: Harvard University Press.

Taylor, S. (2006). *Clinician's guide to PTSD: A cognitive-behavioral approach*. New York, NY: Guilford Press.

Tertullian. (1979). On repentance (S. Thelwall, Trans.). In A. Roberts & J. Donaldson (Eds.), *The anti-nicene fathers* (pp. 657–668). Grand Rapids, MI: Eerdmans.

Toulmin, S. (1990). *Cosmopolis: The hidden agenda of modernity*. Chicago, IL: University of Chicago Press.

Trimble, M. (1985). Post-traumatic stress disorder: History of a concept. In C. R. Figley (Ed.), *Trauma and its wake: Vol. 1. The study and treatment of post-traumatic stress disorder* (pp. 5–14). Bristol, PA: Brunner/Mazel.

van der Kolk, B. A., Weisaeth, L., & van der Hart, O. (1996). History of trauma in psychiatry. In B. van der Kolk, A. McFarlane, & L. Weisaeth (Eds.), *Traumatic stress: The effects of overwhelming experience on mind, body, and society* (pp. 47–74). New York, NY: Guilford.

Wallace, E. R. (2008). Historiography: Medicine and psychiatry. In E. R. Wallace & J. Gach (Eds.), *History of psychiatry and medical psychology* (pp. 3–115). New York, NY: Springer.

Whitehead, A. N. (1964). *The concept of nature*. Cambridge UK: Cambridge University Press.

Young, A. (1995). *The harmony of illusions: Inventing post-traumatic stress disorder*. Princeton, NJ: Princeton University Press.

2

TRAUMATIC ONTOLOGY

Ethical ontologies of finitude

Foucault (1984) argues in "What is Enlightenment?" – an essay concerning the continuing hold of Kant on his thinking – that Enlightenment thought most deeply pertains to its capacity to release us from immaturity. In a manner, Foucault positions himself within the lineage of Kant and this mode of thinking, drawing the ire of Habermas (1996) – expressed at length in *The Philosophical Discourse of Modernity* – and others who detect bare inconsistency in such efforts to both shelter oneself within Enlightenment rationality while exposing its historically contingent collusion with power. What Foucault (1984) appears to aim for, however, is not identification with traditional elements of Enlightenment humanism, but with "a philosophical ethos that could be described as a permanent critique of our historical era" (p. 42). For early modern life, such critique is notably oriented to the immaturity of unreflective submission to *prima facie* warrants of authority, be they theological, political, or scientific. Most provocatively, however, this releasement from immaturity involves an ongoing ethical obligation in interrogating the subject's collusion with limitations of its freedom. Consequently, not only does Kant inaugurate an inquiry into the formal conditions of knowledge, but he associates this move with a " 'critical ontology of the present and ourselves' . . . [which] Foucault maintains, resituates ancient spirituality in a modern context by linking the activity of knowing the present to a transformation in the subject's being" (Raynor, 2007, p. 135). The task in such a relation between the subject and knowledge is the disavowal of any specific historical outcome – such as universal forms of political or economic life – and a renewed acuity of perception towards newer authorities that have entrenched themselves within the nexus of power and knowledge, especially those partaking in the obscuring strategic fusions of political and pastoral subjectification of human being.

As suggested above, restorative temporality shares in the *ethos* of a self-transformational or self-transcendent trajectory, which would surmount our epoch's submission of the subject's being to empirical and disciplinary determinations. Though framed as discourse, the thought of Husserl et al. regarding temporality could, nonetheless, also be said to be contemplative practice; however, as we have seen, as discourse or praxis, each of these ways of addressing the crisis of historicality and temporality retains a nowhere, space, or gap that is exterior to the subject. In each case, an integrative subject, both recalling the humanism of Enlightenment moral and political commitments and aspiring to overcome the problematic descent into the world of which it is a part, projects the fissure outwardly. For these restorative modes, however, no longer is this break, strictly speaking, part of reality itself – as the division between the sensible and intelligible, the problem of God's personality disorder (theodicy, or, framed hysterically, "Does He love us or hate us?"), or in the blindness of the absolute gaze to its representations – but occurs as a theoretical annoyance that must be put up with for a system of thought to work. Phrased differently, as it does in much Marxist thought, restorative temporality makes sense once the impossible, founding fiction – a theoretical nowhere external to the subject – is established (and forgotten). However, the Enlightenment project – in its fully modern incarnation – must take its leave from these mythologies, not only of the intelligible or the absolute, but also the theoretical utopias that persist at the margins; these immaturities deprive the subject of its responsibility for its truth and knowledge, and its location within it.

Modern life requires – for industrial, political, and scientific reasons, as argued *infra* – the capacity for the subject to represent its representations, and the fallen mode of this endeavor involves its ongoing and partial attempts at fulfillment under the disqualified regime of representation. The traversal of this broken epistemology, and the associated fantasies of coming to certain knowledge of itself, entails the possibility that its self-relation would surpass knowledge that manifests on another plane of immanence. Hence, it necessitates the foundation of this inquiry on entirely different ground, a peculiar inversion of transcendent subjectivity, wherein the subject's facticity – its embeddedness in the world, its finitude – is made structural. Additionally, the starkly ethical nature of this access becomes far more apparent. While an ethical dimension is involved in any historically contingent mode of subjectification, what I will call "ethical ontologies of finitude" – wherein the subject's traumatic self-withdrawal, its nothingness, becomes the condition for truth and knowledge – obtains depth heretofore unseen. In what follows, I outline the thought of Heidegger, Levinas, and Lacan as giving – through their ethical ontologies – privileged access to the fundamental structural features of the modern subject. Certainly it is not intended to collapse one theoretical perspective into another, though I am heretically suggesting that to speak of Levinas' "thought" at all means that it is not only agonistically related to ontology.

The later Foucault (1984/1988, 1984/1990, 2001/2005) famously shifted emphasis from the analysis of regimes of knowledge, and the coercive productions of human being pursuant to power, towards a conscious concern with ethics as a process of self-formation and relation. This trajectory is notably manifested in his studies of ancient Greek and Roman sexual ethics in *The Use of Pleasure* and *The Care of the Self* and extends through his later lectures at the Collège de France, such as *The Hermeneutics of the Subject* and certain interviews. Despite the change in emphasis, these practices of subjectification are, naturally, implicated and framed in knowledge (in *savoir* and *connaissance*) and in extrinsic forms of power (that of regulating the conduits of bodies and virtualities of psyche), as Foucault (1994) observes:

> I would say that now I am interested, in fact, in the way in which the subject constitutes himself in an active fashion, by practices of the self, these practices are nevertheless not something that the individual invents by himself. They are patterns that he finds in his culture.
>
> *(p. 11)*

The neo-Heideggerian tone here should be clear – that the possibilities taken up by the subject, as Dasein or being-in-the-world, are simultaneously formed in knowledge, pressed into action by certain forms of power (whether sovereign, disciplinary, or biopower), and also by the self-constituting practices producing the experience of being a certain sort of subject. Yet, the interpretive move in the unfolding of the subject's possibilities – as given but also self-constituting – is configured differently for Foucault and Heidegger. Han (2002) notes that Foucault prefers the notion of "problematization" to Heidegger's pre-reflective understanding of what follows structurally from ontology, or what emerges from the event of appropriation (*Ereignis*). In other words, the subject's ethical life becomes figural or manifest – not in relation to a pure form of experience, but in relation to the referential totality of background practices and discourses that are socio-historically in play. For Foucault (1983, 1994), the four dimensions of one's relationship with self (what is problematized in matters of conduct and selfhood) include ethical substance, the mode of subjection, the means of subjectification, and aspirations of the subject. First, the ethical substance (*substance éthique*) relates to the aspect or part of self concerned with or worked through in one's conduct. In antiquity, and in Greek thought and practice specifically, the ethical substance – linking truth to the coincidence of will and knowledge – associates the unity of pleasure and desire (*aphrodisia*), which must be mastered through the act (Foucault, 1984/1988, 1984/1990). For Christianity, the ethical substance implicates that of the flesh and desire, differently, and is transmuted in Cartesian thought into the passions, which must be reflected upon and controlled. Candidates for an earlier modern ethical substance would include, for Kant, reasoned intention, and for received psychoanalytic thought, that of sexuality. Critically, as will be asserted, for Heidegger, Levinas, and Lacan – as emblematic of the mature subject of modernity – the ethical substance is not, strictly speaking, a substance at all; it is an incompleteness in the subject's temporal being. Their self-transformational sensibilities give the trauma of the subject's temporal self-withdrawal ontological status; however, this withdrawal from self takes on significantly divergent consequences among these ethical ontologies. For Heidegger, it becomes that of a nullity, a futural being-toward-death wherein Dasein's incompleteness opens a clearing where entities appear according to *how they matter* to Dasein. In Levinas' work, the withdrawal concerns the existent's asymmetrical relation to the Other's immemorial past, whose call rescues the subject from its solitude, and provides it with a fecund existence. With Lacan, the subject is itself divided, castrated through symbolic temporalization, which leaves a residue of the Real as set free through a dialectic of desire, and in fragments of *jouissance*. Second, the mode of subjection (*mode d'assujettissement*) is "the way in which people are invited or incited to recognize their moral obligations. Is it, for instance, divine law . . . Is it natural law, a cosmological order . . . Is it a rational rule?" (Foucault, 1983, p. 239). For Heidegger, Levinas, and Lacan, such an ethical mode of subjection entails – at a fundamental level that installs the analytic of finitude – a common concern with language, as the poetic basis of de-cision and unconcealment, the Saying over the Said, or the cutting into the subject by the symbolic order, and its Real remainders. Third, the means of subjectification (*practique de soi* or self-forming activities), deemphasized in this analysis, are contemplative in the case of Heidegger and Levinas; Lacan's means of ethical practice, grounded in a dyadic relation, forms a counterpart to the technologies of self in the clinical discourse of trauma that will be seen to conceal its ontological status. Fourth, the *telos* of ethical self-formation relates to the aspirations of the subject, such as purity, self-mastery, or rational freedom. For Heidegger et al., such ends relate not to knowledge or the abstract potential of moral agency but to the truth of responsibility – to one's ownmost possibilities, to the Other's call within one's being, to assuming the cause of one's own existence – that allows what is known to manifest in the open space of the finite, in the incompleteness of one's being. The ontology of the subject's self-relation is, thus, radically reconfigured. The literatures on Heidegger, Levinas, and Lacan are vast, and the following rendering of their accounts of subjectivity will follow the themes already enunciated – the empirico-transcendental doublet, unthought, fractured temporalization, and ontological trauma as a condition for truth and knowledge – followed by a discussion of their respective ethical visions related to a traumatic ontology.

Heidegger

Because the early Heidegger (1927/1962) is notably concerned with ontological difference, the Being of beings, this leads to an important interpretation of Dasein as mostly a self-interpreting being, as uniquely *the* being whose Being is itself at issue. A recently visible variant of this argument comes from Dreyfus (1991), who cogently emphasizes Dasein's involved coping in the world, its pressing into possibilities that may – in some sense – become intelligible, if not fully known. Importantly, this view consigns Division Two of *Being and Time* – which fleshes out Dasein's existentiality, its being-towards-death – to inconsistency, to error that led the later Heidegger to abandon subjectivity as a domain of his thought.[1] Dreyfus' emphasis will foreground our concern with finitude because to deprive Dasein of its relation with its limit in its own time almost positions Heidegger as a pragmatist of some stripe (Okrent, 1981; Rorty, 1991), and this stance cannot survive the analytic of finitude. Recall that in Foucault's (1966/1973) empirico-transcendental doublet, the transcendental subject and empirical object defer back and forth to each other in a frustratingly mutual reciprocity. Hence, the anthropological subject finds itself constantly redefined as it comes to differently sedimented empirical knowledge related to man (i.e., the accumulated findings of the social sciences); however, Heidegger (1929/1997) insists that his project is *not* anthropological. In other words, the post-Kantian cognitive, transcendental subject does not exceed the scope of knowledge that emerges from the grasp of its competent coping, and makes it all the more prone to falling into psychologized knowledge. What this means is that cognitivism – and other positive accounts of disclosed knowledge – cannot be undone merely by defining Dasein as that being who acts according to some ultimate "for-the-sake-of-which." Dasein as pragmatist simply becomes its projects or possibilities, and *why they matter* becomes merely the heightened skill in coping with how it knows the world, which could arguably be just as effectively accomplished as a positivist or as a cognitivist, computational subject. As Heidegger (1927/1962) writes, though, Dasein is only tangentially related to a predicated teleologically or practically oriented being of entities:

> The formally existential totality of Dasein's ontological structural whole must therefore be grasped in the following structure: the Being of Dasein means ahead-of-itself-Being-already-in-(the-world) as Being-alongside (entities encountered within-the-world). This Being fills in the signification of the term *"care"* [*Sorge*], which is used in a purely ontologico-existential manner.
>
> *(p. 237)*

Care, for Heidegger (1927/1962), relates to these three existential axes: 1) affectedness or *Befindlichkeit* (mood), where Dasein always already finds itself thrown into a factical world, where things show up in their affective impressions; 2) articulation – Dreyfus' absorbed coping – occurring alongside entities bearing shared significations; and 3) understanding – Dreyfus' "know how," that which allows Dasein to make sense of what to do, how Dasein's pressing into possibilities manifests. Heidegger's argument around how what matters is illuminated distinguishes between ontical comportment (discovery), related to the facts, qualities, and traits of entities, and ontological comportment (disclosure), concerning the Being of beings. For being-in-the-world, Dasein's primordial relationship with the world is notably that of equipmentality – that of availability for use (*Zuhanden*), or ready-to-hand, and the derivative present-at-hand (*Vorhanden*), which isolates things into objects, independent of their use. Dasein's ontic relation to what is encountered in the world shows up as a discovery of what is factually true about this or that entity – for instance, the exhibited behavior of animals under certain conditions; however, disclosure involves the use of this knowledge, to what ends, to what purposes. Similarly, for articulation, what is signified about any particular endeavor belongs to a repository of social, linguistic forms, specific forms of talk, but disclosure asks a different question: what could be signified, what should be? Thus, for Heidegger (1927/1962), understanding – as it connects to a privileged future – will come to encompass a further axis of *Sorge*. As such, understanding, in its ontic mode, allows Dasein to cope with what, in fact, is the case, but the ontological mode discloses – through the as-structure (i.e., the forest shows up *as* sanctuary, or *as* timber) – possibilities for Dasein; not what is or is not, but what could be, or could not be. The disjunction between the possible and the impossible, therefore, reveals that disclosure is transcendental in relation to factuality, or the being of beings, but also parallel to ontic discovery – what is present and what is not present. Critically, however, the disjuncture of what is possible over against what is not possible – oft masked by the ontic dichotomy of present/absent – makes the space for Dasein as a clearing for knowledge and truth opened by its own finitude. Its own self-relation revolves more around the possibility that it would have no more possibilities, and less that it chooses its possibilities skillfully or effectively. Consequently, the care structure explicitly manifests the ethical moment that – releasing the subject from immature longings for certain, factual knowledge of itself – puts disclosure or intelligibility on more existential footing. Because Heidegger's subject is not circumscribed by its knowledge of itself, but its possible ways of being, against nothingness, it escapes the analytic of finitude insofar as the failure of an exhaustive accounting of its being becomes its very ground. Circumspectly, Heidegger (1927/1962) writes that "the different epistemological directions which have been pursued have not gone so very far . . . their neglect of any existential analytic of Dasein has kept them from obtaining any basis for a well secured phenomenal problematic" (p. 250). Thus, what allows Heidegger's thinking to escape the strictures of Kant's cognitive – and potentially reductive – understanding of time, and subjectivity, achieves maturity in his well-known treatment of Dasein's *Sorge* as structured through interrelated temporal dimensions of thrownness and affectedness (past), fallenness and articulation (present), and existence and understanding (future).

Lest Heidegger regress towards the restorative temporality of Husserl et al., Dasein's impossibilities – recalling the metaphysical lacunae of integrative temporalization, its binding to various fictions of entry and external supports – will necessarily be made into its own, up against its own arch-impossibility, its death, which underwrites the end of all possibilities. Dasein's ownedness (*Eigentlichkeit*) and unownedness (*Uneigentlichkeit*) relate to differing modes of disclosure – publicness (an inauthentic, fallen mode) and the resoluteness, the authentic mode awakened by Dasein's awareness of *Angst*, that which manifests the uncanniness (*Unheimlichkeit* or "not being at home") of a world that may at any time deprive it of its possibilities: "In existing one takes over Being-guilty; it means *being* the thrown basis of nullity" (Heidegger, 1927/1962, p. 373). Dasein's resolute, authentic, being responsible – being existentially guilty – for its possibilities will turn out to have a directly ethical relation to the question of Being, and which possibilities authorize what knowledge, what facts, what roles, what activities that constitute Dasein, *what brings them into being*. But, it is the question of death itself that has been raised in the same breath as impossibility, and as the gap that separates Dasein from the past and present as it comes *towards itself* from the future.

Death, for Heidegger, has been the subject of many understandings (and productive misunderstandings), so it may serve to enunciate several important ones, in order to relate finitude to Heidegger's ontology. Death, then, clearly does not relate to perishing, which is the cessation of life; however, existential temporality also does not culminate in demise, as an event that romantically concludes the biographical life of Dasein (Sartre, 1956). Guignon (1983) asserts that being-towards-death means to authentically "recognize the gravity of the task to which one is delivered over and to take full responsibility for one's life" (p. 135). Similarly, Dreyfus (1991) argues that death means the fundamental unsettledness of Dasein's identity, and a heroic engagement with one's capacity to stake one's being on any particular for-the-sake-of-which that comes at one from the future. Dreyfus, therefore, makes the claim that Dasein's positive identity is always unsettled by its eventual death. Young (2001), like Dreyfus, sees in being-towards-death Dasein's status as a discloser of worlds, yet he emphasizes Dasein's impersonal ability to affirmatively transcend its own death as a clearing for worlds. Other versions involve the anxiety surrounding, and grounding, one's stake in one's world, in the face of its possible collapse, whether individual Dasein (Haugeland, 1982), or cultural Dasein (White, 2005). Though persuasive and accurate in most respects, these accounts appear to retain the pragmatic performativity, the integral subjectivity, that must be avoided to escape the analytic of finitude. Anything of the kind will be, invoking Derrida, destroyed by the spacing of articulation of what is possible – the joints, and differences that both conceal and reveal. To my lights, death – as the fulcrum of Heidegger's jointed temporality – will necessarily find purchase in a structural and psychologically descriptive *traumatic separation of Dasein from itself*. Along these lines, Carman (2003) argues that death is the perpetual closing down of possibilities, which allows others to ex-sist (to stand out) in their shimmering resonance. The standing out of possibilities against those put to death, whether involving individual Dasein, cultural Dasein, worlds, projects, moods, or significations, relates to "our possibilities . . . constantly dropping away into nullity . . . To say we are always dying is to say that our possibilities are constantly closing down around us" (Carman, 2003, p. 282). As follows, existential guilt means not – in the Sartrean sense – the life one affirmatively and choicefully engages with against an external void (the one replacing God); rather, ontological guilt captures the structural divide, the Nothing separating the possibilities that drop away from the ones taken up, in their heaviness, the weight of their debt. This Nothing fragmenting, while structuring, Dasein's being is the abyss between itself and its futurity, in the distance between itself as projecting and its possibilities, drawn out by the factical possibility of absolute futural impossibility (actual death).

The later Heidegger terminologically turns from Dasein's disclosive capacities related to its being-towards-death to the other side of "Being's determination as presence" (Riera, 1996, p. 60). Heidegger's (1999) guiding preoccupation notably becomes that of *Ereignis*, which may be translated as "the event of appropriation," unifying the dimensions of happening, belonging, and revealing (Malpas, 2006). Heidegger (1962/1972) writes that *Ereignis* "determines both, time and Being, in their own, that is, in their belonging together" (p. 19). This means *Ereignis* not only designates a specific historical epoch's ontological horizon for Dasein's possibilities, but also the originary openness from which phenomena and their horizons arise and are withdrawn. For early Heidegger, truth as *Aletheia* (unconcealment) involves a mode of disclosure more primordial than propositional knowledge, which simultaneously conceals something as it reveals. Truth, thus, involves both what becomes uncovered, revealed, and intelligible but also the subterranean and dark ground of the untruth, which is presumably a larger but inclusive category of the unthought in the history of the West. For later Heidegger (1971b), what withdraws, on the other side of unconcealment, is "the mystery of Being itself" (p. 176). Importantly, the groundlessness of *Abgrund*, the abyss (or what "stays away" from the ground of beings), occasions both the emanations of Being and their withdrawal. *Ereignis*, or the event of appropriation, therefore, relates to the abyssal ground from which Being as presence, and through time, comes into its own. Perspectives on Dasein's disclosing capacity (Dreyfus and other scholars) often miss the mark because they continue to stress Dasein's phronetically involved engagement with entities rather than what gives Being, which is *Ereignis* as a temporal opening of a clearing in human being. As Sheehan (2001) suggests, these Aristotelian and crypto-pragmatist readings participate in the trend to place Dasein over against Being, taking a couple of forms: 1) the story of Dasein as projecting Being, as if it were the illuminating source of entities that appear (this bears similarity to Nietzsche, Schopenhauer, and Husserl – their association of truth and will or intention); and 2) the "Big Being" narrative, where Being is located noumenally and occasionally unveils itself to Dasein (this implies a theological metaphysics). To escape the gravity of the modern problematic – the oscillating of the ontically empirical with the transcendental – as we have seen, it is no use to posit the transcendental subject on one side, and the external world as Being on the other; this merely asserts a kind of phenomenological and hermeneutic Kantianism. As a caveat, however, it is helpful also to remember that Heidegger's project of narrating the history of Being (*Seinsgeschichte*) must, nonetheless, be positioned as historically originating from within modernity itself, which makes the gap between thinking and being an issue for Being, which is central to the order of its world. In other words, pursuing the Foucauldian edge of analysis, it would be folly to attempt a historical analysis of Being – or, more humbly, the epistemic conditions for truth/knowledge in a given epoch – from the grounding of an immemorial past (Schwartz, 2003).

As Sheehan (2001) argues, *Ereignis*, or the event of appropriation, is occasioned alongside Dasein's own self-withdrawal, or finitude. This insight contains several important consequences as consideration for modern subjectivity that would escape the analytic of finitude. First, it means that what opens itself in *Ereignis* is intertwined with both the reciprocal need and belongingness of what is offered in Dasein's historically defined possibilities, and the fundamental structural incompleteness of Dasein required for such a task. In other words, Dasein must exist in a state of intrinsic incompleteness; its lack in being is its finitude, which emerges parallel with its preoccupation with history in the modern period. Second, Dasein's finitude or lack in being is directly related to temporality, the negation of being-towards-death that is a Nothing, an *Abgrund*, the upsurge of time welling up from within Dasein, that which separates itself from itself as the coming im/possibilities of in the future. Importantly, Dasein, as *phronimos*, is upended by being temporally out of joint with itself, with the debt or recompense it owes to what is not manifested as possibility. The openness for Dasein's receptiveness and ability to illuminate the being of entities – *as* this or *as* that – requires both a Nothing or nullity drawing into darkness the possibilities not taken up, and a pointing or de-cision into what can be and what, not only practically, should presence as caring for oneself and the solicitude one expresses to other beings. Third, it is, therefore, language itself – which, like history, grounds knowledge beginning in the nineteenth century – that carries the power of *Aletheia*, or unconcealment. *Ereignis* involves a fundamental aspect of the saying of language, a "showing," that for later Heidegger allows presence to shine forth against what withdraws and disappears. Language surpasses human being as an opening for the event of appropriation – appearance of things in their own terms, and in their own light. Nonetheless, human being remains indispensable for language, which pervades the clearing within which phenomena shine forth: "Man here is not first of all man, and then also occasionally someone who points . . . As he draws toward what withdraws, man is a sign" (Heidegger, 1954/1968, p. 9). Language, through human being, allows things to become present or show up differently in varying contexts and modes of revealing (Spinosa, 2005). In this sense, and through language especially, *Ereignis* may be seen as the very ground of unconcealment, as "revealing as such" (Caputo, 1993, p. 22), for individual Dasein, as well as for historically concrete modes of disclosure that arise and disappear. Fourth, what withdraws from Dasein, in its revealing through language and through its negation as dying to possibilities, is unthought, but not a recurrent paradox accompanying the *cogito*. In other words, to read Heidegger's (1954/1968) more universalist notion of unthought (which relates to the metaphysical pretensions abounding in philosophy's forgetting of Being) in light of Foucault's own use of the term, it is not as if Dasein has its possibilities laid out before it as an absolute subject who may choose this or that way of being or living, as conditioned by madness or dreaming. Rather, the debt of what language poetically creates, the being that it illuminates, necessarily and in Derridean fashion leaves Dasein – as existing on both sides of the *Abgrund* – and withdraws to the other side of Being. The intensity of thought, and what may come to be through language, is directly related to what must pass away; it is not a lack in the positive thought itself, but what must take its leave for positive thought to occur, what is necessarily *un*-thought for thought to happen.

The requirement of death – in its varying manifestations as being-towards-death, nullity or negation, the *Abgrund*, and unthought – for what appears in the clearing of Dasein is succinctly stated by Heidegger (1971a):

> Death is what touches mortals in their nature, and so sets them on their way to the other side of life . . . As this gathering of positing, death is the laying-down, the Law, just as the mountain chain is the gathering of the mountains into the whole of its cabin.
>
> *(p. 123)*

To address the Kantian subject's transcendental grasp of its own being as reason, as submitted to the finitude, *the limit* of cognitive operation manifesting in various aporias and antinomies, Heidegger – as demonstrated – ontologizes such limit as emanating from the subject's own being, that its quandaries no longer rest with what it may concretely and empirically establish as knowledge (Han, 2005). Rather, the subject's most striking questions concerning its own being – its ethical self-relation – shift to the mattering of its own possibilities as they retreat, withdraw, and fall away from the unsettled ground of a fractured temporality.

Levinas

It may, of course, seem strange – preposterous even – to include Levinas' ethical critique of ontology within the ambit of ontology itself. There are many aspects of Levinas' disavowal of a Heideggerian ontology – *inter alia*, temporality, Dasein's implicit antagonism towards others – and central is Levinas' (1961/1969)

> calling into question of the same – which cannot occur within the egoist spontaneity of the same . . . brought about by the other. We name this calling into question of my spontaneity by the presence of the Other ethics. The strangeness of the Other, his irreducibility to the I, to my thoughts and my possessions, is precisely accomplished as a calling into question of my spontaneity, as ethics . . . metaphysics precedes ontology.
>
> *(p. 43)*

The ostensible meaning of "metaphysics" for Levinas does not connect to a theory of supreme essences, but to that which transcends the homogenizing light of everyday consciousness or representation. It is the Other – i.e., the concrete human other of the ethical situation – who metaphysically punctures an ontology of presence that would place everything within Being, whether traditional correspondence theories of representation or the searchlight of Dasein's own understanding via its particular being-towards-death. Nonetheless, as Derrida (1978) incisively maintains, the non-metaphorical intervention of the Other puts Levinas in the precarious position of asserting the "*dream* of a purely heterological thought at its source. A *pure* thought of *pure* difference. Empiricism is its philosophical name" (p. 151). In other words, Levinas cannot mount any challenge to ontology without thereby smuggling in an alternative counter-ontology of pure difference, where the Other bears the alterity beyond the Same; empiricism has nothing to say. In other words, Levinas must reposition the human subject ever more firmly within the onto-logic of a sensuous temporality, wherein its transcendent possibilities emerge from the immanent and phenomenal ground of alterity, which always manifests in relation (Bergo, 2005). In rejoining Levinas within Heideggerian thought, Konopka (2009) notes that Levinas' strident remarks regarding ontology only pertain to early Heidegger's identification with Dasein's encircling comprehension. Both Levinas and the later Heidegger question the priority of Husserlian intentionality or a transcendental subjectivity, giving a privileged place to non-Being (as death or alterity), and make absence conditional to the subject's coming to knowledge of itself, or the languaging of its possibilities. As Konopka (2009) argues, both Heidegger's and Levinas' articulations of absence may be framed as taking up Hegel's injunction to "tarry with negative." Neither Heidegger nor Levinas, though, make the unthought of the *cogito* parasitic upon consciousness, or make it structural in a logic of the negative. Rather, for later Heidegger (1962/1972) refracted through Foucault (Raynor, 2007), as mentioned previously, unthought relates to the radical withdrawal of Being in *Ereignis* as what cannot be thought in the *Abgrund*; it is Dasein's self-withdrawal in death that creates possibility. For Levinas (1961/1969) – similar to Lacanian conceptions of the unconscious, which may not be assimilated through the logic of imaginary consciousness – the abyss occurs between the existent and its unthought, unfathomable, and asymmetrical relation to the Other.

The unthought for Levinas is notably mediated through his discussion of Descartes' Third Meditation, his notion of infinity, and the face. Descartes (1641/2008) begins by establishing the existence of the *cogito* beyond doubt by extending doubt to the very ground of the subject's being. Later, however, the Cartesian subject obtains a proof of God, one that creates an obligation with its infinite source. Levinas (1961/1969), however, observes that the "reference of the finite *cogito* to the infinity of God does not consist in a simple thematization of God . . . The idea of infinity is not for me an object" (p. 211). Levinas, therefore, addresses the analytic of finitude, with the excess of what continually overflows the subject's transparent grasp of itself. Moreover, though Levinas is critical of the moral relativism implicit in Heidegger's giving over Dasein to the finitude of historical facticity (Nelson, 2014), his own subject is, indeed, fastened to its own corporeal limit as an existent before the life-giving infinite call of a divine Other. So, for Levinas, Descartes' use of God as guarantor of subjectivity is a productively misguided substantialization of God as a first order ontic being among others. Rather, the Judaic God of Levinas arrives not from a supposed elsewhere but from the repetition of everyday exigencies of conduct and responsibility, as the immanent alterity of relation with the Other, and the infinite or excess *in the subject* of the Other's proximate and unknowable being. Levinas (1961/1969) describes the intervention of the Other in phenomenological terms, to stake out the subject's non-knowledge as an empirical disruption, as a face that calls into question and limits the existent's powers and possession: "The face is present in its refusal to be contained. In this sense it cannot be comprehended, that is, encompassed. . . . The Other remains infinitely transcendent, infinitely foreign" (p. 194). Moreover, the Levinasian Other, as it resists totalization by the Same of the existent, bears the call of responsibility, of obligation, which releases the subject from its imprisonment in the Same, under the regimes of representational logic, thereby – in relational terms – accessing noumenal (and numinous) freedom by arousing an obligation beyond what may be articulated. As Barnard (2002) argues, the subject's freedom and range of possibilities are constituted in relation to the disruption of encountering the alterity of the face: "Levinas considers consciousness to be the effect of *affect*, that which trauma produces in the place of knowledge" (p. 176). In other words, the encounter with the Other, in phenomenological terms, traumatically gives rise to obligation in that the newly constituted subject orients him/herself to Otherness as address or response to the rupture in the Same. For Levinasian ethics – which are constitutive of the subject rather than extrinsic to an integral subject – the Other comes to the subject as a traumatic opening within its own being, as an alterity who replaces the Judaic God as a source of being and its freedom through obligation; only in taking up or refusing such unfinalized commitment can the subject wrest free of the entanglements of sedimented historical or psychologized explanations.

In allowing the subject to escape its mirrored entrapment within the empirico-transcendental doublet of metaphorical and metonymical ascriptions, Levinas' model of the Saying (*le Dire*) further works out the encounter with the embodied Other. It is, again, only as counter-ontology that Levinas' thought may appear in any intelligible form as a corrective to perspectives deriving from linguistic structuralism or pragmatism. As Derrida (1978) observes, what propels Levinas' work is not what can be definitely understood about the ethical relation as knowledge, not a theory of ethics but "an Ethics of Ethics" (p. 111). In relation to the epistemological crisis of modernity, it would, therefore, not be the question of what depictions empirically circumscribe the knowing subject but, rather in parallel, an empiricism of empiricisms. But, what sense could this possibly have? Levinas (1974/1998) enigmatically gives us a hint, holding that

> when stated in propositions, the unsayable (or the an-archical) espouses the forms of formal logic; the beyond being is posited in doxic theses, and glimmers in the amphibology of *being* and *beings* – in which beings dissimulate being. The *otherwise than being* is stated in a saying that must also be unsaid in order to thus extract the *otherwise than being* from the said in which it already comes to signify but a *being otherwise*.
>
> (p. 7)

For an authentically performative ethics that does not reduce Otherness to simula-tions of the Same, Levinas suggests that the "saying must also be unsaid," or that the Other of Being may only be encountered through suspension or interruption of rhetorical means of demonstration. "Amphibology" here alludes to the produc-tion of ambiguity that would elude both typical representational schemes – i.e., the Cartesian theatre and its word-to-event emplotments – but also ontological difference itself, or the precedence of comprehensible possibility governing the movements of being presencing within identifiable or forsaken futures (Ricoeur & Escobar, 2004). As such, language proceeds in various ways of ontologically clos-ing or suturing the wound that would create the pause, the stutter – that which is speechless in waiting for the Other. For pre-modern thought, the ontotheo-logical burden would fall particularly heavy on the subject's speech; the Said (*le Dit*) would find itself literally etched into an experiential joining of flesh and faint traces of the intelligible order. Undoubtedly, this linguistic proximity to the eternal partakes in the phonocentric – recalling Derrida's (1981) deconstructive reading of Plato's *Phaedrus* – devaluation of the written through the privileging of speech that feels closer to its source, and its affiliation with the being of beings. In a more contemporary vein, however, the Said concerns the specific form of lin-guistic demonstration that would not provide a coincidence of presence, speech, and the signatures of truth. Rather, for earlier Enlightenment thought, the Said presents not truth, but represents it to the subject, placing distance, albeit a trans-parent one, between being and its description via assertive propositions. The Said, therefore, reverberates with an epistemology whose contours track an ontology of cognitively sensible and thinkable statements; these have the outlines of objects, and their determinate relation within a grammar, or within histories of language, within the philological dispersions of modernity proper. Critically, what Levi-nas (1974/1998) proposes, however, is that the Said – in all its concretions – is dependent and made possible by Saying, which always outruns and is more open than what can be Said. Indeed, the Saying is that openness where an infinity of locutions, of possible ways of being, is given to the finite human existent. Say-ing is where in the linguistic encounter with the Other, its alterity escapes Being. For Levinas, the Saying, hence, is an interruption, and the Said bears the trace of previous Sayings with it, though never fully able to be made fully present. This leads to the striking insight that diachrony – drawing in the immemorial time of trauma – constitutes the time of Saying, over the synchronic assertions of the Said. Saying, therefore, places the subject under the question of time that it can-not incorporate, master, or assert; the Other's time is not in memory, cannot be engraved in any way.

As for Heidegger (1927/1962), Levinasian ethics makes temporality central; however, Levinas (1947/1987) predictably reverses Heidegger at many turns while also elevating temporal finitude, as formative of the subject, over ordinary con-ceptions of time. The past, as the synchronic accumulation of the statements, discourses, and assertions of the Said, is disrupted by an immemorial past opening the Saying of the ethical relation. The Other's past is immemorial in that it is a pure one, and can never be captured, made present by the subject; it is not a matter of memory too deep or remote but, rather, an impossibility that may not be recapitulated or gathered within the Said (Levinas, 1974/1998). The Other's time, thus, never permits a contemporaneous relation with the subject because the depths of the Other's past are unfathomable, and unrepresentable to a transcendental subjectivity. Because the subject's own past retains a history of encounters with Others – these historical answers given by discrete alterities to questions of identity – the subject's own past as known reaches its vanishing point. Consequently, the modern subject never finds itself in its own search for lost time; it cannot, as the search itself is not entirely its own. Levinas argues that the immemorial past is never present to the subject, but that it shows itself as a trace, a notion taken up through Derridean grammatology as an inquiry into the ways that language carries with it supplementarity or the traces of Otherness. The trace, appearing in the Saying of language and the ethical encounter, not only reminds the subject that its past is irretrievably not its own, but that its obligation to the Other is ancient, anarchical, infinite – coming from a time before all memory, consciousness, and presence. The linguistic trace of the outside, of the exterior term, bears the mark of ethics within the march of the metaphysics of presence, and within the subject's temporal existence.

By way of recollection, for Heidegger, Dasein in the present is always being-with-another; prior to this relation, Dasein is presumed to be in its solitude a fully constituted subject in the present, and it is Dasein's future that forces its *own* question. In contradistinction, Levinas (1947/1987) shows that "time is not the achievement of an isolated and lone subject, but that it is the very relationship of the subject with the Other" (p. 39). Put differently, temporality cannot be solved as a fissure in the modern subject's search for itself because it does not originate with the subject; it is always the Other's time. So, unlike Heidegger's assertion that Being temporally precedes Dasein, that human being provides the clearing where Being primordially is a giving forth (*es gibt*), Levinas finds the term *il y a* (there is) to describe the impersonal and nocturnal ground from which conscious solitude emerges.[2] Moreover, eschewing the metaphor of a being whose possibilities are illuminated, the existent is the insomniac present to the dark, fearful of its being. Even speaking of the Levinasian "subject" can be somewhat misleading because without the Other's intervention, the subject is merely a being *in potentia*, yet unformed. Hence, the existent for Levinas (1947/1978) is not an "I" but a larval being fastened, enchained, and riveted to itself, where "the present refers only to itself, but this reference, which should have dazzled it with freedom, imprisons it in an identification" (p. 79). The present is, for the existent, an impossibly claustrophobic self-same identification, without the Other, and – consequently – without time. For theories of trauma questioning the memorial capacities of the subject, the Levinasian present remains anterior to the subject and time, and the intervention of the Other, or the intervention of so many Others that doggedly pull us out of ourselves moment-by-moment.

Like Heidegger (1927/1962), Levinas, through death, joins the subject's finite existence to its futurity. Levinas (1947/1987), however, concurrently questions Dasein's heroic being-towards-death while proffering his own version of a relation to death that would remain faithful to an ethical project (in the Foucauldian sense) of finding positive being through its limit in non-Being. In contrast to death as definitively coming-towards Dasein, and disclosing through *Angst* the negation of possibility that constitutes a more existential dimension of death, Levinas (1947/1987) writes of death as an utter mystery, as impenetrable to the subject:

> The fact that it deserts every present is not due to our evasion of death [Heideggerian inauthenticity] and to an unpardonable diversion at the supreme hour, but to the fact that death is *ungraspable*, that it marks the end of the subject's virility and heroism.
>
> *(pp. 71–72)*

Death is not what allows one's ownmost possibilities to come to light, to be possessed, but relates to an absolute alterity, and the subjectification of the existent to that which calls it out of its present solitude. This future – the one held out in the absolute Otherness of death – becomes temporal existence only in the Saying held open by the phenomenal Other, the face. This means the existent's standing out of itself, and into the flow of time, is bound in passivity to its erotic, or voluptuous, encounter with the human other, in a social relation. This may sound somewhat strange; however, Levinas subtly places the subject – in a vein similar to Heidegger – as the gulf between itself as an existent in the present and itself as that called into existence on the other side, in this case not by the other side of Being but by the Other's inexhaustible being, its infinity. The possible ways for the subject *to be* arrive from the future – not from the nothingness of impossibilities that melt away under Dasein's invasion by death, but from the ungraspable non-Being of the Other's call, which completes the existent momentarily in its answer. It is not only, then, one's own death that may not be circumscribed in knowledge, but also the Other's death – and the projects, burdens, and gifts of being – that flow out from that unrepresentable event, which bestows the subject its possibilities.

Lacan

In some ways, Lacanian psychoanalysis most precisely captures the intrinsic division of the modern subject arising from the analytic of finitude, doing so – unlike Heidegger or Levinas – without any penumbra of upward theology. The subversive potential of a Lacanian theoretical perspective and practice rests on its specifically historical grasp of the subject of modernity and science. Indeed, for Lacan (1999), science as a modern practice is subversive of knowledge (*connaissance*); before that, knowledge could not be "conceived that did not participate in fantasy of an inscription of the sexual link" (p. 82). Pre-modern and classical cosmologies indicate where and how knowledges tie imaginary instantiations of the subject and reality, as tethered to the absent depth of the intelligible or the surfaces of what may be represented. For antiquity, the link is established in the inscriptions conjoined – sexually and otherwise – by God, where there is no place for Freud's Copernican decentering, and Lacan's rejoining of knowledge with truth purely as a matter of this world. For Enlightenment scientistic epistemologies, of course, knowledge as severed from truth is given over to a mechanical, and linear, causality. In Heideggerian and Levinasian ethics, as we have seen, language plays a significant role in how the subject's truth manifests, passing beyond empirical knowledge. In Lacanian theory, however, the phenomenology of *poiesis* is rejected, and the trace of the immemorial past borne by the Saying becomes a fragment of the Real as a leftover from the cut of the symbolic. Strangely enough, perhaps, it is just this structuring through language, and its slice, that creates the subject as a speaking, rather than inertly asserted, being.

Before speaking to the subject of enunciation and castration – as symbolic difference or hollowing in the Real – it may serve to recall Lacan's differentiation of the imaginary and symbolic. The imaginary is that which fills out what is taken for conventional reality, and is bound with the scopic formation of the ego in the mirror stage whose drama for a "subject caught up in the lure of spatial identification, turns out fantasies that proceed from a fragmented image of the body to what I will call an 'orthopedic' form of its totality" (Lacan, 1966/2006a, p. 78). Importantly, this imaginary reality is overwritten and structured through the symbolic; however, in the Saussurean sign, it is the signified – allied to a hypnotic visual apparatus – that condenses language production around predication. What follows is the confluence of presented imaginary and interior meaning, and public description that is represented to the subject. The subject's representations, and also the ones carried on in the human science disciplines, share in an imaginary fantasy of the equivalences of what is signified, described, and linguistically sedimented and the real thing – as object, or externality itself. For modernity, classical representation is, as argued *supra*, questioned and given over to the shifting dialectic between the subject and its empirical predications. Nonetheless, as Foucault (1966/1973) reminds us, representation does not cease in modernity; it only loses its unproblematic and ideal status. In its stead, a newer form of signifying reality linked to conceptual limit and historical/temporal succession is sought beyond representation, and its transparent visibility, in the dense and opaque grounding of historical meaning. For Lacanian psychoanalysis, modernist inquiry into the rules that govern the meaning of statements, and the functions governing the norms of psychological notions – though taking their leave from classical representation – thicken the tissue of signification into the conceptual, retaining the hope that some historically founded structure, function, or operational schema will come to suffice for the external referent. From this impossible pursuit, an emergent psychology would continue to rest its machinations concerning a psychologized life on the structural exteriority of language, thus unwittingly resting consciousness and cognition on the fragmented subject of language and science.

Though Lacanian theory clearly bears relation to the structuralism that Foucault (1966/1973) wishes to exhume in the archaeology of *The Order of Things*, the attention Lacanian psychoanalysis accords to the subject, given to three registers, allows it to avoid the stultifying deferral between the transcendental and empirical. Still within the imaginary and symbolic, for the moment, Lacan gives a primacy to the enunciating subject over the enunciated one. Most discernible in everyday speech that implicitly relies on the imaginary register for its social work to be done, the enunciated subject settles and forms around the contours and shapes of the objects that it is predicated *to be*. Not only hard facts (i.e., the behavior of molecules), but also conceptual schemes (i.e., the organizational principles of institutions), morality, and pragmatic wisdom constitute objective reality as conventionally construed between the exterior and interior, concealing its grammatical existence. This stance is the one most relied upon by human science inquiry still nostalgically dreaming of classical representation. Fatefully, mainstream psychology has fastened itself to those strands of nineteenth-century projects disavowing finitude or scission through circumscribing itself within positive knowledge and its tenuous contacts with cognition. In the psychological analysis of speech, this becomes readily apparent in forms of cognitive discourse analysis, where "propositional elements are concepts, rather than words from a text" (Johnson, Storandt, & Balota, 2003). Concepts or ideas (interior) attain a practical tether to an objective reality (exterior). Propositional discourse analysis (e.g., Ghiglione, 1983), thus, lingers within the analysis of communication, depicting psychological reality as an analogue to a physical one. Firmly with the problematic of the modern episteme, however, lies the subfield of discourse psychology (Hepburn & Potter, 2003; Potter, 2003, 2004; Wetherell 2001) questioning this use of language as a transparent medium for rendering interiority. Wetherell (2001) remarks that "discourse builds objects, worlds, minds, and social relations. It does not reflect them" (p. 16). This largely performative view, drawing on Wittgenstein's (1958) notion of language as a tool kit or game, upholds a socially contractual agency through discourse, as it still carries on the erasure of the subject in its pragmatic doings and performances. Though removed from representation, these social constructionist projects endure within the strong gravitational field of the empirico-transcendental doublet where effective agency is bracketed, and remains outside the field of discourse, to be invoked deconstructively.

The Lacanian rejoinder to this overly epistemological picture will clear a path towards an ontology of a divided subject, and away from such linguistic and epistemic entrapments. The subject who cannot but become identified with its normatively defined thoughts, behaviors, and discursive practices is – disclaimers aside – allied with a psychology that "has discovered ways of outliving itself by providing services to the technocracy" (Lacan, 1966/2006g, p. 730). In contradistinction to a speak*ing* subject, the enunciated or spok*en* subject arises from, but does not preexist, the enunciating act – an effect of the telling and generating of knowledge that substantiates the accumulated wisdom filling out the imaginary world. The *enunciating subject* exists out of the incarnate structure of symbolic forms; the grammatical subject is but a "shifter" – such as I, we, or common noun ("depressed person") – that indicates how the subject is caught in the machinery of discourse. The real subject of enunciation, however, rather than being plagued by deconstructive gaps in the logic of discourse, is itself created in the in-between predications, in the gaps, parapraxes, sudden flashes of anger, or sadness, being struck mute, or caught in ironically revealing locutions. For the history of the modern subject, whose unthought resides on the outside of consciousness, one illustrative example concerns that statement of the *cogito* itself, "I think therefore I am." Like the Liar's Paradox ("I am lying"), Descartes presents us with two distinct subjects. The first is the enunciated fact of the subject who is a "being through thinking," a symbolic statement overwritten on the imaginary ego. The second is the enunciating subject of doubt, the one not appearing explicitly in the statement, but one existing within the disjuncture between thinking and being (I think "there I am"). In a more deconstructive mode, it could be argued that the subject as a being directly relies upon what could be said to be non-being, that is *thinking* (i.e., non-substantial brains in vats, Strong AI, scenes from *The Matrix*) – the discourse of the Other – for its own substantial existence. Oriented towards subjectivity, however, rather than disembodied language, Lacan (1973/1981) writes that

> the true remains so much outside that Descartes then has to re-assure himself – of what, if not of an Other that is not deceptive, and which shall, into the bargain, guarantee by its very existence the bases of truth, guarantee him that there are in his own objective reason the necessary foundations for the very real, about whose existence he has just re-assured himself, to find the dimension of truth.
>
> *(p. 36)*

For the subject, the thinking of the Other, *the unthought as the exterior of language* (which stands in for God, who has departed the scene), separates him from the very being it seeks to establish; as it writes the subject, the subject's being recedes from it. Pavón Cuéllar (2010) writes of the "impossibility for Descartes *to be* or *to be the one who is certain of being*" (p. 111). Descartes, thus, exists in the gap between thinking and being, and the tortured obsession over the possibility of an evil genius who would deceive him (i.e., his suffering), rather than his logic of argument, enunciates his subjectivity. The upshot of this pertains both to the philosophical subject and its historical quandaries, but also the real subject of Descartes who has – for reasons we cannot apprehend merely as his readers – staked his own truth on the impossibility between thinking and being, placing God in the gaps.

What allows Lacanian ethics to access the beyond of discourse and knowledge will be the interplay not only between the imaginary and symbolic, but also a third register – that of the Real, which will ground the subject's ontological castration in language. Throughout Lacan's oeuvre, the Real undergoes change. In his first phase, the Real constitutes as a kind of background to imaginary and symbolic relations (Lacan, 1966/2006a). Accordingly, in *Seminar II*, Lacan (1978/1991b) writes that psychological modes of research such as associationism project themselves

> into the real, they imagine that is the elements of the real which are of relevance. But it is simply symbolism which they bring into operation inside the real, not by virtue of projection, nor as a framework of thought, but by virtue of being an instrument of investigation. The real is without fissure.
>
> *(p. 98)*

As articulated, this conceptualization relates to a fabric beyond symbolization that may not be accessed and rewritten through practical means, an abject impossibility rather than a veiled substratum, and obliquely gestures towards Kantian noumena. More directly, later Lacan (1986/1992) notes, "*das Ding* is at the center only in the sense that it is excluded. That is to say, in reality *das Ding* has to be posited as exterior, as the prehistoric Other that it is impossible to forget . . . something strange to me, although it is at the heart of me" (p. 71). This "extimacy" of the Real existing from the subject's being rather than the universe at large is, precisely, how Lacan's formulation accentuates Kant's account of the noumenal. Critically for Lacan, therefore, the Real remainders that the subject's signifiers and imaginary relations encircle pertain most centrally to its own subjectivity, which points to the Real as both presupposed as an original condition and – as Žižek (2006) argues – a retroactive posing of what is missing in the symbolic order itself; it is a hole in the symbolic order and, far from being a Derridean nowhere floating and sliding through textuality at large, *it is a void that itself constitutes subjectivity.*

Castration is part and parcel of the subject's real destitution, but also its creation, which – in one Lacanian clinical formulation – involves two traumatic movements of division from the Real, that of alienation and that of separation. Alienation constitutes the inauguration of the symbolic order for the subject, and presages a progressive symbolization of the subject's Real existence. The subject, as a nascent figment of the Real, slides under the signifier that assigns its place in exchange for relinquishing its Real being:

> The alienation here is radical, it isn't bound to the nihilating signified, as in a certain type of rivalrous relation with the father, but to a nihilation of the signifier. The subject will have to bear the weight of this real, primitive dispossession of the signifier and adopt a compensation for it, at length, over the course of his life.
>
> *(Lacan, 1981/1993, p. 205)*

Otherwise said, rather than being deprived of its being by certain accretions of meaning, the subject is submitted to the alienating signifier, which founds its *manque-à-être* or lack in being, more properly thought of as missing rather than empty. As Fink (1995) notes, citing the work of J.-A. Miller, the subject yields the empty set, in other words constituting a symbol that cannot depict a state of facts, the result of an assertion, etc., but a symbol that stands in for a void. If alienation is the more fundamental trauma, separation involves secondary trauma wherein both the subject and the Other of relation (the mOther) exhibit lack in being, and the subject attempts to superimpose its lack onto hers. The process of symbolization continues with the introduction of a third term – not the matrix of language in general, but the installation of a primordial signifier (the Name-of-the-Father) that will divide the subject from its unity with the mOther. In clinical terms, separation provides the fundamental tying down of the subject's symbolic world, a *point de capiton*, or buttoning of language and meaning through a simultaneous expulsion of the subject's Real being; if the subject manages resistance to separation through foreclosure of the Name-of-the-Father, he or she becomes psychotic where *jouissance* erupts into the imaginary, spawning madness, with illusions of certainty, and delusions of reference (Lacan, 1981/1993). However, the neurotic is the subject of desire, and the substitution of the paternal metaphor allows the desire of the Other to be transfigured into signifiers, into discourse, giving the subject's every statement a desiring function that cannot be met. The operable question is "What do you want from me?" and there is, strictly, no object of desire, but only its cause (object *a*), the remainder of the Real that promises some plenitude or wisp of *jouissance* that would substitute for its loss. Consequently, the desire of the Other, still having no object, is attempted to be assumed for oneself: "Man's desire is the Other's desire" (Lacan, 1966/2006d, p. 525). For the more contemporary Cartesian subject (the one without God's skyhook) – the space between thinking and being manifesting the requisite haunting doubt of neurosis – desire comes in the form of significations that promise, but cannot deliver, selfhood: "It is the [temporal] interval between these two signifiers that resides the desire offered to the mapping of the subject in the experience of the discourse of the Other" (Lacan, 1973/1981, p. 218). The rupture of the subject's entry into its being-in-the-world is recapitulated in every utterance, the subject's desire for reentry into the Real, and contact with the Real event of trauma, of its genesis occurring in a necessarily diphasic temporality.

Predictably enough, the Lacanian subject's oscillation between its imaginary being, the Other's unthought who thinks its being, and the fragments of the Real that ground the subject's unspeakable truth cannot be properly located as timeless; traumatic temporality defines the modern, Lacanian subject, and its relation to itself. As we have seen, so much discourse around temporality, however it grasps the passing of time, remains fixated in a spatialized and atemporally transparent grasp of chronological time as a kind of winding parade of events glimpsed from the window of a high-rise apartment. For their differences, not only pre-modern and classical, but Kantian *a priori* notions of cognitive time, and the discourse of restorative temporality all rest on a similar premise – *the constituted subject understands its relation to the transience of time from an external point beyond time* (whether eternity, the gaze of Newtonian linearity, Kantian paralleling of external time and intuitive time, or the aporetic nowhere of Husserl et al.). In other words, the enunciating subject of temporality is bracketed, or placed out of bounds, while a working subject (who for the modern period simply persists as neo-pragmatist fiction) contemplates the various ways that it – as the enunciated subject – exists in time. Unlike Heideggerian and Levinasian emphases on temporality, however, that underwrite an ontologically finite subject bearing, respectively, an open future and immemorial past, the Lacanian subject does not stand as an openness to be completed in a redemptive act of being-towards-death or in relation to the infinity of a phenomenological Other, but exists as a crossroads within the retroactive and grammatical looping (structured through the discourse of the Other) of time through the Real.

For Lacan (1966/2006f), *après coup* or Freud's notion of *Nachträglichkeit* (deferred action or afterwardness) generally conceives the basis of traumatic temporality. According to this temporal logic, an earlier event would not be traumatic and repressed until it could position the subject through a subsequent event. Lacan (1975/1991a) writes that "history is not the past. History is the past insofar as it is historicized in the present" (p. 12). For Freud (1900/1953), as will be seen, this carries with it a certain epigenetic narrative of development that is ostensibly psychological, as well as interpretive, or structural. Heideggerian or hermeneutic accounts of the past would certainly involve *a posteriori* interpretation in light of later events, and one's futurally open being-towards-death. For Lacan, however, retroaction – whose models are alienation and separation – embodies the subject's structural relation to its past and future, the effect of the cut of the symbolic into the Real. The subject's temporal existence is offered by Lacan in the form of a grammatical tense, the future perfect: "What is realized in my history is neither the past definite as what was, since it is no more, nor even the perfect as what has been in what I am, but the future anterior as what I will have been, given what I am in the process of becoming" (Lacan, 1966/2006c, p. 247). By stating, "By the time you get the message, I will have already gone," the subject is, therefore, suspended between an anticipated future that loops through a contingent past. Importantly, the future anterior relates to the enunciating, castrated subject, who exists neither in the first signifier of the statement (S1), nor in the second (S2), but is strung along by his/her desire for occupying the Other's lack, as if some anticipated and concluding signified meaning could solve the problem – in accessing the Real – that has been created through language itself. The Real remainder is left behind as hollowed out by the space (the barred or divided subject) between S1 and S2. Logical time, for Lacan (1966/2006b), is hence structural for the subject's imaginary crystallization of "objective time [that] condenses here like a nucleus in the interval of the first *suspended motion*, and manifests to the subject its limit in the *time for comprehending*" (p. 171). In other words, time as unfolding, as a flow having discrete moments and points of origin is beholden to an intersubjective economy of desire that – unlike Odysseus – never quite finds its way home.

In clinical terms, the subject's temporal looping in the act of enunciation speaks both to the noumenal, to *das Ding*, the encounter with Real, and the phenomenal subject of predicated meaning calling into action the Lacanian notion of fantasy, which substitutes knowledge for absence. For the neurotic subject who has been separated by the paternal function into ego and unconscious thinking through the strictures of the symbolic, the future anterior yields the fantasmatic movements of object *a* – causing desire from the remnant falling out of the Real. The subject, suspended as above, is propelled to affect a measure of future certainty regarding a past event, whose reality is only defined by his/her very exclusion, and its unspeakable remains. Because the subject's Real being is what is missing in the symbolic order, and not some hyper-real substance that weaves together reality, it means that Lacanian temporality bears unthought as that of the Other's discourse that thinks itself through the subject's void in time. Lacanian subjectivity is temporally between being given to the world by the signifier and its retroactive position in consciousness, or in the dialectic of desire. It would seem that this constitutes something of ground zero for an ontology of trauma, where the subject is constituted by the vacancy it leaves at the scene of its genesis, as looped back through the future. In a Bergsonian vein, its past comes towards it from the future, but (unlike Bergson) the subject itself never comes to subsist *as the subject* – only as its enunciated location in the symbolically overwritten imaginary. Hence, the importance of knowledge as substitute and as fantasy, for Laplanche and Pontalis (1986), in imagining "the origin of the subject himself" (p. 19). The subject's fundamental fantasy is, therefore, one of its specific coming into being, and related to its alienation and separation – the cut of determining signifiers that give it its place, and the signifiers that come to fasten it to a world of meaning that seduces it into particular formations of selfhood. Chronological and narrative histories of identity – whether of cultures or subjects – partake, via their objects of desire, in the fragmentary return of the repressed, of the Real that cannot be, but must be, represented:

> The function of *tuché*, of the real as encounter – the encounter in so far as it may be missed, in so far as it is essentially the missed encounter – first presented itself in the history of psycho-analysis in a form that was in itself already enough to arouse our attention, that of the trauma.
>
> *(Lacan, 1973/1981, p. 55)*

The essentially missed encounter of the other scene, similar to the existent's hypostatic encounter with Levinas' Other, occurs as the event that guarantees the subject's being-in-time – not in an external nowhere out of time, or ideal position beyond time, but in the void, the nothingness, the in-between of perception and consciousness. *Tuché* cannot appear within the temporal field that it opens. Put differently, like the sliding of the earth against itself at a fault plane that gives rise to the rumblings and destruction of an earthquake, subjectivity is the void between materiality that is more than itself, perceptible from its positive reverberations, which are themselves not the subject but the effects it authorizes in its radical self-withdrawal. Temporally, the enunciated subject will always have existed in some remote past, and as an effect of the sliding of the symbolic against the Real – that sliding is the Lacanian subject proper, who flashes between signifiers within this temporal conundrum. Importantly, the subject as out of sync with itself means that it never also appears in the field that governs its emergence, as the sliding of the fault can never directly appear in the effects that it produces, even if only slightly preceding them. "~~What happened~~" was never what happened, though we have to speak of it that way. This, not insignificantly, produces a measure of agency for the subject, whose repetition of the Real "always comes back to the same place – to the place where the subject in so far as he thinks, where the *res cogitans*, does not meet it" (Lacan, 1973/1981, p. 49).

For our historical analysis of trauma, the Lacanian subject – as suggested – bears an increasingly ontologized relation to the modern, Kantian subject of the epistemic doublet. Kant's (1781/2007) transcendental idealism – as an edifice relying on demonstration of the possibility of synthetic *a priori* statements – emblematically gives modernity its epistemological turn, wherein realism and speculative metaphysics are abandoned for the conditions of empirical knowledge. Kantian representation (*Vorstellung*), of course, derives from the same representational episteme of the classical order, shared by both empiricism and rationalism; however, as Foucault (1966/1973) suggests, Kant problematizes representation, giving it its limit, historically authorizing the departure of knowledge and thinking outside the play of correspondences. Because unadulterated representation – that of direct correspondence with reality – is broken, two consequences follow. First, the meaning of representation changes, becoming *the representation of representation*. Put another way, the subject's relation to reality is further removed through its own sensible and conceptual correlation with the outside; its access is governed through the appearance of the world. What is represented to the subject is not the world or thing-in-itself, but phenomena as mediated through the subject's own finitude, limits, and statements. Second, the subject – no longer part of God's imperfectly inscribed markings into the flesh of the world, or as a blind spot in the hegemony of absolute vision – disappears from itself as an intelligible, metaphysical, noumenal being. This latter consequence relates directly to Kant's analysis of freedom in the Third Antinomy of Reason, where he presents a causality of reason poised against empirical causality. The problem is succinctly stated by Kant (1781/2007) as "whether it is a correct disjunctive proposition to say that every effect in the world must arise, **either** from nature, **or** from freedom, or whether **both** can coexist in the same event in different relations" (p. 465). The solution Kant adopts is to suppose that representations of the empirical appearance of causality and the subject's noumenal and rational causality occupy heterogeneous domains; this preserves both freedom and regular happenings of the world. For the Lacanian subject, and the subject's genesis in the Other's time, this difference in the order of realities that inhabit the subject maps directly onto Kant's First Antinomy of Reason, where the thesis that the world has a definite beginning (given to us by reason) is contradicted by its antithesis that the world is infinite. Kant's conclusion is that both are false because the world is an object of experience, and such metaphysical speculations are beyond the subject's ken. For Žižek (1999), Kant's quandaries regarding causality and the beginning of the world result from an obsessional avoidance of *das Ding*, the terrifying glimpse that a structural impossibility may exist at the heart of the Being of being. Žižek, in a manner reminiscent of Hegel, ontologizes Kant through mapping the First Antimony onto subjectivity. The Kantian subject's existence is, hence, neither with nor without beginning because 1) it has a finite origin in the temporal order but 2) it would need to occupy an infinite position preceding its existence to apprehend such an origin. In shifting Kant's epistemological analysis towards an ontology of subjectivity, Žižek (1994a) incisively notes that Kant misleadingly transforms an infinite judgment into a negative one – and for our purposes, the subject as "not mortal" becomes the subject as "not-mortal," or "immortal." This is important because it preserves the epistemically realistic vantage point – if only accessible as a Cartesian fantasy of vision – against a more disquieting possibility that the noumenal relates to an ontological difference between "mortality" and "im-mortality," which is a void rather than an imaginary variation on preexistence, of the subject or the world (Johnston, 2008; Lacan, 1981/1993). The traumatic structure of the modern subject is, ultimately, most poignantly illuminated in the Lacanian dictum that the subject constitutes the missing, noumenal encounter in the Real, who appears (is born and dies) in the Other's discourse: "The hole in the real that results from loss, sets the signifier in [temporal] motion. This hole provides the place for the projection of the missing signifier" (Lacan, 1977, p. 38). The signifieds that precipitate from these signifiers are, indeed, not mortal, as desiccated corpses stand in for being-in-the-world that is only known retrospectively according to transcendental illusion. In other words, trauma authorizes a being in the very extrinsic relation to that being it authorizes, which positions its realities both beyond the subject and inside the subject that it inhabits.

Traumatic ethics

For the ontologies of finitude worked out in Heidegger, Levinas, and Lacan, Foucault's (1983) ethical substance relates, as previously mentioned, to the subject's traumatic withdrawal from itself relating to its dispersal in a fragmented temporality. Reading the early and later Heidegger synthetically allows for a radically ontological discernment of what brings about Being; that is, *Aletheia-Ereignis* – the opening of the clearing where entities can appear in their varying manifestations as knowledge through truth. Though Heidegger often speaks universally on the history of Being, this clearing (*Lichtung*) is itself a recently modern, historical opening in Dasein's intrinsic incompleteness, its lack in being, the tragic nullity of its being-towards-death that stretches into the *Abgrund* or abyss that traumatically separates it from what withdraws as unthought. Heidegger (1962/1972) writes that "insomuch as the modes of giving [*es gibt*] that are determined by withdrawal – sending and extending – lie in Appropriation, withdrawal must belong to what is particular to the Appropriation" (p. 22). Such appropriation is none other than what must withdraw on the other side of Being to light up possibilities that press themselves into Dasein's being. The truth of what is unconcealed as the mattering of possibilities that emerge and manifest together follows from this trauma of existence, the separation of Dasein from worlds, forms of life, heretofore unknown, which are eclipsed in what is given to light. What projects one takes up – the manifold ways of loving, knowing, doing – are grasped, seized against what withdraws, is given up, disappears into darkness. To commit oneself, for instance, to a commercial form of life means foregrounding one's possibilities in a world of exchange, where value is contractually ascertained, which has wide-ranging consequences as to what may or may not presence as knowledge infused with truth, and what must be allowed to recede into the ground (i.e., aesthetic, political, moral realities). But these events that gather our being are not always up to us, and the sudden death of a parent to a small child or the searing events of genocide put to death worlds that *could have been* and *should have been* according to a life lived to the threshold of the Event, which can henceforth only be remembered as shadows of our possible past-futures; trauma forecloses these lost possibilities, bringing other terrifying or alienating worlds into being. And, ontic, propositional knowledge arises from possibilities springing from the widening chasm where Dasein's own being recedes from itself. Importantly, what recedes most deeply may not be comprehended in the light of the Being – those possibilities that must remain unknown to Dasein. What belongs to Dasein (its becoming) – in its particularity or singularity – is made possible only through its own structural finitude, encompassing the arising of Being and its Other limit, the alterity that structures what comes to light as mattering to Dasein. Moreover, Dasein's care of the self explicitly touches what it takes up as presence against the void of its being. This means that a discloser of worlds, authentic Dasein – that is, as cognizant of its traumatic finitude – must reckon with its own truth as what manifests against manifold Otherness brought into the fold of its own being through its own orientation to death.

Perhaps an inheritance of Heideggerian thought, for Levinas, the Other side of Being becomes the focus of his heterological ontology. Levinas brackets ~~Being~~, as does the later Heidegger; however, for Levinas, the existent's pre-ontological ethical relation with an empirical Other, rather than a gulf of darkness that interpenetrates Being, provides the transcendental condition for the subject's formation, and for the moments of truth that reroute knowledge through the Saying. For Levinas, it is not Dasein's own possibilities that disappear into the *Abgrund*, but the emergence of the subject as infinitely obligated to the Other, where the existent's possible ways of being are continually withdrawing into question. The fecundity, or the subject's capacity to reproduce its being in ever-differing contexts and experiences, depends upon the existent never being able to fully grasp the Other's difference – of being always already *subject to* the Other's face and the asymmetrical relation to itself (meaning the existent) that is bound with the Other's call. For Levinas, the non-Being (which here is alterity rather than nothingness) that separates the existent from itself as subject involves that part of itself that must persistently field *the question of the Other*, one that is never fully answerable. The subject's care of self is inextricably related to the Other: "To be responsible is to find oneself always exceeded by what is required of one's being . . . It is to be without a place of one's own, to exist in incessant destitution, displacement" (Lingis, 1989, p. 153). This does not mean that thematized knowledge – of oneself or of human beings in general – is not possible; however, what it does mean is that the ground of possibility as knowledge is made possible through an *a priori* ethical, non-rational relation (Clegg & Slife, 2005). Indeed, for Levinas, there are two moments of truth, the first being what occurs between the subject in relation to the Other's call, or Saying, which is the infinity of justice on which truth proper is founded. A second order of truth as knowledge – what may be factually asserted – occurs within what is said, in the field of exigencies opened by the presence of the Other in its exteriority. MacAvoy (2005) writes that "if truth is the experience with exteriority (perhaps even an experience of exteriority in which the exteriority of the other is preserved), then a relation of heteronomy between interiority and exteriority is required for truth" (p. 27). Accordingly, then, the most primordial and abyssal dimension of truth for Levinas resists the cognitive autonomy of Kant's transcendental subject in favor of heteronomy. Moreover, this relation does not befall the integrative, self-possessed, and self-formed subject over against the Other after questions of epistemology have been opened or settled. In contradistinction, questions of self-knowledge arise from the existent's grasp of its limited, ownmost being as being given over to it through its realization in the eyes of the Other. Hence, as related to truth and knowledge, the subject's trauma is precisely that its very being – as the Same, as autonomy, as what may be stated as mere knowledge – always must span a gulf extending to demands, needs, and requirements of the Other. Intelligibility presences in relation as we respond to communal, interpersonal, and dialogical exigencies that never cease their questioning of our own rift in being. When we respond to a child's question, for example, in explaining the existence of clouds or of rain, this is hardly a scientific enterprise first and foremost, though it is certainly that as well. It is the truth of relation that occasions and makes knowledge possible, which is not irrational but is pre-rational, preexisting of the positivities of the human sciences, or Heideggerian hermeneutics. Writing in a phenomenological modality, Levinas – in his treatment of alterity and persistent interrogation by the Other – bridges Heideggerian and Lacanian self-withdrawal.

As elaborated above, for Lacan, who initially follows a Hegelian (shorn of its teleological absolutism) ontologization of Kant, the subject is constituted as a *manque-à-être*, or lack in being. The Lacanian void in the subject, however, extends beyond the Kantian subject's failure to establish an introspective relation to its noumenal being, its freedom. Consequently, the modern subject's finitude is not a mere epistemological limit (though it is that too), like Heidegger, a nothingness, but against Heidegger (and with Levinas) an encounter with exteriority (especially language, as the discourse of the Other). Self-withdrawal, for Lacan, does not begin with an emerging existent, or Dasein as self-confirming being presencing through its temporal horizons; rather, the Lacanian subject is itself the failure, the void of the withdrawal. Žižek (2000) succinctly states that the "intimate link between *subject* and *failure* lies . . . in the fact that the 'subject' itself is *nothing but* the failure of symbolization, of its own symbolic representation" (pp. 119–120). This means that the subject's destitution never shows up in the field of knowledge (*connaissance*) or as a matter for the human sciences, as Lacan (1966/2006g) argues in "Science and Truth." For the Lacanian, modern subject, then, *truth* reenters from its exile in ancient forms but now as still severed from *knowledge*, yet bearing necessary relation thereto. The traumatic ontology of the subject involves splitting (*spaltung*) of these domains, given over to the law of the material signifier as exteriority governing the unconscious deferral and shifting of thought that thinks without thinker. Unexpectedly, perhaps, it is the inversion of truth and knowledge that provides positive reality itself, as knowledge itself is created and ceaselessly generated only in the negation of the signifier, in its retroactive failure in touching the sublime object that falls out of the Real (Nobus & Quinn, 2005; Žižek, 1989). In *Seminar VII*, Lacan (1986/1992) elliptically strikes at the heart of what exists beyond the symbolic order and the eddies of desire initiated in his discussion of the Thing (*das Ding*), which has both Freudian and Kantian implications, though as in the latter not merely what lies noumenally beyond legitimately epistemic aspirations. *Das Ding*, in its specifically Lacanian formulation, arises as an effect of the intervention of the signifier, which is both the cause of *jouissance* and that which it keeps at a distance; the death drive is, thus, aimed at the Thing, whose obverse is the signifying chain:

> *Das Ding* is that which I will call the beyond-of-the-signified. It is as a function of this beyond-of-the-signified and of an emotional relationship to it that the subject keeps its distance and is constituted in a kind of relationship characterized by primary affect, prior to any repression.
>
> *(Lacan, 1986/1992, p. 54)*

For Lacanian theory, *das Ding* – as the beyond of the symbolic register – is extrinsic to it, but also forms the extimate propulsion of desire through its cause in object *a*, which produces many Real effects within the logic of desire. Nonetheless, as mentioned, *das Ding* may not be signified or represented, and what is so taken amounts to the fantasy of completed knowledge of the world or the subject. As in the "calling" of one's chosen work, we know nothing of the thing doing the calling; it has no name yet its truth is felt, presses into us, and is mistranslated into the many names that desire will hold. Because – in addition to the orbits of desire around others – this signifying chain must obey the law of distortion and flux, that of grammatical time, truth never appears in knowledge. The truth effects – which are within the specific domain of the castrated subject as a void, or flashing through, in the symbolic order – temporally regress and withdraw in time. Consequently, symbolic failure is itself insufficient to synchronically castrate the subject, to divide it against itself (after all, Wittgenstein spoke of a reality beyond language of which nothing could be said). For castration, the nihilating signification takes place through the deferral of *Nachträglichkeit*, or the fragmented temporality of trauma.

For Heidegger, Levinas, and Lacan – in each case – traumatic ethics means that the subject's mature being as subject is made possible only through the self-withdrawal or alienation of itself in a gap in temporality, in missing time. In Heideggerian philosophy, the abyssal ground of Dasein's clearing or opening for Being concerns *futurity as a nullity* that unsettles the past – not an absent but remote present, but the ever-present nihilation of what is not taken up, what becomes an impossibility as unlived. As Heidegger (1962/1972) illuminates in his lecture "On Time and Being," "Past and future are a *me on ti*: something which is not, though not an absolute nullity, but rather something present which lacks something" (p. 11). What is coming towards us, and manifesting particular pasts in its wake, summons the flanking movements of the darkness bearing many absent and unseen futures. So, what is always already lacking in that given by temporal Being tracks what is unlived, which is also necessarily unthought because only in living out one's possibilities can what is unconcealed become actualized as disclosed to thought. As such, the ever-present nullity underwriting the future traumatically separates Dasein from itself – what cannot be lived in death – but it also separates itself from its lived, factical past. Facticity bears the experiential conduits, and common-place knowledge that guides, comforts, and grounds Dasein in its routine observances that the sun will set on the same world that it presided over at daybreak ("I love you and will see you tomorrow"). Bracken (2002) writes eloquently of the ontological dimensions of trauma, which "cannot be grasped through the framework of an 'ontic' science" (p. 149), one consigning facticity to factuality. From a similar perspective, Stolorow (2007), thus, observes that trauma, as befalling Dasein, destroys the "absolutisms of everyday life"; however, as Heidegger (1927/1962) consistently reminds us, anxiety or *Angst* unsettles any such attempt to achieve permanence in one's earthly dwelling, whether these elusive assurances emanate from the worlds of love, work, or systems of ideas, cosmologies, and theologies. *Angst* – bearing traumatic temporality – portends the possibility that searing events may suddenly obliterate our ideological and narrative continuity, signaling to us that we are not at home in the world, and the abject uncanniness of the world. Dasein's being as thrown into a world of particular attunements and attachments is structurally unsettled by temporal flux, change, becoming. Consequently, Dasein's trauma, stretching from the future and into the past, pervades its existence. As Stolorow (2011) writes

> Authentic temporality [for Heidegger], insofar as it owns up to human finitude, is traumatic temporality. "Trauma recovery" is an oxymoron – human finitude with its traumatizing impact is not an illness from which one can recover. "Recovery" is a misnomer for the constitution of an expanded emotional world that coexists alongside the absence of the one that has been shattered by trauma.
>
> *(p. 61)*

Stolorow, thus, links the shattering of what is framed as clinical trauma in our medicalized world with the originary trauma at the heart of its existence; Dasein's thrownness is always in question, and the meaning of its being-in-the-world is always potentially subverted by the threat of nothingness. However, it is just this missing being through time that allows Dasein to retroactively become itself. In anxiously projecting itself into the nothingness ahead, Dasein returns to its determination or assignation of what it will have been destined to be (Lingis, 1989). Consequently, the fissure that constitutes the temporal and structural being for Dasein is the traumatic difference between its embeddedness in being – its being part of a world – and its imminent, uncanny, *Angst*-filled disappearance from this world. And, ironically, only this conflictual relation makes Dasein's selfhood possible as the fallout from temporal destitution.

Levinasian temporality proceeds quite differently from that of Heidegger, as we have noted; however, what it does share is self-alienation through a diachronic relation to Otherness, the non-being of the Other's infinite call, rather than death. Instead of allowing the possession of possibilities as "ownmost," the existent's anarchic relation to time grants the existent its subjective being. Though the Heideggerian ethics of being-towards-death as nihilation, as self-care, upends the ontic conception of time as a linear trajectory within a spatialized container, Levinas radicalizes this project on two fronts.

First, as Barnard (2002) notes for Lacan as well, Levinas surpasses an ontology of the Same through making subjectivity itself founded on its response to the diachronically traumatic question posed by the Other, which would be prior to any formation of knowledge, duty, or moral obligation. The Levinasian subject's relation to time is anarchic, meaning that its consciousness is dispersed through the founding interruption of alterity: "Time is not, then, only a teleological realization of the subject's 'possibilities' . . . but is the anachronistic diachrony produced as the impossibility of incorporating the overwhelming event of the Other in synchronic time" (Barnard, 2002, p. 169). Time, for Levinas (1947/1987), is never one's own, always exceeding the subject's conscious and intentional grasp of its possibilities in a projective axis towards the fecundity of the Other's call. The past is immemorial for Levinas not because it is "out there" somewhere, to be reconstructed in an imaginary unity should we be able to attain an impossible position of God-like mastery or height, or through the rites of therapeutic self-actualization, but because the subject's past is itself an opening, a question by the Other; the exigencies that press themselves on us as gaps in knowledge open up fields of knowledge emerging in the aftermath of trauma. As such, the existent's formation from the traces of the Other's question forms an immemorial past transcendent of the subject's own thought, its own represented self: "The dia-chrony of a past that does not gather into re-presentation is at the bottom of the concreteness of the time that is the time of my responsibility for the Other" (Levinas, 1947/1987, p. 112). We may meditate, for instance, in a purely phenomenological vein on how – as children – we came to be formed in response to questions springing out of the unfinished being of our earliest caregivers (i.e., "What does it mean to be a 'man'/'woman'?"). These interruptions of our being, which set us on the course of answering our interlocutors with *our very existence*, may not be located anywhere in any particular past, as they arise also from other questions in other pure pasts. The subject's past always recedes from itself because, with some similarity to Heidegger, it is embedded in an existence that, temporally speaking, has an Other side – for Levinas, the empirical Other of relation. Moreover, the existent is only ushered into subjectivity in flashes of contact with what futurally surpasses it, which gives over to it its time. The existent is rescued from an immemorial past through the grace of the Other's future and, as such, the subject is the result of a kind of traumatically disjointed temporal interrogation wherein its selfhood – as the Said, what can be represented of itself – arises from the relation of two forms of Otherness remote in time from each other. Unlike the Heideggerian grasp of the past through death, Levinasian temporality, thus, provides erasure on a double horizon, past and future, each exceeding the existent's represented being in different directions, yet granting the existent its being as subject in its own withdrawal from the existent. Knowledge, or the Said, is always the fallout of the subject's constitution as an answering to the Saying – the Other's intervention along present, past, and future axes.

Second, Levinas' radicalization of time vis-à-vis the Other concerns the subject's own self-relation in Foucault's own reformulation of ancient ethics. In other words, apart from Levinasian ethics as an ethics of ethics in response to the Other stands the subject's own self-care, which runs through the Other's position within its own traumatic history. Interestingly, Levinas' own convergence with psychoanalytic theory opens up a theoretical space that addresses what it means to be the modern subject of trauma, as it relates to clinical trauma. Bernet (2000) comes very close to the heart of this issue, arguing that Levinas' subject is "traumatizable" as fragmented and separated from itself through the Other's face and question before the intrusion of latter trauma: "'Traumatizable' does not mean the subject 'is waiting' to be traumatized . . . it means that the subject feels fragile and dependent and that it lives haunted by the possibility of its own disappearance" (p. 169). Said differently, the Levinasian subject – mirroring that of psychoanalysis – is a being deeply founded on its own self-withdrawal in time, and the meaningfulness of its conscious life is predicated on a darkly unknowable self-relation mediated through an Otherness that it is never able to outrun or outstrip; its being-in-time is hostage to the empirical Other of interpersonal relation. That subjectivity would find its formative events hidden in the unmasterable, intimate spaces of everyday life presages the frailty by which we as inhabitants of the Western industrial world are given over to the ravages of automobile accidents, sexual abuse, and wartime trauma. We are no longer able to rely on grand narratives etched into the cosmos to sustain and displace the lacunae in orders of Being, the Other's time requiring us to solve the questions within our own being in knowledge that would ever remain incomplete and incommensurable with the interrogation that dislodges it. Not surprisingly, what may be Said – as the provisional attaining of identity or self-knowledge – easily yields its frail partiality and solvability in the shattering events of later traumatic life.

The temporality of Lacan, I would suggest, most directly speaks to modern subjectivity as bearing an ethically traumatic relation to itself because it places the subject as the failure of symbolization through grammatical time pursuant to separate and distinct movements. As Foucault (1966/1973) argues, representation is not a privileged epistemic mode for modernity, and the position of language begins to turn towards a structural – rather than referential – purchase on what is taken for reality. What reality was for the classical episteme, the noumenal or the Real becomes for modernity; signs of desire are non-signifying in reality, and become signifying only in relation to Lack that emerges as a missing place in the subject's temporal being. For the modern subject, the failure of signification does not pertain to unreason – madness, illusion, error, or the unfathomable lapses in God's benevolence. This is not to say that language does not alienate the classical subject, as the breakdown in transparent representation, but it may be better said that it is not language that alienates but, rather, the aporetic external world that eludes the subject's linguistic depiction, causing the subject to occupy the position of error/madness, or reality to exhibit its external collapse. These external failures may have a devastating effect on the subject (i.e., as shaken faith in God's eternal beneficence, or a world of linear time and correspondences) but they are not – strictly speaking – trauma because they do not bear upon *the subject's particular historical and temporal existence*. Under modern conditions, however, there is no longer the possibility that the subject resides as a void in reality in general (that is the case in the classical episteme). As such, trauma must be understood as ontologically and socio-historically structural in relation to this new relation of time and language. Critically, for the modern subject, selfhood or identity ethically as self-care or relation crystallizes in relation to two distinctly Lacanian moments of trauma, as previously discussed: alienation and separation.

As mentioned *supra*, alienation – allowing the subject to exist in submission to the signifier that assigns a place but leaves a void – is an effect of *tuché* as temporally looped through the future anterior. The subject is constituted as absent to its own origin (i.e., Kant's First Antinomy of Reason), which – in a sense – is what continues to be represented/signified but also lost. The subject is, thus, originally traumatized by its division in grammatical time, which also parallels Heidegger's being-towards-death or the self-withdrawal that occasions Levinas' subject's relation to the Other's time. For each, this constitutes the "traumatizable" subject, who comes to all later experience through a temporal opening in its being and must solve other profound challenges in its being according to this logic. Importantly, the subject's sliding under the signifier allows the yawning space to open between what the *subject ~~was~~* and what the *subject will have been*. The particular sedimented selves (i.e., identities concerning the everyday experiences of being ". . .") are alienated from the conditions of their possibility in time, attaining reflexivity thereto. In other words, alienation creates the possibility for the shifting sands of selfhood. In a sense, our culture's own typically existentialist (if not in theory, then in practice) preoccupations with an extensionless, spatialized distance upon our experiences parallels this Lacanian distance that the signifier brings to reality itself. In a Derridean vein, the signifier spells its own demise, and at the same time bestows its own freedom. In our being's submission to the signifier, something is necessarily lost, as the signifier is, by definition, pointing to something that it is not, which occurs within grammatical time. Every utterance pulls behind it a series of others, and pushes before it a future that is non-identifiable with the utterances themselves; they are disfiguring of "reality" as possibilities come at us, and into the pasts that we leave in the wake of our de-cision(s), liberation as missing being-in-time. These possibilities only properly circulate in the dyadic relation to the Other's Lack.

The moment of separation, I think, helps differentiate what is ontological about trauma from its later effects. If the modern subject is ontologically or structurally temporally traumatized by language retroactively, then the subject is secondarily traumatized by a particular encounter with the imaginary Other (Levinas' Other), whose lack the subject attempts to superimpose its lack onto, and the Other of particular signifiers (Levinas' trace of immemorial past) – the law of the father. It is the paternal function that annuls the subject's unity with the Other, which could be the mOther or the other scene of trauma. For the history of trauma, it may be necessary to enlarge separation to include other kinds of unity with other experience – for instance, the unity one feels at the scene of the accident, or in wartime, as the pervasive sense of being-in-the-world as plenitude, as the Same. If alienation is the primary founding trauma, and separation is a secondary event, then many of the traumas that one encounters in the clinic (i.e., rape, torture, accidents, battlefield experience, also severe childhood deprivation, etc.) constitute tertiary traumas. Not surprisingly, the politics of recent *Diagnostic and Statistical Manual of Mental Disorders (DSM)* revisions reflect this crypto-Freudian understanding among researchers that the reach of traumatic suffering is pervasive in Western culture and should be, thus, incorporated among sensible diagnostic rubrics (van der Kolk, 2014). In distinction to a diagnostic reduction of trauma to the discrete event (i.e., PTSD) or even chronically unfolding events (i.e., "complex trauma" as a proposed diagnostic), however, all traumas may be seen to have ontologically structural and particular factical dimensions, and recapitulate each other if not in their intensities then in a primordial alienation and successive separations of the subject from its embeddedness in the plenitude of Being, in the Real. Drawing a bit on Laplanche's (1999) "general seduction theory," one may see trauma as a message from the Other that must be translated. The answering in the Real of the imaginary Other's question must occur in the discourse of the symbolic Other. Another way to say this is that the subject constitutes the space between the sending and the receiving of a message, one that will never be read in its literal form. In Kafka's (2000) "Imperial Message," the subject is the space between the sending and the impossibility of receiving the message, the one that must be *imagined*, the directive dreamed to oneself when the evening comes. As follows, the subject is seduced to become embedded into the plenitude of Being, but is jolted free through the action of the paternal function, the retroactive Saying of the Other's discourse. We only know we have been traumatized when we name it as such, when later events with their chains of signifiers allow it to manifest that way. Importantly, every trauma, thus, involves: 1) a signifying chain; 2) the originary scene touching the subject through alterity; and 3) the residue of Real, which implicates non-knowledge. In other words, trauma involves interruption in Being or the Real by an Other that is retroactively figured in a certain way – sedimenting *connaissance*, borne of an ontologically intrusive symbolic exteriority relating also to a historically specific, factical alterity.

Despite the Lacanian illumination of the temporality in relation to trauma, and its effects, there is undoubtedly something mysterious in these formulations; a direct philosophical and psychological treatment of temporality lies outside the scope of the present work. It bears noting that Lacan's position regarding the subject's traumatic location within time evolved over the course of his work. Lacan's (1966/2006b) earlier work on the subject, "Logical Time and the Assertion of Anticipated Certainty," involves the well-known scenario from game theory of the prisoner's dilemma (Fink, 1996), his later work focusing on the synchrony of the signifier, and finally his topological meditations and that of *tuché*. As Johnston (2005) notes in his treatise on the relation of the drives and temporality, the binary of synchrony and diachrony encircle each other. Importantly, however, synchrony itself appears as supposed but necessary, due to the static and reifying effects of the signifier. Indeed, the "cause" of trauma only emerges in its *a posteriori* positioning within the effects of language. As subjects, we come to our past traumas futurally, which very strangely almost fill themselves in behind our backs so to speak, but making them no less terrifying, formative, or real. Žižek (1994b) insightfully remarks that:

> This paradox of trauma *qua* cause that does not pre-exist its effects but is retroactively "posited" by them involves a kind of temporal loop: *it is through "repetition," through its echoes within the signifying structure, that the cause retroactively becomes what it always-already was.* . . . . *synchrony* designates such a paradoxical synchronization, coincidence, of present and past – that is, such a temporal loop where by progressing forward, we return to where we always-already were.
>
> *(p. 32)*

The phenomenon of "delayed onset" trauma (Horesh, Solomon, Zerach, & Ein-Dor, 2011), as well as vulnerability studies (Enlow, Blood, & Egeland, 2013), appear empirically confirmative that trauma cannot be construed as a brute fact, as a discretely objective clinical event. For instance, as "Hashim" – a victim of potential political trauma (threats of death and imprisonment), draining the efficacy of his tormentors – remarks: "Because in my community we do communicate and we do talk about events and problems, you know . . . And it's not very secret . . . It's happened to everyone because there was a war" (Johnson, Thompson, & Downs, 2009, p. 413). Hence, what is, or is not, traumatic does not preexist the subject, but rather becomes what it already was. This means, *inter alia*, that the subject's originary alienation, his/her earlier developmental attempts (the fallout of Lacanian separation) to suture the void in his/her being, and the further traumatic effects of other events become enfolded within each other. For the modern subject, original alienation, imperfectly solved through assignation within the symbolic order, gives way to the desire of returning to the scene of rejoining, itself dissolved in the intervening signifiers, which circumscribe the subject's search for itself within identificatory and atomistic symbolic schemes. Especially, however, for the intensities of natural disaster, genocide, torture, or rape, the temporal looping that would ancestrally provide subjects a compromise formation ("Give up your desire for mother, and I'll give you the keys to the kingdom of narcissistic iden-tification") fails, as there are precious few signifiers, or systems thereof, capable of effecting such solutions. Consequently, in the stark cruelty of this existence, the bargain so far manifested through the subject's being is effectively repudiated. Thus, as suggested, the temporal looping of *Nachträglichkeit* locating trauma *coming to us from the past* is attuned to the subject's ownmost, particular desolation of searching within its own temporal being for the shreds of signified realities that would make sense of the impossible – in the absence of communities, traditions, or the ontotheological buttresses that may have historically protected others. Then, it is not the least bit astonishing to find the current purveyors of traumatic remedia-tion advocating for the creation of therapeutic communities promising solidar-ity and connection, however transitory or professionalized they may be – wards against the bidirectional temporality of our inheritance.

The second aspect of Foucault's (1983) ethical analysis of the subject concerns the mode of subjection (*mode d'assujettissement*), which involves the ways one is incited to work out his/her moral obligations. For instance, the mode that uncon-ceals the subject's self-relation, which would also touch its relation to others, would include the pre-modern invocation of natural or divine law, or a universal principle of rationality for classical and early modern, Kantian ethics. For later modernity, however, the subject's relation to language becomes its ethical mode of subjection, which is made possible by the dramatic shift in the capacities of language, no longer ontologically woven into the world (in the Renaissance), nor transparently representing reality. Foucault (1966/1973), therefore, writes of the modern deployment of language as that of its having a history, objectivity, and law-like regularity; linguistic phenomena are able to be discerned as objects of knowledge, while also reflecting the historicity of their being. For modernity, language becomes structural and systematized – rather than representational or as a metaphysical signature marked into the world – but also attains its most original Greek meaning of *poiesis*, allowing the brightness of being to shine forth, to bring phenomena into presence through its division of the noumenal, or Real.

Accordingly, for Heidegger, Levinas, and Lacan, the ethical mode of subjection concerns language as a mode of revelation of selfhood through the subject's division or self-withdrawal into nullity, death, or non-Being through the poetic power of the Saying, of the signifier retroactively producing the traumatic cut. Later Heideg-gerian thought, continuing the tradition of hermeneutic thinking, becomes more and more preoccupied with the role of language in the disclosure of Being through Dasein's finitude, as taken up in *Ereignis*. Language participates in the trauma of being-towards-death, in the nullity of Dasein's future, in its dehiscence – the splitting of Being against nothingness. As Richardson (2003) writes, "There-being's [Dasein's] task is to walk the path of seeming-to-be and, by de-cision in its use of language, to find its way to authenticity" (p. 293). Dasein is, for this reason, always at the knife-edge of language, constituting its possibilities against the impossibility of death only in regards to what may be brought into its fore-having, its existential understanding of what it means for it to be. The later Heidegger (1971c) raises language to a "house of being"; however, the foundation of such structure rests on the subterranean and Other side of death, of nothingness: "Only man dies – and indeed continually, so long as he stays on this earth, so long as he dwells. His dwelling, however, rests in the poetic" (p. 219). Accordingly, the showing or unconcealment of Dasein's own being – its own particularities, projects, identifications, loves, anguish, regrets – through *Ereignis* involves what poetically withdraws and disappears against death, what cannot be said as death is not to be represented, but itself bears the Saying upon which the Said is determined. For Levinas, it is precisely this sense of Saying that ethically opens the existent to itself. Language is, in its most primordial way, an opening to what is otherwise than Being. For Derrida (1974), engagement with the Levinasian Saying relates to *the trace* that mediates the space of hearing through *différance*, through the arch-phenomenon of an immemorial past where the Other's exteriority to consciousness that allows our being as an existent would not emerge "without the nonpresence of the other inscribed within the sense of the present, without the relationship with death . . . The presence-absence of the trace" (p. 71). The death offered by the Saying, then, does not offer the subject its being through a linguistic blade of nothingness that admonishes the subject to cleave its own poetic path through the undergrowth of *Gerede*. Nonetheless, the Saying does relate to a death – here an absence of presence, a void in the spacing of the structural system of language (*langue*):

> Diachrony is the signification itself, an ambivalence which, in the present, is an ambiguity. The inscription of the order in the for-the-other of obedience is an anarchic being affected, which slips into me "like a thief" through the outstretched nets of consciousness. This trauma has surprised me completely; the order has never been represented, for it has never been presented, not even in the past coming in memory.
>
> *(Levinas, 1974/1998, p. 148)*

The theme of death returns again for Levinas as that of murder, where the subject is always threatening a violence to the Other in objectification, totalization, and grasp of the Other's infinity as a determinate position in the Said – not the absence of the structure, but in its intermittent presences, culminations, and solidifications. For Levinas (1961/1969), it is the face – opening the existent's being through the Saying – that says "don't kill me." The subject's traumatic wounding encircles the im-possibility of completing its being without transforming the Other into the dead matter of language.

This, precisely, is where Levinas, as a post-humanist, and Lacan, as a structuralist, become counterparts, enunciating as they do the killing power of *logos*, or the Word, as the Real is murdered by the symbolic order. For Lacan, it bears repeating in a somewhat different tone that the castrated subject only achieves its own eternal and identical Same at the price of deadening, of becoming like the living dead of Hollywood second-grade cinema. Žižek (1997) writes that "for a human being to be 'dead while alive' is to be colonized by the 'dead' symbolic order; to be 'alive while dead' is to give body to the remainder of Life-Substance which has escaped the symbolic colonization" (p. 89). The symbolic register, thus, effects a kind of "cadaverization," wherein the subject obtains its false and transient promise of imaginary selfhood in exchange for the death of its Real being. The symbolic origin of this burial alive is associated with what Lacan (1966/2006e) refers to as "unary trait," the iterable mark of difference, and the insignia of the Other that marks the circulation of desire according to the primary repressed positioning of the Lack left by the signifier. The fragmented temporal field of trauma (as separation) – in the strongest ethical terms, as simultaneously implicating the subject's care of self and its relation to the little Other – disturbs the subject's fantasy of being completed through language, and reopens the ontological wounding in the temporalizing of the signifier (alienation). The Lacanian mode of subjection – as the traumatic, alienating cut of the signifier and the retraumatization of separation – is that which operates to free the subject from the more automatic functioning of the natural world, of the convergence of material and imaginary realities. Moreover, as indicated, the temporal dislocation occurring in all later, or tertiary, traumas discloses the failed retroactive symbolic gestures that never effect full repair, or only after much renarrating within therapeutic enclosures and socially sanctioned spaces are able to clumsily suture the wound in the subject's being. Consider the detonation of an IED (improvised explosive device) in the lives of many American soldiers during the recent U.S. incursions in Iraq and Afghanistan, where a Real Other not only maims or kills the flesh itself but also kills and is killed by the elaborate symbolic systems that promise identification and self. Coming home, thus, becomes profoundly alienating as the past as lived – along many dimensions – is falsified and comes to be seen and navigated differently, as it *always will have been*. Trauma across its axes – historically ontological, subjectively ontological, and as event – calls us to painfully remove ourselves from meaningfully signified engagements in the immersive seduction of Being. Perversely, perhaps, the Kantian antinomy that plagues classical epistemology turns out, on an ontological level, to be the ironically redemptive and traumatic removal of the subject's genesis in time, as the engine of its freedom.

Under Foucault's (1983) ethical analysis, the final dimension concerns the being one aspires to be, the *telos* or working out of the ethical substance and the modes of its subjection. For other epochs, these involved purification (Christianity), or a kind of rational freedom (classical thought through Kant); however, under the maturity of Enlightenment culture of late modernity, the ethical mandate revolves around the subordination of knowledge to the truth of responsibility. As we have seen, the

Kantian–Lacanian temporal paradox of the subject's traumatic genesis is ordinarily given over to the imaginary, enunciated power of language, as the "transcendental illusion is the name for something that appears where there should be nothing. It is not the illusion of something . . . Behind this illusion there is no real object" (Zupančič, 2002, p. 69). As a matter of course, the object circulating does so under the aegis of the traumatic separation that has transpired via the paternal signifier, which initiates a dialectic of desire. Lacan (1966/2006e) writes that "we must add that man's desire is the Other's desire [*le désir de l'homme est le désir de l'Autre*] in which the *de* provides what grammarians call a 'subjective determination' – namely that it is qua Other that man desires" (p. 690). As discussed *infra*, in many technologies for trauma recovery, the imaginary significations that gravitate around object *a* often suture the subject's division through narratives of biographical continuity. In striking contrast to a moment of metaphorization that would provide an identificatory but impossible merger of the fleeing fragment of Real being and sedimented signification, the subject's *traversal of the fantasy* refers to its taking up of its own being-in-time, which necessarily embraces itself as a breach in time rather than precipitate. For Lacan, therefore, this means that the subject assumes the traumatic cause of his or her being. The subject's existence out of the future anterior here brings it to the precipice of its being as a futural past ("By the time you read this message, I will have written my letter to you about our agreement"). The reading of the letter, looped and divided through the future, becomes a traumatic past that is retroactively decided within this temporal sequence that places the noumenal content or reality (the "real meaning") of the message in abeyance, though the Real message is already symbolically deadened by the end of the sentence. Crucially, however, is that the subject potentially takes responsibility for something problematic, an embodied exigency or anxiety heretofore unknown but *more Real than anything*, which – strictly speaking – becomes the cause *après coup* of its symbolically dissected and imaginary being as a sender of messages, a person making agreements, etc. Fink (1995) writes that

> The traversing of fantasy involves the subject's assumption of a new position with respect to the Other as language and the Other as desire . . . Not "it happened to me," or "They did this to me," or "Fate had it in store for me," but "I was," "I did," "I saw," "I cried out."
>
> *(p. 62)*

To my lights, the Lacanian ethical *telos* of traversing the fantasy gives rise to several striking and related insights pertaining to a coming of age of the subject of the Enlightenment. First, it allows the subject to take responsibility for itself as a void, or failure of symbolization of the Real – not as any particular signified self-formation. As Žižek (1989) argues, "the subject is an answer of the Real (of the object, of the traumatic kernel) to the question of the Other" (p. 180). Second, traversal of the fantasy breaks the ideological spell that object *a* creates via its many phallic significations, the illusion that truth effects exist "out there" in the world of imagined objects, social relations, etc. Third, the subject's responsibility for its division amounts to the realization that truth, while being bound with knowledge, does not equate to knowledge. In other words, the truth that the subject comes to is not able to be transcribed, and its *jouissance* evades capture; however, it must be assumed nonetheless and its assumption will also involve the production of knowledge secondary from it.

While Lacanian ethics partake in a kind of structuralist variation on existentiality, Heidegger's own ethical direction is notable for its phenomenological origin. As discussed earlier, Dasein's finitude providing the clearing for the presencing of Being in *Ereignis* and as being-towards-death are central for Dasein's *Sorge*, or care structure. Of course, in many ways, it is its being-towards-death, as a nullity of possibility that functions for Heidegger the way that the void, as failure in the symbolic order, functions for Lacan. Nonetheless, the closing down of possibilities traumatically haunting Dasein's being-in-the-world relates not explicitly to it assuming its cause, but rather to the proximate notion of taking responsibility for the truth of one's authentic, phenomenal existence. Ethically, as self care, the trauma of fragmented temporality reflects Dasein's inability to fully reflect on its life as lived at the end of its days because – in a kind of bookend to the Lacanian-Kantian noumenal impossibility of witnessing one's birth – one never attains the perspective at death; Dasein is always not-yet. Still, Dasein's own existential guilt pervades its being-in-time – i.e., the inevitable price of embracing some possibilities will put others to death – forming the ontological basis for the moral guilt guiding everyday social conduct. Notably, it is *Angst* or Dasein's discernment of the uncanny – the tremor of non-Being accompanying the vanishing of things and other beings – that allows the phenomenon of being-towards-death as anticipation of death at the end of life to become the omnipresent *death in life* (the withdrawal of *Ereignis*) to take its hold on Dasein's conscience: "Exposure to nothingness itself, is utterly positive in its effect: it posits being, the being I am, wholly potential come to itself, wholly power" (Lingis, 1989, p. 117). Indeed, as for the Lacanian subject, Dasein must, in a confrontation with the nothingness that traumatically separates it from the plenitude or embeddedness of being-in-the-world, stake out its being on its own ground. Anticipation allows Dasein to find itself as lost in the they-self, and gives it over to the possibility of being itself – a freedom loosened from the illusions of the "they," as factical (rather than factual) being, and thus anxious in the face of non-Being (Heidegger, 1927/1962). For a Heideggerian ethical sensibility, in listening to the Nothing at the heart of Being, one hears the calling of conscience – the wresting free of one's ownmost possibilities from those cultural and social possibilities of the "they-self," underlying anticipatory resoluteness for the disclosive projection of its factical possibilities that it will take up. As with Lacanian ethics, the existential authenticity of Heidegger offers several potentially subversive consequences for the subject of late modernity, which calls to mind Heidegger's National Socialism as a repressive limit within his own philosophy. First, Dasein takes responsibility for itself against the nullity or nothingness of death, which will not allow for a settled or final solidification of self (as object-like). Along these lines, Dreyfus (1991) writes it is "precisely because resolute Dasein is clear that it can have no final meaning or settled identity, it is clear-sighted about what is actually possible" (p. 320). Second, in parallel with traversal of the fantasy, the call of conscience allows Dasein to draw itself from the fallen and inauthentic, everyday world of "the they" (*Das Man*), whose idle talk and received wisdom paralyzes the transformative possibilities of a being possessed of its own destiny, its own death. Third, as in Lacan, the subject's responsibility for its emptiness of a fundamental nature, and its *Angst*-filled grasping for its own existence, its own resolute understanding and hermeneutic disclosure of its world, deprives objective knowledge – whether scientific, moral, or practical – of its privileged status independent of its socio-temporal, contextual effects on a *deathbound subject*.

As suggested, Levinasian thought is ethical thought *par excellence*, an ethics of ethics; however, its substantial import as self-relation touches the ethical relation to the Other (in a different sense), rather than being an incitation for existential self-possession or differentiation. It would be inaccurate to speak of Levinas' subject as having its aspirations as a moral or ethical being bound to death, nullity, or the void; rather, for Levinas' ethical ontology, the subject's perpetual interruption by the non-Being of the Other is the creative source of its fecundity. The Other, for Levinas, is origin and *telos* of its legitimate projects. In practical/ethical terms, the Levinasian subject's relation to the Other is theological as well as ethical, and not only frustrates an ontology of presence but creates or founds a notion or idea of the good: "The Other qua Other is situated in a dimension of height and of abasement – glorious abasement; he has the face of the poor, the stranger, the widow . . . at the same time, of the master called to invest and justify my freedom" (Levinas, 1961/1969, p. 251). The subject's relation to the Other, then, is one of rescue from solitude followed by theologically minded obligation. The upshot of this, of course, is that the subject must continue to submit itself to the Other as a reward for bringing it out of its prison, for teaching it new things and allowing new knowledge about the world. In speaking for the Other, one must substitute oneself for the Other, advocate for the Other by sacrificing oneself, as the Other becomes the author of the subject's freedom and possibilities of achieving the good. Moreover, "the good" generally carries the Judeo-Christian meaning of sacrifice and charity. The Other, even when it is holding the subject hostage, is conceptualized as beneficent, as a manifestation of the benign will of God, "The idea of God comes only through my relation to the Other" (Manning, 1993, p. 148).

Levinasian ethics – as that which traumatically separates the subject from itself as self-same, as identical to itself – is deeply indebted to a non-conception of God. For Levinasian thought, as with Heidegger and Lacan, knowledge – whether *connaissance*, philosophical thought, or conscious meaning – is made possible by what transcends it. Also for Levinas, the obsessional effort to conflate reality and thought results in a reduction or totalization of reality to the phenomenal light of vision, to representation or depiction, to presence. Importantly, however, Levinas does not oppose thought with faith, which merely asserts an absent presence whose proof may be amenable to depiction; rather, transcendence attains a pre-ontological status. Absolute transcendence – paralleling in some ways the position of death in *Ereignis* for Heidegger or the Real for Lacan – emanates from the God of Abraham, whose commands are unintelligible through reason. God as absolute alterity is, therefore, beyond presence and the immanence of experience. Moreover, God disrupts the self-presence of the existent, as a relation with the infinite that grounds thought or consciousness; however, significantly, the infinite that exceeds the existent's grasp and creates the Levinasian subject is found *within the subject*. In other words, as suggested *supra*, the subject itself is a relation between the self-same existent and the infinite, which gives it its mature being, and its relation to the good. The Levinasian subject is less the Lacanian subject divided against itself as being inhabited by what is utterly alien, but more the subject whose non-Being that runs through is the foreign but positive condition of thought. Consequently, the subject's asymmetrical relation with the infinity of the Other is not purely an external relation. Nonetheless, the subject's own being that traumatically opens the gulf between itself as existent and the infinity of God within awakens the desire, beyond satisfaction, for the good beyond Being. This occurs phenomeno-logically in relation to the Other, who most proximately bears the transcendent infinity of God in human form (which Levinas calls *illeity*, meaning "Himness") (Levinas, 1974/1998). For our inquiry, the traumatic dimension of Levinas' ethical invocations regarding the subject's responsibility for the good of the Other impli-cates not only the subject's own immemorial past in relation to the Other but the Other's immemorial past, and the future inspired by the desire beyond what can be accomplished in substituting oneself for the Other. As counterpart to Lacan and Heidegger, Levinas, thus, argues that the subject's own history does not appear to itself – not because of a noumenal failure of symbolization or the nullity of Das-ein's being-towards-death, but because it is always already related to the Other's history, which guarantees its anarchic, diachronous existence but is unknown. Similar to Lacan and Heidegger, Levinas' subject's responsibility to the Other is only retroactively known in time, as the Said is always being deferred from, falling out from, another time of responsibility, another Saying. Finally, Levinasian eth-ics, despite its theological character, speaks to the same quandaries of Enlighten-ment rationality addressed in Lacan and Heidegger. First, Levinas' subject takes up its responsibility for itself as being-for-the-Other, which predates any particular version of substantial selfhood; the subject is always in the making as responding to the Other's call before the advent of thought. Second, the subject's attention to the awakening of responsibility for the Other and its attendant Saying subverts any attempt to categorize or finally signify any aspect of the Other's being as Said – as *connaissance*, thought, or even consciousness. Third, as in Lacan and Heidegger, the subject's responsibility for its own relation to the infinity of *illeity* brings realiza-tion that truth or reality transcends mere knowledge.

The traumatic ontology of the modern subject

The "ethical ontologies of finitude" of Heidegger, Levinas, and Lacan perhaps only partially reveal the traumatic structure of modern subjectivity, its being emerging from its variegated historical and social conditions that would ostensibly include other ethical sensibilities bearing traumatic finitude, arising from disciplines other than psychology, psychiatry, psychoanalysis, and philosophy. Still, in light of the scientism that continues to haunt the culture of psychology – variants of positivism that nostalgically cling to fulfilling broken promises of the classical episteme, but also varieties of social constructionism, and phenomenological, neo-pragmatist strands of thought – these ethical inquiries into the subject's relation to itself and Others most seriously address the aporias of Foucault's (1966/1973) analytic of finitude because they incorporate a Kantian or noumenal dimension into their inquiries in such a way that, in each case, truth – in relation to *Ereignis*, infinity, or the Real – forms the ground of knowledge. In other words, unlike Foucault's archaeology (which we are attempting to use as a scaffold but to surpass) or deconstructive methodology – which take the gaps in knowledge to be *post*-structural to knowledge – traumatic ethics does not hold to a coincidence or identity between truth and knowledge, and this disjuncture, for all three forms of ethics, emerges from fragmented temporality, a withdrawal from self in time. So, in the barest possible terms, I will attempt to articulate the traumatic ontology of the modern subject, one that will guide the later discussion of the very different paths the human sciences of psychology and psychiatry have taken in approaching traumatic experience:

> *The modern subject – manifesting presence, thought, and knowledge in its expanse – is by this necessity ontologically finite, characterized by its withdrawal from itself in time. Its non-Being arises from its traumatic dis/possession of its being-in-time, wherein its immersion in the noumenal, Real, the plenitude of Being, or its sameness is alienated through the poetic death of symbolic articulation. As transcendent of knowledge, the modern subject's ethical relation to itself implicates its assumption of responsibility for its truth, whose origin in time is unknown to thought and knowledge.*

The traumatic subject of modernity, as given access through the work of Heidegger, Levinas, and Lacan, illuminates structural conditions that – I will suggest vis-à-vis the human sciences – extend beyond the confines of philosophical or psychoanalytic thought. However, within philosophical thought, it is suggested that the traumatic ontology of Heidegger, Levinas, and Lacan is, perhaps, the most penetrating expression of what its speculative realist critics refer to as "correlationism," which

> consists in disqualifying the claim that it is possible to consider the realms of subjectivity and objectivity independently of one another. Not only does it become necessary to insist that we never grasp an object "in itself," in isolation from its relation to the subject, but it also becomes necessary to maintain that we can never grasp a subject that would not always-already be related to an object.

> *(Meillassoux, 2008, p. 5)*

Because correlationism falls in the wake of post-Kantian philosophy, its varieties would include not only so much continental thought – from Kant through Hegel, Heidegger to structuralism and poststructuralism – but also much of the analytic tradition, such as Popper's (2002) post-positivism, or Wittgenstein (1958). Nonetheless, as articulated above, correlationism as governing the *subject's relation to the object, to knowledge* does not tell the entire story because, for a traumatic ontology of the subject – which would be a subset of correlationist thought – knowledge is submitted to *truth*, which, though unknown to the subject, materially resonates in the Real, in Being.

As follows, ethical ontologies of finitude – disclosing the subject's traumatic being – address Foucault's (1966/1973) analytic of finitude, reorienting its quandaries for the subject in ways that edify and support the Enlightenment call to assume responsibility for one's being. It may help to briefly enumerate how this is accomplished for future reference to the technological strategies deployed by techno-capitalist culture that conceal the subject's ontological trauma. Not coincidentally, these refashionings of finitude on the subject's behalf are associated with the traditional subfields in philosophy of metaphysics, epistemology, and ethics, respectively:

Truth

For the modern subject, truth becomes neither the insoluble problem of a fallen relation to the eternal, nor the problematic correspondence between itself and knowledge. Rather, truth is the effect of an Otherness that symbolically and temporally separates the subject from its immersion or infusion in the Real or in Being. Its animating power derives from the subject's embodied occupation of the space where Being passes to non-Being.

Reflexivity

The modern subject, being removed from knowledge in the world through its symbolically effected non-Being-in-time, becomes capable of representing to itself representations of its being without the incumbent problem of its point of access to itself as an object of knowledge. As a consequence, the modern subject never directly appears in its enunciated statements, in what is said.

Autonomy

The modern subject, being temporally removed from its origin, is not submitted to the causality of the world of objective knowledge and thought. Consequently, the subject need not rely on ontotheological conceptions of ontic being that would guarantee its freedom. Its most transformative task becomes that of assuming responsibility for the non-Being that marks the trace of truth for itself and for others in relation.

Notes

1 In "Kierkegaard, Division II, and Later Heidegger," Dreyfus and Rubin (1991) argue that early Heidegger attempts to stake out Dasein's existentiality on Kierkegaard's (1989) account of the self from *The Sickness Unto Death*, wherein Kierkegaard specifies four spheres of existence: the aesthetic (commitment to enjoyment), the ethical (commitment to absolute choice), Religiousness A (self-annihilation before God), and Religiousness B (commitment to cause or project). Briefly, Dreyfus and Rubin (1991) argue that Heidegger wishes to inconsistently secure for Dasein the meaningful existence of Religiousness B while preserving its nothingness in Religiousness A.

2 In some ways, Levinas' critique of Heidegger's temporality resembles that of Blattner (1999), who argues that Heidegger's temporal idealism fails because originary temporality – while explanatory for the human world of meaning, purpose, and end – does not account for events coming from outside of this sphere. The subject both requires an extra-subjective source of its time (an exteriority that for Blattner is sequential time, and for Levinas, the Other's time) and is simultaneously the source of finite temporality that illuminates the world. Levinas (1947/1987), against idealist philosophy (in which he places Heidegger), argues that "existing does not exist. It is the existent that exists" (p. 46). In a somewhat Leibnizian turn, temporality requires the existent's relation to particularity that is Other.

References

Barnard, S. (2002). Diachrony, tuché, and the ethical subject. In E. Gantt & R. Williams (Eds.), *Psychology for the other: Levinas, ethics, and the practice of psychology* (pp. 160–181). Pittsburgh, PA: Duquesne University Press.

Bergo, B. (2005). Ontology, transcendence, and immanence in Emannuel Levinas' philosophy. *Research in Phenomenology, 35*(1), 141–180.

Bernet, R. (2000). The traumatized subject. *Research in Phenomenology, 30*, 160–179.

Blattner, W. (1999). *Heidegger's temporal idealism.* Cambridge, UK: Cambridge University Press.

Bracken, P. (2002). *Trauma: Culture, meaning, and philosophy.* London, UK: Whurr.

Caputo, J. D. (1993). *Demythologizing Heidegger.* Bloomington: University of Indiana Press.

Carman, T. (2003). *Heidegger's analytic: Interpretation, discourse, and authority in Being and Time.* Cambridge, UK: Cambridge University Press.

Clegg, J. W., & Slife, B. D. (2005). Epistemology and the hither side: A Levinasian account of relational knowing. *European Journal of Psychotherapy, Counselling, and Health, 7*(1–2), 65–76.

Derrida, J. (1974). *Of grammatology* (G. Spivak, Trans.). Baltimore, MD: Johns Hopkins University Press.

Derrida, J. (1978). *Writing and difference* (A. Bass, Trans.). Chicago, IL: University of Chicago Press.

Derrida, J. (1981). *Positions* (A. Bass, Trans.). Chicago, IL: University of Chicago Press.

Descartes, R. (2008). *Meditations on first philosophy* (M. Moriarty, Trans.). Oxford, UK: Oxford University Press. (Original work published 1641)

Dreyfus, H. (1991). *Being-in-the-world: A commentary on Heidegger's Being and Time, division I.* Cambridge, MA: MIT Press.

Dreyfus, H., & Rubin, J. (1991). Kierkegaard, division II, and later Heidegger. In H. Dreyfus (Ed.), *Being-in-the-world: A commentary on Heidegger's Being and Time, division I* (pp. 283–340). Cambridge, MA: MIT Press.

Enlow, M. B., Blood, E., & Egeland, B. (2013). Sociodemographic risk, developmental competence, and PTSD symptoms in young children exposed to interpersonal trauma in early life. *Journal of Traumatic Stress, 26*, 684–694.

Fink, B. (1995). *The Lacanian subject: Between language and jouissance.* Princeton, NJ: Princeton University Press.

Fink, B. (1996). Logical time and the precipitation of subjectivity. In R. Feldstein, B. Fink, & M. Jaanus (Eds.), *Reading seminars I and II: Lacan's return to Freud* (pp. 356–386). Albany: State University of New York Press.

Foucault, M. (1973). *The order of things: An archaeology of the human sciences* (A. Sheridan, Trans.). New York, NY: Vintage. (Original work published 1966)

Foucault, M. (1983). On the genealogy of ethics: An overview of a work in progress. In H. Dreyfus & P. Rabinow (Eds.), *Michel Foucault: Beyond structuralism and hermeneutics* (pp. 229–252). Chicago, IL: University of Chicago Press.

Foucault, M. (1984). What is enlightenment (C. Porter, Trans.). In P. Rabinow (Ed.), *The Foucault reader* (pp. 32–50). New York, NY: Pantheon.

Foucault, M. (1988). *The history of sexuality: Vol. 3. The care of the self* (R. Hurley, Trans.). New York, NY: Vintage. (Original work published 1984)

Foucault, M. (1990). *The history of sexuality: Vol. 2. The use of pleasure* (R. Hurley, Trans.). New York, NY: Vintage. (Original work published 1984)

Foucault, M. (1994). The ethic of care for the self as a practice of freedom: An interview (J. D. Gauthier, Trans.). In J. Bernauer & D. Rasmussen (Eds.), *The final Foucault* (pp. 1–20). Cambridge, MA: MIT Press.

Foucault, M. (2005). *The hermeneutics of the subject: Lectures at the Collège de France 1981–1982* (G. Burchell, Trans.). New York, NY: Picador. (Original work published 2001)

Freud, S. (1953). The interpretation of dreams. In J. Strachey (Ed. & Trans.), *The standard edition of the complete psychological works of Sigmund Freud* (Vols. 4–5). London, UK: Hogarth Press. (Original work published 1900)

Ghiglione, R. (1983). Language attitudes and social influence. *Journal of Social Psychology, 121*, 97–109.

Guignon, C. (1983). *Heidegger and the problem of knowledge.* Indianapolis, IN: Hackett.

Habermas, J. (1996). *The philosophical discourse of modernity* (F. G. Lawrence, Trans.). Cambridge, MA: MIT Press.

Han, B. (2002). *Foucault's critical project: Between the transcendental and the historical.* Stanford, CA: Stanford University Press.

Han, B. (2005). The analytic of finitude and the history of subjectivity. In G. Gutting (Ed.), *The Cambridge companion to Foucault* (2nd ed., pp. 176–209). Cambridge, UK: Cambridge University Press.

Haugeland, J. (1982). Heidegger on being a person. *Nous, 16*(1), 15–26.

Heidegger, M. (1962). *Being and time* (J. Macquarrie & E. Robinson, Trans.). San Francisco, CA: Harper. (Original work published 1927)

Heidegger, M. (1968). *What is called thinking* (J. G. Gray, Trans.). New York, NY: Harper. (Original work published 1954)

Heidegger, M. (1971a). What are poets for? (A. Hofstadter, Trans.). In *Poetry, language, thought* (pp. 87–139). New York, NY: Harper.

Heidegger, M. (1971b). The thing (A. Hofstadter, Trans.). In *Poetry, language, thought* (pp. 163–184). New York, NY: Harper.

Heidegger, M. (1971c). ". . . Poetically man dwells . . ." (A. Hofstadter, Trans.). In *Poetry, language, thought* (pp. 211–227). New York, NY: Harper.

Heidegger, M. (1972). *On time and being* (J. Stambaugh, Trans.). Chicago, IL: University of Chicago Press. (Original work published 1962)

Heidegger, M. (1997). *Kant and the problem of metaphysics* (R. Taft, Trans.). Bloomington: Indiana University Press. (Original work published 1929)

Heidegger, M. (1999). *Contributions to philosophy (from enowning)* (P. Enad & K. Maly, Trans.). Bloomington: Indiana University Press.

Hepburn, A., & Potter, J. (2003). Discourse analytic practice. In C. Seale, D. Silverman, J. Gubrium, & G. Gobo (Eds.), *Qualitative research practice* (pp. 180–196). London, UK: Sage.

Horesh, D., Solomon, Z., Zerach, G., & Ein-Dor, T. (2011). Delayed-onset PTSD among war veterans: The role of life events throughout the life cycle. *Social Psychology and Psychiatric Epidemiology, 46*, 863–870.

Johnson, D. K., Storandt, M., & Balota, D. A. (2003). Discourse analysis of logical memory recall in normal aging and dementia of the Alzheimer type. *Journal of Neuropsychology, 17*, 82–92.

Johnson, H., Thompson, A., & Downs, M. (2009). Non-Western interpreters' experiences of trauma: The protective role of culture following exposure to oppression. *Ethnicity & Health, 14*(4), 407–418.

Johnston, A. (2005). *Time driven: Metapsychology and the splitting of the drive.* Evanston, IL: Northwestern University Press.

Johnston, A. (2008). *Žižek's ontology: A transcendental materialist theory of subjectivity.* Evanston, IL: Northwestern University Press.

Kafka, F. (2000). An imperial message (J. Neugrochel, Trans.). In *The metamorphosis, in the penal colony, and other stories* (pp. 263–264). New York, NY: Scribner.

Kant, I. (2007). *Critique of pure reason* (M. Weigelt, Trans.). New York, NY: Penguin. (Original work published 1781)

Kierkegaard, S. (1989). *The sickness unto death* (A. Hannay, Trans.). London, UK: Penguin.

Konopka, A. (2009). The "inversions" of intentionality in Levinas and later Heidegger. *PhaenEx, 4*(1), 146–162.

Lacan, J. (1977). Desire and the interpretation of desire in *Hamlet. Yale French Studies. Literature and psychoanalysis. The Question of Reading: Otherwise, 55–56*, 11–52. doi: 10.2307/2930434

Lacan, J. (1981). *The four fundamental concepts of psycho-analysis* (A. Sheridan, Trans.). New York, NY: Norton. (Original work published 1973)

Lacan, J. (1991a). *The seminar of Jacques Lacan: Book I. Freud's papers on technique, 1953–1954* (J. Forrester, Trans.). New York, NY: Norton. (Original work published 1975)

Lacan, J. (1991b). *The seminar of Jacques Lacan: Book II. The ego in Freud's theory and in the technique of psychoanalysis, 1954–1955* (S. Tomaselli, Trans.). New York, NY: Norton. (Original work published 1978)

Lacan, J. (1992). *The seminar of Jacques Lacan: Book VII. The ethics of psychoanalysis, 1959–1960* (D. Porter, Trans.). New York, NY: Norton. (Original work published 1986)

Lacan, J. (1993). *The seminar of Jacques Lacan: Book III. The psychoses, 1955–1956* (R. Grigg, Trans.). New York, NY: Norton (Original work published 1981)

Lacan, J. (1999). *The seminar of Jacques Lacan: Book XX. On feminine sexuality, the limits of love and knowledge, 1972–1973* (B. Fink, Trans.). New York, NY: Norton.

Lacan, J. (2006a). The mirror stage as formative of the I function as revealed in psychoanalytic experience (B. Fink, Trans.). In J. Lacan (Ed.), *Écrits: The first complete edition in English* (pp. 75–81). New York, NY: Norton. (Original work published 1966)

Lacan, J. (2006b). Logical time and the assertion of anticipated certainty (B. Fink, Trans.). In J. Lacan (Ed.), *Écrits: The first complete edition in English* (pp. 161–174). New York, NY: Norton. (Original work published 1966)

Lacan, J. (2006c). The function and field of speech and language in psychoanalysis (B. Fink, Trans.). In J. Lacan (Ed.), *Écrits: The first complete edition in English* (pp. 197–265). New York, NY: Norton. (Original work published 1966)

Lacan, J. (2006d). The direction of the treatment and the principles of its power (B. Fink, Trans.). In J. Lacan (Ed.), *Écrits: The first complete edition in English* (pp. 489–542). New York, NY: Norton. (Original work published 1966)

Lacan, J. (2006e). The subversion of the subject and the dialectic of desire (B. Fink, Trans.). In J. Lacan (Ed.), *Écrits: The first complete edition in English* (pp. 671–702). New York, NY: Norton. (Original work published 1966)

Lacan, J. (2006f). Position of the unconscious (B. Fink, Trans.). In J. Lacan (Ed.), *Écrits: The first complete edition in English* (pp. 703–721). New York, NY: Norton. (Original work published 1966)

Lacan, J. (2006g). Science and truth (B. Fink, Trans.). In J. Lacan (Ed.), *Écrits: The first complete edition in English* (pp. 726–745). New York, NY: Norton. (Original work published 1966)

Laplanche, J. (1999). *Essays on otherness*. London, UK: Routledge.

Laplanche, J., & Pontalis, J.- P. (1986). Fantasy and the origins of sexuality. In V. Burgin, J. Donald, & C. Kaplan (Eds.), *Formations of fantasy* (pp. 5–34). New York, NY: Methuen.

Levinas, E. (1969). *Totality and infinity: An essay on exteriority* (A. Lingis, Trans.). Pittsburgh, PA: Duquesne University Press. (Original work published 1961)

Levinas, E. (1978). *Existence and existents* (A. Lingis, Trans.). Pittsburgh, PA: Duquesne University Press. (Original work published 1947)

Levinas, E. (1987). *Time and the other* (R. Cohen, Trans.). Pittsburgh, PA: Duquesne University Press. (Original work published 1947)

Levinas, E. (1998). *Otherwise than being, or beyond essence* (A. Lingis, Trans.). Pittsburgh, PA: Duquesne University Press. (Original work published 1974)

Lingis, A. (1989). *Deathbound subjectivity*. Bloomington: Indiana University Press.

MacAvoy, L. (2005). Truth and evidence in Descartes and Levinas. In S. H. Daniel (Ed.), *Current continental theory and modern philosophy* (pp. 21–35). Evanston, IL: Northwestern University Press.

Malpas, J. (2006). *Heidegger's topology: Being, place, world*. Cambridge, MA: MIT Press.

Manning, J. S. (1993). *Interpreting otherwise than Heidegger: Emmanuel Levinas's ethics as first philosophy*. Pittsburgh, PA: Duquesne University Press.

Meillassoux, Q. (2008). *After finitude: An essay on the necessity of contingency* (R. Brassier, Trans.). London, UK: Continuum.

Nelson, E. S. (2014). Heidegger, Levinas, and the other of history. In J. E. Drabinski & E. S. Nelson (Eds.), *Between Levinas and Heidegger* (pp. 51–74). Albany: State University of New York Press.

Nobus, D., & Quinn, M. (2005). *Knowing nothing, staying stupid: Elements for a psychoanalytic epistemology*. London, UK: Routledge.

Okrent, M. B. (1981). The truth of being and the history of philosophy. *The Monist, 64*(4), 500–517.

Pavón Cuéllar, D. (2010). *From the conscious interior to an exterior unconscious: Lacan, discourse analysis, and social psychology*. London, UK: Karnac.

Popper, K. (2002). *Conjectures and refutations*. London, UK: Routledge.

Potter, J. (2003). Discourse analysis and discursive psychology. In P. M. Camic, J. E. Rhodes, & L. Yardley (Eds.), *Qualitative research in psychology: Expanding perspectives in methodology and design* (pp. 73–94). Washington, DC: American Psychological Association.

Potter, J. (2004). Discourse analysis. In M. Hardy & A. Bryman (Eds.), *Handbook of data analysis* (pp. 607–624). London, UK: Sage.

Raynor, T. (2007). *Foucault's Heidegger: Philosophy and transformative experience*. London, UK: Continuum.

Richardson, W. (2003). *Heidegger: Through phenomenology to thought*. New York, NY: Fordham University Press.

Ricoeur, P., & Escobar, M. (2004). Otherwise: A reading of Emmanuel Levinas' *Otherwise than Being or Beyond Essence*. *Yale French Studies, 104*, 82–99.

Riera, G. (1996). Abyssal grounds: Lacan and Heidegger on truth. *Qui Parle, 9*(2), 51–76.

Rorty, R. (1991). *Essays on Heidegger and others: Philosophical papers*. Cambridge, UK: Cambridge University Press.

Sartre, J.-P. (1956). *Being and nothingness* (H. E. Barnes, Trans.). New York, NY: Simon and Schuster.

Schwartz, M. (2003). Epistemes and the history of being. In A. Milchman & A. Rosenberg (Eds.), *Foucault & Heidegger: Critical encounters* (pp. 163–186). Minneapolis: University of Minnesota Press.

Sheehan, T. (2001). Kehre and ereignis: A prolegomenon to *Introduction to Metaphysics*. In R. Polt & G. Fried (Eds.), *A companion to Heidegger's Introduction to Metaphysics* (pp. 3–16). New Haven, CT: Yale University Press.

Spinosa, C. (2005). Derrida and Heidegger: Iterability and ereignis. In H. L. Dreyfus & M. A. Wrathall (Eds.), *A companion to Heidegger* (pp. 484–510). London, UK: Blackwell.

Stolorow, R. D. (2007). *Trauma and human existence: Autobiographical, psychoanalytic, and philosophical reflections*. New York, NY: Routledge.

Stolorow, R. D. (2011). *World, affectivity, trauma: Heidegger and post-Cartesian psychoanalysis*. New York, NY: Routledge.

van der Kolk, B. A. (2014). *The body keeps the score: Brain, mind, and body in the healing of trauma*. New York, NY: Viking.

Wetherell, M. (2001). Themes in discourse research: The case of Diana. In M. Wetherell, S. Taylor, & S. J. Yates (Eds.), *Discourse theory and practice* (pp. 14–28). London, UK: Sage.

White, C. (2005). *Time & death: Heidegger's analysis of finitude*. London, UK: Routledge.

Wittgenstein, L. (1958). *Philosophical investigations* (G. E. M. Anscombe, Trans.). Oxford, UK: Blackwell.

Young, J. (2001). *Heidegger's philosophy of art*. Cambridge, UK: Cambridge University Press.

Žižek, S. (1989). *The sublime object of ideology*. London, UK: Verso.

Žižek, S. (1994a). Kant as a theoretician of vampiricism. *Lacanian Ink, 8*, 19–33.

Žižek, S. (1994b). *The metastases of enjoyment: Six essays on women and causality*. London, UK: Verso.

Žižek, S. (1997). *The plague of fantasies*. London, UK: Verso.

Žižek, S. (1999). *The ticklish subject: The absent centre of political ontology*. London, UK: Verso.

Žižek, S. (2000). Class struggle or postmodernism? Yes, please! In J. Butler (Ed.), *Contingency, hegemony, universality* (pp. 90–135). London, UK: Verso.

Žižek, S. (2006). *The parallax view*. Cambridge, MA: MIT Press.

Zupančič, A. (2002). On love as comedy. *Lacanian Ink, 20*, 62–79.

3
TRAUMA AND TECHNOLOGY

Technology, representation, and trauma

Traumatic ontology potentially gives rise to a revolution in subjectivity. For the subject of trauma as a lapse in its own being-in-time, agency is firmly located within the confines of the historically shifting world itself, without reference to extrinsic, metaphysical guarantors. Consequently, autonomy increasingly arises not in an innate ability residing in the undetermined space of mind, such as Descartes' (1641/1954) assertions of a faculty of judgment originating in God, carrying ancient concerns of what being would lie outside the matrix of causality. Nor does agency come to us by way of God's eighteenth-century surrogates (i.e., Berkeley, 1710/1998; Hume, 1748/1975; Locke, 1690/1975), or even in the form of a special, hard-wired, evolutionary capacity – such as Dennett's (1978) "Valerian" compatibilism. As earlier stated, Kant (1781/2007) pragmatically locates the self-hood of freedom in the noumenal. That is, such a being must be, and can only be, supposed. This, however, leaves the question of how to position noumenal being. Hence, rather than remove such questions as simply out of bounds, to ontologize the question of freedom horizontally within the phenomenal world is to allow it to emerge from a gap or void in the subject's being wherein its reality itself is split in time. For Heidegger, as Žižek (1999) observes, the trace of the "inaccessible noumenal Beyond, is already marked by the horizon of finitude – it designates the way the noumenal Beyond *appears to the subject within his finite experience*" (p. 25), thus having the much-needed effect of removing an implicit reliance on eternity for earthbound temporality as a deficient form of the former. This means that freedom is implicated in the temporal void that occurs for the subject as space or opening for the temporal fold or disjuncture in reality itself as it presences in the space of human finitude.

The subject's agency and truth are related to what cannot appear as knowledge in the field of its traumatic opening. Again to Žižek's (1999) lights, the limitations in our epistemological grasp of reality become the originary condition for coming to knowledge. Phenomenologically, this means that what we take as the flow of experience is itself part of temporal being, taken from our own finite, traumatically open, temporal clearing (*Lichtung*) within understanding. For the later Heidegger (1977a), and as suggested previously, this implicates the move from philosophically ubiquitous confinements of truth to knowledge to that of "unconcealment," or in its Greek form, *Aletheia*. Afterward, "truth," for Heidegger, is increasingly differentiated from knowledge. Unconcealment does not uncover deeper correspondences of idea and thing, but relates to what shows itself, what becomes manifest – as in "phenomenon" (in Greek, *phainomenon*), associated with the visible and what can be brought to light, against the nullity of Dasein, whose traumatic relation to Being allows for the trace of the inaccessible. Such phenomena, thus, stand in relation to darkness (what remains concealed), and the in-between is where truth emerges as lived resonance, or shimmering, and the difference from which freedom arises. As Heidegger (1993) writes,

> Precisely because letting be [disclosure or unconcealment] lets beings be in a particular comportment that relates to them and thus discloses them, it conceals beings as a whole. Letting-be is intrinsically at the same time a concealing. In the ek-sistent freedom of Da-sein a concealing of being as a whole propriates.
>
> *(pp. 129–130)*

This leads Heidegger to the striking insight that what *truth comes to light is itself also a form of concealment or untruth* because that which shows itself may only do so through a kind of banishing of other phenomena into darkness, one that creates a space for the subject. Truth – through the sundering of human being – stretches into darkness, and every de-cision brings both light and darkness to what is not mastered and, thus, concealed (Heidegger, 1971a). This untruth arguably includes both the Heideggerian notion of unthought, as the errancy of philosophical inquiry, and Foucault's understanding of unthought as more aligned with any specific historical epoch's regional ontology. Furthermore, truth as the "opposition of clearing and concealing" bears an inextricable bond to what is made both known and unknown in the becoming of disclosure (Heidegger, 1971a, p. 59). More simply, how and what we have lost or never actualized, or in Freudian terms what has been displaced – both in our proximate existentiell temporalities and in our collective historical time – orients us in how we care for and take up the possibilities that presence amongst the ruins of a pure past.

For later Heidegger (1977c), not only is ontic knowledge historically dependent, but ontological modes of revealing and concealing what it means for truth to exist at all may change radically over time. Importantly, therefore, knowledge and truth are variably permissible under particular historical conditions, and ultimately, vis-à-vis *Ereignis*, Heidegger submits ontology to historicity. As Dreyfus and Rubin (1991) note, "for medieval Christians, reality was the presence of created things as finished products which were simply to be accepted" as part of a divine order (p. 338), and the truth for the medieval subject (as cultural Dasein), and its knowledge – in particular forms of agency relating to the imperfection of its flesh – presenced in relation thereto. Underneath the unbroken chain of creation, theologically and economically visible, lay the impenetrable mystery of the necessity *and* accident of sin and evil in the world. For the classical subject of the eighteenth century, what is real for the subject and its autonomy relates to its ideal relationship with what can be known in correspondence; truth is imagined as coincident with externally aporetic knowledge over against interest or passion, but necessarily suppressing of other truths manifesting as madness and paradox. For the modern traumatic subject, the void that allows erasure awakens a maturely Heideggerian ethics of truth, bearing its call to conscience, responsibility for the alterity that crosses its being (Levinas), and its traversal of its imaginary fantasies of origin (Lacan). This means that truth, in its modern formulation, relates – primordially and with attendant difference – to the symbolic ordering and creative disfiguring of the subject's noumenal Beyond, whose Real traces ignite the retroactive and prospective grasping of freedom for the discrete subject and its functionalist relation to knowledge. In the socio-historical dimension (the truths of particular subjects cannot be easily spoken of in global terms), what comes to light in *disavowing* the tendrils of fleshly noumenal inaccessibility is a return of the classical epoch's paralogism (for instance, in the contemporary debates regarding the nature of consciousness) or in the turn to the obsessional subjectivity hastened in societies of biopower and of control (Deleuze, 1992; Foucault, 2008, 2009). For the later Heidegger, Being is therefore realized as a succession of epochs, each containing its own manner of actualizing what comes to light, what withdraws, and its attendant form of truth and what knowledges follow, but also the manner that threatens or obscures this manifestation.

In his later work, Heidegger (1977a) suggests that the nihilistic destitution of modernity results from metaphysical pretensions of our epoch's mode of concealing traumatic ontology, of our epoch's particular historical opening of the abyss. Indeed, Žižek (1999) remarks that in *Being and Time* Heidegger (1927/1962) encountered a form of existentially disrupted subjectivity foreshadowed in Kantian transcendental thinking. The concealment, however, of this revelation involves a particularly modern form of technology. Greek, premodern *techne* – an expansive notion of revealing or *poiesis* (bringing-forth) – involved skilled unconcealing in the way of calling or coaxing the unmanifest.[1] For instance, a sculptor must respect the reality of the medium in which she works, and the form, which is "slumbering" in the marble. In contradistinction, modern technology does not reveal in the manner of *poiesis*, but as *Gestell* or "enframing." *Gestell* carries meanings of "frame," "shelf," "stand," or "rack," and involves a kind of framing of an object in such a way that it *appears to us* for a certain use. Heidegger argues that *Gestell* involves a horizon of understanding in which objects are "challenged forth" as *Bestand*, or "standing reserve," a way of extracting from them what is needed so that it may be stockpiled and constituted a resource that is on hand. Modern technology, thus, does not embody any particular modality (e.g., nuclear power, television) but is our epochal mode of revealing/concealing that allows reality to manifest in such a way as to be liquidated into homogenized form for calculative exploitation. Importantly, Heidegger (1977a) writes that "Enframing means the gathering together of that setting-upon which sets upon man, i.e., challenges him forth, to reveal the real, in the mode of ordering, as standing-reserve" (p. 20). In other words, not only does the essence of modern technology, as *Gestell*, order natural objects and processes into standing reserve, but human being itself becomes ordered into standing reserve. Even given its resistance, Dasein has increasingly become part of the terrain to be exploited. Moreover, it should be noted that beings in every epoch potentially, and at times, show up as a resource; however, Heidegger (1977a) argues that modern technology is distinct in obscuring its own historically ontological mode of disclosure, no longer allowing unconcealment to be seen as originating in the relation of truth to untruth, and covering over "revealing as such." In other words, modern technology is not unique in its concealment and revealing of Being through beings, as all technological practices and ways of knowing participate therein; however, what is particular for modern technology is its *concealment of concealment*, its unwavering insistence that the surfaces its practices reveal constitute an exhaustive rendering of the realities that are alleged. For instance, witness the rise of "best practice" standards that span strategic management in industry, human services, education, and other domains. The essence of modern technology is, thus, metaphysical reduction of revealing to the ontic being (the factual being) of entities, and an absolutizing of the horizon of world disclosure that is bounded by abject emptiness (i.e., the imaginary counterpart of the space of the physical sciences) rather than the temporal void or nothingness that issues knowledge for the subject. For inquiry into the human sciences, a historically sensitive account of subjectivity grasps the *meaning* or *mattering* of human being that shows up only as a resource in the Lacanian imaginary or the Levinasian Said, which technologically banishes truth for, or merges it with, aporetic knowledge.

Prior to its arrival, modern technology always already tacitly approaches knowledge in conformity with its use as resource. Modern technology, achieving a near hegemony in its way of disclosing reality, allies itself with an epistemology purporting to encounter and totalize a phenomenon through its positive coordinates of knowledge. What is instrumentally figural tends to manifest as "*standing* in representational production" (Heidegger, 1971b, p. 124). It may serve to recall that modern representation differs from the aspirations of classical representation, the former divested of its power to provide correspondence that would comprehensively link between the map and its terrain. Modern representation, no longer seeking an identity of knowledge and the world, settles for producing pragmatic, positive, and probabilistic certainty for a world demanded by need for instrumental knowledge; however, modern representation continues to bear the nostalgic, classical impulse of reproducing the world *under the subject's vision*. The impulse towards mastery requires an objectification as representation for use (Heidegger, 1977c). Phenomena producing uncertainty or knowledge unworthy of collectively standardized manipulation are ignored, or consigned to lesser epistemological status – for instance, irrational desire, political interest, mere opinion, or pathology.

Where phenomena press technological practices into contradiction, or into crisis, such aporias must be integrated into a metaphysics supporting the subject's own capacities for representing the world, and coming to knowledge. The progressive psychologization of human suffering as error, illusion, or mental illness, thus, attempts a reappropriation of experience destabilizing modern technology and representation. The ongoing crisis in representation, carried over from the classical period through the analytic of finitude, and culminating with the traumatic ontological structure of the modern subject, threatens the mastery of modern subject over its being – calling forth efforts to refashion the subject's representational capacities in ever more pragmatic and functional forms supportive of industrial life. Social institutions are, thus, organized around producing and perpetuating certain ontic forms of knowledge (that is, industrial, medical, psychological, etc.), and tend towards incorporating crisis into their discourses, and for their own ends, rather than allow for an unraveling of their own existential premises.

Over against the opening of the modern subject's ontologically traumatic being, the disciplinary ascendancy of psychiatry and psychology allows for an efficiently insufficient solution to the aporetic crises befalling the modern subject under the analytic of finitude. As Foucault (1966/1973) argues, these human sciences follow the structural features of biology, wherein norms circulate within what is functional for the subject or organism, and the latter always embedded in the subject/organism's cultural or environmental milieu – the overall, holistic context within which it is situated, including its history. However, as mentioned, under dominant modes of psychological and psychiatric knowledge, aggregates of human behavior, experience, and cognition revolve around *socio-historically embedded norms or central tendencies*. As fallout from classical failure to orchestrate a coherent project for complete, encyclopedic knowledge of the world, these disciplines assert their relative and normatively governed independence from potentially related philosophical, philological, and historical inquiries. As such, they often draw upon the natural sciences to promulgate their own distinctive methodologies, and – for the most part – those in the human sciences of psychology and psychiatry have demonstrated little impulse to imagine their own pursuits from philosophical, historical, or other perspectives. Consequently, trauma – as an entity for clinical dissection – is submitted to a psychological and psychiatric matrix of norms and diagnostic procedures oriented towards representational knowledge for instrumental use, often as an analogue to physical disease. Because the aporias emerging from the analytic of finitude are assigned to the domain of psychopathology rather than submitted to a more ontologically structural analysis, the empirico-transcendental doublet, unthought, and historicality/temporality are ontically framed in ways that technologically conceal the modern subject's ontologically traumatic status. For instance, for discourse on trauma, the excess arising from the doubling of man achieves the same deferral, the same reciprocal movement as it does in the thought of positivism; however, for psychological or psychiatric thought, the difficulties pertaining thereto are pathologized and used to diagnostically segregate some individuals from others. Likewise, unthought (in the Foucauldian sense) for the subject of clinical trauma resides at a purely psychological level; the outside of thought, noumenally inaccessible to the sufferer, becomes the abnormally missing time from everyday healthy memory. As follows, the difficulties of modern temporality – i.e., the receding origin – encountered frontally but unsuccessfully by the discourse on restorative temporality, and structurally through traumatic ontology, are ontically transcribed into memory that is in principle cognitively and pragmatically, if not veridically, recoverable.

Emergent theories of trauma, therefore, technologically reproduce the struggle with representing the subject's immemorial past on a psychological level. In recent scholarship, Ruth Leys (2000) provides an especially penetrating narrative of refractory tensions occasioning memorial representation in theories of trauma. Inasmuch, Leys' account primarily resonates on an epistemological level. To map her account onto the instant analysis, nostalgia for specular representation – in the Foucauldian idiom, the epistemic conditions of the classical age – provides impetus for memorial or second-order correspondence that Leys (2000) designates "antimimetic" and is forbidden by the return of the subject's "mimetic" immersion in the other scene. For mimesis, traumatic experience involves a form of hypnotic imitation, where the subject identifies with the event. As in hypnosis, the victim undergoes an alteration in consciousness preventing reliance on ordinary memory; in trauma, the victim is overwhelmed, engulfed in the event and loses the capacity to narrate the experience. This produces a kind of blindness, or unconscious relation to one's past. In contrast, the antimimetic theory posits trauma as an externally disruptive event that occurs to a conscious subject who is, ostensibly, a spectator to his/her experience. The antimimetic dimension of trauma theory relies on the subject's capacity for memorial representation and narrativization that has been privileged from Janet to current neurobiological accounts. Nonetheless, as paralleling Foucault's (1966/1973) modern crisis of finitude that aligns with ontological trauma, on a purely ontic or epistemological level, ongoing tension between mimesis and antimimesis is not resolved. The recalcitrant residue of a reductive gaze is – in its capacity for distance from itself – grounded upon what it cannot penetrate. To borrow from Lacan (1966/2006b), its symbolic ascent from the noumenon allows for narrative articulation at the expense of its identification with the undifferentiated Real. A mimetic position of disappearance into worldly phenomena, though required as a foil for reflexivity, is not a place where one can remain, due to the human subject's intrinsic, possibly exaptational, exigencies for symbolic narration. Leys (2000) writes that the

> concept of trauma has been structured historically in such a way as simultaneously to invite resolution in favor of one pole or the other of the mimetic/antimimetic dichotomy and to resist and ultimately to defeat all such attempts at resolution. This is especially palpable in those instances where attempts have been made to formulate a resolutely antimimetic account of trauma by expunging all hint of mimesis, but is equally true of mimetic accounts.
>
> (pp. 299–300)

The deferral from mimesis to antimimesis (and back again) will then turn out to technologically (that is, discursively and pragmatically) concretize the void of temporality in the traumatic subject's being.

Whereas the ethical ontologies of finitude of Heidegger, Levinas, and Lacan open the modern subject's being-for-itself to a temporally abyssal ground, in the human science disciplines of psychology and psychiatry, epistemological tendencies and difficulties of the analytic of finitude are suppressed as technologically refashioned relating to Foucault's analysis of power. As sketched, under Foucault's three axes of historical ontology (knowledge, power, and ethics) (Hacking, 2002), trauma, as constellation of both discourse and clinical practice, spans each domain and follows Foucault's general analysis of modern power that is productive of knowledge rather than repressive, and inextricably linked with various modes of subjectification. As previously mentioned, Foucault's oeuvre contains several movements that track differing concerns (archaeology, genealogy, and self-constitution), but also differing historical modes of power (sovereignty, disciplinary power, and biopower). Consequently, many scholars have maintained an understandable and rigorous attention to the changes in Foucault's method and aims, and in following the evolution of Foucauldian heuristics or analytics (Dreyfus & Rabinow, 1983; Han, 1998, 2005). Accordingly, one may justifiably inquire into the theoretical difficulties and specifics of the shifts in Foucault's overall trajectory in what he variously refers to as "conditions of possibility," the "historical *a priori*," "discursive formations," "power/knowledge," "apparatuses," "regimes of truth," and "the hermeneutics of the self," or other notions. Foucault (1990) himself obviously made these kinds of distinctions, many of them having to do with the shift from his emphasis on language/discourse to that of the material effects of knowledge, and the shift from objectifying technologies to subjectifying ones. Foremost among these changes is that between the anatomo-politics of the body coincident with disciplinary power and biopower. Recall that the former, arising in the eighteenth century, involves the direct training of individual bodies to efficiently effect control over or produce their particular movements (and individual being), yet organizing them in functional groups for work/operation in particular settings (e.g., schools, factories, asylums, prisons) (Foucault, 1975/1995). The latter, that of biopower (and biopolitics as those specific strategies such as the discourse around sexuality or the pharmaceutical research into psychiatric medications), operates to regulate well-being, health, and – above all – security and risk through its interventions in the sphere of biological life itself, which, rather than individualizing with direct action (discipline), aggregates human being as "population" (Foucault, 2008, 2009). Nonetheless, despite the differences in epochal power arrangements, Foucault (2003) writes of the relation of these modes: "Technologies of discipline on the one hand and technologies of regulation on the other, succeeded in covering the whole surface that lies between the organic and the biological, between body and population" (p. 253). This would suggest that on the many fronts on which Foucault writes and thinks, the rules and logic governing discursive formations, the institutional mechanisms disciplining bodies and regulating life, and practices of self-relation interpenetrate each other. Though the ends of biopower for governmentality and its specific mechanisms will be discussed in the next chapter, suffice it to rely for now on Rabinow and Rose's (2016) formulation, holding that the notion of biopower integrates Foucault's three planes of concern whereby individuals subjectify themselves "under certain forms of authority, in relation to truth discourses, by means of practices of the self, in the name of individual or collective life or health" (p. 307). In other words, within industrial and post-industrial worlds where biopower predominates, technologies in the human sciences – such as that of trauma – will simultaneously make discursive claims as to what is or is not true knowledge about human being (as well as to their own scientifically authoritative status), deploy strategies for addressing human being in aggregation (such as methods confirming validity, including case studies or quantitative methodology), and produce practices by which subjects will form ethical self-relation, so-called "technologies of self" (including various forms of psychoanalytic confession and the training of cognitive therapies). To prefigure later discussion on the position of exteriority (psy-discourses as power/ knowledge) within Foucauldian understandings, nothing herein should be construed to mean that the ethical ontologies of finitude – as discourse or as ethical practices for fragmented subjectivity proffered by Heidegger, Levinas, and Lacan – do not themselves exist within networks of power/knowledge. Nevertheless, in pressing an issue that Foucault never opened (and, perhaps, would not have), it is necessary to discern those technologies that access the deep rifts in the subject's being (again, submitted to the failures of the *savoir* of modernity), and those that suture, cover over, or conceal the subject's temporal division through their own positive metaphysical presences.

The historical concealment of traumatic ontology may be seen across several interconnected fronts. First, the historical ontology of trauma, which is grounded in non-Being, absence, and temporal fragmentation as manifested by the modes of subjectification articulated by Heidegger, Levinas, and Lacan, is transformed by productive power into positive, discursive knowledge of the subject and its condition. Notably, Foucault (1980) writes of such intertwining of power/knowledge: "What makes power hold good, what makes it accepted, is simply the fact that it doesn't only weigh on us as a force that says no, but that it traverses and produces things, it induces pleasure, forms knowledge, produces discourse" (p. 119). Though perhaps distinct from the *savoir* that would govern the deep knowledge of the age (and the subject's finitude), as a discursive formation, the literature on trauma constitutes a set of statements with rules to which speakers or advocates unwittingly adhere (Foucault, 1969/1972). Of the elements for a discursive formation (object, enunciative modality, concept/theory, and theme/strategy), the following analysis is mostly concerned with concept and theme. In conceptual terms, the logic of mimesis and antimimesis appears to govern what Foucault (1969/1972) would call a field of presence, which presides over – includes and excludes – the range of statements or knowledge that may be made about traumatic experience according to various theories that extend from early psychiatry through various forms of psychoanalysis to neurobiology and cognitive-behavioral therapies. Second, Foucault markedly enlarges his concerns with power/knowledge to also consider non-discursive means of production, the ensemble of discourses, institutions, and material practices that he refers to as the *dispositif*, or apparatus – the "grid of intelligibility" that would allow trauma to positively surface as a clinical entity at the intersection of psychiatric/psychological knowledge and medical and institutional practices. Here, the traumatic subject framed in part by the modern *techne* of trauma, visible in the epistemically oscillating principles of mimesis and antimimesis, becomes a target for institutional production and control through the technological incorporation of the aporetic spaces of the analytic of finitude in clinical discourses and material practices. Thus, the subject of knowledge – and its reflective consciousness – is remade, reproduced through the positive structuring and mediation of limit, which ties discursive boundary or failure to the subject's embodied suffering, disturbing the functioning of the social order, and the everyday life of love and work. As will be seen, this is accounted for in the ubiquitous possibility for *pathological breakdown* in neurophysiology, memory, temporality, and language. Relatedly, the traumatic ontology of the modern subject is suppressed because its pervasive hold on its being is reduced to power/knowledge of the psy-disciplines, and trauma is segregated, separated, or divided as an abnormal experience befalling only certain individuals undergoing extreme suffering. Foucault (1983) writes that "in what I shall call 'dividing practices' . . . the subject is either divided inside himself or divided from others. This process objectivizes him. Examples are the mad and the sane, the sick and the healthy" (p. 208). For the clinical apparatus of trauma, distinguishing healthy versus unhealthy remembering – and externally disciplining the latter through the psy-disciplines' institutional conduits – becomes a way of objectivizing and promulgating visions of selfhood that promote industrial values. Third, suppression of ontological trauma (and its ethical potential in radical forms of psychoanalysis) is concealed through what Foucault (1988) calls certain technologies of self, permitting subjects to work on themselves (their bodies, conduct, souls, thoughts) so as "to transform themselves in order to attain a certain state of happiness, purity, wisdom, perfection or immortality" (p. 18). For the history of the subject's ethical relation to itself, the ancient subject's care of the self (*epimeleia heautou*), the cultivation of habits, dispositions, and character enabling it to achieve *gnomé*, and the Christian injunction to achieve purification through publication of one's sins through one's behavior or verbally through confession all involve a self-transformation of the subject to access its truth. In distinction to these practices and aforementioned ethical ontologies of finitude, and for the technologies of trauma advocating the antimimetic reintegration of memory, confessional practice is recontextualized for a pragmatically oriented, positive, and "realistic" self-relation, thereby obscuring the void that structures the subject's being-in-time, and relieving the subject of the transformational possibilities it may take up as assuming responsibility for its non-Being in time. Fourth, a certain "parasitism of masking" coincident with biopower – the concealing function of the apparatus – allows ontic conceptions of clinical trauma that are productive of particular enunciated selves to mask the ontological conditions of their arrival. In Heideggerian terms, the ontological structure of disclosure always involves grasping possibility against impossibility – calling forth Dasein's nullity or being-towards-death; however, ontic knowledge involves what is in fact, or not in fact, known. The ontological structuring of possibilities – gathered by death as "the laying down, the Law" (Heidegger, 1971b, p. 123) into temporal impossibility – is always covered by the more visible, psychologized, and biomedical factual state of affairs that exists against a ground of the emptiness of space. In other words, an abject spatial absence appearing environmentally or geographically though remote in time – pathologized to produce concrete selves – tightly covers over the temporal void that makes representation, over against the subject's perpetual non-appearance to itself, possible.

Technology, historical enframing, and the apparatus of trauma

The subject's division in time and being would not only manifest in the deep thought structures of the nineteenth century, but would be replicated in the emerging human science discourses – touching both psychology and psychiatry – in the doubling of consciousness. Put differently, the doubling of consciousness as *savoir* would parallel that of *connaissance* in the nascent psy-disciplines. As prefiguring the rise of both hypnotism and memory science, magnetism descends from its origins in late eighteenth-century conflict between the exorcist Johann Joseph Gassner and Franz Anton Mesmer, son of Enlightenment thought, and promoter of a cure for mental and physical suffering via manipulation of the subtle magnetic fluid pervading human and non-human worlds. Nonetheless, it was Mesmer's disciple, the Marquis de Puységur, who would contribute to the development of dynamic psychiatry (Ellenberger, 1970). Puységur discovered that the fluid theory of Mesmer was less important than the sleep that was coincidently induced for the cure, which occurred in the case of Victor: "There were no convulsions, no disorderly movements . . . he fell into a strange kind of sleep in which he seemed to be more awake than in his normal waking state" (Ellenberger, 1970, p. 71). Strikingly, in their trance-like states, his patients were able to diagnose their own illnesses, predict their courses, and generate treatments. Beyond this rudimentary division between trance-like states and normal waking consciousness, and for the eventual foundation of psychoanalysis and dynamic psychiatry generally, hypnosis demonstrates in a domain outside of philosophical thought the structure of the empirico-transcendental doublet. Aside from the Nancy school of hypnotism, represented by Hippolyte Bernheim, wherein hypnosis was normalized, for Charcot (1889), ever inquiring into more fundamental states of pathology in order to explain their differential manifestations, hypnosis shares with hysteria many features – somatic characteristics (i.e., anesthesia, paralysis, catalepsy), the appearance of "second mental states" (i.e., somniloquism, somnambulism, amnesia), and the heightening of suggestibility. As to the latter, Charcot (1889) surmises that in cases of traumatic hysteria and in hypnotic trances, the patient enters into a state of increased suggestibility wherein trauma is imprinted into experience as a fixed idea (*idée fixe*) of involuntary autosuggestion. Charcot's use of hypnosis as a parallel to hysteria and also to traumatic paralysis signals the division of unhealthy and healthy remembering, of the patient's in/capacity to represent to herself the ostensibly traumatic idea that is lodged in her memory. Against this, the patient might dangerously inhabit rather than represent or remember/reconstitute the event. Leys (2000), thus, argues that hypnosis so threatened to dissolve self and other that such mimetic identification was given over to that of antimimesis, so that the patient could experientially represent herself in the scene of trauma. This fundamentally irresolvable deferral of representation as mimesis and antimimesis, as return of the classical failure but at the level of the modern finite subject, thus shadows the subject of hypnosis and hysteria. As Hacking (1995) notes, the *dédoublement de la personnalité* involving the doubling, splitting, or dividing of consciousness becomes a discursive trope, or formation, for nineteenth-century French culture spanning the domains of psychiatric medicine, psychology, and philosophy. The Cartesian lineage insisted on the integrative "I" or *moi* that would endure over time; however, the Comtean positivist tradition, as well as the emergent psychiatric movement towards articulating unthought as unconscious or subconscious, implied a clinical substrate that would explain a variety of conditions – the second states of somnambulism, fugues, hysteria, hypnotic trances, and multiple personality. Notably, the latter phenomena co-emergent with clinical trauma are admirably sketched in Leys (2000) and, of course, in Hacking's (1995) *Rewriting the Soul*. These various forms of clinical knowledge, in varying degrees, eventually intersect with the genesis of Freudian thought, with which they share the central and defining notion that what cannot be thought consciously, what is missing, especially in time or memory, becomes central to selfhood; such experiences constitute *maladies de la mémoire*.

Trauma as a *dispositif* – incubated from emergent technological enframing through its guiding preoccupation with pathologies of memory and representation – attains far-reaching cultural and historical power for the creation of identity/selfhood through increasing medicalization. As a specifically medical technology of subjection, trauma appears in the mid-nineteenth century with Erichsen's medical examination of patients involved in railway disasters, whose horrors the Victorian imagination attributed to the industrial age. Erichsen's (1866) explanations foreground a material continuity between sufferer and a world of visible and fungible things:

> If the spine is badly jarred, shaken, or concussed by a blow or a shock of any kind communicated to the body, we find that the nervous force is to a certain extent shaken out of the man . . . One of the most remarkable phenomena attendant upon this class of cases is, that at the time of occurrence of the injury the sufferer is usually quite unconscious that any serious accident

has happened to him . . . When he reaches home, the effects of the injury that he has sustained begin to manifest themselves . . . His friends remark, and he feels that "he is not the man he was."

(pp. 73–75)

For Erichsen (1859), the tremors, cold sweats, fluttering pulse, and other similar symptoms parallel this distinctly psychological interruption of experiential continuity, including "great mental depression and disquietude; the disturbed state of mind revealing itself in the countenance, and in the incoherence of speech and thought" (p. 106). Victorian medical discourse, thus, depicts an electromagnetic force invisibly interpenetrating psychological reality (Harrington, 2001). Furthermore, medical and forensic subjects of trauma are interpolated into a neurological discourse whose mathematized medical contours mirror legal reality, where suffering is monetized. Initially, homogenous causal explanation in antimimetic distance appears decisive in its exhaustive explanation of the phenomena. Nonetheless, such seemingly neutral descriptions figure against a background of what is disturbed, what is made incoherent – how the subject is separated from the plenitude of its being-in-the-world – by the violence of mechanized life: "The rapidity of movement, the momentum of the person injured, the suddenness of its arrest, the helplessness of the sufferers, and the natural perturbation of mind that must disturb the bravest" (Erichsen, 1866, p. 22). The mimetic disappearance of this subject coincides with a state of helplessness, with a kind of simultaneous experience of seduction into an immersive relation with one's being-in-the-world, but also a violent rupture that occurs only coded after the fact, *après coup*. Mimetic immersion cannot persist because the subject's own claims to self-mastery involve an antimimetic move, a telling to oneself and others of what happened, of "how I survived." As Laplanche (Caruth, 2002) argues, even an earthquake or train accident constitutes and disrupts the subject's seduction into embeddedness in the world, the event constellating a message that must be translated in the deferred and second moment. As a result, a certain separation or deworlding allows the enunciated or crystallized "brave" agentic self to grammatically occur out of its potential dissolution. Victorian selfhood – ordinarily represented as courageous, consistent, and virtuous – is, in this instance, technologically and psychiatrically assembled from its experiential and biographical effacement. Importantly, however, the tremors of the inaccessible noumenal Real signal that the exteriority of discourse cannot articulate such "natural perturbation . . . of the bravest" (Erichsen, 1866, p. 22). Problematically, then, the man of Victorian realism and moral self-possession, with its wide-angle representational vision, finds its own being foregrounded in its traumatic residue – what is temporally unknown to the subject about his or her experience. The sovereign consciousness taking a direct and Lockean "instrumental stance" (Taylor, 1989) towards itself as empirical object must emerge from its inescapable but possible and helpless immersion and disappearance in the event, the blind spot in its own interior hermeneutic.

Similarly, in the work of Page (1883), a critic of Erichsen and medical expert for railway concerns, the scientistic distancing of medical discourse may also be seen to betray the subject's non-knowledge of itself. Though Page (1883) would locate railway trauma within the nascent discourses of hysteria, neuromimetic disorders, and evolutionary accounts of shock, he also suggests that many, if not all, trauma victims harbor "unconscious motives" that

> colour the course and aspect of the case, with each succeeding day to become part and parcel of the injury in the patient's mind, and unwittingly to affect his feelings towards, and his impressions of, the sufferings he must undergo.
>
> *(p. 255)*

Unlike Erichsen, who entirely places trauma in the world of jolting bodies and nerves, Page increasingly aligns such phenomena to unseen lacunae, the non-knowledge, of legal advocacy where the self is determined as an unconscious malingerer. Consequently, traumatic experience being hidden, or unconscious, not only threatens the individual sufferer's moral integrity for brave, Victorian personhood, but legal, civic personhood as well. Now, it is no longer clear what the subject's intentions or motivations might be, and whether suffering merely factitiously imitates neurological disease. Significantly, however, the effacement of the subject's determination in scientific and legal discourse is required for its agency. The forensic subject's powers of coming to knowledge, therefore, arise from its failure to fully represent itself to interior vision, to remain free of being fixed as knowledge. Put another way, the exile of the traumatic subject from its own experience – *as embedded in the Real or Being* – gives itself over to normative agentic functioning, which necessitates a fissure in the subject's history for the generation of its being. Medical and legal discourse reveals antimimetically, and at a distance, the subject as empirical object (whether helpless victim of shock, hysteria, or unconscious malingerer) to itself for institutional and instrumental use. Nonetheless, the exile of the traumatic subject from its own experience within an orderly functioning and usual social world recurs as a fissure in the subject's history productive of its selfhood. In other words, the work of technology in early trauma theory involves not simply an objectification of the subject, but rather the effective incorporation within the subject's being of a pathologized yet generative tension in the limits of what is representable. Importantly, for the present argument, however, is the concealment of traumatic ontology effected through Victorian legal and medical discourses that segregate trauma as an unusual experience befalling accident victims, and also one supportive of living a certain kind of life within an industrial culture – that of a claimant forensically asserting legitimate economic interest. Of course, a tension persists in the power/knowledge that externally acts upon the subject in constituting a clinical entity – which might be impressed by fear and actualize as hysterical symptom or malingering – and the temporal void itself that the subject must ethically appropriate for its freedom. Traumatic ontology is thus concealed through the giving over to the subject its possible being as various subject positions (or selves) – as Victorian moral agent, or legal personhood – through the ontic, pathologized limits of traumatic neuro-physiological and legal collapse.

As suggested, as forms of epistemic and ontically formed intelligibility, the metastases of trauma colonize adjacent discourse and institutional practice. The failure of any one discourse (i.e., legal or surgical) to subsume the phenomena of trauma allows it to circulate among knowledge that touches both physiological and more psychological domains. Charcot (1889) remains significant for trauma, not only because both his theory of "hystero-traumatism" and his location within the dynamic psychiatric movement challenge the integrity of consciousness. First, Charcot (1889) extends traumatic hysteria beyond the stereotypical female patient, conducting studies with working class men at Salpêtrière, which are set in con-siderable medical detail from his own first-person examinations in a number of transcribed clinical lectures. From these reports, a typical case – similar to railway spine – involves a slight bodily injury (one without far-ranging or catastrophic physical consequences) with common effects of anesthesia, hyperesthesia, paralysis, contracture, and, *inter alia*, sleep disorders, headaches, fatigue, and confusion. This insertion of hysteria into a continuum of traumatic experience not only broadens the conceptual reach of trauma outside of the medico-forensic context but also installs a depth of suffering that would underlie seemingly divergent diagnostic categories. Second, and relatedly, Charcot – though clearly asserting a hereditary component or *diathèse* – opens the way for trauma to become more intrinsically related to what it means to be human. As Micale (2001) argues, "While the cases that Charcot described as traumatic hysteria usually occurred in association with physical accidents and were manifested through physical symptoms, they were mediated, he came to believe, by the psyche" (p. 123). Indeed, Charcot's work becomes an early visible indication of the psychologization of traumatic experi-ence; however, an understanding of the imprinting of the *idée fixe* during hypnotic autosuggestion becomes further heightened:

> The idea, or group of ideas suggested, are met with in a state of isolation, free from the control of that large collection of personal ideas long accu-mulated and organised, which constitute the conscience properly so–called the *ego*. It is for this reason that the movements which exteriorly represent the acts of unconscious cerebration are distinguished by their automatic and purely mechanical character. Then it is truly that we see before us the *human machine* in all of its simplicity, dreamt of by De la Mettrie.
>
> *(Charcot, 1889, p. 290)*

The logic of mimesis/antimimesis is, of course, at play across the surface of Char-cot's account, yet the pathological interruption of the event, as pressed into the psyche of the sufferer, allows for a further effect – the giving over of certain expe-riences to an automatic realm of psychological life against the agentic, personal domain of everyday consciousness. Such a division of consciousness, with a causally determined ideational substrate governed by affect, would be taken up through psychoanalytic discourse; however, even in Charcot, this trajectory becomes figural. Thus, under the influence of Ribot, discussed later, Charcot adapts the notion of partial memories, which – as mentioned – would inform his understanding of how a lesion in memory would segregate healthy memories from unhealthy ones (Goetz, Bonduelle, & Gelfand, 1995). As Foucault (1966/1973) makes clear, psychology and psychiatry among the human sciences especially would fall under the modern episteme and its *savoir* – that of organic structure, with functional elements (i.e., organs) that allow the organism to historically adapt to its environment. Dysfunctions, under this regime, would specifically involve a departure from normative temporal or memorial functioning. Isolated, encapsulated memories laden with affect or unconsciously automatic actions (i.e., paralysis) would precisely identify and locate an individual whose own memorial and temporal reality is damaged. Of course, as argued *supra*, the historicity and temporality at stake for the subject pursuant to this episteme becomes concretized and submitted to an abnormalizing tendency that leaves normal, egoic, and conscious life suspiciously free from impinging events; yet, such mimetic effects of buried memories associated with affects allow for lost antimimetic capacities for representation as forming agentic "control of personal ideas." For Charcot, such psychologized and functional control could be asserted over the pathogenic lesion in memory, which is the intense fear of imminent demise producing mimetic and somatic effects, but removed from any necessary antecedent physical contact with the sufferer.

Though continuing the overall psychic movement of trauma, fear as a functional construct is submitted to the experimental sensibilities of Crile (1899) and Cannon (1914), who synthesize strands of thought containing dimensions touching the psychology of emotion and the physiology of response, as well as evolutionary biology. For Spencer (1855), fear is the memory of pain obtained ontogenetically (the organism's idiographic history) and phylogenetically (the organism's instinctual or inherited fears) that is retrospectively connected with prospective desire; the history of the behaviors produced by desire "have been previously presented in experience; and the representation of them is the same thing as a memory of them" (p. 597). Consequently, memory as a somewhat fragile form of representation is able to internally affirm external reality in a purely functional manner consonant with environmental demand. Nonetheless, as Young (1995) argues, what really sets Crile and Cannon apart from Spencer is the distinctly physiological location of trauma, wherein emotional experience is depicted according to how it affects the internal organism's adjustment to external environment. Cannon (1914) writes, regarding the sympathetic nervous system: "The bodily changes which occur in the intense emotional states – such as fear and fury – occur as results of sympathetic discharges, and are in the highest degree serviceable to the organism in the struggle for existence" (p. 275). As Young (1995) notes, though Crile and Cannon in some measure accomplish, as does Charcot, a universalization of the potentiality for traumatic experience, the impulse for pathologizing trauma through an evolutionary account of emotion and memory preserves the division between adaptation and dysfunctionality. Hence, the mobilization of the sympathetic nervous system becomes a fork of outcomes, capable of both "all of the offensive and defensive activities [fight or flight] that favor the organism" (Cannon, 1927, p. 187) and non-adaptive freezing or fusion with experience in the scene. As with Charcot, the recurrent thematic presence of death, and its position as both trigger for possible survival and an aberration of the organism's workable existence, is emblematically manifested in the phenomenon of "voodoo death":

> In records of anthropologists and others who have lived with primitive people in widely scattered parts of the world is the testimony that when subjected to spells or sorcery or the use of "black magic" men have been brought to death . . . The phenomenon is so extraordinary and so foreign to the experience of civilized people that it seems incredible.
>
> *(Cannon, 1942, p. 169)*

It turns out that a victim rendered into the death-like state of "voodoo death" brought on through the flight/fight/freeze mechanism initiated by fear remarkably parallels that of trauma. The victim for both "voodoo death" and trauma is immersed in his or her experience through the effects of overwhelming fear, and fear of death especially; in either case, representation becomes impossible in the void of the trance. Moreover, a barely visible fulcrum, that of natural selection, works both on the subject's behalf and against it, linking also the "extraordinary and so foreign" division between the normal and pathological, what is natural and what is anomalous, which arise from the very same substrate of possibility.

In the discourses of Crile and Cannon, and psychiatric practice of Charcot, the problematic ontological structure of trauma is concealed through scientific and clinical architecture that technologically reduce non-Being to the presence of unwanted emotional states. Not surprisingly, especially for Lacan (Fink, 1997) and Heidegger (1927/1962), trauma touches the Real or draws out the *Angst* of being-towards-death through embodied effects that are not, strictly speaking, simply calculable. Lacanian analysts speak of interpretations that "hit the Real" of trauma, producing tearful outbursts, sudden mutism, stuttering, or even laughter that is strangely out of place. Most precisely, these emergences do not relate to essential emotional states circulating like humors that would interfere with the sound workings of reason, or – alternatively – become a helpfully cognitive means of shorthand. Rather, what hits the Real, and its earthquake-like reverberations, relates to specific signifiers. In other words, for the subject, such embodied resonance, such "falling apart," is radically particular to the subject's castration by the symbolic. Though Soler (2016) specifically refers to anguish in connection with the Lacanian subject of castration as destitute, and makes reference to the many affects in the Lacanian register (sadness, joy, guilt, shame, etc.), she also returns to the Lacanian suspicion of a generalized, psychologized taxonomy of affect or emotion:

> Affects are subject to history . . . This can easily be understood: since they fluctuate with the status (or mode) of jouissance, they are impacted not only by the effect of language but also by the effects of discourse. The

latter – insofar as they regulate the modalities of jouissance characteristic of a social bond – generate affects that could be called concordant, or in any case dominant, in a given era. They are the affects with which everyone can easily identify.

(p. 79)

For Heidegger, however, affectivity and emotion differ for another reason. As follows, *Befindlichkeit* is the *a priori* existential by which Dasein has moods, such as fear, and as such it discloses the way that Dasein is *affected* in its being-in-the-world in a phenomenological sense. Fear is, thus, disclosive of what is threatening, though differentiated from *Angst*, which persistently places Dasein's being in question. More to the point, mood – as an ontological axis of human embodiment – is prior to any particular ontically framed category or naming.

In contradistinction to Lacanian notions and Heideggerian conceptions of affect and mood, as related to the non-Being that deprives the subject of its origin in time, Charcot, Crile, and Cannon's accounts of fear-induced trauma create a positive account of the subject of trauma defined by a neurophysiological breakdown in emotional processing. As touched on, Charcot's traumatic hysteria – as well as Crile and Cannon's evolutionary formulations – is founded on a division between healthy and unhealthy emotional fear that forbids working representation or anti-mimesis. Besides precipitating the subject of "emotional breakdown," and subject positions (or selves) that are implied by its suture – the healthy, adaptive organism as able to carry on without the effects of the troublesome *idée fixe* – Charcot, Crile, and Cannon participate in an imaginary (in the Lacanian sense) discourse on emotions. Lacan (1988a) writes that "the affective is not like a special density which would escape an intellectual accounting" (p. 57). Put differently, in the imaginary register, affects such as "fear," "sadness," and "joy" are always named afterward, and are submitted to cultural and linguistic coding for their import, though they may be historically and structurally concordant or ascendant. As such, this is not to repudiate traditional psychological research into emotional life; however, as Danziger (1997) implies, the replacement of *passion* with *emotion* is embedded in the Western history of mental life as an increasing domain of instrumental, rational control over mental agitation or motion that would conceptually preserve calmly considered *interest* as the locus for a virtuous, economic actor within an emergent culture of capitalism. Ostensibly, emotion could be said to represent the range of experiences that would at first problematize, and later augment, the modern subject's capacities for action. In this vein, emotion as an ontically shared dimension of mental life provides measures of solidarity in everyday life (that is a common visible currency for exchange), but – critically for our purposes – obscures the radical particularity that occurs for the subject of trauma, covering Real effects with imaginary ones. Technologies that foreground such emotional states suppress other experiential modalities as well as the ontological ground from which they rise. In this way, they foreclose more unrestrained understandings of affect as relating to the passage from one experiential intensity to another, given over to an expansion or diminution in capacity to act (Deleuze & Guattari, 1987). In this manner, they absolutize psychological horizons allowing selfhood to become revealed merely as suited to the organism, whose emotional "fit" with environment may be submitted to forms of discipline, that is "a 'physics' or an 'anatomy' of power, a technology" (Foucault, 1975/1995, p. 215). Ostensibly, this revealing participates in a Pavlovian economy, an instrumental stance towards human being, where the latter may be explained, whose orderly and natural movements may be predicted, and whose sentiments may be controlled.

Under the analytic of finitude, nowhere is the tension and slippage between what can be represented, narrated, and reconstructed (and explained), and what is blind and unknown (and not amenable to prediction or control), more perceptible than in the rising sciences of memory. As we have seen, what becomes clear for Kant (1781/2007), and for Foucault (1966/1973) – in the failure of representation – is that apparent difference between rationalist and empiricist philosophy collapses under a shared philosophical horizon of the adequation of idea with object; a more nuanced and pragmatic outlook on representation is required. And as argued *supra*, the Kantian and modern "epistemological turn" transforms Newtonian and Leibnizian conceptions of space/time as fundamental, hypostatic relations among objects in the external world into a dimension of the *subject's relation to the world through its own capacities*. While the discourse of restorative temporality of Husserl et al. ostensibly offered a path towards a traumatic ontology, dominant cultural tendencies have moved in neither direction, and have supplanted any ethical stance involving self-transformation with the mandate that only the fluorescent light of dispassionate reason may yield self-knowledge. Because Kantian time is conceived neither empirically nor conceptually, but as *a priori* intuition – the framework of all perceptions (Hoy, 2009) – it becomes the most fundamental of cognitive filters that would frame the modern subject's understanding of itself. Nonetheless, as a structuring of outer experience as intuition, the Kantian must as well admit that something escapes between the empirically real and transcendentally ideal. In other words, Kant's cognitivism must itself traumatically lose time, but is enabled to represent its own remembered representations as a kind of *post hoc* examination of film footage of an event. Consequently, though memory had been philosophically associated with the mind's isomorphic relation to corporeal or intelligible reality (as it is in Aristotle), rendering time into cognitive finitude makes possible ontic research into memory. Memory, as a psychological construct, is not tethered to a truthful relation with self or events in the world, but *the engraved experience of time*, the representation (conscious appropriation) of representation (mind's etched correlation with the passing time of the external world).

The increasing scientific isolation of memory as a capacity and experience related to, but distant from, the passage of time would have several important effects related to the clinical formation of traumatic suffering. As Danziger (2008) argues, in the eighteenth and nineteenth centuries, memory becomes simultaneously detached from knowledge itself (as secondary copies of more primary experiences) and devalued in terms of its reliable access thereto, but privileged – nonetheless – as central to personhood: "Memory became interesting again because it provided access to an object of ever-greater cultural significance, the individual personality, and especially its inner private life" (p. 103). This is, of course, manifest in the Lockean conflation of identity and memory, but also emblematically in Rousseau's (1782/2008) *Confessions*, and more generally in the rise of the novel as a literary form centering on the narration of the individual existence, and the preponderance of diaries and journals as means of a sanctified expression of inner, emotional life. Still, what would be intimate to the individual would be opposed to what could be objectified and submitted to the rational, instrumentalist mastery of the human sciences along two related, but different, fronts. First, emergent sciences of memory – such as the experimental studies cultivated by Ebbinghaus (1885/1913) – newly constellated a domain oriented towards understanding retention and reproduction in forms of decontextualized quantifications of knowledge, or neurological location (Broca). Interestingly, Danziger (2008) notes that Ebbinghaus' work, and those who took up his methods in varying degrees, frame "the question of retention in terms of *Arbeit* (quantity of work) necessary go from zero production to perfect reproduction" (p. 129). In this light, the mnemo-technologies of the industrial world become clearly visible as relating to the improvement of memory performance in the most efficient and productive manner for the ends of pedagogy and the scientific management of work. Second – in connection with identity – discourses treating alienation in memory proliferate. Of course, Locke (1690/1975) is troubled with the notion of alienated states of consciousness – i.e., drunkenness, somnambulism, madness, etc. – because these conditions implicate and complicate moral and legal responsibility. A new discourse, thus, appears – progressively captured by an emergent psychiatric field – and one specifically conceptualizing memory as susceptible to injury or being diseased. As Hacking (1995) suggests, it is the more psychodynamically conceived notion of memory as capable of harm, division, or splitting that would have lasting influence in Western culture. Nineteenth-century cases involving the doubling of the personality demonstrate that apprehending the unitary *moi*, or self, could not exhaust the field of psychological inquiry (e.g., Charcot, 1889; Prince, 1905). Psychodynamic explanations of memory form a substitute field, holding potential for understanding what had been previously regarded as untouchable by science – soul. Still, division in consciousness portends an uneasy indeterminacy around past events, especially those events bearing intense suffering. The resolution occupying discourse around traumatic memory is simply to juxtapose what may be represented (antimimesis) with what is forgotten or simply not registered as pathological, defective, or unrepresentable (mimetic blindness). The polar movements of the memorial and immemorial are technically appropriated to ironically underwrite selfhood, premised on what is unavailable to the subject in time within the overall faculty of memory.

Broken in its totalizing vision, representational thought – chained to its "unconscious" for subjugation – perseveres in knowledge produced by nineteenth-century psychological and medical institutions. The formation of memory prominently appears in the thought of Ribot (1882), who held the chair of experimental and comparative psychology at the Collège de France, and his successor, Pierre Janet. The "new psychology" of Ribot rests on the premise that positivistic, methodological inquiry into psychological phenomena would uncover the relation of consciousness, memory, and reasoning to its organic substrate. More specifically, what interests Ribot is the axis of self-awareness and memory, including pathogenic memory. Importantly, Ribot's (1882) *Diseases of the Memory* articulates our now familiar theme of the empirico-transcendental disjuncture between consciousness and what is silently and automatically transcribed in the mind, or in the brain as a stand-in for the external world:

> The brain is like a laboratory full of movement, where thousands of occupations are going on at once. Unconscious cerebration, not being subject to restrictions of time, operating, so to speak, only in space, may act in several directions at the same moment. Consciousness is the narrow gate through which a very small part of all this work is able to reach us.
>
> *(pp. 38–39)*

In this psychic economy, ordinary memories fade and become integrated into webs of remembrance. Indeed, the constant renewal of self is only possible because of this effect of fading, making room for new memories, new life – a process in harmony with late Enlightenment values of finding one's life according to its own, rather than borrowed, terms. As Ribot (1882) writes, "forgetfulness, except in certain cases, is not a disease of memory, but a condition of health and life" (p. 61). Nonetheless, under this outlook, memorial dissolution attains sufficient intensity to disrupt the flow of life. Diseases of the memory brought on by epilepsy, syncope, physical trauma, or hysteria (or other second states of consciousness such as railway spine) involve, for Ribot, both amnesia and hypermnesia (both elements of traumatic memory), and constitute a kind of parasite of the psyche. Hacking (1996) notes that Ribot's law of regression – wherein the dissolution of memory (paralleling Janet's "dissociation") progresses according to a certain logic of erasure – points to Ribot's historical signaling of the soul's final capture by the psy-disciplines. Yet, what is more striking in a way is not the loss of the subject's untouchable inner substance, but what is produced in the aftermath amongst these metaphysical ruins – the subject's possession of its own duration in memory and time. Young (1995) states "the diachronic self, the 'conscious personality' according to Ribot, is known and experienced in its continuity with the past. It is the *self as the subject of its own history*" (p. 29). And, precisely, diseases of the memory interrupt and obstruct – and make manifest – the subject's self-relation as continuous in its own time.

Similar to Ribot, Janet (1925) seeks an integration of pathological or traumatic memory into that of healthy, narrative memory. In contrast to ancient admonitions of the subject to unify itself with knowledge touching a transient, degraded temporality mirroring eternity, or Enlightenment treatments of memory as adequation of representation with an event, Ribot and Janet's psychologization of memory lowers its capacity for an epistemically faithful depiction of an event, while elevating its power for placing patients in renewed engagement with their lives. For conversion, or "presentification," of traumatic memory to narrative memory, what is imperative

> *is the action of telling a story* . . . independent of our attitude towards the happening . . . [which is] capable of being perfected in various ways. The teller must not only know how to do it, but must also know how to associate the happening with the other events of his life, how to put it in its place in that life-history which each of us is perpetually building up and which for each of us is an essential element of his personality . . . the chapters in our personal history.
>
> *(Janet, 1925, pp. 661–662)*

Antimimetic self-representation, therefore, must attain a distance from the event of trauma vis-à-vis pragmatic reflexivity. This imagined vision must wrest itself from the "happening" itself, and adaptively associate the traumatic event (the hole in memory) with everyday biographical memories. For instance, an event of sexual abuse would be drained of its radically alienating effect of delivering the subject into its uncanny relation to being-in-the world. This is accomplished through the mundane signification of what "really" happened – an event typically framed through signifiers promising moral absolution ("it is not your fault"), affirmation of experience ("you have every right to feel rage"), and uninterrupted time ("you can tell me again"). Traumatic narratives recursively reconstructed may once again – as a wrinkle in time, a stutter, or scar, no doubt – rejoin the populated reserve of healthy experiences for day-to-day social functioning, and mastery over one's ordinary life. Traumatic memory is worked through in its recital, not towards understanding of what happened, in entering the event itself, its blindness or its intensity, which runs counter to the overall *ethos* of integration. By necessity, such projects recapitulate loss or blindness in their forms of forgetting.

On a theoretical or epistemic level, or within the subject's own engagement with its trauma, the vicissitudes of lived time are not so easily mastered through sanitized memory, and violently return in the form of pathological counterparts to idealized life. Janet's (1925) presentification, allowing pathogenic memories to become washed in narration and to fade, is undermined in the exemplary case of Irène, who suffered trauma after the death of her mother. Irène was unable to actualize her loss, the effects appearing as somnambulism and amnesia relating to the event, and was "incapable of associating the account of her mother's death with her own history" (Janet, 1925, p. 662). Leys (2000) argues that such a case requires Janet to abandon naïve tactics of exhorting patients to "speak the unspeakable," as contemporary theorists advocate (e.g., Herman, 1992). Rather, Janet's (1925) pragmatism suggests another trajectory for the cure:

> Irène's case is of special interest because her absurd behavior was so out of place in the circumstances, and because of the lacunae in her interior assimilation which found expression in her amnesia . . . Irène . . . became capable of bringing about a necessary liquidation . . . because she succeeded in performing a number of actions of acceptance, of resignation, of rememorisation.
>
> *(pp. 680–681)*

Janet begins to see the cure to trauma, therefore, involves both integration and liquidation – a remembering and a forgetting. Resignation, of accepting one's sightless and tragically lived relation to traumatic loss and the distance required for its depiction, renews the interpretive project as at once impossible but necessary. By "interpretive" what is meant is the recurrence of the gap between the event that intervenes in the subject's being and the subject's memorial representations. As encountered through Irène, Janet must account for the epistemic rupture in the traumatic subject's interiorized mastery of pathogenic memory that parallels, as Foucault (1966/1973) argues, the modern failure of finding human being in its history.

For the work of technology, for enframing of human being in the memorial discourses of trauma, the positive structuring of limit is incorporated into the binary of healthy versus pathogenic memory, and the practices that encourage the solidification of the former, and the management of the subject's ontological trauma. Under the regime of memory and the work of its narration, antimimesis and mimesis attain a remarkably impenetrable disguise. What returns is an irreducible excess of the subject's spatialized mapping of time, and its reproduction in miniature in the psyche, as traumatic or parasitic mimesis, or immersion in the event, is itself structured as the necessary collapse to produce representation of representation. For narrative memory to forge *new and biographically functional memories*, truthful memorial access must necessarily fail, requiring the possibility for blind, mimetic disappearance in the event of trauma. Naturally, the dividing practice of segregating normal from abnormal allows a deepening of this suppression because the project of facilitating the subject's search for its own biographical unity, one that may alleviate its suffering by giving it substantial personal, social, and interpersonal identity, becomes invisible in its cultural ubiquity. After all, few would legitimately question such a technology, especially if it could validate its methods in some rhetorically persuasive idiom, such as the tropes of positivistic discourse and psychiatric medicalization. Moreover, such technologies would serve contemporary, not ancient or even classically modern, social ends. Following Foucault's (1983) historical modernization of confession, such pastoral power does not call the subject to a position of absolute depth, to a deep truth necessary for its spiritual salvation. Rather, as will be further elaborated, for modern psychological and medical communities, pastoral power is instantiated differently, salvation taking the form of security, the maintenance of well-being, and the management of risk (Foucault, 1983). Consequently, the pragmatism inherent in such pursuits is lost to the naked eye because functionalist practice has become synonymous with coming to knowledge, and truth has lost its unique disposition requiring the subject to transform him or herself in preparation for accessing what is beyond it, in death, extimacy, Otherness. Truth *has become* what can be distanced as knowledge, and it is precisely knowledge – not having any relation to previous understandings of truth, but only sought in its imaginary equivalences – that is operative in sedimented biographical outcomes of the clinical theory and praxis of Ribot and Janet (and their cognitive-behavioral heirs). We can detect the concealment in these processes because, unlike the traumatic and ontological conditions of their possibilities, such technologies reduce truth to facts, reflexivity to objective distance, and autonomy to flexible performance. In all of these forms, trauma loses its traumatic status, becoming instead a way of suturing what is always missing in the subject's time, and its being, its *manque-à-être*; trauma is transformed – in some Orwellian fashion – into its opposite, an aporia in knowledge allowing the attainment of identity, but an aporia that erases itself. Nonetheless, this discursive parapraxis arising in the light of mnemo-technology carries with it a "saving power" (Heidegger, 1977b), providing possibility for insight, and opportunity for enframing to be ontologically revealed in its essence.

For the history of trauma, Freud establishes psychic trauma both psychologically and culturally, and as definitive of the modern, divided subject. Along with Marx and Nietzsche, Freud completes the triumvirate, whose thought Ricoeur (1977) famously designated "the hermeneutics of suspicion," questioning the mastery of disinterested rationality in its own house. Inasmuch, psychoanalysis would itself be overdetermined by regressive tendencies for scientistic solidification, but also capable of a radically different manifestation of subjectivity, including the revelation of traumatic ontology through permutations of its own thought. Importantly, memory as a cognitive or rational construct would insufficiently articulate, or contain, the crisis of subjectivity at hand. For psychoanalytic thought, the relation of trauma and memory becomes an imbrication of truth, subjectivity, and temporality on an entirely different scale.

Certainly, despite its periodic meditations around its own scientific status, Freud's thinking – from its genesis until his death – persistently returns to the notion of subjectivity as fundamentally traumatic in nature. Very early on, Breuer and Freud (1895/2000) write that "memory of the trauma . . . acts like a foreign body which long after its entry must continue to be regarded as an agent that is still at work . . . *Hysterics suffer mainly from reminiscences*" (pp. 6–7). In proximity to Charcot (1889), Freud and Breuer recount a psychological genesis of hysteria in seduction, but also prefigure a striking revision of the temporal logic of memory. In his final phase of work, Freud (1940/1964a) returns to this fundamental insight that "no human individual is spared . . . traumatic experiences; none escapes the repressions to which they give rise" (p. 185). Along the way, in the intervening years, Freud (1895/1954) continues to tether his theoretical revisions such as the "Project for a Scientific Psychology" and other works (Freud, 1894/1962a) to a traumatic and retroactive temporality. As sketched therein and as mentioned in relation to the Lacanian subject, trauma – as submitted to *Nachträglichkeit* – results from the co-constitutive relationship between two events, neither of which is intrinsically traumatic. As an illustration from *The Interpretation of Dreams*, Freud (1900/1961b) writes of a young man speaking of the beauty of the wet nurse who had suckled him as a baby, expressing regret that he did not make more of the opportunity. Ostensibly, some latent, libidinally charged potential for sexuality had been present in his childhood experience, which later theory would take to manifest in the older man's perspective as a mature relation to his embodiment, which had developmentally passed through the requisite psychosexual stages of conflict and resolution. Otherwise, the adult simply interprets presexual infantile experience in retrospect, according to the distance of more mature sexuality, and the resultant ego position. As Freud (1918/1959a) writes:

> At the age of one and a half the child receives an impression to which he is unable to react adequately; he is only able to understand it and to be moved by it when the impression is revived in him at the age of four; and only twenty years later, during the analysis, is he able to grasp with his conscious mental processes what was then going on in him. The patient justifiably disregards the three periods of time, and puts his present ego in the situation that is so long past.
>
> *(pp. 516–517)*

Classical psychoanalytic thought, thus, engages the opening of the traumatic rupture in the subject's being-in-time – the gap between the impression and the retroactive arrival of the later ego or consciousness; however, this is accomplished in clinical terms, without the explicit effort to formulate a general theory of temporality, or without strict adherence to a mechanistic theory of the psyche. As Mieli (2001) clarifies, "It [*Nachträglichkeit*] does not signal a delay in action or in reaction, but rather an event that in the very act of positing itself, reinvests a past inscription and takes on the status of a revelation" (p. 268). This is important because it allows psychoanalysis to speak to the subject's enigmatically and historically embedded being, without philosophical or clinical erasure of the trauma – that is, a rationalistic accounting. Late in his work, Freud (1937/1964b) suggests that neurosis, or psychosis even, harbors within its delusions or fantasies a "historical truth which it inserts in the place of the rejected reality" (p. 268). Accordingly, Laplanche (1999) asserts that neither realistic depiction nor agentically narrative reconstruction of an event is able to do justice to the compelling truth of an event or experience that presses itself forward in our being. The subject's history, insofar as it implicates its truth, is not *history* in any usual sense of the word – neither an epistemically objective nor subjective enterprise.

At this juncture, it appears that psychoanalytic thought itself harbors a mode of inquiry into an analysand's experience of temporality that would escape technological enframing. Because Freud (1916–17/1963b) brackets the epistemic reality of childhood traumatic events, holding "we have not succeeded in pointing to any difference in the consequences, whether fantasy or reality has had the greater share in these events of childhood" (p. 370), the distinction between pathological and healthy remembering appearing under the medical gaze becomes, thereby, threatened. A more expansive understanding of subjectivity – founded on the twin forks of immersion into the Real and the alienation given through alterity – becomes possible. A distinctly mimetic turn, where the subject is placed into contact with ever-differentiating and remote events, apparently overturns the leveling of the particularities of the subject's existence to the uniform and brightly visible surfaces of scientific knowledge. In response to wartime trauma, and the inexplicably destructive repetition compulsions plaguing the lives of so many analysands, psychoanalytic discourse performs an immanent critique (cf. Deleuze & Guattari, 1972/1983) of its own doctrine, sketching subjectivity beyond the *Eros* of the Oedipal relationship. Leys (2000) writes that the subject's originary invasion or alteration would create a

> vacancy of the traumatized subject or ego in a hypnotic openness to impressions or identifications occurring prior to all self-representation and hence to all rememoration . . . This would explain why the traumatic event cannot be remembered, indeed why it is "relived."
>
> *(p. 32)*

For Laplanche (Caruth, 2002), more recently, what is elemental for trauma concerns an Otherness, outside of time and representation, which is unaccountably implanted in one's being. As suggested earlier, even an earthquake victim is addressed in his/her embodied openness – the perceptual, affective, chiasmic intertwining – to such horrifying experience. Consonant with Freud's notion of historical truth, Laplanche (1999) strategically avoids the conflation of his method with a facile subjective reconstruction of fact. Rather, in elevating the psychoanalytic project over methods espousing representation or their surrogates (integration, memorial reconstruction, etc.), he supplants interpretivism with translation, which befits the more ontologically oriented dimensions of psychoanalytic theory: "What is *translated*, specifically, is not a natural, or even historical sign, but a message, a signifier or a sequence of signifiers . . . I am again resorting to the category of the *message* of the enigmatic *signifier* [of the Other]" (Laplanche, 1999, p. 157). Problematically for scientific and philosophical understandings, such messages surpass the capacities of language yet require the alienating effects of language to make their mark. This is evident, for instance, in Freud's (1919/1955) paper "A Child is Being Beaten," wherein the inscribed prohibition of the law and the unspeakable masochistic *jouissance* of being beaten by one's object of love coalesce (Mieli, 2001). The paradox of masochism closes in on that of traumatic experience, which may not be depicted, but can only be translated; it comes to the subject as address rather than knowledge.

Psychoanalysis would itself, of course, suffer its own trauma though Freud's (1920/1961a) momentous revision in *Beyond the Pleasure Principle* that would provide a vanishing point for subjectivity, potentially arresting the recalcitrant technological tendencies harbored within its own doctrine. As is well known, during and after the First World War, the stream of soldiers leaving the battlefield and coming home with "shell shock" required that Freud consider a different outlook, more inclusive of these experiences. Wartime trauma had deeply problematized an economy of the unconscious formed entirely around the pleasure principle: "The term 'traumatic' has no other sense than an economic one. We apply to it an experience which within a short period of time presents the mind with an increase of stimulus too powerful to be dealt with or worked off in the normal way" (Freud, 1915–16/1963a, p. 275). More generally, the persistence of painful and destructive experiences could be submitted to an alternate schema with another, different generator of psychic energy – the death drive. Overall, Freud (1920/1961a) grounds this possibility in three different clinical domains. First, as mentioned, are traumatic neuroses, where dreams reproduce traumatic memories rather than wish-fulfillments. Second, Freud famously reports his observation of his grandson's behavior when his mother left him for a few hours; the boy would stage his mother's appearance and disappearance – and his existential mastery thereof – with a game of *fort* and *da* ("gone" and "there"), involving a wooden reel and a piece of string. Third, in transference, patients appear to the analyst to be "pursued by a malignant fate or possessed by some 'daemonic power'" (Freud, 1920/1961a, p. 23), while at the same time this being somehow arranged by the patient him or herself to override the pleasure principle and determined by early childhood experience. Freud's (1920/1961a) comprehensive solution to this tripartite problem – conjoining originary, secondary, and tertiary traumatic effects – bears the indicia of the technological appropriation of human being under the antimimetc signal of external *quanta* impinging on the psyche's exterior barrier:

> We describe as "traumatic" any excitations from outside which are powerful to break through the protective shield . . . At the same time, the pleasure principle is for the moment put out of action. There is no longer any possibility of preventing the mental apparatus from being flooded with large amounts of stimulus, and another problem arises instead – the problem of mastering the amounts of stimulus.
>
> *(p. 33)*

What unites the various dimensions of the death drive would be the aim of restoring an initial state of inorganic homeostasis that precedes life (the Nirvana principle). Strikingly, however, as Laplanche (1976) asserts, the physicalistic metaphors inherited from Helmholtz – concerning the relative balance of free and bound energy – and enlarged through the second law of thermodynamics run into trouble. In late classical psychoanalytic discourse, it would appear that psychic energy is offered two different routes. *Thanatos* aims at a degree zero state via the radical unbinding of energy, and *Eros* aims at a state of homeostatic equilibrium achieved through binding or cathexis. But, as Laplanche (1976) makes clear, the radical anti-life experiences of frenetic *jouissance* press themselves into the subject's being, as the repetition compulsion, in ways that may not be accounted for in naturalistic depictions: "The death drive . . . is present, in Freud's final formulations, not as element in conflict but as *conflict itself* substantialized" (p. 122). Life is death. Pleasure is unpleasure. Appearance is disappearance. Or, desire is the Other's desire. As Reisner (2014) writes, "Freud's discovery is that *the other desire* is not the mere negation of desire but *an originary radical of other-desire, equal in intensity to all the adoration of oedipal love*" (p. 45). Therefore, by necessity, Otherness may not be made intelligible but must be translated, answered, addressed – portending the flashing of truth that must be approached in non-philosophical and non-scientific practices. It should not be the least bit surprising, then, to find that the death drive becomes central for Lacanian theory and practice, Lacan (1966/2006b) writing that "to evade the death instinct in his [Freud's] doctrine is not to know his doctrine at all" (p. 679). Significantly, Lacan's (1988b, 1966/2006a) own trajectory in relation to the death drive tracks the shift in his relative historical emphasis from the imaginary to symbolic registers – the former involving a lost harmony for pre-Oedipal fusion (in the imaginary), and the latter relating to the symbolic order itself producing repetition under the logic of castration; lastly, the death drive is an element of every drive. For the clinical apparatus of trauma as a refusal to ontologically position alterity as embedded in the subject's being – that is, in the technical adherence to the encircling binaries of mimesis and antimimesis – we no doubt find the scientific aspirations of psychoanalysis themselves in conflict.

Trauma, as the radical unbinding of the death drive, comes to theoretically interpenetrate the mechanisms of repression in Freud's (1926/1959b) later theory, as manifested in *Inhibitions, Symptoms, and Anxiety*, giving rise to more fundamental pre-Oedipal psychic states. Freud (1926/1959b) writes that "Anxiety is not newly created in repression . . . Affective states have become incorporated in the mind as precipitates of primaeval traumatic experiences" (p. 93). Of course, object relations theory – discussed *infra* – would give rise to many formulations relating to separation and loss, which would also manifest the uneasy tension between mimesis and antimimesis. Earlier on though, for Ferenczi (1933), the sufferer of trauma is forced into reengagement with such primitive conditions, and the difficult discernment of how "not-me" elements of experiences may be rejected aggressively or taken in as an "identification with the aggressor," wherein a person adopts the perspective of another, perhaps aggressive or malevolent, subject/object. Thus, Ferenczi (1995) strikingly states "this kind of mimicry, this being subject to impressions without any self-protection, is the original form of life" (p. 147). Traumatic events, therefore, are constituted not by a mere forgetting of an external event but, in parallel with the unbinding of the death drive, by causing an erasure of the subject and object positions, insofar as a person loses his/her ego in a complete identification with the other – person, scene, or event. This revision of psychoanalytic theory not only merges to some extent *Eros* with *Thanatos* but places the ego in a site of constant vigilance ensuring the subject will not be enveloped or lost in the being of another. Indeed, subjectivity becomes primordially related to Otherness, the subject being written through bits and fragments of an Other consciousness. Increasingly, finding one's true being is less a matter of disclosing a specific experience of sexuality than speaking one's own, self-same truth – suspended between the vicissitudes of erotic and destructive impulses – directed towards others/objects for cathexis or identification. The subject called to speak is reflected through a world of others, in varying degrees benevolent, malevolent, or indifferent, who give us the materials with which to build, attain, or construct our own selves, to individuate or become enveloped by the outside. Leys (2000), however, dissects the corpus of Ferenczi's writings to discern – in addition to the originary or developmental understanding of trauma – a postoriginary model of trauma wherein an event befalls an already constituted ego and, in due course, a splitting occurs that results in a subjective emotional tie to the traumatic event and an objective intellectual system that cannot master the intensity of the former. Consequently, Leys (2000) asserts that this very ambivalence around what foundational principle – that of mimetic blindness or antimimetic representation – would guide psychoanalysis is present not only for Freud, and Ferenczi, but also for prominent critics of psychoanalysis, such as Borch-Jacobsen (1988), due to a pervasive suspicion that the patient would be drawn into a form of hypnotic simulation. Whether through active collusion with the analyst's suggestion of certain confessions or through the analyst's use of play-acting and the cathartic reliving of emotionally charged memories, the transferential relationship itself becomes endangered as a kind of performative game, whose outcomes are more aligned with social pragmatics than memorial archaeology. What is fascinating and incisive about Leys' (2000) analysis is the manner in which she follows the seeming intractability of the mimetic/antimimetic dilemma both in psychoanalytic discourse proper and the contemporary commentary it has spawned. For instance, in her assessment of Borch-Jacobsen (1988), she sketches the shift in his thinking about hypnosis from believing that psychoanalysis was invested in a mimetic position that results in unmasterable experiences and interminable analysis to that of an outright game played by a fully conscious subject. Rather than attempt an answer to this machinically and theoretically emplaced riddle, Leys (2000) wisely demonstrates again and again "that with respect to the episodes and cruxes treated in this book the tension or oscillation between mimesis and antimimesis I have been tracking cannot definitively be resolved by choosing one over the other" (p. 181). As a result, what is preserved is the possibility for ontologically traumatic subjectivity, as sketched herein, as well as the disquieting possibility that – as conflictual as its technological apparatus may be – the clinical discourse of trauma obeys a common logic of a subject whose attainment of its being is submitted to linear temporality, with its epistemically realistic and medical grasp of its own realities.

Though classical psychoanalytic thought and therapeutic practice would often privilege the subject's blind, mimetic immersion into the scene of trauma, both in the notion of *Nachträglichkeit* and in the transference – in the relationally formed affective charge – of the session itself, its edifice would consistently yield under the gravity of its scientific pretensions, an ineluctably antimimetic move. The epistemic ground of representation no longer holds the older Enlightenment promise of absolute mastery, but rather has a more practical aim in relation to the biomedical knowledge emerging in nineteenth-century *savoir*, as chronicled by Foucault (1966/1973). Rather than pure correspondence, what Freudian theory aims for is a positive correlation, which would yield practical results. Freud's (1914/1958) project of cure is nothing less than a recollection, and a working through of associations to the ends of interpretation, which the patient would need to accept in order to move beyond the repetition compulsion. Representation, therefore, overturns blind repetition in search of an epigenetic explanation for the patient's suffering. Concerning the colonization of historiography by natural science, Heidegger (1977c) writes that "there is no other historiographical explanation so long as explaining means reduction to what is intelligible and so long as historiography remains research, i.e., an explaining" (p. 123). An antimimetic turn, where patients's struggles are strongly depicted in etiologies foregrounding remote yet discrete events, effects a leveling of experiential multiplicity to a "univocity of concepts and specifications" (Heidegger, 1954/1968, p. 34). The subject's own historically traumatic being is enframed by, and interpolated into, scientific metaphors – specifically those concerning the embodiment of sexuality and the transformations of somatic energy in the psyche.

Traumatic suffering, for classical psychoanalysis and its further permutations thereafter, would continually find itself tethered to the subject's primordially privative experiences of erotic embodiment. Freud's earliest texts, as are widely known, frame the subject's arc of life squarely within the procrustean bed of early childhood sexual experience, formed on "*an analogy between the pathogenesis of common hysteria and that of traumatic neurosis*" (Breuer & Freud, 1895/2000, p. 5). From Charcot through Freud, as Roth (2001) observes, hysterical subjects are enjoined to recollect an event bearing upon their earliest lives, and then – paradoxically – being allowed to forget, in "wiping away these [traumatic] pictures" (Breuer & Freud, 1895/2000, p. 53). As Freud, however, abandons the seduction hypothesis for a developmental understanding of childhood sexuality, his earlier and more mimetically inclined practices premised on the disappearance of the symptom through abreaction increasingly give way to explanation via interpretation. The theoretical devices for such ascriptions of trauma expand considerably after Freud (1897/1966, 1905/2000) elevates the fantasy to the status of reality, and works out theories of sexuality that considerably deepen his earlier conceptions of *Nachträglichkeit*. On the relation of traumatic temporality and sexuality, Laplanche (1976) inquires:

> *Why sexuality?* Freud's answer is that sexuality alone is available for that action in two phases which is also an action "after the event." It is there and

there alone that we find that complex interplay – midst a temporal succession of missed occasions – of "too early" and "too late." Fundamentally, what is at stake is the relation in the human being between his "acculturation" and his "biological" sexuality, on the condition that . . . the latter is already, for its part, partially "denatured."

(p. 43)

Freudian sexuality, hence, precociously predicts its own critique in Foucault's (1980) notable argument of sexuality as socio-historical deployment – aiming at establishing a depth of being – whose domains span the hysterization of women's bodies, the pedagogization of children's sex, the socialization of procreative behavior, and the psychiatrization of perverse pleasure. Simultaneously, the delayed effects of sexual trauma arrive too late alongside mature understanding of eroticized adult relationships, and are increasingly projected backward in time as explanation. These latter representations, no doubt, play their part in the subject's ethical self-relation; however, for the instant argument, they conjoin two external dimensions of power/knowledge – sexuality as knowledge of subjectivity that is the scientific surrogate of the soul with childhood as fundamental element for selfhood. Indeed, Foucault (2004) remarks that "childhood as a historical stage of development and a general form of behavior becomes the principal instrument of psychiatrization" (p. 304). Psychoanalytic theories of sexuality – as they bear upon traumatic suffering – implicate a continually retroactive scientific positioning of knowledge of individual subjects. These knowledges fix the subject to the archives of personhood, the dossiers kept in psychiatrists' offices, in prisons, in schools; they memorialize antimimetically who the subject is, according to the putative fundaments of his or her embodied being, and they do so in light of current experiences that bear immanent marks in relationship to the analyst. As the patient as subject understands the analyst's explanation or suggestion around her traumatic experience, she is at that very moment given public address; such *connaissance* always arrives too late.

Undoubtedly, Freud's metapsychological equation of mental energy with physical energy, and his hydraulic/mechanical mapping of its movement, would hold the most promise for a purely representational and antimimetic understanding of trauma, though this would prove to be conceptually fragile. As early as *Project for a Scientific Psychology*, Freud (1895/1954) seeks an integrated model of the psyche wherein neurons freely transfer excess energy, which is considered a primary process, whereas the constancy principle keeps such energy bound via a secondary process of binding. Such energy *in potentia* exists in a stratified limbo; however, traumatic memories may be recalled exactly on the basis of later excitations. As Freud (1895/1954) goes on to explain, the primary process may be unbound through the retroactive unconscious association of memory traces: "As in the case of the hysterical *proton pseudos* [initial falsehood], the release of unpleasure is occasioned by a *memory* . . . *the retardation of puberty makes possible the occurrence of posthumous primary processes*" (p. 416). Freud (1894/1962a, 1896/1962b) continues his efforts to seamlessly assimilate repression and traumatic memory into his physicalistic formulations, holding that residual excitations are converted into symptoms, such as hysterical conversion and obsessional thinking; however, trauma would not itself be capable of accounting for repression, requiring again the notion of deferral. In his papers on metapsychology, and "Repression" especially, Freud (1915/1957) – further illuminating the unconscious processes elaborated in his works on dreams – offers a remarkable and bidirectional understanding of the nature of traumatic memory. Noting the existence of both the primal repression of an ideational/psychic representative of instincts and the repression proper of the associated mental derivatives of the repressed representative, Freud (1915/1957) writes:

> Psycho-analysis is able to show us . . . that the instinctual representative develops with less interference and more profusely if it is withdrawn by repression from conscious influence. It proliferates in the dark, as it were, and takes on extreme forms of expression, which when they are translated and presented to the neurotic are not only bound to seem alien to him, but frighten him by giving him the picture of an extraordinary and dangerous strength of instinct.
>
> *(p. 149)*

This striking passage appears to indicate that what is repressed is always – in some important sense – a fantasy of sorts, that primary repression remains unknowable and always supposed, and that the originary scene of trauma is always submitted to the proliferations "in the dark" of derivative representatives, continually displaced in everyday life. Moreover, this means that repression itself is nothing other than deferred action (Quinodoz, 2005). From Charcot through Janet, memorial access to knowledge had assumed a salubrious and functionally pragmatic tethering, and Freudian doctrine continues this naturalistic tendency through his desire to explain the associative traces of memories that constellate and allow a certain triangulation of a ground zero for therapeutic interpretation of trauma, at arriving at the original scene. Nonetheless, against the mapping of the unconscious that would possibly allow a fully cogent and final understanding, Freud betrays a fully antimimetic solution through his infusion of memory into temporality itself, of refusing to locate memory as a place for storage, or as an ideal container for ordinary autobiography that could be cleansed of the polluting effects of suffering, loss, and mourning.

Classical drive theory – when submitted to a biologically reductive and antimimetic narrative made intelligible through energetic movements of physical entities – is paralleled by the ascendancy of an ego and object-oriented psychoanalysis that would theorize the subject's relation to trauma in the frame of reference governed by experience-near consciousness over against others as external objects. Theoretical rendering of the unintelligible into the *lingua franca* of ontically grounded, scientific explanation is also precociously evident in psychoanalytic theory and practices that abandon conflict as structural for human being for an ever-expanding interpretively transparent self or ego. One trajectory of psychoanalytic thought, drawing its breath from Freud's (1926/1959b) *Inhibitions, Symptoms, and Anxiety*, as well as Anna Freud's (1936/1966) *The Ego and the Mechanisms of Defence*, would instantiate a psychoanalytic ego psychology. For Hartmann, Kris, and Loewenstein (1951), the ego constitutes an evolutionary extension of consciousness, serving as the mental equivalent of a physical organ, whose purpose is to facilitate social adaptation, integration of experience, and personality organization. Moreover, such an enterprise, because it conceptualizes the ego as potentially without conflict, allows it to provide a transparent space of representing its own problematic origin, its instinctual vicissitudes, and the intensities of its experience with others. Hartmann (1955) eventually separates the ego entirely from Freud's instinctual drive model, thereby finalizing his theoretical hegemony of self-possessed representation, which retains the pragmatist strain of the modern episteme. For her part, in "Comments on Trauma," Anna Freud (1967) reinforces the position of epistemic realism in analytic practice, holding out the egological space for knowledge and, crucially, placing the analyst on high ground as land surveyor above the experientially dark terrain of psychic suffering. To the former, Anna Freud (1967) borrows from Sigmund Freud's own locution that it is in the ego's helplessness that lies the essence of trauma: "The entire defense organization of the ego is endowed with the characteristics of a protective shield and drawn into orbit of potential traumatic onslaught" (p. 236). As follows, ego is normatively defined as a locus for the accurate grasping of reality rather than as a suturing of originary or secondary trauma as in Lacan and other psychoanalytic discourses privileging a more ontological account of trauma (e.g., Brothers, 2008; Stolorow, 2011). In its fundamental orientation, Anna Freud's approach to trauma focuses on a medico-forensic investigation into both the original scene of trauma and into the patient's psychological, egoic capacities of managing the distress. Not surprisingly, ego psychology is able to well augment the latest neurobiological research such as that conducted and reviewed by van der Kolk (2014) and others (e.g., Chertoff, 1998). A thorough assessment of the patient's traumatic reality is, thus, entirely possible, with inquiry being suggested into: the nature of the event (i.e., "Was it really sufficiently traumatic?"), the patient's history of prior suffering and trauma (i.e., "What did the current event trigger for the patient?"), the effect of hereditary factors on functioning (i.e., "Is the patient's ego intrinsically weak?"), the developmental history of the patient (i.e., "Is the trauma related to a particular stage of development?"), and interpersonal environment (i.e., "What was the relative danger/safety of the social world in which the event occurred?") (Chertoff, 1998; A. Freud, 1967). Importantly, these questions appear to be oriented to ascertaining the nature, location, and realistic grasp of the traumatic event. In this way, the subject's own traumatic facticity (as an axis of its ontology) – as lived and dispersed against his/her own temporal horizons – is given over to factuality. Of course, along the way, the patient must – at some level – identify his or her ego with that of the analyst if there is to be the appropriate arrival at knowledge that will produce the distance of healing, the integration of memory, and the settling of a narrative that will reclaim the forward project of identity.

In keeping with spatial tropes positing a subject's history that can, in principle, be known or represented, object relations theory provides more traditional medical iterations of the psychoanalytic project's complementary consideration of the various ways that the subject fashions him or herself from phenomenal others, who are given the status of "objects" in the subject's inner world (Fairbairn, 1952; Winnicott, 1965). As theorized by Winnicott (1965), the mother's lingering intrusion into the child's early existence, coupled with the latter's attunement to the mother's needs and desire results in fragmentation of a "true self" and "false self," notions that have influenced neo-Freudian (e.g., Horney, 1937), humanistic, and existentially oriented psychologies (e.g., Laing, 1960). Importantly, these currencies of authenticity bearing the stamp of truth do not do so in relation to temporal non-Being – except as the void of pathological states – but rather to an idealized and essentialized locus of agency, gesture, and spontaneity. For an account of trauma from an object relations perspective, it will serve to outline the theoretical contributions of Kohut (1971, 1984, 2011a), who continues the overall trend of conceptualizing the human being as intrinsically related to its earliest enduring dyadic relationships – termed "selfobjects" – and their effects of mirroring or affirming the subject's existence and providing a source for an idealized self. It may be important to signal that Kohutian theory and practice, in its considerable influence over the history of psychoanalysis (in North America, especially), offers differing paths on which to travel. One theoretical trajectory becomes congruent with contemporary psychoanalytic understandings of relationality and intersubjectivity, maintaining a dialogue with the existential-phenomenological insights of Heideggerian and Levinasian thought (e.g., Stolorow, 2011). Despite Kohut's (2011b) training in neurology, shortly before his death he disavowed "such a misalliance as psychobiology, or biopsychology" (p. 529), yet another trajectory within self psychology maintains a closer bearing to neurobiology, neuropsychoanalysis, and attachment theory (Schore, 2002).

Kohut's self psychology, at its center, maintains a modest epistemological stance in its commitment to clinical knowledge as accumulated in analytic practice, and thus – while not accessing the modern subject's traumatic ontology – discursively and practically balances mimetic or antimimetic sensibilities. In recounting his own influences and basic outlook, Kohut (2011a) states that it "was especially the study of Kant, in particular *The Critique of Pure Reason*, that established in me . . . the conviction that the essence of reality, of external and internal reality as I would now put it, was unknowable" (p. 448). Though eventually abandoning drive theory, Kohut's self psychology in its metapsychological moments often reproduces itself as psychiatric knowledge organized around norms of well-being defined as the flourishing of affective self-expression and engagement with more mature selfobjects. Its explicit theoretical orientation is that of impressionistically representing how and where a subject's trauma began. At the outset, it is quite clear that self psychology most aptly characterizes developmental trauma, where early self-forming relationships lead to fragmentation. Trauma in this idiom, thus, may pertain to a discrete event but more often to an ongoing failure to provide the conditions for the subject's own developmental self-solidification. Kohut (1971) writes that

> if, for example, a narcissistic parent . . . considers the child as an extension of herself . . . it may lead to the development of a sensitive psychological super-structure . . . Or, the early excessive exposure to the psychological overcloseness may, on the contrary, lead to a defensive hardening or blunting of the perceptive surfaces in order to protect the psyche from being traumatized by a pathogenic parent's anxiety-provoking responses.
>
> *(pp. 277–278)*

The subject's enduring and cohesive sense of self is, therefore, dependent on selfobject experiences that affirm the self's fundamental existence through time. Along these lines, Wolf (1995) observes that Kohut's conceptualization moved away from an early reliance on energetic overstimulation consistent with the unbinding of the death drive. According to Wolf (1995), this transformation involves several alterations of emphasis: the etiology of trauma moves from inside the subject to outside the subject (its interpersonal milieu in selfobjects); location shifts from events to relationships; the injurious force changes from intensity of stimulation to the responsiveness of the milieu; and the observer's attention shifts from objectively viewing intrapsychic events to being intersubjectively attuned to the patient's experience. Consequently, the analytic situation itself – the transference and countertransference – is seen to be a curative element in analysis or therapy, and also the epistemic ground from which the patient's unbearable affect in the here and now is attuned. In an important sense, Kohut (1984) arguably does not hold that a realistic understanding of the subject's originary or primary trauma, even if developmentally conceived, would even be possible or necessary in the formation of new and healthy relationships. Indeed, for the practice of self psychology, the deficits of selfobject trauma are – at some level – inaccessible to the subject, and its reconsolidation only occurs within the specific confines of the analytic situation, within transference. Accordingly, Kohut appears to bracket trauma as unreachable, and turns to effect an analytic cure within an affirming relationship with the patient, one promising a realistic appraisal of one's life, relational reparation, and creative fulfillment (Goldberg, 1980). Significantly, however, the practice of self psychology offers the subject an empathically immersive setting that would encourage the mimetic reliving of the traumatic event or failure; however, the analyst's empathic attunement is utilized to broker a certain self-understanding vis-à-vis the analyst's explanations, which are dynamic, relational, and suggestive (Kohut, 1984). Self psychology, therefore, allows, in the same breath, a mimetic and antimimetic move. In some parallel with Janet and Ribot, a more psychologized psychoanalysis interests itself not in the truth-effect of the remote event itself or chronic emergence of trauma but the ends of self-fashioning that would occur in its aftermath. Correspondingly, ego and object-oriented psychoanalysis technically appropriate the subject's wounding through time for social adaptation, normalization, and the maintenance of bourgeois ideals of self-discipline and bounded self-mastery. Cushman (1990, 1995) and others (e.g., Layton, 1990) have persuasively asserted that Kohut's vision of selfhood privileges the subject's triumphs of ambition, attainment of self-esteem, independence, and neo-Romantic expression of feeling. More pointedly, Cushman (1995) argues that Kohut interprets the appearance of emptiness, confusion, and isolation as the discrete pathology of individual subjects, over against the clinical standard of intrapsychic substance and resilience. Fink (2004), therefore, writes of the possibility that "psychoanalysis could now be brought back into the fold of general psychology . . . and the positive achievements of the ego as it masters languages, mathematics, science, everyday tasks, and so on" (p. 40). Accordingly, a psychologized psychoanalytic practice heightens capacities for telling one's story, and relating to others, through a socially meaningful narrative of self-repair, arising from an inevitably unresolved crisis of representation for a subject ontologically dispersed in temporal discontinuity.

For modernity, psychoanalysis – in its different permutations – manifests contradictory tensions related to ontological trauma and its ontic, clinical concealment, thus placing it at the crossroads of the epochal disclosure of the phenomenon itself. As argued *supra*, Lacanian theory especially, but also that of Laplanche work at the level of ontology because they have taken their leave from trauma as understood through an inaccessible temporal synchrony. Sketched previously, for Laplanche, there are – heuristically speaking – two moments of trauma. In the first moment, there is the implantation of something outside (the Other's intervention). The second moment involves the signified revision of the first moment of implantation (for Lacan, separation by the paternal signifier). What is initiated through the subject's being is an enigmatic message, which bears truth but not knowledge, truth that must be translated in the second and successive moments. For this ontology of trauma, which would obtain resonance also for Levinas, the subject is blind to the other scene because *the other scene is not a place* but diachronic dispossession of the subject's being, stretched out, broken up in time. In contrast, more traditional and psychologized psychoanalysis conceives of the subject of trauma through its power/knowledge as the ontic, factual being who is pathologically gripped, and rendered blind and mute, by otherly intrusions remote in spatialized time – the other scene, *that other place*, where "it happened." Much traditional psychoanalytic discourse on trauma, in distinction to Janet or van der Kolk positing a subject in principle capable of generating workably representational memories, adheres epistemically to the mimetic pole where the other scene is inaccessible due to the radical unbinding of the energies of the death drive (later Freud), primary pre-Oedipal identification (Ferenczi), or an originary fusion with others as objects (Winnicott and Kohut). These theories are not indebted to the ontologized Kant of Lacan, but are closer to the epistemically oriented Kant, where the scene of trauma as spatio-temporally noumenal (immersive) facilitates the segregation of psychopathology from health in certain terms. Unlike an ontological understanding of trauma, whose trajectories implicate the subject's truth, reflexivity, and autonomy emerging from its diachronic absence to itself in time, the breakdown in a synchronic temporality adhering to a mimetic epistemology divides the subject between neurotic/sublimated, depleting selfobject relations/edifying selfobject relations, weak ego/strong ego, etc. Overall, these technologies – through a background of pathologized identification of the subject with another place in time – foreground an idealized conception of selfhood organized around attaining character or ego strength, or the discharge of one's industrial duties of love and work (to produce other beings, and to manufacture objects) with the utmost spontaneity, joy, fortitude, consistency, and realism. As a result, unlike technologies of self that enjoin the subject to attain a Cartesian, antimimetic distance, or representational reflexivity regarding one's "punctual self," traditional psychoanalytic confessional practice does return somewhat to an ethics of transformation, reminiscent of the *epimeleia heautou*. After all, in the main, these therapies require the relationship of another person (the analyst), not for guidance as to what should count for realistic depiction of one's suffering, but for the "borrowed ego," the insight from the repetition of transference in analysis, or Kohutian reparenting. The purification required in Christian penitential or confessional technologies is reoriented away from purging the soul of its originally sinful mark into its flesh, and towards healing the original wounding arising from its thrownness into less than hospitable conditions. Nonetheless, traditional psychoanalytic technologies participate in the enframing of the subject because they – though hinting at ontological trauma – retain the masking effects of synchronic over diachronic temporality. Put differently, they continue to draw on an aporetic, inaccessible past, but one mapped via linear time, itself the devalued counterpart to eternity. The ontic, synchronous, and mimetically oriented spatialization of trauma, present in antimimetically oriented theories as well, masks or covers an ontology of trauma very neatly because it conceptualizes psychic trauma as a place of psychological devastation and dispersal, thereby giving its warrant for rebuilding the subject as self, an imaginary and solidified social being whose integral appearance forms afterward.

The influence that psychoanalytic discourse and practice would have for approaches to traumatic suffering throughout two world wars and afterward can hardly be overstated. Significantly, however, discourses constelling traumatic neurosis as shell shock during the First World War would continue to contain an undercurrent of evolutionary biologism. These outlooks included those of W. H. R. Rivers (1920) – who lectured on Freud and favored a naturalism derived from Hughlings Jackson (1931/1958) and Spencer (1855) – conjoined with understandings of mimetic autosuggestion as an explanatory mechanism for traumatic neurosis and counter-suggestion as a cure (along with various physical treatments). The wartime disciplining of memory would also be taken up by Brown (1920, 1923) and McDougal (1920), among others, who promoted the technique of autognosis, which would seek to translate the intensity of memory into the past tense, in the words of Brown (1920) as progress "from a state of relative dissociation to a state of mental harmony and unity" (p. 19). Notably, however, for the theoretical lineage that van der Kolk would find in Janet – and others such as Herman (1992) – it is Kardiner (1941) who would begin to formulate a visibly contemporary account of the symptomology of trauma. As Young (1995) observes, Kardiner's list of symptoms (including those characterizing sensitivity to fear-inducing stimuli, psychological contraction, loss of consciousness/dissociation, and loss of interest in the world) prefigure those currently prevailing in the *Diagnostic and Statistical Manual of Mental Disorders* (American Psychiatric Association, 2013). Moreover, in *The Traumatic Neuroses of War*, Kardiner (1941), though working from a largely psychoanalytic theoretical frame, signals an important shift away from a reliance on the potential for egoic mastery of intolerable intrapsychic experience:

> The traumatic event creates excitations beyond the possibility of mastering, inflicts a severe blow to the total ego organization. The activities involved in successful adaption to the external environment become blocked in their usual outlets . . . As a result of the trauma, that portion of the ego which normally helps the individual to carry out automatically certain organized aggressive functions of perception and activity on the basis of innumerable successes in the past is either destroyed or inhibited.
>
> *(pp. 116–117)*

Though Kardiner (1941) rejects earlier psychoanalytic explanations that foreground libinal repression, and sanctions traumatic neurosis as the unbinding of the death drive – linking the scene of trauma with a pre-Oedipal Other as Ferenczi or birth trauma as Rank (Leys, 2000) – traumatic memory, as mimetic immersion, becomes inscribed into the adaptive physiology of fit between organism and the world itself. What begins to surface in Kardiner's account, thus, is an increasingly close symptomatic correlation between traumatic symptoms themselves and the disjuncture between the original environment of trauma and the latter environments in which the subject would find him or herself located, and, crucially, a shift from Freudian metapsychology to the observation of embodied, biomedically framed, states of experience, that of *physioneurosis*, which "describes more precisely the province of the ego involved, that connected with organ function, and the specific psycho-physical integrations" (Kardiner, 1941, p. 195). Of course, the watershed publication of the *DSM-III* would cement a metatheoretical diagnostic language beholden to a neo-Kraeplinian psychiatry foregrounding mental disorders as analogous to organic disease, closely associated with visible and statistically verified constellations of symptoms, and ultimately having neurobiological origins. The Vietnam-era politics of the entry of PTSD into the *DSM-III*, and its effect on the Veteran's Administration in the United States and access to treatment for veterans, is well recounted by others (Scott, 1990; Young, 1995). Additionally, critique of the syndromal matrices of contemporary psychodiagnostics is beyond the scope of the present work; however, what bears emphasizing is the rigorous and systematic fixing of collective traumata to the dysfunctional effects of neurological processes evolved to ensure the subject's physical survival, and the institutional accumulation of this data in populations as a prominent biopolitical strategy. Recall that case history, a staple of psychoanalytic practice owing in part to a hermeneutic privileging of the idiographic nature of the subject's suffering, is remarkably inefficient in its capacity to aggregate and revise findings and replicate knowledge. What is needed in industrial societies are diagnostic rubrics facilitating both a physicalistic determination of the subject's memorial and biographical rupture and the capacity for widespread production and dispersal of that data for instrumental use in medico-juridical and other economic contexts (i.e., circulation among insurance companies and governmental agencies). Under the increasingly administrative and institutional assumption of psychological well-being coincident with the nation state's pastoral relationship with its citizenry, Janet's fundamental insights regarding trauma as a pathology of memorial representation would resurface, increasingly allied to an embryonic neurobiological revolution.

Foremost among the current neurobiological perspectives on trauma, van der Kolk's (1996a, 1996b) work partakes in the organicist account of mind, and prevailing discourses of evolutionary psychobiology. What Rose and Abi-Rached (2013) refer to as a "neuromolecular style of thought" retains a number of common principles, including among them structural modularity corresponding to psychological function, an emphasis on neurotransmission, exhaustive correlation of neural states with mental states, and putative observability of material processes. Undergirding these assumptions, and the numerous scientific and clinical research agendas they have spawned, is a conception of the brain as an organ like any other, which is mostly geared for survival. This outlook often models neuropsychological processes on complex, human-created machines (i.e., electric relays, or the various forms of formalized reasoning engineered within the field of artificial intelligence). Under this account, functional pathways specified by location and neurochemical connection perform several important tasks in an organism's interface with the external world, among them to produce signals registering need, maps of the world to satisfy those needs, plans (and adjustment thereof) to achieve potential success in satisfaction, and warnings of danger. Evolutionary understandings of psychobiology find these deeply inscribed capacities in the long history of the human, cognitive archifossil (Meillassoux, 2008). This is, of course, the triune brain – its development from more a reptilian brain (regulating the elemental activities of arousal, sleep, hunger, breathing, defecation/urination), to a mammalian mid-point, the limbic system (regulating the appreciation of danger, emotional-social relevance, and perception/categorization relating thereto), and finally the neocortex (the developmentally late prefrontal cortex regulating temporal perception, censorship, and empathic relation). Central to traumatic suffering is the operation of the reptilian and limbic systems in apprehending danger. Sensory input is routed by the thalamus to the amygdala in order to assess its significance as threat. As LeDoux (2012) observes, if the threat is severe, the amygdala (checking against emotional memory patterns in the hippocampus) sends messages to the hypothalamus to secrete stress hormones to initiate a response via the autonomic nervous system (call for help, fight/flight, freeze); this is the so-called "low road" whose duration is relatively short. The alternative neural pathway – the "high road," which takes longer – extends from the thalamus through the hippocampus and anterior cingulate to the prefrontal cortex, for conscious assessment of danger. In the aftermath of trauma, a person whose functional response has largely been determined through the need for a heightened response will experience symptoms that predetermine his or her response to certain stimuli, which split, divide, or dissociate emotional memory from narrative understanding. Problematically, thus, trauma as PTSD is associated with the segregation of emotional memory in hypermnesia, hyperactivity to stimuli, reexperiencing of the event, and psychic numbing, avoidance, amnesia, and anhedonia. The seeming contradiction between hyperarousal and numbing, which is characteristic of PTSD suffering, is explained in reference to the norms governing said organismic information processing. For sufferers of trauma, the more typical state, wherein emotional responses to stimuli subside once a person is able to make cognitive and narrative sense of the situation, is lost. As van der Kolk (1996a) suggests, "people with PTSD do not seem to serve their usual alerting function – namely as warning signs to take adaptive action" (p. 219). Trauma victims who later encounter intense but neutral stimuli, or that relate in some way to the event, become paralyzed and/or overreactive, which refers back to the dissociation occurring at the event. Under contemporary psychobiological discourse and in neurochemical terms, the distress of extreme arousal is accompanied by the massive release of endogenous, stress-responsive neurohormones (i.e., norepinephrine and epinephrine), serotonin, hormones of the hypothalamic-pituitary-adrenal axis (i.e., cortisol), and endogenous opioids. Some of these substances act as a kind of "brake" on the stress reaction (i.e., cortisol) in order to facilitate goal-directed coping and avoid the fury of a fight/flight response; others, norepinephrine especially, trigger the amygdala's overconsolidation of emotional memory (during the event) and the long-term potentiation of traumatic memory traces. The overstimulation of the amygdala – an anti-Cartesian center of irrational action for neuropsychological discourse – interferes with the integration of external and internal representations. The mammalian evolutionary mechanism, whereby the strength of memory laid down correlates with the strength of the accompanying hormonal stimulation, bears the danger that in dire circumstances the organism's conscious capacity to cope will be overwhelmed (McGaugh, 1992, 2004). Ademac (1991) suggests that the extreme stimulation (indicative of trauma) of the amygdala interferes with the usual operation of the adjacent hippocampal system, which records spatial and temporal elements of experience necessary for explicit or declarative memory. These indelible subcortical emotional memories become etched in the place where healthy, narrative memory would ordinarily reside. This, for van der Kolk (1996b) and others (Pitman & Orr, 1990), constitutes the "black hole" in the memorial life of the trauma victim.

For van der Kolk (1996b) and others (e.g., van der Hart, Steele, Boon, & Brown, 1993) – drawing up the legacy of Janet – the void or black hole of traumatic remembering, with little surprise, relates to the separation of healthy from pathogenic memory. Though recently, strong arguments are made for a specific dissociative subtype for PTSD (Frewen & Lanius, 2015), the dominant, medically oriented discourses around trauma make use of a more conceptually global understanding of dissociation. In this regard, it may help to consider dissociation as the sudden division in two fundamental types of remembering, an interruption of the ordinarily reciprocal, orderly, and complementary systems of declarative or explicit memory and non-declarative or implicit memory. The former refers to memory that allows for the conscious awareness of facts indexing a world, and what can be rendered linguistically and ordered narratively in ways that makes sense or meaning. The latter refers to memory of habits, skills, emotional responses, and somatosensory experience and, for van der Kolk (1996b) and his poststructuralist allies (Caruth, Felman, et al.), this form constitutes an imprinting of the event in its perceptual and sensory literality into the mind of the victim. During conditions of high arousal, the flooding of neurochemical messengers disrupt hippocampal function leaving traumatic memories as dissociated from ordinary functional and biographical memories, but – strangely – indicate a kind of heightened veridicality:

> Memories of trauma may have no verbal (explicit) component whatsoever. Instead, the memories may have been organized on an implicit or perceptual level, without any accompanying narrative about what happened . . . experienced as fragments of the sensory components of the event.
>
> *(van der Kolk, 1996b, p. 287)*

Verbal memory, which is clearly valued in this and the cognitive-behavioral literature in parallel (Brewin, Dalgleish, & Joseph, 1996; Ehlers & Clark, 2000; Follette & Ruzek, 2006; Grey, 2009; Resick & Schnicke, 1993), is set against emotional/somatic/perceptual memory ostensibly *more real* than the verbal memory that would therapeutically supplant it. Such memory is inherently disorganized (i.e., unarticulated in language) as well as being uncondensed, and prone to intensely intrusive effects but also to produce amnesia. The debates surrounding the validity of repressed memories – of childhood sexual abuse, particularly – are well-documented (Loftus, 1993; Williams, 1995); however, as van der Kolk (2014) points out, the practices of research psychologists in privileging decontexualized laboratory settings that cannot replicate the natural environment of the clinic have resulted in an unjustifiable suspicion towards such experience. For our purposes, though, what is more interesting is the hinge between dissociative or traumatic memory and narrative or ordinary memory, and the privileging of the latter as having normative status. In a remarkable statement, van der Kolk (2014) writes that "the traumatic enactment serves no function. In contrast, ordinary memory is adaptive; our stories are flexible and can be modified to fit the circumstances" (p. 182). What manifests is the devaluation of a basic psychobiological process that is intrinsically natural and adaptive in evolutionary terms. Leys (2000) seizes on this fold in van der Kolk's account, noting that psychobiological discourse (and that of Caruth, *infra*) simultaneously holds two contradictory positions: first, that traumatic memories, such as flashbacks or the recovery of repressed memories, are veridical representations of events; and second, that these repetitions or literal replicas of the event somehow stand outside representation. In therapeutic terms, the tradition from Janet, to van der Kolk, to cognitivism is to engage these dissociated literal "flashbulb" memories in the manner of "presentification," integration, and assimilation in biographical meaning-making – which would, as said earlier, falsify the literal etching. Certainly, psychobiological discourse gives away its manifestly antimimetic aspirations, that trauma as an external event occurs to a temporally integrative and constituted subject who in principle may remember or recover functional memory of the event, given effective therapy, working time, etc. Nonetheless, this possibility is always set against, dependent on mimetic blindness to representation, the subject's disappearance into the literal event. Again, similar to Janet's engagement with trauma, at the level of knowledge or epistemology, bearing neither pre-modern coincidence nor classic correspondence with the world, *memory must itself become conceptually traumatized*, split into privileged and devalued counterparts that attempt, but never attain, either realistic narrative concerning the event or the event-in-itself. Pursuant to the epistemological frame of trauma under the analytic of finitude, an excess always remains, even where therapeutic interventions have successfully integrated traumatic memory into narrative memory. The price of gaining narrative distance is the loss of an imprint of literal reality.

For the concealment of a historical ontology of trauma, and ethical practices and discourses that follow in its wake, neurobiological discourse betrays a certain epistemic, antimimetic vision – both methodologically and for the subject's biography – that partakes in the hold of biopower in our current epoch. More generally, Levin (1988), following a Heideggerian path, discerns in our current regime of perception the representational reflections of modern *techne* intent on the lighting of Being as image, as a visible texture, a recording of ontological difference in the harsh but partial light of the surfaces of things seen at a distance. More specifically, in *The Birth of the Clinic*, Foucault (1963/1994) writes of a certain change in the medical gaze from that bound to the density of tissue and symptom to that form of perception that allows, in principle, for a totalizing view of an illness to be taken in:

> In a clinical medicine *to be seen* and *to be spoken* immediately communicate in the manifest truth of the disease of which it is precisely the whole *being*. There is disease only in the element of the visible and therefore statable.
>
> *(p. 95)*

The previous, classical nature of disease, conveying the nature of disease as having an impenetrable essence that may yield sign or symptom is given over to modern medical perception whereby the sign and symptom are collapsed into signifiers that may form statements that correspond with reality. Such positivities attain evidentiary weight as conjoined with medical vision that would open bodies and peer into operationally discrete processes of illness, an emergent probabilistic reasoning, and a new conception of disease not as a force against life, but as a pathological form of life. The shift that would render the bodied illness visible would require a layered viewing of the constituent structural elements for a more comprehensive clinical practice that could isolate – in the convergence of anatomy, chemistry, and technical devices for seeing – the lesion in a certain anatomical site. Gilman (1982) proposes that from the sixteenth century, to understand madness was to visualize it; however, consistent with the aforementioned shift in medical perception and anatomo-clinical isolation, the essentialist rendering of black bile or the surface images of the hysterical *arc de cercle* give way to the inquiries of Gall, Broca, and Ferrier. In our contemporary milieu, neuroimaging, despite expressed concerns over limitations in scale (Logothetis, 2008) and strict localization (Poldrack, 2008), participates in this tyranny of vision, this "illusion that visualization itself has – or could – resolve the questions of the relations between minds and brains" (Rose & Abi-Rached, 2013, p. 81). Nonetheless, not surprisingly, trauma research has taken great pains to demonstrate to us the speechless horror in fMRI imaging – such as decrease of activation in Broca's area and the left hemisphere more generally (Joseph, 1995; van der Kolk, 2014) or dysfunction in the medial prefrontal cortex, amygdala, and hippocampus (Pitman, Shin, & Rauch, 2001) – during experimentally recreated traumatic stimuli. Unremarkably, perhaps, such clinical vision parallels the figuration of selfhood as a putatively realistic, memorial depiction or narration of lived, linear time. The modern clinical gaze, hence, directs its view both to the research activities required to register the statistical regularities of traumatic suffering for populations, and encoded into the discourse of evolutionary mechanism, and also to the particularized biographical existences of individual subjects. In this way, such a gaze connects the antimimetic pole of psychobiological discourse – as a pervasive point of seeing and saying, of collapsing embodied capacities for sight into descriptive statements regarding the deep reality of traumatic pathology – with the traumatic temporality of the suffering subject him or herself. Put differently, the hegemony of seeing – as anatomo-clinical technology – replicates itself in the subject's own experience, where his/her fragmented being-in-time is translated into the Newtonian linearity of a past that may be paradoxically grasped in its non-literality. Pathological time – the sickness in life itself – is diverted from its due course, in salvaging narration, and marked through the grasp of a future that could be known, or at least managed. Forecasting later discussion, such discourses and technologies of remediation and repair undertake such a reaching into the past through a future governed by taming chance and probability (Hacking, 1990) in reference to norms generated by clinical medicine and justified by economic and political outcomes. In this way, the subject's temporal fissure enters into that of the social body, whose need to forensically look into the facts and circumstances, the clinical evidence of past events, takes precedence, and whose political future could only be guaranteed by a subject that would accept the responsibility for therapeutically taking charge of its own health.

Trauma's irreducibility

For the Foucauldian enterprise of seeking *savoir* that exists in the interstices of *connaissance*, Caruth's (1995) work on trauma occupies a unique position because it draws insight from recent neurobiological research (van der Kolk, 1996a), psychoanalytic theory (Lacan, 1981; Laplanche, 1999), and deconstructive literary theory (de Man, 1979). Fundamentally, what Caruth accomplishes is a sort of deconstructive permutation of van der Kolk's neurobiological theory of trauma, wherein overwhelming environmental impingement in the subject's experiential world results in a blinding of representation through the inscription of the literal real as a *différance* between the capacity of representation and its repetition as flashback, nightmare, etc. Indeed, Caruth's (1996) own deconstructive views on language derive from de Man's (1979) notion that the materiality of the signifier severs the speech act, drawn from Kantian disruption in self-presentation. The recurrence of representational discourse, and its Kantian limit, occurs prominently in the contemporary studies of trauma that intertwine social reality, history, and language (Caruth, 1996; Felman, 1995; Laub, 1995), as well as the considerable literature on intergenerational trauma in the context of the Holocaust (Auerhahn & Laub, 1998; Rapoport, 2011). Parallel to the Derridean analysis of restorative temporality, discussed earlier, Caruth (1996) writes that

> in his analysis of Kant, de Man identifies this break specifically as a disruption in the phenomenal self-representation of language, or in the appearance in language of a performative dimension . . . Knowing itself as a grammar or a system of tropes, philosophy must, and yet cannot, fully integrate a dimension of language that not only shows, or represents, but acts . . . It is paradoxically in this deathlike break, or resistance to phenomenal knowledge, that the system will encounter the resistance, de Man suggests, of reference.
>
> *(p. 87)*

Language – in Foucault's (1966/1973) analytic of finitude, Derrida's (1974) deconstruction, or de Man's (1979) performativity – accomplishes its task of representation, of reference, or depiction by the ironic failure of correspondence. Again, citing de Man's work regarding language materially severed from its own empirical and mechanical signification, Caruth (1996) writes that "recognition that direct or phenomenal reference to the world means, paradoxically, the production of a fiction; or, otherwise put, that the reference is radically different from physical law" (p. 76). Language is, thus, intrinsically incapable of accessing reality directly, or in an unmediated fashion that would not create distortion. Traumatic experience, as an emblematic breakdown in language, unable to be symbolized or represented, only attests to unspeakable reality in return of the literal (i.e., "flashbulb," imagistic, or nondeclarative memory).

Provocatively, Caruth (1996) maintains "that history can be grasped only in the very inaccessibility of its occurrence" (p. 18). On the other side of representation – what, for Kant, would be noumenal – Caruth (1996), citing Lacan, situates the "*ethical* relation to the real" (p. 102). The horror of trauma may be found in its nonrepresentation, where the capacities of language are constantly surpassed. Language, thus, rises to its scientific aspirations only in being unlocated in a temporal origin that may be recounted because the groundlessness presumed by correspondence requires it. If the historical origin of representation is actually engaged, actually found, its thought falls into contradiction because it becomes identified with something other than itself, part of the terrain it desires to survey (Foucault, 1966/1973). Still, the return of the literal in the Real – the memorial etching of the incomprehensible event (Caruth, 1995; van der Kolk, 1996b) – strangely mirrors the referential representation that it purports to escape. For Caruth as it is for van der Kolk, the Real is almost "hyperreal," reproducing the event so vividly it escapes representation, as well as the problem that it attempts to theoretically solve. In other words, though Caruth (1996) invokes the Lacanian Real as a coordinate for traumatic experience, the Real becomes not the castration of the subject-in-time but, yet again, the problematic other scene as a Real place, a Real relation. Allied to van der Kolk's neurobiological discourse betraying the conceptual trauma of memory (narrative versus emotional), Caruth's language attains its performative and antimimetically pragmatic function as dependent on its supplementary traumatic potential as the Real truth of the event. Unlike van der Kolk, Caruth (1995), thus, emphasizes the importance of preserving the mimetic incomprehensibility of the traumatic event so as not to disfigure the truth of trauma with narration:

> The transformation of the trauma into a narrative memory that allows the story to be verbalized and communicated, to be integrated into one's own, and others' knowledge of the past, may lose both the precision and the force that characterizes traumatic recall . . . The danger of speech, of integration into the narration of memory, may lie not in what it cannot understand, but in that it understands too much.
>
> *(pp. 153–154)*

Caruth's (and de Man's) interesting formulations concerning referentiality, the natural world, and trauma are potentially disclosive of our ontological predicament. Structural finitude, however, reasserts itself in epistemic descent into ontic sedimentations of clinical discourse, having aspirations towards a more general theory of language and knowledge. Such universalism does not account for more recent genesis of a traumatic subject whose temporal privation of being is internalized and given responsibility for working his/her suffering according to canons of objectivity and scienticity, and the rise of a professional class of clinicians promulgating techniques (pharmacological and behavioral self-monitoring, and self-correction) that bind the subject's truth to assertoric knowledge. Put differently, Caruth appears to largely remain within the modern epistemological structure of finitude, where her theory mimetically compensates for the psychiatric tendency for antimimetic representation. That is to say, Caruth's expansive understanding of trauma tethered to the normative aspirations of clinical theory comes to mostly augment a deconstructive, performative theory of language (Leys, 2000), which obscures the historical specificity of trauma as co-emergent with modern technology.

The neurobiological renderings of trauma and postmodern approaches, as juxtaposed, oddly participate in similar technological concealment of ontologically traumatic subjectivity because they constitute complementary remediations of late Enlightenment obsessions with the problematic status of knowledge for a subject persistently imagined as *potentially immune* or untouched by epistemic failures appearing to emanate from peripheral and intermittent disjunctures between the inside and the outside world. Unlike the ethical ontologies of Heidegger, Levinas, and Lacan, which disperse the subject along the diachronic axis of temporality, admonishing that the subject owes his or her truth, reflexivity, and freedom to non-Being, the psychiatric power/knowledge of van der Kolk (1996a, 1996b) and others continues to assert an integrated, fully formed subject descending from the classical epoch whose powers for vision and antimimetic representation depend on memorial tethering to reality. For these theories, as suggested, memory itself – as existing at one remove from correspondence – is bifurcated into opposite forms of originary contact with the world. The external correlation as narrative, explicit, or declarative memory is, by definition, less literal, *less Real, but more realistic.* Mimetic immersion into the event correlates to memory *more Real, but less realistic.* At root, these memorial theories rest upon biological formulations – the legacy of Charcot, Crile, and Cannon – positing a neuroanatomical and neurochemical substrate wherein lies the juncture between adaptive and non-adaptive experience, which can only be known retrospectively or prospectively as what will be or will have been necessary for the flourishing state, and the well-being of its citizenry. The homeostatic theories around arousal regulation and memorial encoding, thus, implicitly hinge on a nature/culture binary, paralleling mimesis and antimimesis, respectively. Without a doubt, for psychiatric and psychological technology – i.e., presentification to cognitive-processing – what is privileged is the antimimetic realism of the cultural world over the natural world, a realism that allows the subject to enframe his/her own experiences as biographical memory. *Trauma is the pathological breakdown in realistic representation, to be remediated through civilizing narration.* And, what is "civilizing" occurs always as division within societies as institutions – political, economic, juridical, and medical – come to constitute their programmatic aims in light of the future. Caruth (1995) and the postmoderns, relying on exactly the same distinction – the literality of emotional memory as a black hole or void in representation – recapitulate the same swirling vortex of mimesis around antimimesis, yet constitute the subject of trauma as iconic for their perspectives on language; however, more importantly is the sense that the truth of trauma, of the Real, exists in the spaces between representation and must be indexed in cultural practices preserving such incomprehensibility. This comes to fore, in particular, with reference to Holocaust testimony: "The gaping, vertiginous black hole of the unmentionable years . . . Parents explained nothing, children asked nothing . . . It was a silence that swallowed up the past, all the past, the past before death, before destruction" (Fresco, 1984, pp. 417–427). These discourses around the impossibility of representation that do not rely on their own erasure also privilege the postmodern subject of trauma as a photographic negative of the psychological one – *the pathological breakdown in representation is constitutive of a marginal subject, who must be cared for as a hole in the individual and collective memory.* Such discourses – though not calling for the individual remediation seen in many therapies – position themselves as archivists and caretakers for the monuments of memory left through the Holocaust, and other genocides and forms of cultural and historical violence. While the later Caruth's (2013) understanding of trauma almost reaches the ontological structure of traumatic subjectivity (for instance, her discussion of the archival dimensions of contemporary history), her overall project yields to the technological march of psychiatric normalization, of privileging an antimimetic reflexivity that must constantly defer/differ from its mimetic absorption. For both van der Kolk and Caruth, the subject's ethical relation to itself involves the management of the spatialized literal, Real – the repetition of pathologized traumatic memory in forms that appear to contaminate or infect the subject's own fragile powers of representation.

Note

1 Heidegger (1975), contra Foucault, would assert that his fundamental ontology was partially, but not fully, anticipated in pre-Socratic thought. As one would expect, Foucault consistently holds to a more rigorously historicist framework where ontological modes of disclosure, and their associated epistemes, change radically through time.

References

Ademac, R. E. (1991). Normal and abnormal limbic system mechanisms of emotive biasing. In K. E. Livingston (Ed.), *Limbic mechanisms* (pp. 405–456). New York, NY: Plenum Press.

American Psychiatric Association. (2013). *Diagnostic and statistical manual of mental disorders* (5th ed.). Washington, DC: Author.

Auerhahn, N. C., & Laub, D. (1998). The primal scene of atrocity: The dynamic interplay between knowledge and fantasy of the holocaust in children of survivors. *Psychoanalytic Psychology, 15*(3), 360–377.

Berkeley, G. (1998). *A treatise concerning the principles of human knowledge* (J. Dancy, Ed.). Oxford, UK: Oxford University Press. (Original work published 1710)

Borch-Jacobsen, M. (1988). *The Freudian subject* (C. Porter, Trans.). Stanford, CA: Stanford University Press.

Breuer, J., & Freud, S. (2000). *Studies on hysteria* (J. Strachey, Trans.). New York, NY: Basic Books. (Original work published 1895)

Brewin, C. R., Dalgleish, T., & Joseph, S. (1996). A dual-representation theory of post-traumatic stress disorder. *Psychological Review, 106*, 670–686.

Brothers, D. (2008). *Toward a psychology of uncertainty: Trauma-centered psychoanalysis.* New York, NY: The Analytic Press.

Brown, W. (1920). The revival of emotional memories and its therapeutic value. *British Medical Journal, 1*(1), 16–19.

Brown, W. (1923). *Talks on psychotherapy.* London, UK: University of London Press.

Cannon, W. B. (1914). The interrelations of emotions as suggested by recent physiological research. *American Journal of Psychiatry, 25,* 256–281.

Cannon, W. B. (1927). *Bodily changes in pain, hunger, fear and rage.* New York, NY: D. Appleton & Company.

Cannon, W. B. (1942). "Voodoo" death. *American Anthropologist, 44,* 169–181.

Caruth, C. (1995). Recapturing the past: Introduction. In C. Caruth (Ed.), *Trauma: Explorations in memory* (pp. 151–157). Baltimore, MD: Johns Hopkins University Press.

Caruth, C. (1996). *Unclaimed experience: Trauma, narrative, and history.* Baltimore, MD: Johns Hopkins University Press.

Caruth, C. (2002). An interview with Jean Laplanche. In L. Belau & P. Ramadanovic (Eds.), *Topologies of trauma: Essays on the limit of knowledge and memory* (pp. 101–125). New York, NY: The Other Press.

Caruth, C. (2013). *Literature in the ashes of history.* Baltimore, MD: Johns Hopkins University Press.

Charcot, J. (1889). *Clinical lectures on diseases of the nervous system delivered at the infirmary of la Salpêtrière* (Vol. 3, T. Savill, Trans.). London, UK: New Syndenham Society.

Chertoff, J. (1998). Psychodynamic assessment and treatment of traumatized patients. *The Journal of Psychotherapy Practice and Research, 7*(1), 35–46.

Crile, G. W. (1899). *An experimental research into surgical shock.* Philadelphia, PA: Lippincott.

Cushman, P. (1990). Why the self is empty: Toward a historically situated psychology. *American Psychologist, 45*(5), 599–611.

Cushman, P. (1995). *Constructing the self, constructing America: A cultural history of psychotherapy.* Boston, MA: Da Capo Press.

Danziger, K. (1997). *Naming the mind: How psychology found its language.* London, UK: Sage.

Danziger, K. (2008). *Marking the mind: A history of memory.* Cambridge, UK: Cambridge University Press.

Deleuze, G. (1992). Postscript on societies of control. *October, 59,* 3–7.

Deleuze, G., & Guattari, F. (1983). *Anti-Oedipus: Capitalism and schizophrenia* (R. Hurley, M. Seem, & H. Lane, Trans.). Minneapolis: University of Minnesota Press. (Original work published 1972)

Deleuze, G., & Guattari, F. (1987). *A thousand plateaus: Capitalism and schizophrenia* (B. Massumi, Trans.). Minneapolis: University of Minnesota Press.

de Man, P. (1979). *Allegories of reading: Figural language in Rousseau, Nietzsche, Rilke, and Proust.* New Haven, CT: Yale University Press.

Dennett, D. (1978). *Brainstorms: Philosophical essays on mind and psychology.* Cambridge, MA: MIT Press.

Derrida, J. (1974). *Of grammatology* (G. Spivak, Trans.). Baltimore, MD: Johns Hopkins University Press.

Descartes, R. (1954). *Philosophical writings, a selection* (E. Anscombe & P. T. Geach, Trans.). Indianapolis, IN: Bobbs-Merrill. (Original work published 1641)

Dreyfus, H., & Rabinow, P. (1983). *Michel Foucault: Beyond structuralism and hermeneutics.* Chicago, IL: University of Chicago Press.

Dreyfus, H., & Rubin, J. (1991). Kierkegaard, division II, and later Heidegger. In H. Dreyfus (Ed.), *Being-in-the-world: A commentary on Heidegger's Being and Time, division I* (pp. 283–340). Cambridge, MA: MIT Press.

Ebbinghaus, H. (1913). *Memory: A contribution to experimental psychology* (H. A. Ruger & C. E. Bussenius, Trans.). New York, NY: Teachers College, Columbia University. (Original work published 1885)

Ehlers, A., & Clark, D. M. (2000). A cognitive model of persistent posttraumatic stress disorder. *Behavior Research and Therapy, 38,* 319–345.

Ellenberger, H. (1970). *The discovery of the unconscious: The history and evolution of dynamic psychiatry.* New York, NY: Basic Books.

Erichsen, J. E. (1859). *The science and art of surgery.* Philadelphia, PA: Blanchard and Lea.

Erichsen, J. E. (1866). *On railway and other injuries of the nervous system.* London, UK: Wallace and Maberly.

Fairbairn, W. R. D. (1952). *An object-relations theory of the personality.* New York, NY: Basic Books.

Felman, S. (1995). Education and crisis, or the vicissitudes of teaching. In C. Caruth (Ed.), *Trauma: Explorations in memory* (pp. 13–60). Baltimore, MD: Johns Hopkins University Press.

Ferenczi, S. (1933). Confusion of tongues between adults and the child. In M. Balint (Ed.), *Final contributions to the problems and methods of psychoanalysis* (pp. 156–167). New York, NY: Brunner/Mazel.

Ferenczi, S. (1995). *The clinical diary of Sándor Ferenczi* (J. Dupont, Ed.). Cambridge, MA: Harvard University Press.

Fink, B. (1997). *A clinical introduction to Lacanian psychoanalysis: Theory and technique.* Cambridge, MA: Harvard University Press.

Fink, B. (2004). *Lacan to the letter: Reading Écrits closely.* Minneapolis: University of Minnesota Press.

Follette, V., & Ruzek, J. (Eds.). (2006). *Cognitive-behavioral therapies for trauma.* New York, NY: Guilford.

Foucault, M. (1972). *The archaeology of knowledge, & the discourse on language* (A. M. Sheridan, Trans.). New York, NY: Pantheon Books. (Original work published 1969)

Foucault, M. (1973). *The order of things: An archaeology of the human sciences* (A. Sheridan, Trans.). New York, NY: Vintage. (Original work published 1966)

Foucault, M. (1980). Truth and power. In C. Gordon (Ed.), *Power/Knowledge: Selected interviews and other writings* (pp. 109–133). New York, NY: Pantheon.

Foucault, M. (1983). The subject and power. In H. Dreyfus & P. Rabinow (Eds.), *Michel Foucault: Beyond structuralism and hermeneutics* (pp. 208–226). Chicago, IL: University of Chicago Press.

Foucault, M. (1988). Technologies of self. In L. H. Martin, H. Gutman, & P. H. Hutton (Eds.), *Technologies of the self: A seminar with Michel Foucault* (pp. 16–49). Amherst: University of Massachusetts Press.

Foucault, M. (1990). *Politics, philosophy, culture: Selected interviews and other writings, 1977–1984* (A. Sheridan, Trans.). New York, NY: Routledge.

Foucault, M. (1994). *The birth of the clinic: An archaeology of medical perception* (A. Sheridan, Trans.). New York, NY: Vintage. (Original work published 1963)

Foucault, M. (1995). *Discipline and punish: The birth of the prison* (A. Sheridan, Trans.). New York, NY: Vintage. (Original work published 1975)

Foucault, M. (2003). *"Society must be defended": Lectures at the Collège de France 1975–1976* (A. Fontana, Trans.). New York, NY: Picador.

Foucault, M. (2004). *Abnormal: Lectures at the Collège de France 1975–1976* (G. Burchell, Trans.). New York, NY: Picador.

Foucault, M. (2008). *The birth of biopolitics: Lectures at the Collège de France 1978–1979* (G. Burchell, Trans.). New York, NY: Palgrave.

Foucault, M. (2009). *Security, territory, population: Lectures at the Collège de France 1977–1978* (G. Burchell, Trans.). New York, NY: Picador.

Fresco, N. (1984). Remembering the unknown. *International Review of Psycho-Analysis, 11,* 417–427. Retrieved from http://www.anti-rev.org/textes/Fresco84a/

Freud, A. (1966). *The ego and the mechanisms of defence*. London, UK: Karnac. (Original work published 1936)

Freud, A. (1967). Comments on trauma. In S. S. Furst (Ed.), *Psychic trauma* (pp. 233–245). New York, NY: Basic Books.

Freud, S. (1954). Project for a scientific psychology (J. Strachey, Trans.). In M. Bonaparte, A. Freud, & E. Kris (Eds.), *The origins of psycho-analysis* (pp. 347–466). New York, NY: Basic Books. (Original work published 1895)

Freud, S. (1955). A child is being beaten (A contribution to the study of the origin of sexual perversions). In J. Strachey (Ed. & Trans.), *The standard edition of the complete psychological works of Sigmund Freud* (Vol. 17, pp. 175–204). London, UK: Hogarth Press. (Original work published 1919)

Freud, S. (1957). Repression. In J. Strachey (Ed. & Trans.), *The standard edition of the complete psychological works of Sigmund Freud* (Vol. 14, pp. 141–158). London, UK: Hogarth Press. (Original work published 1915)

Freud, S. (1958). Remembering, repeating, and working-through. In J. Strachey (Ed. & Trans.), *The standard edition of the complete psychological works of Sigmund Freud* (Vol. 12, pp. 145–156). London, UK: Hogarth Press. (Original work published 1914)

Freud, S. (1959a). From the history of an infantile neurosis (A. Strachey & J. Strachey, Trans.). In *Collected papers* (Vol. 3, pp. 473–605). New York, NY: Basic Books. (Original work published 1918)

Freud, S. (1959b). Inhibitions, symptoms, and anxiety. In J. Strachey (Ed. & Trans.), *The standard edition of the complete psychological works of Sigmund Freud* (Vol. 20, pp. 75–174). London, UK: Hogarth Press. (Original work published 1926)

Freud, S. (1961a). *Beyond the pleasure principle* (J. Strachey, Trans.). New York, NY: Norton. (Original work published 1920)

Freud, S. (1961b). The interpretation of dreams. In J. Strachey (Ed. & Trans.), *The standard edition of the complete psychological works of Sigmund Freud* (Vol. 4). London, UK: Hogarth Press. (Original work published 1900)

Freud, S. (1962a). The neuro-psychoses of defence. In J. Strachey (Ed. & Trans.), *The standard edition of the complete psychological works of Sigmund Freud* (Vol. 3, pp. 41–61). London, UK: Hogarth Press. (Original work published 1894)

Freud, S. (1962b). Further remarks on the neuro-psychoses of defence. In J. Strachey (Ed. & Trans.), *The standard edition of the complete psychological works of Sigmund Freud* (Vol. 3, pp. 157–185). London, UK: Hogarth Press. (Original work published 1896)

Freud, S. (1963a). Introductory lectures on psycho-analysis (Parts I and II). In J. Strachey (Ed. & Trans.), *The standard edition of the complete psychological works of Sigmund Freud* (Vol. 15). London, UK: Hogarth Press. (Original work published 1915–16)

Freud, S. (1963b). Introductory lectures on psycho-analysis (Part III). In J. Strachey (Ed. & Trans.), *The standard edition of the complete psychological works of Sigmund Freud* (Vol. 16). London, UK: Hogarth Press. (Original work published 1916–17)

Freud, S. (1964a). An outline of psycho-analysis. In J. Strachey (Ed. & Trans.), *The standard edition of the complete psychological works of Sigmund Freud* (Vol. 23, pp. 139–208). London, UK: Hogarth Press. (Original work published 1940)

Freud, S. (1964b). Constructions in analysis. In J. Strachey (Ed. & Trans.), *The standard edition of the complete psychological works of Sigmund Freud* (Vol. 23, pp. 256–269). London, UK: Hogarth Press. (Original work published 1937)

Freud, S. (1966). Extracts from the Fliess papers. In J. Strachey (Ed. & Trans.), *The standard edition of the complete psychological works of Sigmund Freud* (Vol. 1, pp. 175–279). London, UK: Hogarth Press. (Original work published 1897)

Freud, S. (2000). *Three essays on sexuality* (J. Strachey, Trans.). New York, NY: Basic. (Original work published 1905)

Frewen, P., & Lanius, R. (2015). *Healing the traumatized self: Consciousness, neuroscience, treatment.* New York, NY: Norton.

Gilman, S. (1982). *Seeing the insane:* New York, NY: Wiley.

Goetz, C. G., Bonduelle, M., & Gelfand, T. (1995). *Charcot: Constructing neurology.* Oxford, UK: Oxford University Press.

Goldberg, A. (1980). Self psychology and the distinctiveness of psychotherapy. *International Journal of Psychoanalytic Psychotherapy, 8,* 57–70.

Grey, N. (2009). *A casebook of cognitive therapy for traumatic stress reactions.* London, UK: Routledge.

Hacking, I. (1990). *The taming of chance.* Cambridge, UK: Cambridge University Press.

Hacking, I. (1995). *Rewriting the soul: Multiple personality and the sciences of memory.* Princeton, NJ: Princeton University Press.

Hacking, I. (1996). Memory sciences, memory politics. In P. Antze & M. Lambek (Eds.), *Tense past: Cultural essays in trauma and memory* (pp. 67–88). London, UK: Routledge.

Hacking, I. (2002). *Historical ontology.* Cambridge, MA: Harvard University Press.

Han, B. (1998). *Foucault's critical project: Between the transcendental and the historical* (E. Pile, Trans.). Stanford, CA: Stanford University Press.

Han, B. (2005). The analytic of finitude and the history of subjectivity. In G. Gutting (Ed.), *The Cambridge companion to Foucault* (2nd ed., pp. 176–209). Cambridge, UK: Cambridge University Press.

Harrington, R. (2001). The railway accident: Trains, trauma, and technological crisis in nineteenth-century Britain. In M. Micale & P. Lerner (Eds.), *Traumatic pasts: History, psychiatry, and trauma in the modern age, 1870–1930* (pp. 31–56). Cambridge, UK: Cambridge University Press.

Hartmann, H. (1955). *Essays on ego psychology.* New York, NY: International Universities Press.

Hartmann, H., Kris, E., & Loewenstein, R. (1951). Some psychoanalytic comments on "culture and personality." In G. Wilbur & W. Muensterberger (Eds.), *Psychoanalysis and culture* (pp. 3–31). New York, NY: International Universities Press.

Heidegger, M. (1962). *Being and time* (J. Macquarrie & E. Robinson, Trans.). San Francisco, CA: Harper. (Original work published 1927)

Heidegger, M. (1968). *What is called thinking* (J. G. Gray, Trans.). New York, NY: Harper. (Original work published 1954)

Heidegger, M. (1971a). The origin of the work of art. In A. Hofstadter (Trans.), *Poetry, language, thought* (pp. 15–76). New York, NY: Harper.

Heidegger, M. (1971b). What are poets for? In A. Hofstadter (Trans.), *Poetry, language, thought* (pp. 87–139). New York, NY: Harper.

Heidegger, M. (1975). *Early Greek thinking: The dawn of Western philosophy* (D. F. Krell & F. A. Capuzzi, Trans.). San Francisco, CA: Harper.

Heidegger, M. (1977a). The question concerning technology. In W. Lovitt (Trans.), *The question concerning technology, and other essays* (pp. 3–35). New York, NY: Harper.

Heidegger, M. (1977b). The word of Nietzsche: "God is dead". In W. Lovitt (Trans.), *The question concerning technology, and other essays* (pp. 53–112). New York, NY: Harper.

Heidegger, M. (1977c). The age of the world picture. In W. Lovitt (Trans.), *The question concerning technology, and other essays* (pp. 115–154). New York, NY: Harper.

Heidegger, M. (1993). On the essence of truth (J. Sallis, Trans.). In D. Krell (Ed.), *Basic writings: From Being and Time (1927) to The Task of Thinking (1964)* (pp. 115–138). New York, NY: HarperCollins.

Herman, J. (1992). *Trauma and recovery.* New York, NY: Basic Books.

Horney, K. (1937). *The neurotic personality of our time.* New York, NY: Basic Books.

Hoy, D. C. (2009). *The time of our lives: A critical history of temporality.* Cambridge, MA: MIT Press.

Hume, D. (1975). *Enquiries concerning human understanding and concerning the principle of morals* (L. A. Selby-Bigge, Ed.). Oxford, UK: Clarendon Press. (Original work published 1748)

Jackson, J. H. (1958). *Selected writings of John Hughlings Jackson: Vol. 2* (J. Taylor, Ed.). New York, NY: Basic. (Original work published 1931)

Janet, P. (1925). *Psychological healing: Vol. 1.* New York, NY: Macmillan.

Joseph, R. (1995). *The right brain and the unconscious.* New York, NY: Plenum.

Kant, I. (2007). *Critique of pure reason* (M. Weigelt, Trans.). New York, NY: Penguin. (Original work published 1781)

Kardiner, A. (1941). *The traumatic neuroses of war.* Washington, DC: National Research Council.

Kohut, H. (1971). *Analysis of the self.* New York, NY: International Universities Press.

Kohut, H. (1984). *How does analysis cure?* Chicago, IL: University of Chicago Press.

Kohut, H. (2011a). Four basic concepts in self psychology. In P. H. Ornstein (Ed.), *The search for the self: Selected writings of Heinz Kohut* (Vol. 4, pp. 447–470). London, UK: Karnac.

Kohut, H. (2011b). On empathy. In P. H. Ornstein (Ed.), *The search for the self: Selected writings of Heinz Kohut* (Vol. 4, pp. 525–535). London, UK: Karnac.

Lacan, J. (1981). *The four fundamental concepts of psycho-analysis* (A. Sheridan, Trans.). New York, NY: Norton.

Lacan, J. (1988a). *The seminar of Jacques Lacan: Book I. Freud's papers on technique, 1953–1954* (R. Grigg, Trans.). New York, NY: Norton.

Lacan, J. (1988b). *The seminar of Jacques Lacan: Book II. Freud's papers on technique, 1954–1955* (S. Tomaselli, Trans.). New York, NY: Norton.

Lacan, J. (2006a). The function and field of speech and language in psychoanalysis (B. Fink, Trans.). In *Écrits: The first complete edition in English* (pp. 197–265). New York, NY: Norton. (Original work published 1966)

Lacan, J. (2006b). The subversion of the subject and the dialectic of desire (B. Fink, Trans.). In *Écrits: The first complete edition in English* (pp. 671–702). New York, NY: Norton. (Original work published 1966)

Laing, R. D. (1960). *The divided self: An existential study in sanity and madness.* London, UK: Penguin.

Laplanche, J. (1976). *Life and death in psychoanalysis* (J. Mehlman, Trans.). Baltimore, MD: Johns Hopkins University Press.

Laplanche, J. (1999). *Essays on otherness.* London, UK: Routledge.

Laub, D. (1995). Truth and testimony. In C. Caruth (Ed.), *Trauma: Explorations in memory* (pp. 61–75). Baltimore, MD: Johns Hopkins University Press.

Layton, L. (1990). A deconstruction of Kohut's concept of the self. *Contemporary Psychoanalysis, 26*(3), 420–429.

LeDoux, J. (2012). Rethinking the emotional brain. *Neuron, 73*(4), 653–676.

Levin, D. M. (1988). *The opening of vision: Nihilism and the postmodern situation.* London, UK: Routledge.

Leys, R. (2000). *Trauma: A genealogy.* Chicago, IL: University of Chicago Press.

Locke, J. (1975). *An essay concerning human understanding.* Oxford, UK: Clarendon. (Original work published 1690)

Loftus, E. F. (1993). The reality of repressed memories. *American Psychologist, 48*(5), 518–537.

Logothetis, N. K. (2008). What we can do and what we cannot do with fMRI. *Nature, 453*, 869–878.

McDougal, W. (1920). The revival of emotional memories and its therapeutic value. *British Medical Journal, 1*(1), 23–29.

McGaugh, J. L. (1992). Affect, neuromodulatory systems, and memory storage. *Annual Review of Neuroscience, 2*, 255–287.

McGaugh, J. L. (2004). The amygdala modulates the consolidation of memories of emotionally arousing experiences. *Annual Review of Neuroscience, 27,* 1–28.

Meillassoux, Q. (2008). *After finitude: An essay on the necessity of contingency* (R. Brassier, Trans.). London, UK: Continuum.

Micale, M. (2001). Jean-Martin Charcot and *les névroses traumatiques*: From medicine to culture in French trauma theory of the late nineteenth century. In M. Micale & P. Lerner (Eds.), *Traumatic pasts: History, psychiatry, and trauma in the modern age, 1870–1930* (pp. 115–139). Cambridge, UK: Cambridge University Press.

Mieli, P. (2001). On trauma: A Freudian perspective. In M. Dimen & A. Harris (Eds.), *Storms in her head: Freud and the construction of hysteria* (pp. 265–280). New York, NY: Other Press.

Page, H. W. (1883). *Injuries of the spine and spinal cord without apparent mechanical lesion, and nervous shock, in their surgical and medico-legal aspects.* London, UK: Churchill.

Pitman, R. K., & Orr, S. (1990). The black hole of trauma. *Biological Psychiatry, 26,* 221–223.

Pitman, R. K., Shin, L. M., & Rauch, S. L. (2001). Investigating the pathogenesis of post-traumatic stress disorder with neuroimaging. *Journal of Clinical Psychiatry, 62*(17), 47–54.

Poldrack, R. A. (2008). The role of fMRI in cognitive neuroscience: Where do we stand? *Current Opinion in Neurobiology, 18*(2), 223–237.

Prince, M. (1905). *The dissociation of the personality: A biographical study in abnormal psychology.* New York, NY: Longmans, Green.

Quinodoz, J.-M. (2005). *Reading Freud: A chronological exploration of Freud's writings* (D. Alcorn, Trans.). London, UK: Routledge.

Rabinow, P., & Rose, N. (2016). Biopower today. In V. W. Cisney & N. Morar (Eds.), *Biopower: Foucault and beyond* (pp. 297–325). Chicago, IL: University of Chicago Press.

Rapoport, E. (2011). Growing up in the shadow of the holocaust: A psychoanalyst addresses intergenerational transmission of trauma in her family. *Issues in Psychoanalytic Psychology, 33,* 43–49.

Reisner, G. (2014). The compulsion to repeat as death-in-life. *Psychoanalytic Review, 101*(1), 39–69.

Resick, P. A., & Schnicke, M. K. (1993). *Cognitive processing therapy for rape victims: A treatment manual.* Newbury Park, CA: Sage.

Ribot, T. A. (1882). *Diseases of the memory: An essay in the positive psychology.* London, UK: Kegan Paul, Trench.

Ricoeur, P. (1977). *Freud and philosophy: An essay on interpretation* (D. Savage, Trans.). New Haven, CT: Yale University Press.

Rivers, W. H. R. (1920). *Instinct and the unconscious: A contribution to a biological theory of the psycho-neuroses.* Cambridge, UK: Cambridge University Press.

Rose, N., & Abi-Rached, J. M. (2013). *Neuro: The new brain science and the management of the mind.* Princeton, NJ: Princeton University Press.

Roth, M. S. (2001). Falling into history. In M. Dimen & A. Harris (Eds.), *Storms in her head: Freud and the construction of hysteria* (pp. 169–184). New York, NY: Other Press.

Rousseau, J.-J. (2008). *Confessions* (A. Scholar, Trans.). Oxford, UK: Oxford University Press. (Original work published 1782)

Schore, A. (2002). Advances in neuropsychoanalysis, attachment theory, and trauma research: Implications for self psychology. *Psychoanalytic Inquiry, 22,* 433–484.

Scott, W. (1990). PTSD in DSM-III: A case in the politics of diagnosis and disease. *Social Problems, 37,* 294–310.

Soler, C. (2016). *Lacanian affects: The function of affect in Lacan's work* (B. Fink, Trans.). London, UK: Routledge.

Spencer, H. (1855). *Principles of psychology.* London, UK: Longman, Brown, Green & Longmans.

Stolorow, R. (2011). *World, affectivity, trauma: Heidegger and post-Cartesian psychoanalysis.* New York, NY: Routledge.

Taylor, C. (1989). *Sources of the self: The making of the modern identity.* Cambridge, MA: Harvard University Press.

van der Hart, O., Steele, K., Boon, S., & Brown, P. (1993). The treatment of traumatic memories: Synthesis, realization, and integration. *Dissociation, 6,* 162–180.

van der Kolk, B. A. (1996a). The body keeps the score: Approaches to the psychobiology of posttraumatic stress disorder. In B. van der Kolk, A. McFarlane, & L. Weisath (Eds.), *Traumatic stress: The effects of overwhelming experience on mind, body, and society* (pp. 214–241). New York, NY: Guilford.

van der Kolk, B. A. (1996b). Trauma and memory. In B. van der Kolk, A. McFarlane, & L. Weisath (Eds.), *Traumatic stress: The effects of overwhelming experience on mind, body, and society* (pp. 279–302). New York, NY: Guilford.

van der Kolk, B. (2014). *The body keeps the score: Brain, mind, and body in the healing of trauma.* New York, NY: Penguin.

Williams, L. M. (1995). Recovered memories of abuse in women with documented child sexual victimization histories. *Journal of Traumatic Stress, 8*(4), 649–673.

Winnicott, D. (1965). *The maturational process and the facilitating environment.* New York, NY: International University Press.

Wolf, E. S. (1995). Psychic trauma: A view from self psychology. *Canadian Journal of Psychoanalysis, 3*(2), 203–222.

Young, A. (1995). *The harmony of illusions: Inventing post-traumatic stress disorder.* Princeton, NJ: Princeton University Press.

Žižek, S. (1999). *The ticklish subject: The absent centre of political ontology.* London, UK: Verso.

4

TRAUMA, SUBJECTIVITY, AND BIOPOLITICS

Biopolitics, governmentality, and security

For an inquiry into the technological concealment of the modern subject's ostensibly fragmented temporality, it will be necessary to expand upon the forms of biopower prevailing in contemporary post-industrial societies in order to excavate the strategies of governance of this subject's being-in-time. Since Foucault's (2003, 2008, 2009) initial exploration of these themes, biopower and biopolitics have become *au courant* in continental thought (Agamben, 1998; Esposito, 2008, 2009, 2011; Hardt & Negri, 2000); however, arguably, Foucault's own accounts remain unparalleled in their depth. In his Collège de France lecture *Society Must be Defended*, Foucault (2003) opens with the suggestion that "in order to make a concrete analysis of power relations, we must abandon the juridical model of sovereignty" (p. 265). Instead of becoming mesmerized by an understanding of power wherein an ideal, juridico-political subject would have its transparent capacities limited through political or economic compromise, Foucault advocates that we continue to focus on the more contemporary political relation of the subject and knowledge. Biopower – as a historically emergent form of mediation among the triad of power, right, and truth – may be distinguished from both traditional concepts of sovereign power (the deprivation of life, liberty, and property through divine right or social contract) and disciplinary power (the production of certain individuals through the separation, serialization, and surveillance of bodies). Rather, this newer form of power, touched on previously, infiltrates and embeds itself in existing disciplinary technologies, and inhabits ethical forms of self-relation or technologies of self. Importantly, however, what distinguishes biopower is that it is addressed to human life itself, *en masse*, in the aggregate. Biopower appears in parallel (as radicalized, perhaps) to what Deleuze (1992) calls "societies of control," where hyper-rapid free-floating control replaces the closed enclosures of the barracks, schools, hospitals, and asylums. Against these analogical spaces, where the referential point is always the metaphorical power of the prison to form the subject into predetermined molds of action and thought, this form of power operates to track metastatic risk. As Deleuze (1992) writes, "Individuals have become '*dividuals*,' and masses, samples, data, markets . . . [substituting] for the individual body or numerical body the code of the 'dividual' material to be controlled" (pp. 5–7). As recounted by Foucault (1976/1990), and others such as Hacking (2016), such a shift begins in the late eighteenth century with the keeping of statistical records regarding birth rates and mortality, incidence of disease, and accidents. The natural realities so targeted involve the health, hygiene, and well-being of populations (rather than discrete bodies or selves) as the various coordinates of these functional concerns extend over chronological time. What preoccupies Foucault (1976/1990) in this relatively early expression as a guiding principle for biopower is the regularization of certain preferences for the welfare of said populations, an established equilibrium resistant to accidents, random events, and preventable illnesses. Any particular steady state would require a baseline; however, as always, such normalization of conduct, or states of mind, affect, or body, is addressed by body-organism institutions (such as asylums or hospitals) and population-biological process regulatory mechanisms (such as medical and psy-discourses). Moreover, a nuance of this relationship would be that individual subjects would increasingly become located according to their place within knowledge extending beyond the early Enlightenment or classical order (i.e., natural history) into time itself, as the human sciences – tethered to biology for their operative principles – would submit the organisms' maladies and maladjustments to their own histories. Then, it would be of the order of such logic to expend such institutional energies around projects – using ever-expanding capacities to collate data and produce knowledge – to attempt to prevent the loss of health and well-being, as a predictive "archiving of the future" (Anthanasiou, 2003, p. 144). Just as Foucault discusses regarding sexuality, and as will be elaborated, traumatic temporality intersects both the metrics of populations and the specific techniques of intervention in the individual life; the biographies of populations can be said to contain contaminants and exteriorities that may be defended, or guarded against.

Biopower may seem at first glance to bear the vestigial aims or functions of sovereign power, manifesting the stamp of domination; however, this view is to miss not only its historical contingency but also its necessity. In his Collège de France lecture *Security, Territory, Population*, Foucault (2009) traces in some detail what he calls the "art of government," which arises in the sixteenth century. This newer form of governmental rationality (*raison d'État*) would have ever-tenuous contact with older forms of legitimacy premised on divinely ordained, or natural, law. Rather, such *raison d'État* would have a different relationship to time and history:

> With this analysis of *raison d'État* we see the emergence of a historical political temporality with specific characteristics in comparison with the

temporality that dominated the thought of the Middle ages, and even the Renaissance, because it is an indefinite temporality, the temporality of a government that is both never-ending and conservative.

(Foucault, 2009, p. 259)

Consequently, the state's legitimacy is no longer tied to the salvation of subjects in the hereafter, but instead on a form of ever-renewing and changing necessity. Nor does such a state mostly find its legitimacy in safeguarding its inhabitants' fundamental rights against encroachment on liberty. The installation of governmentality within political economy would give the question of legitimacy over to utilitarian effects of policy, of knowledge, or technical apparatus – all of which involve the vitality of the governed. As Foucault (2008) would later write, "there will be either success or failure; success or failure rather than legitimacy or illegitimacy, now become the criteria of governmental action" (p. 16). At the same time, a reflexivity accompanies this inflection on the legitimate basis of governing – which does not any longer reference the cosmic or divine orders – always indexing the internal limitations of the effects of its practice and policies. Its own rational and instrumental consistency, then, becomes its principal concern.

In more contemporary terms, the history of biopower further intersects with both the question of legitimacy during the hegemony of liberal and neo-liberal governmentality and the position of the subject. As Foucault (2008) goes on to argue, liberalism – as a complex politico-economic formation – becomes a correlate for both intervention in and nurturing of the natural and spontaneous market mechanisms that provide a standard for correctness in governmental action. As such, these actions/locations become sites for the production of knowledge as truth (veridiction) immanent to a functional situation. For the modern subject, who must flourish or decline, agency – as a traditionally protected form of civic personhood in various guises – must be addressed under newer conditions. Freedom, thus, becomes not a universal, naturalized, and preexistent abstract right but a measure of the actual relations between procedures of governance and the governed. Increasingly, agency is operationally constituted by management of institutional apparatuses that address overtly economic issues such as free trade versus protectionism and anti-monopoly interventions but also the fostering of "security" as a calculative principle. For instance, contemporary public health campaigns – oriented to populations at risk – raise awareness concerning the prevalence of autistic spectrum disorders, sexually transmitted diseases, or diabetes. Foucault (2008) avers that mechanisms of control that protect liberal and neo-liberal subjects against disease, poverty, criminality, etc. are no longer counter-forces to freedom but the source of freedom itself, which represents a stark departure from classical understandings of political and economic liberties. One fallout from the turn from liberalism to neo-liberalism – apart obviously from the radicalization of the former project, the minimization of official state intervention, monetarism, etc. – is an epistemological transformation in the field of economics. The subject, rather than being subsumed as a mediating factor in the play of capital and production or idealized as one who pursues his/her own interests, is cast a new form of *homo economicus* – one who is a rational actor, a self-entrepreneur who produces a return on his/her own possessions, especially the capital of his/her own being, the body, the mind, the soul. Consequently, this permits an economic analysis of virtually everything this subject may commit his/her possibilities towards – family time, education, marriage, etc. What cannot be understood, or analyzed, however, would concern the seemingly random, or ordered but opaque, events coming to the actor from without his or her sphere of agentic possession. In other words, disease or accidents – always the bane of predictable, countable economic activity, the reliance of others in contract – would recur as a familiar problem, yet cast anew under the technologies of prediction, control, and aggregation of human populations. In Patton's (2016) words, security mechanisms "deal with probable rather than actual events . . . on the basis of cost and in terms of a norm of acceptable outcomes rather than a binary division between the permitted and prohibited" (pp. 106–107). Furthermore, Foucault (2008) would propose, according to the schemata of economic and political history enunciated, that a regime of truth under the aegis of governmentality would "make what does not exist (madness, disease, delinquency, sexuality, etcetera), nonetheless become something . . . It is not an illusion since it is precisely a set of practices, real practices" (p. 19). The reality of the phenomena continuing to stalk the modern subject as *homo economicus* from the margins of life, of vitality, are precisely those that threaten its freedom as risk, as the deprivation of security, its predictable outcomes, for the maximization of immanent possibilities.

The political epicenter of "risk societies" premised on continued security and acceptable risk, coincident with biopower, foregrounds recent discussions of subjectivity and its frailties within modern life in the West (Beck, 1992; Giddens, 1990). Though Giddens is wary of post-structuralist theory, his understanding of late modernity as giving rise to societies of risk runs parallel in many respects to Foucault's notion of biopower and Deleuze's idea of societies of control. In the main, Giddens (1990) suggests that modern societies have – as Foucault (2005) demonstrates in his illumination of the demarcation between the *epimeleia heautou* and *gnothi seauton* – disembedded the subject from its proximately lived existence through an increasing Weberian rationalization of institutions governing life, and removal of the subject from local contexts of lived space, time, and intersubjective relation. Importantly for the instant analysis, one element of disembedding of the subject from its lived world is that of time-space distanciation:

> The separating of time and space and their formation into standardised, "empty" dimensions cut through the connections between social activity and its "embedding" in the particularities of contexts of presence. Disembedded institutions greatly extend the scope of time-space distanciation and, to have this effect, depend upon coordination in time and space.
>
> *(Giddens, 1990, p. 20)*

Hence, the subject's temporal existence in a pre-modern world loses its bearings – its reliance on the habitus of circumscribed roles, within their crystalline hierarchies and affective bonds – requiring another warrant for the maintenance of day-to-day reality. In other words, something else besides an experiential grasp of a proximate relationship (e.g., the expressed solidarity of field workers) must guarantee the immediate basis for social interaction, and security must obtain a certain measure of epistemically externalized trust for the subject. For Giddens (1990), the various systems that disembed the subject from what would have been a more communal or theologically grounded existence, such as financial institutions and expert authority, will be the very ones that also will be called on to mediate among security versus danger, and trust versus risk. In modern life – and heightened in societies of biopower and control – dangers (whether they be vehicular accidents, the contraction of polio, domestic abuse, market downturns, or depressive illness) are mediated through conduct at the level of the subject and institution through calculable risk, a management of future contingencies. Accordingly, security, maintained as a variable and contextual end of governmental conduct and the basis for legitimacy in contemporary Western societies, involves a highly differential (in terms of the technical expertise required) regulation of risk. Where risk is successfully ascertained and managed, Giddens (1990) asserts that trust may be established between actors in various contexts – including financial analysis and health policy analysis, as well as subjects engaged in intimate personal relationships. As such, trust relates to both risk and the confidence that security is attained in relation to spatial and temporal distance, contingency, the empty transience of time: "What is seen as 'acceptable' risk – the minimising of danger – varies in different contexts, but is usually central in sustaining trust" (Giddens, 1990, p. 35). Obviously, patterns of risk may be given over to institutional analysis and expert systems, but, pressingly, the issue of trust appears for the subject as one of the most intimate installations of biopower, as the coordination of discourse, discipline, and ethics.

Biopolitics and trauma: governing temporality

As Western societies began the process of modernization – including both early Enlightenment and late modern periods – characterizing the acceleration of scientific and physicalistic perceptions of time, certain tensions would have profound effects in social systems where biopower and its various strategies for assuaging such difficulties predominates. Recall that Newtonian conceptions of time, which contributed to a disenchantment and to a nihilistic impulse, also made possible the precise and objective measurement of happenings in the external world for technological mastery. Moreover, as previously suggested, the homogenous or empty time of modernity overturned the pre-modern cosmic, eternal orders of time coexistent with the will of God, the natural telic unfolding of events, and the repetitive or cyclical repetitions of myth; however, history itself would also become radically contingent. Koselleck (2004) suggests that such contingency, under the modern historico-temporal regime of *Neuzeit*, is expressed in the widening divergence in the "space of experience" from the "horizon of expectation" – that life as premised on the habitus of tradition and custom would be divided from the future, which could overturn constellated certainties in both threatening and promising ways:

> Two specific temporal determinants characterize the new experience of transition: the expected otherness of the future and, associated with it, the alteration in the rhythm of temporal experience: acceleration, by means of which one's own time is distinguished from what went before.
>
> *(p. 241)*

This account of continual temporal openness to the future, severance with the past, and perpetual revitalization intensifies the experience of transience at the level of the subject, and – via the ends of governmentality – raises the stakes of discernment of risk and the establishment of security. Moreover, we could say that what the discursive formation of restorative temporality could not accomplish in its own various forms of temporal logic (in terms of the collective or the subject) would have to be submitted to other means. Additionally, widespread facilitation of an ethics of traumatic temporality, bearing the unsettling effects of retroactive temporality or *Nachträglichkeit*, would arguably be disruptive of the necessary predictive control required to manage risk. Giddens (1990) suggests that the project of modern expert systems in managing risk is itself a process of sleepless reflexivity – the constant monitoring of new information as well as new models of apprehending the efficacy of monitoring itself. Drawing upon Weber's distinction between value-rational (directed towards overriding ideals) and purposive-rational (directed towards ends that are not rationally adopted) action, Hammer (2011) extends an analysis of the subject's reflexive self-mastery according to modern forms of temporality. In the main, Hammer avers that what matters to the subject is the satisfaction or actualization of a particular end, and whatever separates the subject from this end – such as the searing events of trauma (e.g., sexual violence from a trusted parent, the roadside bomb in wartime, the head-on collision that kills one's child) – must be overcome; purposive-rational action must control or deny this finitude. Such purposive-rational action is future-oriented, unconstrained by the thick tissue of past histories, and submitted to life projects of continual improvement – as training, discipline, and ethical obligation. The benefits of our temporal condition, this unmooring from value-rational truths – in reflexivity, autonomy, or liberation from oppressive traditions – are paid for, are balanced with reciprocal obligations of trust. This trust is far from that accruing from sacred bonds that tie the subject to collective meaning and shared futures but, rather, relates to "reasons for action . . . only valid in so far as they satisfy abstract, procedural constraints" (Hammer, 2011, p. 56). Along these lines, in separating the subject from a world guaranteeing its salvation in another world, Giddens (1990) draws on Laing, Erikson, and object relations theory, especially

Winnicott, to sketch an account of "ontological security" as relating to questions of existential and socially contractual trust. Critically, we may see – in the field of trauma studies – this purposive rationality, bearing procedural technologies of normalization of the psy-disciplines brought to bear on forming the trust necessary for ontological security in our epoch. This rationality comes to target biography for such a shoring up of trust: *Are you the same person you have always been? Can I trust you? Are you faithful in your disclosures about yourself, your history? Do you discharge your obligations to know yourself, to be aware of your wounds, your struggles, your trauma?* Beck (1992) writes persuasively that the modern, industrial subject, removed from the commitments and protections of traditional collective arrangements, is placed into a contradictory position of being an agent who must fashion a biographical existence yet is dependent on the constraints of institutions that standardize such biographies. Hence, societies of biopower, risk, and control are exactly premised on the necessity of governing the subject's temporal, biographical being. And, such are the requirements that the subjects themselves take up for these projects – to manage temporal disruptions (death, loss, catastrophe, trauma), and at the same time to articulate their lives in ways that yield to the biographical autonomy of others and functioning of an industrial world where risk, even one's own, may be calculated. Risk, security, and trust arrive in their forensic formulations, but they must always be submitted to expert systems, ones that would naturalize biographical risk as historico-biological function, to determine anchoring correlates within aggregate knowledge, while still preserving the ethical injunction.

In order to perceive in depth the logic of the technological concealment of ontological trauma – as a manner of governing the traumatic temporality of the modern subject – it is necessary to further examine this function within biopolitical arrangements. To do so, we may extend somewhat the Foucauldian analysis as it is well known that biopower has been further developed and quite significantly. Nonetheless, some of this rethinking – while quite penetrating in its own right – stands somewhat at odds with Foucault's attention to historical change. Of course, the clearest reference point here is Agamben's (1998) *Homo Sacer: Sovereign Power and Bare Life*, which is often criticized for its anti-historical tendencies to universalize the sovereign governance of "bare life" (Lemke, 2011) and, relatedly, in its reigning, and limited, metaphor of the Holocaust as central to the operation of biopower (Rothberg, 2009). In an entirely different vein, but similarly problematic, Hardt and Negri (2000, 2004) propose an expansive vision of biopower premised on an absolute and far-reaching hegemony of the current mode of capitalist production, one involving immaterial or cognitive labor where life itself and biopolitical production are coterminous. Their notion of the network of actors who creatively inhabit and potentially provide resistance to this vast machine – the "multitude" – owes to a Spinozist monism holding there is nothing outside the biopolitical Empire that Hardt and Negri describe; however, as generative as their analysis may be, it is subject to critique for blurring central distinctions. For instance, the variable, intermittent, and often inconsistent workings of language (as representation or discourse) and power itself appear to be flattened out. Lemke

(2011) points out that there is such an ontological privilege given to immanence that biopolitics becomes "so comprehensive that it remains unclear in what way it may be circumscribed" (p. 74). Moreover, it becomes unclear how older, ancestral forms of subjectivity brought into relation to modernity – such as that proposed by Levinas (1961/1969) – might operate differentially in contemporary socio-economic contexts.

Less at odds with Foucault's more finely grained historical studies of power, and possessing greater capacity to access the question of temporality for the modern subject, are perspectives offered by Roberto Esposito (2008) in *Bios: Biopolitics and Philosophy* and other works. Esposito seizes on a disjunctive and problematic issue that appears to escape Foucault's analyses. That is, biopower appears as both a set of practices – discursive, institutional, subjectifying – that emerges from life, and simultaneously as a constrictive and destructive possibility of eliminating life and its expansion:

> What is the *effect* of biopolitics? At this point, Foucault's response seems to diverge in directions that involve two other notions that are implicated from the outset in the concept of *bios*, but which are situated on the extremes of semantic extension: these are *subjectivization* and *death* . . . Either biopolitics produces subjectivity or it produces death.
>
> *(Esposito, 2008, pp. 31–32)*

Esposito, thus, seeks to address an issue critically related to that of resistance. How does the subject whose existence is circumscribed by power resist power itself? Put differently, how does biopower itself both oppose and support life? Generations of scholars and commentators have found this quite vexing. In Foucauldian fashion, Esposito (2008) conducts such further analysis through drawing out a distinction for studies of modernity – that of *communitas* and *immunitas*. Esposito suggests that *communitas* – or public and collective life – involves a gift that incurs an obligation; however, modern societies have granted *immunitas* to the individualized subject, who has received a dispensation (*dispensatio*) against this obligation. Enlightenment political theories – drawn from Hobbes, Locke, or others – preserve life through creating a bordered subject, an encapsulated individual whose property and liberty are continuations of their created personhood that will grow or expand only insofar as this subject has been granted an exemption from the incursions of the collective (for instance, the sovereign's treatment of body, life, and property of the condemned prisoner as its own body). The modern period, hence, for Esposito, generates a regime of knowledge and political life where immunization as strategy for preserving life has become dominant. One may observe that the dynamic between *communitas* and *immunitas* – their very inextricable relation – may possess a certain historical variability, yet under modern regimes where biopower predominates, immunization comes to bear society's "most intimate essence . . . the need for a different defensive apparatus of the artificial sort that can protect a world that is constitutively exposed to risk" (Esposito, 2008, p. 55). But, what of the apparatuses that bear such artifice, or construction? In societies where security is the basis of legitimate governmental action, institutions must mobilize knowledge and the instrumentalities of its policing function to manage risk on many fronts. Managing risk, for the psy-disciplines, then, means extending political reciprocity on a deeply psychological basis heretofore unseen in the intensity of its measures. The confidence in one's own rights, and the capacities for the expansion of the work of one's body, further the emergence of possibility immanent in one's organism and its health mirrored by those of others. Consequently, the modern subject, while inevitably participating in *communitas*, must be given dispensation against the risk of injury to his or her biographical being, and he or she is required to recognize similar dispensation given to others. Because juridico-political bases for immunization are mostly formal and no longer pertain to the heart of governmentality, traumatic injury must be immunized against pursuant to the artifice, to the handiwork of technologies that protect growth, development, and futural possibility.

Psychological and psychiatric practices and discourses that suture the subject's traumatic temporality, as more directly accessed by the ethical ontologies of finitude of Heidegger, Levinas, and Lacan, may – according to the workings of biopolitical systems – be said to form immunitary technologies (Vermeulen, 2014). Recall that for Heidegger, modern technology enframes (*Gestell*) human being through challenging it forth as *Bestand*, or "standing reserve" for particular kinds of instrumental use. Moreover, the history of trauma expresses a technological form that conceals itself, and for studies on trauma it purports to exhaust the field of its investigations through its representational capacities supplemented through biopolitical gatherings of data consisting of populations and resultant statistical correlations among their traits and qualities. Nonetheless, for Heidegger, *techne* could only be considered as part of the unfolding of Being, rather than something imposed from without; it is, rather, the *techne* or artifice spoken of by Esposito that would create a fold or opposition within life or Being. This would have indirect similarities to Nietzsche's well-known transvaluation of slave morality, which would itself carry the very will-to-power it masks. Accordingly, ontically enframed discourse/practice around trauma effects an immunization for the modern subject in industrial and post-industrial societies reliant on biopower (Vermeulen, 2014). While it may be overstating the case somewhat to identify ontological trauma with *communitas* itself (Luckhurst, 2014) – because ontological trauma not only emanates from any organized collective but from what escapes it, in its vulnerability to external contingency – such positioning may, nonetheless, allow us to further understand the relationship between ontological trauma and its technological remediation. Following Esposito, Vermeulen (2014) writes that "immunization does not consist in the outright exclusion or negation of community. In order to master the excessive and contagious dimensions of community, the process of immunization 'homeopathically' includes what it excludes" (p. 149). Esposito (2008) conceptualizes the implicit life-affirming and life-denying poles of Foucault's analysis as fused together, as immunization seeks to secure life against its own self-destructive potentialities. Vermeulen (2014) reads the death drive of the late Freud (1920/1961) in *Beyond the Pleasure Principle* as indicating both *communitas* and the immunizing process; repetition compulsion involves *both* a collective "cut" into the subject (as Lacan demonstrates) *and* a homeopathic strategy where life contains its self-destructive drive by repeating trauma. This appears somewhat aligned with the present argument, which is that ontological, factical, and ontic dimensions of trauma converge. More importantly, for inquiry into a historical ontology of trauma and its concealment, however, is the acknowledgement of the necessity of the double valence of trauma – both the incorporation of aporetic spaces within the subject's temporal being and its technological remediation via the logic of mimesis/antimimesis in the interests of security, in the alleviation of undue risk, and the establishment of interpersonal trust, and trust in oneself. The axis of traumatic temporality, as demonstrated, serves the ends of the subject's reflexivity, autonomy, and particular truths, whereas the axis of technological immunization – in tension – serves the ends of determinate identity and self-hood through social co-creation and registration of discrete biographical narrative achieved through normalized aggregation of information.

In the regulating of temporality, we have seen these twin axes of chronological representation and temporal dissolution manifest in the technologies of trauma from Erichsen to Caruth, though in the main it appears that traumatic ontology is obscured and working from the margins. The modern subject's possibilities for immunizing self-representation appear as a necessary counterpart to an immemorial past – what cannot be depicted, remembered, or integrated. The historical origins of trauma depicting the sufferer's experience physio-medically, as electromagnetic shock, and monetized, as it is in Erichsen (1859, 1866) and Page (1883), would necessarily spawn unknown and unruly counterparts to reductive medical and economic knowledge. Such consciousness nostalgically adopts a Lockean, "instrumental stance" (Taylor, 1989) towards itself as "punctual self," requiring possible but inescapable immersion and disappearance into the event of trauma. Only such an absence in knowledge would maintain the agency of the forensic subject, who would be overrun should his/her most profound experiences be reducible to homogenous explanations. Further, it should not be the least bit astonishing to find Ribot (1882) and Janet's (1925) psychologization of memory to diminish correspondent proximity to the truth of history, which returns in the pathogenic identification with an event more real than memory. Assimilation, or presentification, would precisely require a form of forgetting – a negation of the temporal relation to the event, or a deficiency in memory as the truth of history – for memory as biography to function. The theoretical elucidation offered by Caruth (1996) and van der Kolk, (1996) of dividing representation into privileged and debased forms of memory ends with a parody of narrative representation – literal "memory." Moreover, Freud and his more scientistic successors struggle to reconcile a subjectivity that is structurally divided in its mimetic identification with the Other, and one whose history must be represented in alienating narration. Ultimately, emptiness reigns as a gap in memory, collapse in language, and necessary absence allows for the possibility of attaining certain referential presence for the depiction of one's possibilities according to the norms of everyday life, which brings with it a host of valued ends necessary for "healthy" individuality in societies of risk (e.g., guilt-free living, the ability to experience pleasure, etc.).

Even as biopolitical strategies seek to install the capacity for mastery of traumatic suffering to achieve their governmental ends, such technologies also rely on an ontology of trauma to ground the successor to the juridico-political subject and its agentic being. The potentially disruptive or chaotic effects of traumatic ontology or ethics, such as that embodied in the thinking of Heidegger, Levinas, and Lacan, require mediation through knowledge and practice that have biopolitically redemptive effects in relation to the subject's fractured being-in-time. Historically, for Christendom, as Foucault (1983a) observes, pastoral power – as that oriented towards salvation (perhaps in the life to come) – is one that expends itself to safeguard the entire community, and also one that must obtain knowledge of the souls of its flock; such power is interested in eliciting the truth of the individual. Foucault (2005) points out that Christian forms of subjectification stand close, in some ways, to the *epimeleia heautou*, as there continues a relationship to self-knowledge as truth and care, which is inscribed into a divinely eternal and eschatological order; however, the circulation of such truth no longer pertains centrally to civic and political life but to the nature of the soul, the psyche, and its particular mark in the flesh. Christian hermeneutics of desire, hence, requires the subject to articulate a particular truth, "the objectification of the self in a true discourse" (Foucault, 2005, p. 333). Here, the ontotheological grounding for the Christian subject's temporal being is quite clear – the mind of God, coextensive with both the eternal and temporal orders. Importantly, however, the modern state with an entirely different basis for governance – where the aims of security allow the dominion over bare life to eclipse traditional juridico-political sovereignty – takes aim at an entirely different order of salvation in the form of protection from worldly contingency. The dimensions of modern biopower that govern the subject's being-in-time – massifying/globalizing, individualizing, and subjectifying – find another ideal subject by which to submit the ravages of fragmented temporality. Already, conceptions of sovereign power through the Enlightenment retain grounding in what Fitzpatrick (2006) refers to as "quasi-deific," pointing to Hobbes' (1651/1982) leviathan as manifestation of God's tremendous power, to the divine qualities of Rousseau's (1762/1968) law-giver in *The Social Contract*, and to Kant (1797/1996) who writes in *The Metaphysics of Morals* of a "law that is so holy (inviolable) that it is already a crime even to call it in doubt *in a practical way* . . . as if it must have arisen not from human beings but from some highest, flawless lawgiver" (p. 95). Such theological underpinnings in Enlightenment political theory are hardly surprising given the utopian epistemological leanings of the classical age, and the Cartesian coincidence of the subject's truth with knowledge, yet also with the reference to an invisible guarantor of such knowledge outside of chronological or linear time (the aporia, again, of the classical episteme). Fitzpatrick (2006), relying on Derrida (2001), argues that more contemporary political arrangements permit a continued ontotheologically oriented (self) referent. More specifically, along these lines, sovereignty may never be absolutely detheologized (or secularized):

> With modernity, sovereignty is not constituted in transcendent reference. Rather it is entirely self-constituted in what Derrida would call an "autopositioning," in a complete ipseity. That, of course, goes to confirm sovereignty as neo-deific, the outcome being that the very "sovereign" claim . . . becomes the assertion of ontotheology.
>
> *(Fitzpatrick, 2006, p. 169)*

According to such a formulation, modern pastoral power, and its address of individuality of the subject and its particular being-in-time, attains an ontotheological warrant for its "autopositioning." But, how is this possible if such authority is not conferred through a transcendent reference? It would appear that – for the subject of trauma – biopolitical technologies would rely on the very receding origin of traumatic temporality itself, only recast in the human sciences as the aporia existing in the empirico-transcendental doublet. In institutional terms, the expression of such political authority resides in the pragmatic fiction of technical and administrative expertise, the objective, impartial, and dehistoricized methods of the psy-disciplines. Here, to neutralize the alterities that temporally invade the subject's biographical being to produce suffering, misery, and dysfunction, the subject's interlocutor (i.e., therapist, psychiatrist, social worker) must adopt a pragmatic position of beneficence, trust, and clear vision – and one occupying a fictional moment outside of history – not only for the subject him or herself, but for an entire domain of public policy, of validated treatments, of addressing populations. To translate the truth of traumatic suffering into knowledge requires a spatalized observer (Romanyshyn, 1978) located precisely in the fulcrum of the temporal juncture, both attentive to the well-being of biographies of the afflicted and mindful of the change, the agency needed to marshal the needed techniques of correction and their internalization, their subjectifying potentialities.

Biopolitics and cognitive-behavioral *techne*

To trace a genealogy of the cognitivist subject of psychology (which has subsumed the strictly behavioral one), as it would inform and inhabit the various techniques of cognitive-behavioral therapies, would lie outside the scope of the present work. However, to historically contextualize the ascendency of cognitive-behavioral technology – as concealing traumatic ontology while forming a specific aggregated, disciplined, and subjectified being – we may provisionally find its emergence in the confluence of several epistemic and material appearances. First, cognitivist approaches – though obviously revised in light of Darwinist borrowings, and the more recent turn to affect (Demasio, 1994) – retain a strongly Cartesian inheritance in the privileging of a representational, procedural rationality founded on the premise of empty or substitutable elements or terms having no necessary relation with specific content or valued endpoint (akin to Weber's purposive rationality operating on a more institutional scale). To this influence of Descartes' conception, Taylor (1989) writes that "despite all of the scorn which has been heaped on him from the dominant empiricist trend in modern scientific culture, the conception of reason remains procedural" (p. 156). Moreover, though cognitivism declares its independence from strict Cartesianism, it continues to privilege an individualist mode of thought, while still aligned with a deterministic outlook in the form of "intentional causality" (Bolton & Hill, 1996). Second, under contemporary cognitivist accounts of consciousness, representation loses its early Enlightenment absolutist epistemic pretensions while retaining a pragmatic realism in terms of the relative closeness of "cognitive mapping" and reality. Mental schemata, corresponding with the external world, fluctuate between becoming more abstract and complex and more compact and moderate (Fiske & Taylor, 1991), and increasingly fitted to reality itself (Rosch, 1978). The standpoint for perception of effective cognitive schemata is of the objective and neutral scientist-observer – one free from bias, or the darkness that would dim the vision in the clear light of a procedural rationality. Gergen (1994) asserts that such an objectivist subject is paradoxically achieved in a rhetorical fashion through certain "distention devices." These would include depersonalizing language, the suppression of affect, and the statistical methods that make up dominant approaches to understanding psychological suffering and psychiatric treatment. Gergen (1994) writes that "in this way, the compendium of terms within an objective science should be an inventory of the world. Or, to put it more metaphorically, an objective description should furnish a map or a picture of the world as it is" (p. 171). Not surprisingly, recent psychological discourse, especially in its cognitivist iterations, conceives of the psychological subject him or herself as a scientist, who must confirm or disconfirm erroneous interior states of mind that obstruct pragmatic capacities to mirror the world as it is. That is, the means by which the psychological subject may be apprehended are replicated in the fabrication of this operative subject as outcome, and, as it goes, certain ways of knowing are invisibly reproduced. Partly responsible for this outlook, though by no means identical to it, would be the development of artificial intelligence, and – more generally – the view of the mind as having a computational foundation (Dennett, 1991; Pinker, 1997) whose aim it is to model a reality that will always be in some ways remote from it. Third, though cognition itself would not historically be its first province, personality or self becomes the successor to ancient conceptions of soul, or early Enlightenment preoccupation with person as a forensic placeholder for memory and culpability. More importantly, personality – like living tissue – could be diseased, which would include, among other maladies, the diseases of the memory commented on by Ribot, Janet, and Prince (Danziger, 2008). Much later, after the cognitive revolution in the late twentieth century, memorial pathology would become framed as maladaptive interpretive schemata around networks of fear, errors regarding one's past, present, and future, or time as experienced. Fourth, the norms that would come to guide adaptive cognition originate, as Foucault (1966/1973) argues drawing on Canguilhem (1989), from human sciences patterned from the life sciences of the nineteenth century owing to thoroughly empirical, positivistic, and naturalistic methods of inquiry. These sciences are conceptually regulated through the discontinuity of life forms, the environmental system in which the organism exists, and its specific history within those ecologies. Norms that arise in such contexts relate to an ongoing functional response to the organism's press for continued life; however, what may be termed "pathological" prefigures such flourishing as a boundary condition determined through the organism's history and trajectory. The human sciences only heighten the contextualism at hand, fastening norms to the infinite play of needs, conceptual frames, and material creations of the socio-historical world. Still, Hacking (2016) points out that human life as a statistical concern ("the avalanche of printed numbers") becomes the object of "bureaucracies of counting" in early nineteenth-century Europe, including early private associations of life and health insurance as well as the nation states' concerted efforts to collect, classify, and collate particular kinds of data regarding the health of populations: "Disease, madness, and the state of the threatening underworld, *les misérables*, created a morbid and fearful fascination for numbers on which the bureaucracies fed" (p. 73). Deviancy, or departure from the ecological norm, becomes the threshold of both interest and locus of instrumental control for an array of phenomena disclosing disordered life including, *inter alia*, affect, cognition, and relationships with others. In summary, the cognitivist subject appears historically formed amongst its productive and pragmatic difficulties – a subject possessed of imperfectly representative capacities of exterior reality, but only as measured against its normative fit with its environment, which is rapidly changing technologically, morally, and economically. Giddens (1990) and Beck (1992) speak of the reflexivity characterizing modern forms of life, and the cognitivist subject as an institutionally created operational and normative space for conscious adaptation ostensibly embodies such a notion.

The technologies providing immunization against psychological trauma, demonstrated in the last chapter, privilege antimimetic depiction or realistic representation of the subject's experienced reality; however, in addition to allied neurobiological renderings, cognitive-behavioral interventions approach the apotheosis of enframing such suffering according to the ends and logic of biopower in our epoch. The ontic apparatus of trauma – its historical path as a constellation of discourses and practices – would never attain requisite operational efficiency in maintaining the well-being of populations, in facilitating the equilibrium of mental health, in the varied and ad hoc, idiosyncratic practices of psychoanalysis or humanistic therapies. To address the pervasive risk that temporal destruction brings not only to the subject whose life is destroyed in the tornado, or in the witnessed suicide of one's father, but to others in proximity, the stabilizing of cognitive and affective processes and biographical history would further call forward normalizing and massifying institutions and their agents. Moreover, to provide the ontological security for the modern subject in its everyday existence – necessitating its disembedding from a world of tradition, its own all-too-close relation to alterity, its own temporality – a certain severing must be accomplished for a renewed horizon of expectation, consistent with demands of *homo economicus*. Accordingly, cognitive-behavioral technologies hold the promise of merging the subject of trauma's representation, realistic mapping of reality (its past and future, present difficulties) with the contours of data collected on how such subjects – on average – manage such feats. This project may be productively analyzed along three dimensions that inform Foucault's (2008, 2009) overall approach to biopower. First, discourses and empirical methodologies *massify* a universally operative subject – in terms of neurobiology, cognitive function, and normative development. This generally corresponds to "emotional process theory" (Foa & McNally, 1996), and the underlying logic of the social cognitive theory of assimilation and accommodation of schemata relating to traumatic events (Resick, Monson, & Chard, 2008). Second, relatedly – as the efficacy of therapies are also massified – certain practices or techniques (skills, strategies of appraisal, confrontations) *discipline* or individualize the subject's experiences around belief, meaning, and memory. That is, they perform a kind of shaping, and description, of the subject's experience in orthopedic conformity with their own mechanisms. Third, the knowledge and discipline bearing upon the subject's trauma – though having an explicitly purposive-rational and amoral orientation – *subjectify* him or her according to a discrete form of ethics and implied basis for personal and social agency (this will be addressed in the final section of this chapter). In other words, they enjoin the subject to relate to itself and others according to certain preferred ways of being.

Massifying the operative subject's trauma

Over the past several decades, there has been growing expansion in the production – theorization, testing/trial, and instituting – of cognitive-behavioral therapies for PTSD, which remains the reigning conceptual framework for addressing traumatic suffering (set forth in *DSM-V* and *ICD-10*). Still, the diagnostic winds continue to shift, as in the debates surrounding the inclusion and existence of complex post-traumatic stress disorder (C-PTSD) or developmental trauma disorder (DTD) as proposed by van der Kolk (2014) and Herman (1992), among others. Nonetheless, though the scientific validity of *DSM* rubrics remains contested (Kirk, Cohen, & Gomory, 2015) – due in part to the disavowed yet residually categorical syndromes that mirror organic disease – the proliferation of techniques and standardized treatments for PTSD persists. Unremarkably, the viciousness of life and intensity of events depriving people of their most cherished memories and assumptions demands address, and societies governed through biopower become ever more vigilant in funneling information into the corridors that would produce knowledge required for remediation and prevention. Technologies relying on medicalized neuroscientific and neurobiological evidence are obviously not confined to cognitive-behavioral approaches (i.e., EMDR or sensorimotor psychotherapy), yet the former forms the decades-old tradition that is still viewed by many clinicians as the standard for practice and scientific credibility. Notably, these therapies include such modalities as prolonged exposure (PE), cognitive processing therapy (CPT), and stress-inoculation training (SIT). Overall, these discourses (and the interventions following) mostly occupy the same conceptual terrain and rely on similar understandings of causal mechanisms in operation, while emphasizing differing aspects of these shared underpinnings.

In the theoretical lineage of Crile, Cannon, and Charcot, especially, behavioral theorists emphasize the role of fear reactions in the formation of post-traumatic reaction. Early on, Mowrer's (1960) two-part theory holds that classical conditioning accounts for the pairing of traumatic stimuli with a fear response, and operant principles account for the subject's avoidant behavior as negatively reinforced. More recently, the role of fear is greatly expanded to encompass not only externally observable behavior but also verbal and physiological responses, as well as the meaning attached to fear states. In elaborating this more cognitively inflected emotional processing theory (Foa & Kozak, 1986), Riggs, Cahill, and Foa (2006) write of the interconnection of these elements into a fear structure that "serves as a blueprint for escaping and avoiding danger; as such, it supports adaptive behavior when a person is faced with realistically threatening situations" (p. 70). However, such a structure becomes maladaptive when the associations among stimuli lose their accurate representation of the world as escape or avoidant responses are triggered by harmless events in the present through the subject's distorted interpretations. In this vein, Foa, Steketee, and Rothbaum (1989) assert that traumatic events are depicted in memory as a fear structure containing a number of benign elements that are not realistically sensed, perceived, or interpreted by the victim of trauma. In most contexts, individuals recover naturally from exposure to traumatic events (Atkeson, Calhoun, Resick, & Ellis, 1982; Harvey & Bryant, 1998); however, a minority of victims do not recover, this failure due "to inadequate activation of the fear structure in the wake of trauma and/or the unavailability of corrective information" (Riggs et al., 2006, p. 71). Research under this model also indicates that other emotional states – for example, sadness, anger, horror, helplessness – are also implicated in such associational webs of memory (Pitman et al., 1990). Correcting maladaptive traumatic fear or other emotional structures means imparting information disconfirming of the structure, and habituation through the exposure of the subject to stimuli that recall the original event(s). Habituation arguably allows the victim of trauma to differentiate present realities from past realities and to tolerate distress that is temporary and unrelated to previous events. In biopolitical terms, this operative subject – which is formed by the immense methodological, economic, and professional efforts of the psy-disciplines – exists by and through a certain norm where the past is disavowed for an almost utopian and open future, where events in the present are washed of their previous resonance or significance. Such a normalized relation to the past and future is *empirically derived* (i.e., it is the case that most contemporary Western subjects desire to be released from the affective intensities of memorial associations) and, also, this relation is *valued*, matters, and is to be desired. Perhaps, this seems invisible to us now as modern subjects, as we are admonished, not only by cognitive-behavioral therapies but also traditionally psychoanalytic ones, to "move on," to "work through" our past traumas and struggles, to explain them, account for them in ways that place them firmly in the antimimetic mode of depiction – to avoid living through them, to wash ourselves of the past, to open ourselves for progress, to the future. But without invalidating a modernist operative subject of cognition, desiring to efface the web of associated memories that maintain its mimetic immersion in the events of its suffering, we may ask if this kind of institutionally mandated relation to one's past is universally desired or empirically grounded. In examining a variety of wartime suffering, arguably enframed as "traumatic stress," Summerfield (1998) argues that this is not always the case, citing many examples where victims desire to maintain connection with wartime memories of violence and atrocity, and specifically of prisoners in a Second World War Burmese death camp who

> spoke freely of grief and horror but seemed to be attesting not to long-term psychological effects but to an overriding concern to bear witness. They could still shed tears, but so they should, they implied. Japanese atrocities were unforgettable, but so should they be.
>
> *(p. 28)*

Certainly, such guarded protection of traumatic memory recalls the inexorable presence of truth at the heart of the subject's disjointed temporal and historical existence, what cannot be made sense of in disrupting one's most fundamental sense of self, yet what is held on to for dear life, what must not be forgotten. The Real effects of intervening alterities, and necessities of speech in distorting these realities, have such consequences, as damning as they may be for security, trust, and governance. Nonetheless, the efforts of biopolitical technologies in crafting an operative subject for instrumental control of the past would root out vestiges of irrational fear and horror, replacing them with the harmless stimuli of everyday life in an industrial world of work, production, consumption, within the pragmatic orientation required for these pursuits.

Janet's (1925) prescription that his patients perform a "presentification" of trauma, and Freud's (1914/1958) own impulse towards interpretation prefigure the shift away from strictly automatic modes of traumatic suffering already surfacing in the revisions of behaviorist approaches, as codified in emotional process theory earlier. Under the necessities incumbent upon an interpretative outlook to be technically precise, valid, and replicable, any hermeneutic uncertainties arising from temporal finitude – occasioned through ontological trauma – would need to be tamed, immunized, and operationalized. Pursuant to this mandate of the psy-disciplines to naturalize their procedures, the modern, industrialized subject's thinking and beliefs would be naturalized as well. Consequently, over the past several decades, several cognitive theories have emerged to account for suffering in PTSD (Beck, Emery, & Greenberg, 2005; Ehlers & Clark, 2000; Janoff-Bulman, 2010; Resick et al., 2008). Emblematic of the cognitive approaches oriented towards meaning and belief, social cognitive theory (Resick et al., 2008; Resick & Schnicke, 1992) addresses the developmental integration of mental schemata after a traumatic event, especially regarding the dynamic of logic, uncertainty, and probability in the subject's thinking. Two common cognitive-developmental processes inform this line of theorization: proper accommodation and assimilation required to effect an equilibrium of experienced selfhood, of the continuity of past biographical forms into an open temporal horizon. Social cognitive theory holds that the processing of traumatic experience is sometimes not properly accommodated but problematically assimilated into existing beliefs about self, other, and the world. For instance, a person who believes that the world is a fundamentally just and moral place – the "just world hypothesis" (Lerner, 1980) – may overly attribute blame to him or herself ("I had this coming to me because we all get what's coming to us in the end"). Other forms of problematic assimilation include hindsight bias (Fischoff, 1975) and the false sense of control that sometimes persists, creating more guilt and responsibility in the wake of trauma. For example, sexual assault victims may feel they could have prevailed if only they had fought their attacker more ferociously, despite perhaps there being numerous attackers, or the existence of surprise, or a relative disparity in physical strength. Problematic assimilation, as represented by social cognitive theorists, tends to preserve the subject's overly ideal and biographically continuous relation to the world – which is just, knowable, and controllable in action – at the expense of a more realistic appraisal. It bears pointing out that this relation to world is exactly what the subject is asked to aspire to in neo-liberal societies; that is, where the subject internalizes a certain responsibility for his/her life. The other threat to accommodation is that of overaccommodation, where maladaptive beliefs about self, other, and the world become overgeneralized or amplified after a traumatic event ("I will never trust my judgment of people again" or "The world is an unsafe place where catastrophe may strike at any time, a place of evil and violence," etc.) (McCann & Pearlman, 1990). Overaccommodation tends to overemphasize the untrustworthiness of the world and its inhabitants, including often those of the victim in perceiving danger. Therefore, overaccommodation replicates in the subject the apprehension and wariness that societies of risk themselves institutionally foster – constant monitoring and assessment as an obsessional attitude against Type II errors. Though these underlying logical dynamics explain mechanism, what cognitive therapies have in common – in treating PTSD and other conditions such as depression – is an emphasis on attaining equilibrium of self-control and apprehension of risk. Apart from emotional networks derived from an information processing model, unrealistic and illogical thinking are said to be at the core of the victim's troubles – overgeneralized, exaggerated, and unreliable appraisals. Consider an exemplar case of a young man in his mid-30s who had been sexually assaulted multiple times as a young child (beginning at age 7), and then again more recently:

> The overall feeling of what it means to have been assaulted is the feeling that I must be bad or a bad person for something like this to have occurred. I feel it will or could happen again at any time . . . The world scares me.
>
> *(Shipherd, Street, & Resick, 2006, p. 106)*

A cognitive-behavioral therapist's task here should by now be relatively clear, to help his or her patient or client examine the evidence for such far-reaching and damaging interpretations of his life, being, relations with others, and the world at large, and to avoid the confusions and misattributions at hand – including self-blame (versus the acceptance of limited and situational helplessness) and assessments projecting catastrophic certainties (versus probabilities). Clearly, such theoretical and practical conduits of action lend themselves to an antimimetic, ontically technological stance, solidly in line with the apparatus of trauma charted over the past two centuries; however, the valued endpoints of this brand of pragmatic realism remain founded on shifting, epistemic sands.

The massified, operative subject of trauma in its cognitivist guise manages the ravages of the traumatic temporality, its lack in being, and the Otherness to which it owes its being through fixing its biographical continuity and hope for the future to a realism lined with the promise of health. As argued, the ethical ontologies of finitude of Heidegger, Levinas, and Lacan yield a traumatic ethics where the subject's being is made possible through self-withdrawal as a gap in temporality. Along Heideggerian lines, Stolorow (2011) observes that clinical trauma recalls or recapitulates such disruption, paralleling the experience of *Angst* in the strongest terms. There is no recovery from the worlds one is severed from, from the forms of identity destroyed, from the uncertainty trauma brings us. For the victim of sexual assault, the world as a welcome place where one's embodied, sensual, generative being is inviolable is irremediably lost, and the truth arriving in its place speaks of different worlds to come, and those that will be fashioned out of the ruins of a past never to return. Different pasts, those that will have been retroactively, take their place, placing the victim – in the existentially ontological sense – in a more authentic position vis-à-vis his or her suffering than the technologies that seek to suture these wounds. In contradistinction, the cognitivist's antimimetic move is to enframe the traumatic subject's experience of the past as one of passive responsibility, as legitimately helpless in the face of inexorable forces beyond his or her control, and to confine this subject's future as circumscribed through probabilities calculated to ensure his or her continued practicable peace of mind, and efficacious grasp of his or her own being. An epistemic outlook so aligned with the ends of health, and so formative of the empirical subject of psychological and psychiatric research, could only be morally undergirded by a utilitarian and hedonistic bent towards a consequentialist understanding of its own practices. Moreover, for a disembodied subject existing through the emptiness of clock time, awareness of the ontological predicament afforded through *Nachträglichkeit* – the deep uncertainties bestowed as gifts and curses alike – are covered over in the immunizing stability borne of a coherent past and promising future. What is real becomes what works, and what works best works for a population's mean, in any given domain of struggle. The subject's truth in the Real, or in its *Angst*, and its relation to others is substituted by a newer arrangement, one with brighter overall consequences for most. In other words, in practice, these strategies have participated in a large-scale deterritorializing of the juridico-political subject, premised on formal or principled judgments on the nature of a precarious reality in relation to others, moving to a biopolitical one, wherein freedom mostly pertains to the increased vitality of the governed according to the powers of increased probability of health or functioning *en masse.*

Disciplining the operative subject's trauma

The nexus between psychological life and disciplinary power begun in *Discipline and Punish* and *Psychiatric Power* has been continually renewed (Hook, 2007; Rose, 1990, 1998) however, what has not been consistently emphasized is how the individualizing function of this new form of power necessarily, in part, forms the contours of a meaningful world for the modern subject. Indeed, Foucault's elaboration of a disciplinary power that would metaphorically, panoptically operate in almost every corridor of life (famously in prisons, barracks, schools, and asylums) has often been seen as contributing to socio-historical reduction of complex phenomena to a metaphysics of power (Burkitt, 1993). Still, though this reading is often pursued in hardline social constructionist thought, Foucault (2006) is clear that the "soul," an antiquated term used to indicate the historically psychologized being of self, ego, identity, etc., is formed or projected beyond its material architecture:

> Disciplinary power is individualizing because it fastens the subject-function to the somatic singularity by means of a system of supervision-writing, or by a system of pangraphic panopticism, which behind the somatic singularity projects, as its extension or as its beginning, a core of virtualities, a psyche.
>
> *(p. 55)*

This "core of virtualities" maps more or less well onto Heideggerian possibility, the ways the subject meaningfully projects its being into the future, to take up projects that matter, that implicate itself and its fellow beings in relation. Indeed, as Foucault (2006) would suggest, the subject formed under the eye and material applications of modern systems of thought would be mirrored in the formal, juridico-political subject of the later Enlightenment: "The discourse of the human sciences is precisely to twin, to couple this juridical individual and disciplinary individual, to make us believe that the real, natural, and concrete content of the juridical individual is the disciplinary individual" (pp. 57–58). Towards this aim, under the regime of disciplinary power, which differently persists in societies of control or biopower, specific conditions are emplaced that co-constitute the subject's being-in-time – its coherent narrative (the dossier), present capacities to fill the roles offered in the current order, and future capabilities. One might say that the juridico-political subject is formal and abstract, a successor agent of sovereign dominion now conceptualized as social contract, and the disciplinary subject is a naturalized one (no longer a created body-soul). That is, it is a technically somatized body with implicitly potential capacities (psyche) that – being able to be continually trained, formed, and changed – necessarily surpasses the static embodiment of agrarian orders and political arrangements. In accomplishing its immunizing function in relation to and through individual Dasein, but also increasing its fitness for assignment in the wards of its then emergent industrial but now post-industrial enterprises, Foucault (1975/1995) specifies several features of disciplinary power with far-reaching institutional scope: distribution and enclosure (the partition of the space of subjection/objectification); control of the somatic-virtual subject's elaboration of action (i.e., the time table); evolutive, linear time towards a desired endpoint or equilibrium; means of the correct training (i.e., normalizing judgment, examination); and, never-ending surveillance that is internalized as well as enacted. In all of these dimensions that have been taken up by psychology and psychiatry as a "moral orthopedics" (Foucault, 1975/1995), the individualizing function of discipline works in tandem with the normalizing one, to ferret out deviance in respect to the singularity of Dasein, to find its preemptive potentiality for future formation, its cure being to fully reenter the population, only in its particular pathways, its scars, its history, its trauma.

The technicality of the individualizing function of disciplinary power – over against the aggregation of the being of the subject of trauma – may be seen first and foremost in instrumental approaches that form cognitive-behavioral approaches in processing emotional memory. Bringing forward the older modern, philosophical concerns of memory as harnessing the subject's ownmost personal reality – for instance, the notion that what can be remembered about one's experiences is most central to who one is – and also the nineteenth-century psychiatric discourses around diseased memory, cognitive-behavioral therapies focusing on memorial association microscopically catalogue, intensify, and leverage procedures aimed at identifying and remediating "stuck points" in their patients' traumatic experience. First, as to the issue of distributive space, it may be said that disciplinary power operates anew in settings dominated under biopolitical strategies; the asylum or hospital in contemporary life is less commonly where these therapies are carried out, as they are more likely found in neo-liberal economies amongst the cubicle spaces of counselors, social workers, and psychologists' practices. Second, as to issues of control, it should again be said that biopolitical augmentations resemble coaching or the kind of training one would find in a corporate, business setting; or, as for the older, almost Taylorist fashion, the subject-patient's suffering is given over to a discrete time-table of events, each with their own agenda. For instance, for Prolonged Exposure (PE) therapy, Foa and Rothbaum (1998) provide for x sessions, each lasting x minutes and incorporating several elements: psychoeducation regarding PTSD, imaginal and repeated exposure to the traumatic stimulus, breathing exercises to reduce distress, and setting up in vivo exposure as an out-of-session activity. In imaginal exposure, throughout the session, the act of retelling of the trauma again and again effects the temporal elaboration of the act of memorializing under control of the therapist, and according to the rhythmic back and forth of past and present ("How much distress are you feeling now?" "You're in a safe place here in my office. Please go on."). Thus, the act of speaking, and the training to reduce anxiety through proper breathing, drains the traumatic memory through embodied articulation and modulation – as if one is tuning the incremental elements of the subject's traumatic narrative with particular correlates of the body's gestures in imprinting a presently sanitized reality onto specific problematic memories. Additionally, the principle of efficiency operative in disciplinary power maintains a maximum speed and minimal use of effort, meaning the correct sequence has been experimentally verified as bearing on the operative subject of trauma (what works, on average). For example, in some exposure therapies, especially problematic memories are identified according to a subjectively reportable but numerical scale (Subjective Units of Distress or SUDS), which will allow a precise, purposive-rational, homogenized temporal mapping of the intensity of memory throughout the session:

> Graphing a client's distress ratings throughout the imaginal exposure is also helpful. This can be done by designing a graph with *time* on the x-axis and *SUDS* on the y-axis, which allows client and therapist to see how the client's distress changes across the exposure . . . concrete graphing of distress reduction across the session provides clients with additional information on their ability to tolerate distress (integration of new information), as well as the fact that their fear response is reduced with continued exposure.
>
> *(Monson & Shnaider, 2014, p. 29)*

The identification of problematic stuck places (so called "hot spots") in this process of retelling furthers the march towards what Foucault (1975/1995) refers to as an "evolutive" time, a convergence of a macrophysics and microphysics of power where social progress mirrors the progress of the individuality-cell, where a certain stable, terminal point is aimed for. Here, the individual's specific memory – his or her unique associations, i.e., the smell of the rapist's body, the sound of the bomb's shattering blast, the visual image of others running during the earthquake – is differentiated from its retelling or its parallels in daily living (the in vivo exposure). The past, once forensically determined and processed, must be the past because the future must be open; the subject's temporality must continue uninterrupted and flowing against an open horizon. His or her individuality as an organism will be that which, as documented, prevents this movement – this deviance from the neutral "now" moment of memory.

In the social cognitive aspects of therapy, the disciplinary features of hierarchical observation, normalizing judgment, and examination just alluded to take somewhat different form in indexing the subject as an individuality-cell. Again, in addressing madness (or later, mental illness), the disciplinary power that Foucault describes most squarely operates in a world, such as that of the asylum, where geographical spaces of segregation permit a pervasive, physical surveillance. In more contemporary clinical contexts, the relationship between therapist and patient has attained a more discretionary status; however, a diagnosis itself is often necessary in attaining reimbursement for private health insurance or under state-sponsored programs (for instance, for veterans in requiring a PTSD diagnosis). Thus, elements of discipline may be found manifest in the various talking cures that have arisen in the privatized therapies of the late nineteenth and twentieth centuries. For instance, in classical psychoanalytic practice and its heirs, as mentioned, the patient is enlisted into a working alliance with the analyst, wherein he or she says whatever comes to mind, yet places his or her experience at issue within the various developmental, libidinal, or object-related interpretive schemes. In these practices, the subject observed or monitored (summoned in for regular sessions that bear relation to, and modify, an outside life) is examined (associations are tested, cut short, or elaborated) and normalized (placed under diagnostic rubrics and narrative arcs that remediate suffering). Nonetheless, the subject's turmoil as confronted by the analyst is one of conflict and inner destitution, whose evidentiary tethering in the external world is that of renewed capacities to experience joy, and to fluidly and unobstructedly participate in love and work. In other words, the psychoanalytic subject is brought to enjoy life, whose truths are far afield from both the original impulse behind disciplinary power – to effect conformity with an institutionally preferred exterior reality unconcerned with the truths of madness – and more recent iterations. In a sense, in contemporary social cognitive therapies, disciplinary practices rejoin their high Enlightenment concern with a confrontation over the reality the subject and therapist inhabit, and the crisis that yields must point towards a demonstration of sorts that would solve this quandary through a technical realism. Yet, as expressed, this newer arrangement combines also the refinements of the psychiatric nosologies developed over the past century, which concern less the supervisory relays in nineteenth-century asylum culture in favor of a system of perpetual training described by Deleuze (1992). For traumatic suffering – which is mostly enframed as PTSD, wartime trauma being its prototypical formation – hierarchical observation finds its purchase not in enforced participation but in the reliance and trust in sanctioned experts, whose credentials are publicly verified and scrutinized as marking competence. Insofar as social cognitive therapies, concerned as they are with belief and its attribution, relate to the process of examination, there is explicit use of what is called "Socratic questioning"; however, it becomes quite obvious that such interrogation has a much different end in post-Enlightenment contexts, which is explicitly forensic and reality-oriented rather than aiming at ancient conceptions of truth, or the "truth event" of trauma that informs traumatic temporality and ethics. Monson and Shnaider (2014) set forth several kinds of questions cognitive therapists use when approaching clients suffering with PTSD. Clarifying questions typically establish the factual narrative of trauma itself, as well as illuminating the state of the mind of the client (such as, "What was happening just before the bomb exploded?" or "How were you feeling on the night you were raped – tired, hungry, anxious walking home?"). Questions that challenge assumptions often directly implicate some aspect of reality that the subject struggles to accept, and that negatively colors their perceptions of themselves, others, or the world (for example, "What could you have done really to avoid the accident?"). Questions of evaluation are often addressed to present threats, which are said to be overestimated (for instance, "What do you think the actual probabilities are of you being assaulted on a daily basis?"). Finally, questions that challenge underlying beliefs are said to strike at the heart of the client's maladaptive appraisals (as in, "Why do you think it's so hard to give up blaming yourself for what happened?"). As Foucault (1975/1995) notes, the examination, with clear medical parallels in the daily routines of hospital life, locates the subject's struggle as both visible and publicly accountable, constituting the individual as a "case" or particular pattern. Put differently, for trauma, the subject's individuality-cell is called forth through the forensic process of questioning, the confession less a secret desire or unfathomable truth one is harboring and more that of a subject constituted by certain errors in appraising a reality that the therapist is called on to rectify. In contrast to psychoanalytic formulations, diseased memory is no longer a purely singular instance of experiential and embodied absolute difference but, rather, an understandable and externally validated difference of narrative.

Social cognitive approaches to PTSD engineer together a massified, dividualized operative subject – i.e., harboring the cognitive processes of assimilation, accommodation as a dynamic process – with a normalizing judgment by which the individual is identified in accordance to *both* its own particular histories and virtualities *and* a standard of conduct and/or thinking referencing a transparently rendered world. As Foucault (1975/1995, 2006) observes, the psy-function establishing the boundaries of normalization, which is only heightened under biopower, is the engine at the heart of disciplinary power itself. The correction that must be summoned, here not the physical correction of the soldier's manual of arms or the madman's ways of taking meals, concerns the vestiges of thought that do not serve the modern subject's own narrative, and putatively *realistic* appraisal of its being-in-time. It should be emphasized, especially under a Heideggerian-Foucauldian analysis, that the individuality coming into light under the contributing effects of biopower and disciplinary power are hardly repressive, but rather safeguard, protect, and nurture a certain kind of being. The psy-function, as it comes to serve biopolitical strategies, seeks to sustain political legitimacy only insofar as the subject's agency or freedom is created or actively brought into being by the expansion of its possibilities. The macroscopic projects of alleviating risk and creating security in the subject's personal and interpersonal lives require the subject's open future and the survival of its prospects for satisfying and meaningful pursuits in labor and in relationships. The trust needed in oneself, in one's own efficacy and powers to self-fashion, and in others, relies upon a biographical and memorial narrative that may be unknotted, or unstuck, and is also forensically amenable – that is, submitted to methods of proof foregrounding representation or demonstration. In the main, as already foregrounded, these practices seek to objectify the client's being-in-the-world, to replace or alter thoughts that appear lacking evidence or a rational footing in reality itself; however, the touchstone for this clinical realism is always what is more helpful, pragmatic, healthful, and beneficial – what reduces suffering. Zayfert and Becker (2007) well illustrate this practical trajectory with reference to a young woman who had been raped at a college party after ignoring her parents' general advice against going, and the therapist's dilemma in how to address her overwhelming sense of guilt and "badness":

> Emilia's therapist now faced a choice. Emilia identified a series of important thoughts and beliefs, many of which she used to support one another. Emilia's therapist identified two paths that might be very helpful. First, she could challenge the *my fault* thought . . . In other words she could try to help Emilia shift some blame to her rapists. Alternatively, she could tackle Emilia's beliefs about obeying her parents . . . Ultimately, the therapist chose the former path first . . . There are no right answers in choosing a thought to challenge.
>
> *(p. 168)*

At issue is the question – the vexing problem – that cognitive therapists face in remediating the effects of PTSD, which is how to intervene as an agent of external narrative reality that preserves the subject's own continuity, as a validated being with beliefs, knowledge, and memories themselves that should be preserved. This means that the traumatic suffering would be both memorially integrated (i.e., assimilated) into past identities and representing of a new world (i.e., accommodated), balancing the subject's sense of self with a heightened rational grasp of his or her past, and future risk or contingency. The observer-less reality here is simply *unknown* or *unknowable*, and the therapeutic challenges originate mostly in synthesizing a particular normative (in moral, juridical, and political terms) interpretation of the past (i.e., one is not responsible for physical events done to one's person against one's will), and a securely open future (i.e., one should not worry about events unlikely to take place in the pure aggregate, even if personally experienced). But what *is known*, intersubjectively through the testimony of the patient herself in a clinical forum, concerns the palpable and horrific effects of events that deprive the subject of intimate being. Significantly, however, the objectivist project of establishing an independently verified external record of events – which is premised on the dissociative paradigm of trauma from Janet (1925) through contemporary neuro-cognitive understandings – technologically obscures the interpretative clearing that may illuminate a particular, lived relation to the historico-cultural world, in all of its promises and betrayals, and its traumatic destruction. Accordingly, in the context of gender, Foucault (1976/1990, 2006) historically links hysteria – with putative traumatic origins in gendered traumatic temporality – with psychiatric knowledge in such a way that manifests a marginalized sexuality as co-constituted in *pouvoir*, or the possibilities grounding both psychiatric category and the embodied defeats, victories borne out by the modern subject in relation. Psychoanalytic discourses, in their more expansive forms, preserve the symbolic, temporally retroactive dimensions of traumatic experience, which would appear to preserve the feminine subject's resistance against acts of violation, which are submitted to the logic of her own experiences. Again in the context of trauma and gender, Haaken (1998) notes the concealment of the feminine subject's suffering in more recent antimimetic accounts: "To be anointed with this newly anointed label, the patient must produce evidence of trauma of sufficient magnitude to account for the symptoms" (p. 67). Nonetheless, in distinguishing how disciplinary power operates to not only conceal but technologically disclose a meaningful world for a particular individuality to be documented in public knowledge as having been victimized, or transgressed against through human or natural forces, is to see the redemptive task at its heart. The freedom bestowed extrinsically in the Socratic examinations of the scene of trauma arises from clinically normalizing judgment as challenges to thoughts leading to guilt, shame, fear, anxiety, and resulting incapacities. These expanded possibilities follow from seeing oneself as in principle free as a rational actor, a neo-liberal subject, yet only constricted through the mishaps of chance, and the affects and thoughts that are mistakenly clung to in preserving unrealistic appraisals of one's life. Subjects are, thus, rendered unique by virtue of the marks, the patterns of error and their bondage, the contingencies befalling them.

The ethics of redemptive rationality

The technologies concealing the modern subject's relation to traumatic temporality via the ethical ontologies of finitude do not preclude, or even entirely supplant, a deeply ethical existence in relation to time and history. Because traumatic temporality, both as an aporia in knowledge and experienced self-knowledge, produces distressing effects on subjects and their sociality, what I will call "the ethics of redemptive rationality" – characterizing forms of subjectification as related to trauma – becomes a historical counterpart to traumatic ethics. In the main, this development avoids the project of immersive transformation, as ancient systems manifest, and does not seek a holistic synthesis of temporality, as the discourse of restorative temporality would attempt. As Foucault (1994) remarks, and as suggested, spiritual forms of care continue during the early Enlightenment period in a highly modified form: "We notice that this mode of being is entirely determined by knowledge . . . it superimposes the functions of spirituality on an ideal based on scientificity" (p. 14). Recall that the *epimeleia heautou* involves a substantive truth of being that one inhabits, the transformative effects of *technai* or virtue attained in political and civic life – a life well lived towards certain communal ends. The suffering surmounted, thus, becomes a settling of accounts related to the kairotic instantiations, the truth-telling harboring one's word and will according to implicit unfoldings of a *polis* in step with the movements of an ordered finality. The discourses of restorative temporality – arising in the nineteenth and early twentieth centuries – attempt a parallel maneuver, though obviously operating in far different socio-historical milieux. Here, the impulse is to recover lost time. As argued *supra*, the thought of Husserl et al. submits the subject's knowledge of itself in time through a process of transformation to alleviate the disjointedness of modern temporality. For instance, Husserl (1991) attends to the subject's ideal grasp of time, lived in "transverse intentionality." For technologies concealing traumatic temporality, outcomes for the subject relate not to transformation but a pragmatically oriented perspectival realism; the subjects of these latter forms of self-relation are not necessarily transformed but buttressed in their histories and capacities. Nonetheless, as sketched below, what oddly connects the ethical ontologies of finitude with the ethics of redemptive rationality is a more direct address of the temporal fragmentation of our epoch. In other words, these opposing perspectives – that of traumatic ethics and redemptive rationality – occupy the same historical moment. Hence, cognitive-behavioral therapies addressing trauma arguably, implicitly, and necessarily partake in, while also concealing, traumatic temporality, yet they do so towards the ends of pragmatic and biopolitical solutions to the quandaries manifested, and they mostly imperceptibly present those suffering the contingencies of trauma with the questions of what ethical stance to adopt, which will alter the ensuing knowledge and subjectification.

The biopolitical capture of trauma in its many technical manifestations, and to the ends of managing risk, creates the conditions for forms of subjectification that necessarily escape the frame of panoptic discipline – in ways consonant with post-industrial sociality bearing reflexive modernization. In an epoch where in dominant economies the production of physical goods (the Fordist factory being its prototypical image) is subordinated to production of knowledge, increased desire for consumption, and the production of human capital/resources, the reflexive stance identified as central to earlier modern subjectivity (Taylor, 1989) attains a hyper-reflexive position. *What does this mean, this transition from reflexivity to hyper-reflexivity?* As Bauman (2000) argues, a condition of "liquid modernity" heightens the perpetual state of transgression (in Nietzschean terms) resulting in two departures from earlier forms of modern consciousness. First is the collapse of the belief that there is an end to human history (i.e., the just society to come), and the second relates to the deregulation and privatization of the process of becoming an individual: "To put it into a nutshell, 'individualization' consists of transforming human 'identity' from a given into a 'task' and charging the actors with the responsibility for performing the task and for the consequences (and also the side-effects) of their performance" (Bauman, 2000, pp. 31–32). Thus, individualization – as a project of re-embedding the subject in successor contexts of significance (as communities founded upon religious meaning, or economic interest) – gives way to the perpetual project of *individuation*. From an epistemic vantage point, what is required is another, further distancing on one's experience, selfhood, or subject position. Giddens (1990) points out that the reflexivity of modern life involves a particular development in knowledge, wherein social practices are continually investigated in light of newly accumulated knowledge (for instance, in the human sciences). Giddens (1990), Beck (1992), and Bauman (2000) reference sociological knowledge as indexical of this increased distance (the way, for instance, we might speak of our interpersonal struggles in light of the "disintegration of the nuclear family"). However, for biopolitics – as a post-panoptic front – it is the subject's self-distancing through the psy-function that bears most directly on the experience and discourse of trauma. Rose (1998) makes this case adroitly, that the subject's relation to itself, in Foucault's (1983a) idiom "action upon action," does not pose a psychologized being against a freer, authentic, humanist subject; rather, the

> diverse fragments and components of psy have been incorporated into the "ethical" repertoire of individuals, into the languages that individuals use to speak of themselves and their own conduct, to judge and evaluate their existence, to give their lives meaning, and to act upon themselves.
>
> *(Rose, 1998, p. 65)*

In other words, the Cartesian reflexivity of rational distancing from the contents of one's consciousness – the thoughts, passions, and intentions that float through the stream of awareness – is radically refigured into the injunction to take hold of the nature of one's psychological being. Psychological knowledge is necessarily related to the modern subject's ethics because it intersects with both the expert institutional systems charged with understanding human being and with the warrant of legitimacy in societies where governmentality is premised on freedom opened through healthy development and satisfaction rather than preexistent right or authority.

In light of the technical mastery of human being in various psychologized forms – in the moves to calculate the aptitude of the individual for endeavors in work and education, but mostly in the epistemic negatives of the clinic – we may inquire into the axes of Foucault's ethics as they correlate to the ascendancy of cognitive-behavioral technologies as oriented to traumatic suffering. As may be recalled, for Foucault (1983b), the four dimensions of one's relationship with self include ethical substance (*substance éthique*), the mode of subjection (*mode d'assujettissement*), the means of subjection (*pratique de soi*), and aspirations of the subject (*teleologie*). In the interest of space, I will mostly sketch out an ethics of redemptive rationality according to the first and fourth dimensions; the means of subjection concerning technique are substantially treated above, and the mode of subjection (narrativity) deserves a treatment elsewhere (e.g., Gergen, 1994). Cognitive-behavioral *techne* – as a biopolitical solution to trauma – reaches its antimimetic apotheosis, not in its extrinsic relation to the subject as power/knowledge (in the cumulative statistical effects of its treatments, for instance), but in its departure from collusion with coercion, in its centrality in the ethical injunction for self-governance. In this context, Foucault's (1983b) ethical substance, therefore, relates specifically to the requirement that the subject attain and maintain a history of its own being. It is well chronicled that autobiographical memory emerges, in its forensic and fictional sedimentations, in the early modern era; however, as Bauman (2000) argues, the early modern subject retains the project of re-embedding its individual being within traditional socio-economic forms (the estates had given way to class membership, whose existence continued to bear the indicia of a static order). However, the reflexive distance necessary to revise selfhood more comprehensively tracks the conversion of linear temporality to that of the historicality of the analytic of finitude. Consequently, it is hardly coincidental that redemptive rationality, as the subject's capacity in writing any number of histories, relates to the ethical mandate that is structural to traumatic ethics, as fragmented temporality (or historicality) – the openness of the subject's being-in-time – constitutes the modern condition for rewriting the history of selfhood pursuant to the arrival of differing interpretive knowledges of the subject. For redemptive rationality, the mode of subjection (*mode d'assujettissement*) as narrativity founds both the manifold ways history may be told and the metanarrative distance assumed. Put differently, the ethical stance so described requires that subject to adopt an awareness of its own history as variably written, which inhabits the same historical spaces occupied by social constructionist psychology with its analysis of subject positions within conversation and discourse as speech acts or practices of signification (e.g., Gergen & Gergen, 1983; Shotter, 1993).

Histories that cognitive-behavioral therapies initiate are, clearly, differently oriented to an overtly psychologized process of individuation that do not foreground the social construction of past experiences, but rather the clinical construction of narratives portending a more vital and resilient future. The antimimetic move pervading the ethics of redemptive rationality considerably raises the ante of Janet's (1925) suggestion that traumatic suffering is ameliorated by the "action of telling a story," as the subject's histories are submitted to vigorous and striking transformations of fact. One way in which histories are changed pertains to the shift from affectively intense memories to those that are putatively "neutral" via their being placed firmly within the past – "Remember, it is just a memory, and a memory on its own can't hurt you" (Monson & Shnaider, 2014, p. 36). As Grey, Young, and Holmes (2002) would address to a typical patient with PTSD the rationale for converting SAM (Situationally Accessible Memories) into VAM (Verbally Accessible Memories): "What we need to do is to activate this trauma memory and update it, using the information you know now in the arguments we have rehearsed. This will help make it more like your normal memories" (p. 43). Nonetheless, the implicit reliance on the historicality of the subject's being is most visible in cognitive reappraisals of past events, their revision in light of the subject's suffering. For instance, in the case of an individual involved in a motor vehicle accident in which another person was killed, Moulds, Hopwood, Mastrodomenico, and Bryand (2009) describe a therapy session in which the patient asserts that he could have averted the accident by driving off the road to miss the oncoming vehicle, yet the therapist persuades the patient otherwise:

Mark: Yeah, but if I could have done something . . .
Therapist: OK, let's just slow down for a moment and review what we have discussed. When you have the thought "if I had done something differently the driver of the car would not have died," it leaves you feeling guilty and depressed. However, when you think it through, it seems like the reality is that at the time there was no other feasible course of action that you realistically could have taken instead. Is that right?

(p. 24)

In Heideggerian terms, the factuality of the patient's past – the impact of his vehicle killing another human being as trauma, as destruction of a certain world involving, perhaps, assumed beneficence of action towards others (e.g., Stolorow, 2011) – is founded upon a more primordial, ontological condition of care, wherein what is or is not past rests on certain future possibilities. Yet, temporality as ethical substance, and language itself as an ethical mode of creation/destruction, is obscured in favor of a rationalized stance taking a particular view towards factuality, aimed at certain ontic realities that may be narratively established. Indeed, as to the above example, it is not at all clear that the patient might not have prevented the accident through a different action; most deeply, this reality as possibility is implicit within the past, yet unavailable to direct knowledge. However, the past comes to be what it always will have been in light of the alleviation of his suffering – the reduction of guilt and depression – which are laudable projects pursuant to biopolitical logic. Another similar example illustrates the historicality of the subject's past in terms even more suggestive of a specifically psychologized rationality. Taylor (2006), drawing upon a clinical vignette provided by Kubany (1997), describes the intractable guilt arising from Vietnam wartime experience wherein the patient had participated in atrocities involving "overkilling" or mutilating the corpses of enemy bodies so as to produce a measure of intimidation in an already violent context. Kubany goes on to recommend suggestions to patients that: 1) soldiers are impaired, numbed in their capacities to experience empathy or compassion; and 2) research indicates aggressive acts (i.e., of being fired upon by enemy troops) cue or trigger aggressive responses that do not yield to limits set in conventional moral codes. In these clinical discourses, therefore, the subject adopts a hyper-reflexive stance over against its position as discontinuous, immoral, and plagued by dissociated affect through the exercise of psychologized rationality as that which forms a normative past premised on psychological functioning first and foremost. In contrast to the pure forms of asylum discipline described by Foucault (1975/1995), the contemporary subject of trauma adopts or borrows a form of self-relation from the therapist, who questions the subject in such ways that establish an ongoing ethical sensibility so that the subject's past may be redeemed of its suffering through the subject's own ongoing clinical efforts to purify the past, to free it from the disease of personality and memory.

If traumatic temporality yields an ethics penetrating the fundamental questions of the epoch – the subject's access to its reflexivity, freedom, and truth – then redemptive rationality, as applied to traumatic suffering, projects its *telos* across the surface of these domains. As treated *supra*, the hyper-reflexivity of redemptive rationality – the referencing of a psychologized subject as a touchstone for narrating one's history – simultaneously conceals a more primary ontological reflexivity (that is, the reflexivity produced as distance from the disjuncture in lived time) and also sutures the wounds arising from the destruction of lived worlds. As Goodman and Marcelli (2010) persuasively argue, significant epistemological shifts during the modern period result in a profound division or severing of ethics as traditionally conceived – either in relation to transcendent knowledge, to tradition, or others in the community. Accordingly, these transformations have several specific effects: the autonomy of reasoning as a relatively amoral and secular enterprise, unconnected with any particular vision of "the good" (Taylor, 1989); the restriction of moral claims to knowledge immanent with the natural order (MacIntyre, 1984); and the instantiation of autonomous reason of the natural order, and its "moral" sense, within the individual (Goodman & Marcelli, 2010). Though Enlightenment approaches to ethical life include deontological approaches, what increasingly manifests in modern psychological thought, as already suggested, contains a strong consequentialist or utilitarian bent (Tjeltveit, 1999). Moreover, such an immanentization of moral being concerns precisely the translation of principle or the relationship with one's suffering, as it pertains to a life with others, into a procedural technology, or means of addressing what is presumed to be the organism's natural ends – functional well-being and adaptation:

> Ethics does not shape rationality; it is a unidirectional relationship. In this system, detached reason allows for the possibility of determining "adaptive" and "normative" thought and behavior, which is then conflated with ethics. Principles are formed from the observation of natural processes and these principles determine what is "good."
>
> *(Goodman & Marcelli, 2010, p. 575)*

As an illustration of the rational means and ends of cognitive-behavioral approaches to trauma, one may well continue consideration of the role of psychologized rational reflexivity in ameliorating the effects of guilt and shame as experiential fallout, which appears highly correlated with PTSD within clinical literature (Kubany, Abueg, Kilauno, Manke, & Kaplan, 1997). In philosophical and theological contexts, guilt – as the felt burden of responsibility for the capacity to act otherwise – may be approached in principle as a substantive matter, that is, as a principle to live by, uphold, implying certain thresholds one should not violate (e.g., to needlessly or recklessly do harm to others, to murder, render falsehoods, withhold protection from those helpless, etc.). Nonetheless, though it is clear these more traditional understandings form a kind of background for discerning the trauma victim's experience of guilt, the clinical address of such experience largely brackets the burdens of selfhood borne by guilt. Rather, what is aspired to is a heightened awareness in monitoring one's own thoughts, feelings, and self-talk: "We may say 'There are certain words and phrases that if you never use again, you will be a happier person' . . . if they [clients] are not aware of negative things that they say to themselves, they are out of control and cannot regulate how they feel" (Kubany & Ralston, 2006, pp. 266–267). Such rationalized awareness involves standing back from experiences, words, thoughts, and affects, and neutrally evaluating them in reference to their ultimate effects on one's being; in other words, not *living through them* or *going into them* but living apart from them, seeing them from the cold light of the efficient calculation of impact. In relation to the Cartesian or classical episteme – in the sense discussed by Foucault (1966/1973) – the subject's knowledge of trauma (his or her revised account), as instantiated in such rational awareness, does not pertain to close correspondence with reality; rather, positive statements are matched against the probability such statements will obtain psychological benefit to the subject in the future. Importantly, such awareness inculcates in the subject an instrumentalist/purposive rationality oriented towards solving questions of guilt, shame, or other negatively charged belief, or affect through modifying these experiences almost entirely within the technical capacities to alleviate suffering, which – by its very nature – is undesirable, and antithetical to the ends of immanent organic reality, which is to thrive with minimal unpleasantness, to grow without the impediment of physical or psychological damage.

According to its *telos*, redemptive rationality for trauma revitalizes – in biopolitical terms – the subject's being along two further dimensions. First, one may recall that under the aegis of traumatic ethics, freedom itself is premised on the subject's self-withdrawal or alienation as a gap in temporality, in missing time. The pragmatic agency pertaining to the subject of redemptive rationality, as it emerges from cognitive-behavioral *techne*, rests on the subject's historical time as unsettled – as being disrupted by later events and relationships to others – yet this primordially fragmented temporality is unacknowledged. For cognitive aspects of trauma therapy, Briere and Scott (2015) write that "trauma-related cognitions should be treated not as products of client error or inherent neurosis, but rather as initial perceptions and assumptions that require updating in the context of safety and support" (p. 159) (see also Chard, Weaver, & Resick, 1997; Resick & Schnicke, 1992). The revision of harmful self-appraisals concerning one's traumatic past as may be projected into the future as expectation requires a past that may be rewritten in light of intervening events, including the ethical mandates of one's relationship with the Other of the clinic, the therapist who helps produce a different narration. Thus, as indicated, the cognitive solutions to trauma rely on traumatic subjectivity itself, which means that the health-giving activities of such therapy amount to a kind of *anti-trauma;* that is, akin to the orthopedic surgeon who must break a bone to reset it, the therapist invokes another rupture or break with traumatic reality in order to allow for healing to occur. For instance, towards technological efficiency in providing pragmatic agency, Resick and Schnicke (1992) advocate for an approach that would "activate memories of the event and will also provide corrective information regarding conflicts and fault attributions or expectations that interfere with complete processing" (p. 750). Consequently, the subject must be mimetically reimmersed into the memory of the event for another antimimetic distancing to occur. Previous depictions that uneasily attempted the assimilation of the traumatic event into the preexistent world(s) – the dissociated world of trauma – must be challenged by this introduction of further trauma. *The traumatic world itself must be de-worlded* through the intervention of an Other bearing another injunction, another message, which is concealed through a principal reliance on technical expertise rather than the desire of the Other as the source of potential transformation. Second, one may also recall that the subject's truth – for traumatic ethics – is unknown to thought, meaning it may not be reduced to knowledge though its effects reverberate, problematize, and in some sense form the tissue or flesh underneath the surface of knowledge. For the technological ethics of redemptive rationality, the truth effects of trauma – meaning the embodied, visceral living out of the beyond of reason – are translated into more logic-oriented forms of experience. Frewen and Lanius (2015) remark that, in cases of dissociative experience, the traumatic event intervenes into normal waking consciousness causing self-referential awareness to be converted into "non-self-referential" or "other-referential" processing, the solution to which is the reestablishment of a personal narrative, one involving a translation of Otherness into *connaissance*, received understandings, sedimented meanings pertaining to one's own life lived. In the context of complex trauma, Courtois, Ford, and Cloitre (2009) write that one principal task of processing or reappraising traumatic memory is the "safe self-reflective disclosure of traumatic memories and associated reactions in the form of progressively elaborated and coherent autobiographical narrative" (p. 93). In such practices, which are befitting of the hedonistic ends of late capitalism, paradox, contradiction, and the ambiguity inhabiting the truth of non-knowledge – the Other's message that must be translated (Laplanche, 1999) – are given over to a scientifically transcendent discourse of adaptive change, and more specifically, about one's own storied being. Accordingly, this ethical subject – while never able to fully efface its being-in-the-world and the trace of Otherness that marks its flesh through time – nonetheless aspires to an ideal position of complete self-recognition ascribed to in the ordinary meanings of words about things. Put differently, what cannot be said but only stuttered, or lived, or taken up is given over to knowledge that may be represented as an unfolding of an own-world (*Eigenwelt*), whose history may be realistically narrated to oneself. Yet what propels the subject of traumatic temporality – as an answer in the Real to the question of the Other, in the Lacanian sense – to forsake its unyielding yet situated freedom for the cold safety of pragmatic agency and autobiographical continuity? Perhaps, in so doing, for the *telos* of redemptive rationality, subjects' truths are tethered, made intelligible as a coherence of the past portending a future of mundane pleasure, satiety, and interest. Knowledge of the world in its realistic pretensions, and the subject's own coherent knowledge of itself in the world after all, bear a residual enjoyment, a substitute for a world that once was but was destroyed. And, in biopolitical terms, satiation, well-being, and interest remain the ends and form the legitimacy of governing.

Trauma and obsessional subjectivity

Due to the prevalence of medicalized thought in the psy-disciplines, we are accustomed to approaching psychological suffering as categorical in nature, where discrete boundaries between disease-like conditions parallel the contours of physical illness. Of course, the correlation of, the concurrence of, psychiatric conditions has a long and troublesome history, as the various correspondences between wildly disparate conditions suggests the disease model is intrinsically flawed, and this insight has even made its way into institutional corridors usually apologetic of reigning diagnostic regimes (American Psychiatric Association, 2013). The typical research solution is to ascertain a more fundamental condition underlying the different surface manifestations, clusters of symptoms – for instance, in the field of trauma studies, "complex trauma" has been postulated as a more central diagnosis for some, which would connect events of trauma with depression, personality disorders, etc. (Courtois & Ford, 2009; van der Kolk, 2005). Yet, despite these debates, another perhaps more disquieting possibility exists, that some forms of psychological struggle appear, almost, to be solutions to others. That is, traumatic subjectivity may itself be addressed, countered by instilling in the subject another, different form of experience that itself contains a pathological limit, as well as a pragmatic or useful end. Though a thorough working out of this line of argument is beyond the scope of the present work, the following is suggestive that obsessional subjectivity, not specifically the categories of OCD (Obsessive Compulsive Disorder) or OCPD (Obsessive Compulsive Personality Disorder), but the structure of experience making them possible, is institutionally available for the suturing of traumatic temporality and subjectivity.

Current cognitive-behavioral perspectives on obsessionality, while tracking the psychoanalytic concerns with pathological doubt, orient themselves to what may be understood on an epidemiological plane. On the contrary, as noted, Lacanian psychoanalysis orients itself, through its conception of traumatic subjectivity, to *ontological doubt* ("What am I beyond thought?") rather than *epistemological doubt* ("What am I that may be thought?"). Consequently, the subject's conscious life is not tracked as psycho-biography but as a fantasy of identity deriving from the desiring subject entwined in a symptomatic thought process. As such, the obsessional subject's concern with both doubt and knowledge persist structurally for the modern, Lacanian subject. Emblematic of the traumatic subjectivity that would include the thinking of Heidegger (1927/1962) and Levinas (1961/1969), Lacanian subjectivity as mentioned is precipitated from a being's submission to the alienating effects of the symbolic order, and separation from an imagined return to a position of plenitude within an economy of the Other's desire (Lacan, 1966/2006; cf. Laplanche, 1999). Specific to the Lacanian account of foundational trauma, as previously argued, the modern subject's lack in temporal being (*manque-à-être*) gives rise to differing strategies towards impossible rejoining with Being, and the fulfillment of its desire thereof. As a result of differing pathways in cultivating desire in the face of potentially unbearable loss, hysterics and obsessionals have differing orientations to the object cause of desire (*petit objet a*) and differing relations to knowledge. As Lacan (1966/2006) observes, the obsessive, in a Cartesian manner – by thinking – "negates the Other's desire, forming his fantasy in such a way as to accentuate the impossibility of the subject vanishing" (p. 698). Where the hysteric notably identifies his/her coming to knowledge with what the *other wants from him/her*, the obsessional subject fantasizes that she/he may come to knowledge *outside of this relation*, as a non-divided subject fantasizing about an unmediated relation with the object cause of his/her desire. Consequently, the obsessional subject's link with the Other is dissimulated, and his/her desire follows the conduit within the confines of his/her knowledge pursuant to the phallic function. Accordingly, Soler (1996) notes that the return of the repressed – as desire-infused thinking – sutures the gap in the obsessive's temporally divided being.

Obsessionality is implicated not only in the suffering it often produces, in its feverishly unattainable understanding of its own being, but also for the work it undertakes on behalf of technocratic institutions, and the mode of its production of knowledge. Concerning Lacan's four discourses, unlike the discourse of the hysteric, there is no discourse of the obsessive (Fink, 1995); however, the obsessive subject's desire ostensibly aligns with the ends of the university discourse in his/her attempt to exhaustively represent the world (and his own selfhood) to him or herself. For Lacan (2007), the structure of university discourse is schematized as $S_2/S_1 \rightarrow a/\$$. Thus, the signifier as knowledge (S_2) substitutes for the master signifier (S_1) in the position of agent that addresses the Other – marking and intervening into one's temporal being as object a, or the surplus value over what may be said, represented, or known in the event of trauma. The split subject is so produced, but also barred, and the master signifier (the force of authority) becomes the truth that underwrites said relations of knowledge. In other words, knowledge undergirded by governmental authority comes to the unknown event to translate it or convert into a realistic medium.

Psychological, obsessional discourses on trauma (S_2) partake in the ever-receding final accumulation of theoretical knowledge concerning the phenomenon of trauma collectively and for the particular subject. For Parker (2001), the psychological Other (object a in university discourse) – as the addressee of this power/knowledge in the Foucauldian sense – escapes the epistemic frame. What is produced or falls out of this relation is the subject ($\$$) beyond that of psychology, whose divided being may not finally be circumscribed in knowledge. The impossibility of achieving such epistemic mastery reveals the fundamental difference between representation/thinking and what is represented/being, a difference borne through historicality, which is precisely the condition of possibility for revising the post-traumatic selfhood wracked by guilt, shame, disgust, and recurrently searing memories of the event of trauma (Monson & Shnaider, 2014; Resick & Schnike, 1992). This interpretive turn requires an openness in the subject's being – the chasm between mimetic immersion and antimimetic depiction – that would allow for new understandings to emerge but also newly formulated discourses on the clinical phenomenon of trauma itself. Yet, university discourse, including technologies addressing suffering, must obey – in the Lacanian idiom – the structurally libidinalized knowing of selfhood as a matter of pure knowledge, pursuant to the biopower: "In the University discourse, is not the upper level ($S_2 - a$) that of biopolitics (in the sense deployed by Foucault to Agamben)?" (Žižek, 2004, p. 399). Because the obsessional subject partakes in our culture's fantasy of completeness, biographical continuity (even retroactively established), and the power of technical reason to ascertain the nature of things, its traumatic being is concealed. This subject inquires into the mystery of its open being-in-time from the perspective of theory, data, what can be known and communicated. From a Lacanian perspective, a society of biopolitics would not only work on our bodies and consciousness to form its habits of action and thought, but also to obsessively structure our unconscious relation to knowledge, to infuse into us a desire to enjoy our own epistemological self-regulation, to attain scientific knowledge to the ends of its own security.

Obsession in the age of biopower requires a double movement of Oedipal subjectivity to achieve its ends, to suture the temporal void at the heart of the subject's being. The doubt instantiated in epistemological questioning of psychologized being – i.e., to inquire into the more wholesome understandings of one's past and future – requires a certain fantasy of desire, or coming to knowledge that is *obtainable* and *unobtainable* at the same time. From the Lacanian view on neurotic structure, the obsessional subject's lack or division is temporarily solved through coming to psycho-biographical knowledge of selfhood, but one that constantly escapes. Current technological approaches to trauma actively collude with this fantasy of producing knowledge that will increasingly facilitate this subject's own self-monitoring – all of the various forms of processing traumatic memory, of cognitive reappraisal already discussed. On the one hand, for societies of control, such knowledge as university discourse ($S_2 \rightarrow a$, the upper half of the formula) must address the fantasy as potentially realized. On the other hand, reflexive doubt requires an openness or lack in the subject's being ($) that would escape any particular form of *connaissance*. The various master signifiers at work in biopower (the S_1s) – beholden to the ethics of redemptive rationality – must simultaneously afford the benefit of closing down the subject's being for purposes of tracking, while opening the aperture for its circumscribed escape for ongoing work and consumption without losing grip, in the terminology of Deleuze and Guattari (1972/1983), on a fully nomadic subject. In other words, societies of control need to effectively manage epistemological doubt, maintaining the subject's openness in being and time without triggering ontological doubt, which would revolutionize subjectivity itself.

References

Agamben, G. (1998). *Homo sacer: Sovereign power and bare life* (D. Heller-Roazen, Trans.). Stanford, CA: Stanford University Press.

American Psychiatric Association. (2013). *Diagnostic and statistical manual of mental disorders* (5th ed.). Washington, DC: Author.

Anthanasiou, A. (2003). Technologies of humanness, aporias of biopolitics, and the cut body of humanity. *Differences, 14*, 125–162.

Atkeson, B. M., Calhoun, K. S., Resick, P. A., & Ellis, E. M. (1982). Victims of rape: Repeated assessment of depressive symptoms. *Journal of Consulting and Clinical Psychology, 50*(1), 96–102.

Bauman, Z. (2000). *Liquid modernity*. Cambridge, UK: Polity Press.

Beck, A. T., Emery, G., & Greenberg, R. L. (2005). *Anxiety disorders and phobias: A cognitive perspective*. Cambridge, MA: Basic Books.

Beck, U. (1992). *Risk society: Towards a new modernity*. London, UK: Sage.

Bolton, D., & Hill, J. (1996). *Mind, meaning, and mental disorder: The nature of causal explanation in psychology and psychiatry*. Oxford, UK: Oxford University Press.

Briere, J. N., & Scott, C. (2015). *Principles of trauma: A guide to symptoms, evaluation, and treatment: DSM-5 update* (2nd ed.). Los Angeles, CA: Sage.

Burkitt, I. (1993). Overcoming metaphysics: Elias and Foucault on power and freedom. *Philosophy of the Social Sciences, 23*(1), 50–72.

Canguilhem, G. (1989). *The normal and the pathological* (C. Fawcett, Trans.). New York, NY: Zone Books.

Caruth, C. (1996). *Unclaimed experience: Trauma, narrative, and history*. Baltimore, MD: Johns Hopkins University Press.

Chard, K. M., Weaver, T. L., & Resick, P. A. (1997). Adapting cognitive processing therapy for child sexual abuse survivors. *Cognitive and Behavioral Practice, 4*, 31–52.

Courtois, C. A., & Ford, J. D. (Eds.). (2009). *Treating complex traumatic stress disorder*. New York, NY: Guilford Press.

Courtois, C. A., Ford, J. D., & Cloitre, M. (2009). Best practices in psychotherapy for adults. In C. A. Courtois & J. D. Ford (Eds.), *Treating complex traumatic stress disorders* (pp. 82–103). New York, NY: Guilford Press.

Danziger, K. (2008). *Marking the mind: A history of memory*. Cambridge, UK: Cambridge University Press.

Deleuze, G. (1992). Postscript on societies of control. *October, 59*, 3–7.

Deleuze, G., & Guattari, F. (1983). *Anti-Oedipus: Capitalism and schizophrenia* (R. Hurley, M. Seem, & H. Lane, Trans.). Minneapolis: University of Minnesota Press. (Original work published 1972)

Demasio, A. (1994). *Descartes' error: Emotion, reason, and the human brain*. New York, NY: Putnam.

Dennett, D. (1991). *Consciousness explained*. Boston, MA: Little, Brown & Co.

Derrida, J. (2001). A discussion with Jacques Derrida. *Theory and Event, 5*(1). doi: 10.1353/tae.2001.0004.

Ehlers, A., & Clark, D. M. (2000). A cognitive model of posttraumatic stress disorder. *Behaviour Research and Therapy, 38*, 319–345.

Erichsen, J. E. (1859). *The science and art of surgery*. Philadelphia, PA: Blanchard and Lea.

Erichsen, J. E. (1866). *On railway and other injuries of the nervous system*. London, UK: Wallace and Maberly.

Esposito, R. (2008). *Bios: Biopolitics and philosophy* (T. Campbell, Trans). Minneapolis: University of Minnesota Press.

Esposito, R. (2009). *Communitas: The origin and destiny of community*. Stanford, CA: Stanford University Press.

Esposito, R. (2011). *Immunitas: The protection and negation of life*. Cambridge, UK: Polity.

Fink, B. (1995). *The Lacanian subject: Between language and jouissance*. Princeton, NJ: Princeton University Press.

Fischoff, B. (1975). Hindsight ≠ foresight: The effect of outcome knowledge on judgment under uncertainty. *Journal of Experimental Psychology: Human Perception and Performance, 1*, 288–299.

Fiske, S., & Taylor, S. (1991). *Social cognition*. New York, NY: McGraw-Hill.

Fitzpatrick, P. (2006). "What are the gods to us now?": Secular theology and the modernity of law. *Theoretical Inquiries in Law, 8*(1), 161–190.

Foa, E. B., & Kozak, M. J. (1986). Emotional processing of fear: Exposure to corrective information. *Psychological Bulletin, 99*, 20–35.

Foa, E. B., & McNally, R. J. (1996). Mechanisms of change in exposure therapy. In R. Rapee (Ed.), *Current controversies in the anxiety disorders* (pp. 329–343). New York, NY: Guilford Press.

Foa, E. B., & Rothbaum, B. (1998). *Treating the trauma of rape: Cognitive-behavioral therapy for PTSD*. New York, NY: Guilford Press.

Foa, E. B., Steketee, G., & Rothbaum, B. (1989). Behavioral/cognitive conceptualizations of post-traumatic stress disorder. *Behavior Therapy, 20,* 155–176.

Foucault, M. (1973). *The order of things: An archaeology of the human sciences* (A. Sheridan, Trans.). New York, NY: Vintage. (Original work published 1966)

Foucault, M. (1983a). The subject and power. In H. Dreyfus & P. Rabinow (Eds.), *Michel Foucault: Beyond structuralism and hermeneutics* (pp. 208–226). Chicago, IL: University of Chicago Press.

Foucault, M. (1983b). On the genealogy of ethics: An overview of a work in progress. In H. Dreyfus & P. Rabinow (Eds.), *Michel Foucault: Beyond structuralism and hermeneutics* (pp. 229–252). Chicago, IL: University of Chicago Press.

Foucault, M. (1990). *The history of sexuality: Vol. 1. An introduction* (R. Hurley, Trans.). New York, NY: Vintage. (Original work published 1976)

Foucault, M. (1994). The ethic of care for the self as a practice of freedom: An interview (J. D. Gauthier, Trans.). In J. Bernauer & D. Rasmussen (Eds.), *The final Foucault* (pp. 1–20). Cambridge, MA: MIT Press.

Foucault, M. (1995). *Discipline and punish: The birth of the prison* (A. Sheridan, Trans.). New York, NY: Vintage. (Original work published 1975)

Foucault, M. (2003). *"Society must be defended": Lectures at the Collège de France 1975–1976* (A. Fontana, Trans.). New York, NY: Picador.

Foucault, M. (2005). *The hermeneutics of the subject: Lectures at the Collège de France 1981–1982* (G. Burchell, Trans.). New York, NY: Picador.

Foucault, M. (2006). *Psychiatric power: Lectures at the Collège de France 1973–1974* (A. Davidson, Trans.). New York, NY: Picador.

Foucault, M. (2008). *The birth of biopolitics: Lectures at the Collège de France 1978–1979* (G. Burchell, Trans.). New York, NY: Palgrave.

Foucault, M. (2009). *Security, territory, population: Lectures at the Collège de France 1977–1978* (G. Burchell, Trans.). New York, NY: Picador.

Freud, S. (1958). Remembering, repeating, and working-through. In J. Strachey (Ed. & Trans.), *The standard edition of the complete psychological works of Sigmund Freud* (Vol. 12, pp. 145–156). London, UK: Hogarth Press. (Original work published 1914)

Freud, S. (1961). *Beyond the pleasure principle* (J. Strachey, Trans.). New York, NY: Norton. (Original work published 1920)

Frewen, P., & Lanius, R. (2015). *Healing the traumatized self: Consciousness, neuroscience, treatment*. New York, NY: Norton.

Gergen, K. J. (1994). *Realities and relationships: Soundings in social construction*. Cambridge, MA: Harvard University Press.

Gergen, K. J., & Gergen, M. M. (1983). Narratives of the self. In T. R. Sarbin (Ed.), *Studies in social identity* (pp. 254–273). New York, NY: Praeger.

Giddens, A. (1990). *The consequences of modernity*. Cambridge, UK: Polity.

Goodman, D., & Marcelli, A. (2010). The great divorce: Ethics and identity. *Pastoral Psychology, 59*(5), 563–583.

Grey, N., Young, K., & Holmes, E. (2002). Cognitive restructuring within reliving: A treatment for peritraumatic emotional "hotspots" in posttraumatic stress disorder. *Behavioural and Cognitive Psychology, 30*(1), 37–56.

Haaken, J. (1998). *Pillar of salt: Gender, memory, and the perils of looking back*. New Brunswick, NJ: Rutgers University Press.

Hacking, I. (2016). Biopower and the avalanche of printed numbers. In V. W. Cisney & N. Morar (Eds.), *Biopower: Foucault and beyond* (pp. 65–81). Chicago, IL: University of Chicago Press.

Hammer, E. (2011). *Philosophy and temporality from Kant to critical theory.* Cambridge, UK: Cambridge University Press.

Hardt, M., & Negri, A. (2000). *Empire: The new world order.* Cambridge, MA: Harvard University Press.

Hardt, M., & Negri, A. (2004). *Multitude: War and democracy in the age of empire.* New York, NY: Penguin.

Harvey, A. G., & Bryant, R. A. (1998). The relationship between acute stress disorder and posttraumatic stress disorder: A prospective evaluation of motor vehicle accident survivors. *Journal of Consulting and Clinical Psychology, 66,* 507–512.

Heidegger, M. (1962). *Being and time* (J. Macquarrie & E. Robinson, Trans.). San Francisco, CA: Harper. (Original work published 1927)

Herman, J. (1992). *Trauma and recovery.* New York, NY: Basic Books.

Hobbes, T. (1982). *Leviathan.* London, UK: Penguin. (Original work published 1651)

Hook, D. (2007). *Foucault, psychology and the analytics of power.* New York, NY: Palgrave.

Husserl, E. (1991). *On the phenomenology of internal time consciousness* (J. B. Bough, Trans.). Dordrecht, the Netherlands: Kluwer.

Janet, P. (1925). *Psychological healing: Vol. 1.* New York, NY: Macmillan.

Janoff-Bulman, R. (2010). *Shattered assumptions.* New York, NY: Free Press.

Kant, I. (1996). *The metaphysics of morals* (M. Gregor, Trans.). Cambridge, UK: Cambridge University Press. (Original work published 1797)

Kirk, S., Cohen, D., & Gomory, T. (2015). DSM-5: The delayed demise of descriptive diagnosis. In S. Demazeux & P. Singy (Eds.), *The DSM-5 in perspective: Philosophical reflections on the psychiatric Babel* (pp. 63–81). New York, NY: Springer.

Koselleck, R. (2004). *Futures past: On the semantics of historical time* (K. Tribe, Trans.). New York, NY: Columbia University Press.

Kubany, E. S. (1997). Application of cognitive therapy for trauma-related guilt (CT-TRG) with a Vietnam veteran troubled by multiple sources of guilt. *Cognitive and Behavioral Practice, 4,* 213–244.

Kubany, E. S., Abueg, F. R., Kilauno, W. L., Manke, F. P., & Kaplan, A. S. (1997). Development and validation of the sources of trauma-related guilt survey: War zone version. *Journal of Traumatic Stress, 10*(2), 235–258.

Kubany, E. S., & Ralston, T. C. (2006). Cognitive therapy for trauma-related guilt. In V. M. Follette & J. I. Ruzek (Eds.), *Cognitive-behavioral therapies for trauma* (pp. 258–289). New York, NY: Guilford.

Lacan, J. (2006). The subversion of the subject and the dialectic of desire (B. Fink, Trans.). In *Écrits: The first complete edition in English* (pp. 671–702). New York, NY: Norton. (Original work published 1966)

Lacan, J. (2007). *The seminar of Jacques Lacan: Book XVII. The other side of psychoanalysis* (R. Grigg, Trans.). New York, NY: Norton.

Laplanche, J. (1999). *Essays on otherness* (pp. 138–165). London, UK: Routledge.

Lemke, T. (2011). *Biopolitics: An advanced introduction* (E. F. Trump, Trans.). New York, NY: New York University Press.

Lerner, M. J. (1980). *The belief in a just world: A fundamental delusion.* New York, NY: Plenum Press.

Levinas, E. (1969). *Totality and infinity: An essay on exteriority* (A. Lingis, Trans.). Pittsburgh, PA: Duquesne University Press. (Original work published 1961)

Luckhurst, R. (2014). Future shock: Science fiction and the trauma paradigm. In G. Buelens & R. Durrant (Eds.), *The future of trauma theory: Contemporary literary and cultural criticism* (pp. 157–168). London, UK: Routledge.

MacIntyre, A. (1984). *After virtue.* Notre Dame, IN: Notre Dame University Press.

McCann, W. J., & Pearlman, L. A. (1990). *Psychological trauma and the adult survivor: Theory, therapy, and transformation*. Philadelphia, PA: Brunner/Mazel.

Monson, C. M., & Shnaider, P. (2014). *Treating PTSD with cognitive-behavioral therapies*. Washington, DC: American Psychological Association.

Moulds, M. L., Hopwood, S., Mastrodomenico, J., & Bryand, R. A. (2009). Cognitive therapy for acute stress disorder. In N. Grey (Ed.), *A casebook of cognitive therapy for traumatic stress reactions* (pp. 14–30). London, UK: Routledge.

Mowrer, O. H. (1960). *Learning theory and behavior*. New York, NY: Wiley.

Page, H. W. (1883). *Injuries of the spine and spinal cord without apparent mechanical lesion, and nervous shock, in their surgical and medico-legal aspects*. London, UK: Churchill.

Parker, I. (2001). Lacan, psychology, and the discourse of the university. *Psychoanalytic Studies, 3*(1), 67–77.

Patton, P. (2016). Power and biopower in Foucault. In V. W. Cisney & N. Morar (Eds.), *Biopower: Foucault and beyond* (pp. 102–117). Chicago, IL: University of Chicago Press.

Pinker, S. (1997). *How the mind works*. New York, NY: Norton.

Pitman, R. K., Orr, S. P., Forgue, D. F., Altman, B., de Jong, J. B., & Herz, L. R. (1990). Psychophysiologic responses to combat imagery of Vietnam veterans with posttraumatic stress disorder versus other anxiety disorders. *Journal of Abnormal Psychology, 99*(1), 49–54.

Resick, P. A., Monson, C. M., & Chard, K. M. (2008). *Cognitive processing therapy: Veteran/military version*. Washington, DC: U. S. Department of Veterans Affairs.

Resick, P. A., & Schnicke, M. K. (1992). Cognitive processing therapy for sexual assault victims. *Journal of Consulting and Clinical Psychology, 60*(5), 748–756.

Ribot, T. A. (1882). *Diseases of the memory: An essay in the positive psychology*. London, UK: Kegan Paul, Trench.

Riggs, D. S., Cahill, S. P., & Foa, E. B. (2006). Prolonged exposure treatment of posttraumatic stress disorder. In V. M. Follette & J. I. Ruzek (Eds.), *Cognitive-behavioral therapies for trauma* (pp. 65–95). New York, NY: Guilford.

Romanyshyn, R. (1978). Psychology and the attitude of science. In R. S. Valle & M. King (Eds.), *Existential-phenomenological alternatives for psychology* (pp. 18–47). New York, NY: Oxford University Press.

Rosch, E. (1978). Principles of categorization. In E. Rosch & B. B. Lloyd (Eds.), *Cognition and categorization* (pp. 27–48). Hillsdale, NJ: Erlbaum.

Rose, N. (1990). *Governing the soul: The shaping of the private self*. London, UK: Routledge.

Rose, N. (1998). *Inventing ourselves: Psychology, power, and personhood*. Cambridge, UK: Cambridge University Press.

Rothberg, M. (2009). *Multidirectional memory: Remembering the Holocaust in the age of decolonization*. Stanford, CA: Stanford University Press.

Rousseau, J.-J. (1968). *On the social contract* (M. Cranston, Trans.). London, UK: Penguin. (Original work published 1762)

Shipherd, J. C., Street, A. E., & Resick, P. A. (2006). Cognitive therapy for posttraumatic stress disorder. In V. M. Follette & J. I. Ruzek (Eds.), *Cognitive-behavioral therapies for trauma* (pp. 96–116). New York, NY: Guilford.

Shotter, J. (1993). *Conversational realities: Constructing life through language*. London, UK: Sage.

Soler, C. (1996). Hysteria and obsession. In R. Feldstein, B. Fink, & M. Jaanus (Eds.), *Reading seminars I & II: Lacan's return to Freud* (pp. 248–282). Albany: State University of New York Press.

Stolorow, R. (2011). *World, affectivity, trauma: Heidegger and post-Cartesian psychoanalysis*. New York, NY: Routledge.

Summerfield, D. (1998). The social experience of war and some issues in the humanitarian field. In P. J. Bracken & C. Petty (Eds.), *Rethinking the trauma of war* (pp. 9–37). London, UK: Free Association.

Taylor, C. (1989). *Sources of the self: The making of the modern identity.* Cambridge, MA: Harvard University Press.

Taylor, S. (2006). *Clinician's guide to PTSD: A cognitive-behavioral approach.* New York, NY: Guilford Press.

Tjeltveit, A. C. (1999). *Ethics and values in psychotherapy.* London, UK: Routledge.

van der Kolk, B. A. (1996). *Trauma and memory.* In B. van der Kolk, A. McFarlane, & L. Weisath (Eds.), *Traumatic stress: The effects of overwhelming experience on mind, body, and society* (pp. 279–302). New York, NY: Guilford.

van der Kolk, B. (2005). Developmental trauma disorder. *Psychiatric Annals, 35*(5), 401–408.

van der Kolk, B. (2014). *The body keeps the score: Brain, mind, and body in the healing of trauma.* New York, NY: Penguin.

Vermeulen, P. (2014). The biopolitics of trauma. In G. Buelens & R. Durrant (Eds.), *The future of trauma theory: Contemporary literary and cultural criticism* (pp. 141–156). London, UK: Routledge.

Zayfert, C., & Becker, C. B. (2007). *Cognitive-behavioral therapy for PTSD: A case formulation approach.* New York, NY: Guilford Press.

Žižek, S. (2004). The structure of domination today: A Lacanian view. *Studies in East European Thought, 56*(4), 383–403.

CONCLUSION

What is the question to which "trauma" is the answer? Or, what does it mean to be the historical subject of trauma? This has been the abiding question for the foregoing inquiry, with implications for diverse domains of thought and practice. As related, another question emerges that will guide these final remarks: *How does traumatic subjectivity participate in our current epoch's manner of unconcealing Being?*

The confluence of a Foucauldian analysis inflected with a later Heideggerian perspective on the nexus between history and Being may allow us a closing view. Though the Heideggerian notion of *Ereignis* is often translated as "enowning" or "the event of appropriation," Sheehan (2015) offers evidence that Heidegger rejects any interpretation involving that of a discrete event or happening. Rather, as Sheehan (2015) points out at length, such an event is more aptly said to be an occurrence or appearance that is also a bringing-into-its-own: "Ereignis means that ex-sistence has always already been brought into its own as the thrown-open clearing, and 'occurs' precisely in that" (p. 234). In other words, the event of appropriation brings phenomena into their own, as appearing and occurring in their own right. As stated earlier, the later Heidegger moves towards identifying Dasein itself (now Da-sein) with the historical manifestation of the opening of the clearing of Being, involved in his history of Being or *Seinsgeschichte*. As such, Heidegger (1969) writes that "Man [Da-sein] and Being are appropriated to each other. They belong to each other" (pp. 31–32). Intimately tied with *Ereignis* and Da-sein's relation to Being is *Seinsvergessenheit* or the forgetting of Being, the ways that the originary clearing of Being has been obscured in Western thought, which – according to Heidegger – spans from the pre-Socratics (the missing of the clearing) through the metaphysical concealments of Western metaphysics (the forgetting of Being) (Sheehan, 2015). In *Contributions to Philosophy*, Heidegger (1999) elucidates further elements of the technological concealment involved in *Gestell* or enframing, as discussed in relation to the scientistic renderings of traumatic suffering. That is, Heidegger sketches out machination (*Machenschaft*) as a matter of three concealments in the abandonment of Being: calculation (the dominance of orderability), acceleration (the increase of technical speed), and massiveness (the primacy of commonality). As argued throughout this work, trauma – as a clinical discourse and practice – orders or calculates suffering in a fashion that accelerates the speed at which the subject may retain an open futural horizon, and accomplishes this feat through massifying the subject's distress and formulating standardized procedures in address thereof. Yet, there is a tension here in Heidegger's attempt to circumvent metaphysical thinking, and – more particularly – in a distinction between what occurs, unfolds, or is unconcealed in its most originary opening in Being and Da-sein's activities in concealing *Ereignis*, assuming that Da-sein is itself a clearing within Being rather than apart from, or over against Being. In escaping the residual transcendental or metaphysical gravities of this analysis, which Foucault attempts, a certain immanentist move is necessary. As Raynor (2007) provocatively indicates, Foucault's (1984/1990) notion of "problematization" as both the historical occurrences that give being and truth (e.g., the emergence of sexuality in the nineteenth century) and the critical maneuvers that analyze their grounding for a "history of the present" appear to parallel *Ereignis* as "eventalization" (*événementialisation*). Arguably, Foucault's three axes of analysis (discourse, power, and ethics) participate in his effort – like that of the later Heidegger who moved away from privileging the subject of phenomenology or intentionality – to demonstrate how positivities of Being manifest through Da-sein, how exteriorities of the possible inversely condition the moment, the opening of "here," in its presence. Put differently, certain phenomena, due to their historical position, become problematized in such a way as to become figural for the subject and its constitution. The referential totality of background practices, in a Heideggerian idiom (Dreyfus, 1991), equate with Foucault's three axes that problematize particular forms of experience, bringing them into Being, into the clearing.

While the work of Heidegger and Foucault converge on the thrownness of the subject – and the ultimate impossibility of getting behind the subject's submission to history – the question of trauma, however, calls us to attend to how the subject's epochal being is eclipsed through its dispersal in temporality. As Young (2000) asserts, an important shift occurs in Heidegger's (1927/1962) thought from that of *Being and Time*, where the theme of meaning/nihilism dominates, to the later Heidegger's concern with dwelling/homelessness:

> There is some ontological transformation which lies at the heart of the passage from early to later Heidegger: ontological insecurity . . . has been transformed into ontological security. Why has this sea change occurred? The answer, I would argue, lies in Heidegger's gradual, but radical, reappraisal of the character of the "the nothing."
>
> *(Young, 2000, p. 190)*

As suggested, nihilation – as being-towards-death – was even for the early Heidegger an ever-present condition rather than demise, and what Young (2000) suggests is that the *Abgrund*, the other side of the clearing at the heart of the mystery of Being, is not finally for Heidegger an emptiness but a plenitude, a reservoir of Being that awaits *in potentia* to issue forth. Therefore, death or trauma as nihilation attains a specifically historical status in grounding possibility in the clearing of Being. As such, the withdrawal of Being only manifests as nihilation in a particular epochal form. Moreover, the relation of Heidegger's history of Being and Foucault's archaeological and genealogical pursuits are well known (Schwartz, 2003); however, whatever similarities might be drawn between Being and power (as possibility), differences exist as well, foremost among them Foucault's antipathy towards universalizing gestures. Nonetheless, what is ostensibly left untreated for each thinker involves a theme of common interest, which is that of a subject who is a finite being circumscribed not only by knowledge and material practices, but also given over to its epochal mode presencing and withdrawal. Traumatic suffering, as argued *supra*, discloses a specific historical mode of withdrawal founded within the particular historicity of Da-sein's being. The pre-reflective historicality of the modern subject becomes the precondition for its traumatically temporal being. From a late Heideggerian perspective, this becomes a change in the manner of temporal withdrawal in *Ereignis*. The withdrawal of Being no longer occurs as a disjuncture between an outer, cosmic order and existence (the mode for antiquity), in the alienation of the flesh from its creation spurring various theological dilemmas such as theodicy (the mode for medieval Christianity), or the expulsion of unreason from the absolute gaze of rationality (the mode for the early Enlightenment). For the modern subject, its relation to knowledge connects that of the early Heidegger, Lacan, and Levinas where fragmented temporality becomes the clearing for the presencing of the subject's truth in the ruins of sedimented meaning of everyday talk or what may be Said. The aforementioned "traumatic ethics" structurally governs the subject's traumatic self-withdrawal in relation to what is Other within its being-in-time. This fissure in the modern subject's temporal being creates the conditions for autonomy, reflexivity, and truth – the fallout of the shift in our epoch's mode of withdrawal. Trauma constitutes, before it becomes an ontically framed clinical entity, the coming home of the subject's own being – and capacities for knowledge and relation – within its own temporal horizons. The dawn of our selfhood – including our cherished projects, and the meanings we ascribe to our moral and interpersonal worlds – arises from the night of our being-in-time, from our own irretrievable pasts, which press into us, unspeakably.

Given the rise of biopolitical, clinical strategies that both preserve the modern subject's open futural horizon and suture temporal fragmentation, the position of a traumatic ethics becomes figural as a pathway into the embedded tissues of traumatic suffering. In addressing the difference of such perspectives and practices – i.e., psychoanalysis or existential psychotherapy versus cognitive and behavioral forms of therapy – discerning the dimensionality of traumatic suffering offers a grasping of the specific historical clearing within which our possibilities come to light and recede into darkness. Historically, ontological trauma, as the most invisible and perhaps deepest structure described herein, in its most emblematic formulation – though not exhausted through it – may be understood vis-à-vis Foucault's analytic of finitude as manifestation of the subject's temporal receding from itself as excess between transcendental and empirical conditions for knowledge. As Han (2005) notes, the transformations of subjectivity necessary to attain truth were excluded under the Cartesian and later Kantian concerns with knowledge; here, a gap remains in the subject's being as what may be known. Hence, the return of the requirement for transformation necessary for accessing truth beyond knowledge, which would not be given over to the wounds of sin, the flesh of creation (pre-modern knowledge/truth), or the problems attending aporias in correspondence (classical knowledge/truth). Within a horizontal world, with no external guarantees for knowledge, truth would necessarily have a different origin. Under a Lacanian lens, which is most precise in its illumination of traumatic ontology – this offering a reclamation of the embodied truth while residing within the horizon of temporal finitude – the subject is most primarily and primordially submitted to alienation, which we may recall involves the fundamental expulsion of the subject from its Real being, the signifier losing purchase on the probative meanings and statements made on behalf of the subject's being. As discussed, the alienated subject's being remains a *manque-à-être* or lack in being, surpassing – for modernity – the signifiers regulating the subject's being, and as such remain representations of representations. The subject does not appear directly in these statements, being dispersed *après coup* or through *Nachträglichkeit* whereby the subject is marked and disrupted, retroactively borne, by the Other's symbolic order, its Saying, its *poiesis* (for Lacan, Levinas, and Heidegger, respectively). For the Lacanian trajectory, separation – as arising from the factical or contingently typical way of being in Western interpersonal and familial worlds – refers to a secondary trauma, a further deprivation where the subject attempts to position its own lack in being with that of the Other (being), giving rise to the eddies of desire. Laplanche (Caruth, 2002), as mentioned earlier, articulates a general seduction theory whereby the victim of trauma is seduced into the scene itself. This secondary trauma of separation may be equally well asserted by Stolorow (2007) or Bracken (2002), who argues for a distinctly Heideggerian appropriation of traumatic suffering as *Angst*, existential trauma as a fundamental phenomenological disembedding or de-worlding for a subject who desperately wants to find its being merged with the world, to find its home. In secondary trauma, the symbolic signification of the real Other intervenes into the phenomenal being of the subject, depriving the subject of its status as part of the world or (m)Other. For Lacan, this symbolic cut is itself the paternal intervention as a factical matter in Western familial contexts. For acute, event-based trauma downstream of alienation and the barred seduction into the world itself, such as that manifested in the conceptual architecture of PTSD and related technical understandings, trauma would involve an Other (e.g., enemy combatant, sexually aggressive parent, oncoming automobile) as an intervening cause into the ways that the subject has phenomenologically, hermeneutically, and historically fastened together his or her world over against the impossibility of signification. These dimensions are embedded in one another. One way to think through how historical, primary, secondary, and tertiary traumas interweave through each other in our age is through what might be called "world destruction." Granted, such an idiom privileges a hermeneutic ground for traumatic phenomena at the expense of other, more structuralist approaches. Nonetheless, it could be said that, for modernity in the West, our worlds are extended through and founded upon temporally receding horizons, as our being stretches away from itself as statements of knowledge or signified positivities through our own time, given the absence of external and cosmic guarantors. This excess or escape of fundamental grounding finds its displacements of our being in our earliest interpersonal and familial worlds, and the other various "absolutisms of everyday life" (Stolorow, 2007). We persistently seek to align ourselves with the receding plenitude of Being, to find our home in the arms of others, in certain places, according to understandings of the way the world has held us, or should hold us, and most poignantly as fantasies thereof. The dramatic and intensive deprivations of event-based trauma – as emanating from symbolic and material Others – befall a subject whose originary charge it is to solve the problem of the destructions of its worlds within its own being-in-time, within the history of previous wounds, within the horizons of the founding trauma of thrownness, of being subject to historicality – rather than eternity, rather than fate, rather than creation and its fallen correspondences.

Yet, what meaning are we to make of the relation between traumatic ontology – even as structural to our epoch's mode of unconcealing Being – and the technological concealment through the clinical apparatus of trauma? To address this question is to consider traumatic ethics over against a neo-liberal ethics of redemptive rationality. Engaging the question of ethics is to position the subject within the openness in Being, wherein his or her possibilities recede and are expressed within his or her own being-in-time. Techno-capitalism needs this subject's radical openness emerging from its traumatically temporal dispossession, but it also desperately needs its subjects for the dutiful assignments in a widely dispersed network of governmental relations, in the Foucauldian sense. Accordingly, the truth of the subject's trauma, as well as the reflexivity and autonomy pertaining thereto, must conform to visible and cognizable forms of knowledge. In other words, the modern subject's openness in time – as given over to the technological and obsessional suturing of knowledge – allows it to express, make manifest, and reconstitute forms of individuality through an epistemic modulation of symbolic alterity over against the event itself. To borrow a Deleuzian turn of phrase, the technology of clinical trauma – relying on an ontology of trauma – allows a recoding of what is radically singular concerning the subject's existence, refashioning into what is "individual" (Deleuze & Guattari, 1972/1983). As we have seen, the theories of Erichsen and Janet, as well as more contemporary cognitive-behavioral interventions, instantiate a limit threshold that will locate the subject of trauma according to a particular and privileged hierarchy of knowledge. From a perspective foregrounding power/

knowledge as an outside to subjectivity, this positions the subject within the regulative strategies of biopower – that is, placing the subject's suffering and reconsolidation within "populations" under the rule of functionality and *bio-graphy*, interpolated in birth and death records, in medical records that register the subject's selfhood in the public domain. As a form of ethics, technologies of trauma participate in the concealment of our being-in-the-world, our submission to the Otherness of language and the event in favor of an ideal horizon; it is as if the temporal gap in being has been positioned as a perfect future, free of suffering, and free from the mortal contingencies of this world.

To take seriously the prospect of traumatic ethics, however, is to rise to the maturity of our predicament as ontologically traumatic subjects, requiring a collective traversal of the fantasy that someone else, be it a psychiatrist, psychotherapist, or institution, may somehow bear the burden of our own truths, the Otherness that has traumatically dispossessed us of our own being-in-time. The nihilism in denying the hold the world has upon us is surmounted in owning the experience, or subjectifying the cause of the being that emerges from the destitution of the subject in its relation to alterity. Traumatic ethics entails coming to terms with truth as an effect of Otherness that separates the subject from its immersion in the Real, or in Being, as well as the failure of knowledge that renders the subject in its radical openness in time, yet only in its ineradicable contingent positioning within the world, and the chaotic and unfathomable unfolding of events beyond the ken of *connaissance*. Here, freedom and reflexivity – what of the subject that always escapes the statement or representation – is given to the radical contingency of the past as unsettled by the event. This retroactively given agency does not offer us the hedonistic comfort of metaphysical finalities, even technical ones. Rather it is to own being-in-the world, where Otherness or Being passes to non-Being and always marks the return paths to ourselves. Taking up traumatic ethics is to embrace a socio-historically situated solidarity with those beings who share our epochal mode of withdrawal (e.g., Stolorow, 2007), align ourselves with practices that touch the ontological structure of trauma (e.g., Lacan, 1966/2006), and question the exportation of technologies that would traumatize others in non-Western contexts (Bracken, 1998; Summerfield, 1998), as well it is to cease our own collusion with the "fascism in us all, in our heads and our everyday behavior, the fascism that causes us to love power, to desire the very thing that dominates and exploits us" (Foucault, 1983, p. xiii). Raynor (2007) argues that, in a post-Kantian vein, both Foucault and Heidegger situate the subject in the heart of the present by reflecting on, and questioning, the present situation – and its problematizations – which transforms the subject in relation. A critical ontology of the present, thus, only attains its radical potential through its discernment of the problematic fundaments of the subject's historical being, rather than a regressive and comfortable turning away. As progeny of the Enlightenment, we consistently admonished that we are free, but for whom? Who do we allow to imagine *for us* these, our own messages, directed to us through our traumatic time?

References

Bracken, P. (1998). Hidden agendas: Deconstructing post traumatic stress disorder. In P. J. Bracken & C. Petty (Eds.), *Rethinking the trauma of war* (pp. 38–59). London, UK: Free Association.

Bracken, P. (2002). *Trauma: Culture, meaning, and philosophy*. London, UK: Whurr.

Caruth, C. (2002). An interview with Jean Laplanche. In L. Belau & P. Ramadanovic (Eds.), *Topologies of trauma: Essays on the limit of knowledge and memory* (pp. 101–125). New York, NY: The Other Press.

Deleuze, G., & Guattari, F. (1983). *Anti-Oedipus: Capitalism and schizophrenia* (R. Hurley, M. Seem, & H. Lane, Trans.). Minneapolis: University of Minnesota Press. (Original work published 1972)

Dreyfus, H. (1991). *Being-in-the-world: A commentary on Heidegger's Being and Time, division I*. Cambridge, MA: MIT Press.

Foucault, M. (1983). Preface. In G. Deleuze & F. Guattari (Eds.), *Anti-Oedipus: Capitalism and schizophrenia* (R. Hurley, M. Seem, & H. R. Lane, Trans., pp. xi–xiv). Minneapolis: University of Minnesota Press.

Foucault, M. (1990). *The history of sexuality: Vol. 2. The use of pleasure*. New York, NY: Vintage. (Original work published 1984)

Han, B. (2005). The analytic of finitude and the history of subjectivity. In G. Gutting (Ed.), *The Cambridge companion to Foucault* (2nd ed., pp. 176–209). Cambridge, UK: Cambridge University Press.

Heidegger, M. (1962). *Being and time* (J. Macquarrie & E. Robinson, Trans.). San Francisco, CA: Harper. (Original work published 1927)

Heidegger, M. (1969). *Identity and difference* (J. Stambaugh, Trans.). New York, NY: Harper & Row.

Heidegger, M. (1999). *Contributions to philosophy (from enowning)* (P. Enad & K. Maly, Trans.). Bloomington: Indiana University Press.

Lacan, J. (2006). The subversion of the subject and the dialectic of desire (B. Fink, Trans.). In *Écrits: The first complete edition in English* (pp. 671–702). New York, NY: Norton. (Original work published 1966)

Raynor, T. (2007). *Foucault's Heidegger: Philosophy and transformative experience*. London, UK: Continuum.

Schwartz, M. (2003). Epistemes and the history of being. In A. Milchman & A. Rosenberg (Eds.), *Foucault & Heidegger: Critical encounters* (pp. 163–186). Minneapolis: University of Minnesota Press.

Sheehan, T. (2015). *Making sense of Heidegger: A paradigm shift*. London, UK: Rowan & Littlefield.

Stolorow, R. D. (2007). *Trauma and human existence: Autobiographical, psychoanalytic, and philosophical reflections*. New York, NY: Routledge.

Summerfield, D. (1998). The social experience of war and some issues in the humanitarian field. In P. J. Bracken & C. Petty (Eds.), *Rethinking the trauma of war* (pp. 9–37). London, UK: Free Association.

Young, J. (2000). What is dwelling? The homelessness of modernity and the worlding of the world. In M. A. Wrathall & J. Malpas (Eds.), *Heidegger, authenticity, and modernity: Essays in honor of Hubert L. Dreyfus* (Vol. 1, pp. 187–203). Cambridge, MA: MIT Press.

PSYCHOANALYTIC POSTSCRIPTS

Science, the subject, and hysteria

Kareen R. Malone

Science and the subject

Trauma and the Ontology of the Modern Subject can be characterized as an elaborate meditation on Ian Hacking's (1995) impudent observation, "One feature of the modern sensibility is dazzling in its implausibility: the idea that what has been forgotten is what forms our character, our personality, our soul" (p. 209). Roberts seems to believe that neither philosophers nor psychologists need be moralists, normative in intent, or idealists in order to successfully investigate this historical implacability, which is true enough, if "implausible." He does warn that a social praxis can be opportunistic in response to such meanderings of history. Exemplary in this case, psychology's current academic and disciplinary aims in "treating" and rehabilitating memory and trauma show little reflective genius. The field's erasure of temporality as a subject's province by referring its vicissitudes to the measure of time management and adaptive or maladaptive retrieval defer to either ideals of productivity or simply efficiency in information processing. The compression of temporality manifest as personal and cultural histories into proliferating social identities and support groups resorts to "reifying human beings . . . [leading] to crimes next to which those of the physicist's scientism would pale" (Lacan, 1966/2006a, p. 177). The spectrum of slots may be wide. Nonetheless, contemporary disciplinary blinders leave the psychological field to the most slender slice of a question not to say an approach when it comes to the subject. Where, amid handing out badges and implementing whatever either alleviates or improves, is the appearance of a subject recognized, outside of a functionary of social utility or outcome variable personalized with a bio blurb? To see just what the missing piece may be, for a moment, one can rush into Foucault's (1999) arms:

> Not a critical philosophy that seeks to determine the conditions and the limits of our possible knowledge of the object, but a critical philosophy that

seeks the conditions and the indefinite possibilities of transforming the subject, of transforming ourselves.

(p. 161)

If a human subject is still a question, it is not immune to the historical "revolutions" that define its production and parameters. As Roberts poses it, a problem
within human temporality continues to fester within modernity and a particular
form of its expression can be traced as can be what necessarily emerged within a
break that marked the modern and its sidekick, science. Of course, this is further
tribute to Foucault's influence on this text. On this note, Roberts' book also serves
to recall what can be done if we take Foucault at his best, or at least pursue further
his most vibrant project.

Those seeking universals or satisfied with the constructionist preoccupation
with manifest content will be disappointed. The book collects what one might see
as the debris that swirl and make visible a displacement of foundation (the water
around a sinking ship as example); there has been a rupture and when the most
basic elements of the human vessel return to the surface, one grabs hold if one
has survived the vortex. But what has been spit out from the expanse of the sea is
like Queequeg's coffin, carved with hieroglyphics that reproduce what was first
tattooed on the man's body without his understanding. Once the written message
of a pagan prophet, the inscription survives this new theological context, if unde-
cipherable. Perhaps Melville's tale of a whale is a bit too theological for Roberts'
text. Is the empty coffin still inscribed with the mythological and biblical tropes
of life and death, as dictated from the viewpoint of the heavens? Or is there only a
singular person, clinging to a set of inscriptions, where an empty coffin indicates
the referent. Subject of much speculation, from Christian to Zodiac, Queequeg
"had written out on his body, a complete theory for attaining truth" (cited in
Leiter, 1958, p. 250). But of course, the visionary tattoos that mark Queequeg's
body and the coffin's message are no longer a code originary to the heavens nor
is a prophet there to explain their meaning. It is a re-inscribed remnant that pops
out of an abyss, a rupture, and now serves as both lifeboat and coffin. Lest one
think this pop-up coffin is simply a nice allegory, I must mention Jamieson Webster's (2015) somewhat theatrical, ethical revision of hysterical amnesia: "This act
of self-eclipse, the faint, is an act wed to the *mise en abyme* of the unconscious"
(para. 20). The analyst, in her position or rather desire, will support the subject's
encounter with that abyss, not as the undercurrent of the defenses and revelations
of a hysteric's symptomatology, but as indicative of the subject's opaque relationship to his desire (Gherovici, 2015).

Roberts' troika of Foucault, Levinas, and Lacan are not without ethical com-
pass, in relationship to a truth, even if one can only work within the logic of what
appears to be left to the bewildered subject who remains.

If one starts with Foucault, the book's closest companion, there is nothing acci-
dental or spurious about how Foucault is methodologically or conceptually integrated. How does the subject appear as a weird incarnation of its self-erasure? That

question is clearly espied in Foucault's meditations on sexuality, confession, and on bio-politics. In his inaugural volume of sexuality, plainly a subject is extracted through a series of technical and intersubjective interventions presumingly aimed at an interior qua locus of truth (Foucault, 1976/1990). And at first glance, psychoanalysis is guilty of the same strategies. Moreover, its practice is more than complicit with a power formation within the modern state through its simultaneously misconceiving the ideological shift to bio-politics in its focus on law and repression. Yet even in light of these reservations, Foucault and psychoanalysis comingle; Foucault's distinction between psychoanalysis per se and the institutions of psychoanalysis in alliance with psychiatry is often facilely obscured, in both theoretical terms and in terms of the *polis* (Dean & Lane, 2001; Foucault, 2001).

Instead of rehearsing these debates, Roberts backgrounds the broader shift that defines the work of Lacan/psychoanalysis and Foucault. In so doing, he makes another turn to Foucault, following the seriousness of his query into classical and philosophical meditations on the self, on the cultivation of a self, of its place in the public domain, of its subjective constitution. Given this backgrounding (Foucault, 2005), what has become possible or ethical? *The Care of the Self* (Foucault, 1986) indexes the husbandry of bodily discipline, interrogates, by implication, the cusp of psyche and soma; the acolyte is pursuing a path, natural yet schooled, where self-transformation and thus subjectivity can be assumed, a subjectivity who, if referenced beyond itself, is still able to align itself with truth in a dialectic with concrete existence.

Psychoanalysis itself is geared to a certain practice of particularity. Psychoanalysis "is applied, strictly speaking, only as a treatment and thus to a subject who speaks and hears" (Lacan, 1966/2006c, p. 630). In a clinical enterprise, in which the space of self-exile leaves an analysand to her encounter with a knowledge rapidly disappearing under its effects, there are moments when a subject recognizes itself, hears itself, in a momentary self-difference. From this space, which can be so easily squandered, but in this emptiness of an erasure where the position of knowledge is held differently, there is a moment of freedom. The alterity, from which the heard (or written) comes home to its speaker, is an act of remembering, however troubled and unpredictable. One might agree with Hacking (1995) that it is the forgotten or repressed that now inaugurates the subjective. This is so true: that forgetting is the manifest of a self-division that can never be fully undone. Nonetheless, psychoanalysis leverages a troubled remembering, with no beginning, except as it implicates the subject, who must contend with when, how, and what he has no longer forgotten: "The lack of forgetting is the same thing as the lack in being since being is nothing other than forgetting" (Lacan, 1991/2007, p. 52). Put in well-known terms, "Hysterics suffer mainly from reminiscences" (Freud & Breuer, 1893/2004, p. 7).

It is important to speak about the subject who would come to be in an act of transformation. The transformative effects of a subjective truth or transformative effect as one key to truth must still refer to the historical horizon of its possibility. It must be excavated or deduced from the circumstances from which it may arise and can only be variously guaranteed. The effects are fleeting; their assumption as an expression of a subject is an act of self-constitution. But this self-transformation, when packaged as the promised outcome of the current panoply of products, therapies, and regimens that offer transformation back to itself, is oxymoronic, as one has already placed oneself along the plane of an object, instrumentalized by the very gadget he employs. The contemporary individual becomes an avatar of the rubble of data, data into algorithm, algorithm into best practices and market forces. One is equally empty-handed seeking a line of direct descent from any transcendent template or phenomenology of agency. Rather, the truth is half-said, giving the operation of knowledge a different set of aims and results (Lacan, 1991/2007).

This interrogation of knowledge and the subject is not as academic as one might think. It certainly exercises all intellectual fields, but its cultural dissemination is not without its hitches. Knowledge, now so literally at our fingertips, may not operate as one ideally would have hoped. Information, as presumably an emissary from a (vetted) knowledge paradigm that can encompass that of which it speaks, holds no accountability to truth. We might explicitly embrace or ontologically rejoin values and knowledge to constrain its obscene proliferation to some account (Morawski, 1994; Polanyi, 1958). Roberts has brought forth some fairly powerful arguments against any ontological reclamation through one's immediate presence in the world. For those whose choice has been to triage domains of meaning (e.g., the personal is the political), it could be said that a view proposed in such debates has already presumed some sort of subject, rather than understanding that a relation to knowledge actually lies within the constitution of a subjective stance (as does time) prior to such choices. Despite Jacques-Alain Miller's accusations, Foucault (1980) makes it clear that the history of sexuality is not the same as the history of bread; it is about the conjuncture of knowledge, subjectivity, and truth. Insisting on this historical project, Roberts makes this point carefully. So if we are drawing on a subject as an effect of political power or a subject who has a variety of paths to spiritual redemption, or a subject who revives classical values (particularly in advising others), or enters into a cosmological universe now technologically enhanced, we may be rehearsing formations of subjective posturing. Yet in the West, at least, we must notice that such ethical options occur in a context wherein a broader episteme reigns, wherein knowledge, as produced in modern science, has changed the rules of the game. We are not all the same, huddled around the bell-curve (Soler, 2016), but that normative notion of a subject is not altered when presented with a cornucopia of scripted choices, plucked from every tradition imaginable. One's options within this sea of knowledge are not sufficient to answer the place from which we already would choose this path. These technologies of change are still infused with scientism, escapism, and their inchoate relationship to a person's "health" as mediating any relationship to truth, singular or otherwise. If an ethical claim can plausibly insist on subjective transformation in relation to truth even after that cut named afterward, modernity, trauma may well be the placeholder that marks this subject. If the traumatic intrusion into time is telling, its exact wording leaves open a moment of translation we might mark as subjective.

It is well known that Lacan (1966/2006e) noted that psychoanalysis worked with the subject of science; this rather facile remark about subjectivity partly indicates the aftermath of certain Cartesian dilemmas, but extends to an entire interrelated set of reflections on science by various French thinkers, from Koyré to Canguilheim (Milner, 1991). The status of truth is not dismissed here nor is there a retreat either from subjectivity or science. With Freud as one exemplar, the relationship between truth and formalism, contingency, and logic were introduced beyond repair into the human sciences. In defending Lacan's work from those who saw its terms as reactionary, deterministic, or apolitical, Foucault (2001) made these remarks:

> Lacan's whole trajectory: To take up again the philosophical landscape he had in common with Sartre (Lacan had been Hegelian, and Hyppolite had participated in his seminar); he had been Heideggerian . . . Heidegger put into question the entire philosophy of the subject . . . Armed with all this Lacan's encounter with linguistics . . . showed a play of signification on material objectifiable in terms of knowledge that was no longer assimilable to the intentionalities of consciousness; something happened in the subject, through the subject . . . which allowed Lacan to ask the question of the subject again.
>
> *(p. 58)*

Now one might, with different ears, hear Lacanian discourse differently than Foucault, as an intense dialogue with clinical work and psychoanalysis. But Lacan's linguistic move was twofold. It was not that psychoanalysis fulfilled the ideals of science but rather that the precepts of science reside within its plane of praxis. As one might see in reading Lacan's (1978/1998) *Seminar XX*, and in any number of clinical observations, there is a way in which psychoanalysis must, always like science, work within the necessary and the contingent. The aim is perhaps closer to Feyerabend (2010) than applied psychological theory. Science does not leave the structure of the subject untouched, for instance as derivative from a Kantian distinction between that subject and the empirical individual or the reframing of sensible qualities as revelatory of knowledge. The scientific interventions on the status of knowledge are inherent to psychoanalytic practice (Milner, 2000). Moreover, the access of knowledge is one that is not generated through self-consciousness, but in a speaking, a literation, wherein "it speaks." If there is an unconscious that does speak or cogitate, its significations do not reference specific qualities or attributions. In one of many takes on the *cogito*, Lacan (1966/2006b) writes:

> Is the place that I occupy as the subject of the signifier concentric or excentric in relation to the place I occupy as subject of the signified? That is the question . . . The point is not whether I speak of myself in a way that conforms to what I am but rather to know whether, when I speak of myself, I am the same as the self of whom I speak. And there is no reason not to bring

in the term thought here. For Freud uses the term in a way to designate the elements at stake in the unconscious.

(p. 430)

This may be said many times and many ways, but the words of the subject are not of an empirical individual: *a signifier* represents that subject for another signifier. Words as signifiers are representative and not a matter of representation of any intentional synthesis or perception. Certainly, words can do many things, including representing. Nonetheless, when Freud refers to the dream as a rebus, a game of charades, which analysis must decipher, he evokes not words as vehicles for representation or images as meaning-saturated messages of inner psychic turmoil or release. Rather the images operate, in league with free association, like letters in a foreign language, where through juxtaposition, pattern, and the rhetorical form of their articulation, a subject is thinking, an unconscious is thinking. Such a formulation of thinking is impossible without the advent of science, as knowledge is exiled from the ambit of consciousness, not inherently full of sense or coherence. Unconscious knowledge functions more in terms of its algebraic interrelations, or in clinical work, even puns or jokes. Regardless of whether one would not say that formulas are being devised on the blackboard, the method, within the waves of affect and passion, is close to the formulaic rearrangements of the play between signifiers and letters. It is acephalic; there is no self-conscious subject to moderate it or calibrate its values. But this is not fake news, postmodern fragments of momentary adherence. The knowledge harvested in this project lies within the ethical difficulties laid out by Foucault, that is of subject, who is positioned differently towards his enjoyment. "Where it was, I come to be" bears a relation to truth.

The unconscious as a source of knowledge or even truth refers to a subject and its transformation in terms of speaking, deciphering, and writing. A subject's translation of the real, which most certainly for humans entails a body and its intensities – herein earmarked through trauma – can be posited as a knowledge that does not know itself, lying with the episteme of science (Morel, 2016). Anyone familiar with debates within the philosophy of science is aware that the determination of truth in relationship to knowledge is hardly a matter of agreement, whether one takes a realist stance (Kitcher, 1993), a more problem-solving/pragmatic standard (Laudan, 1977), or a position proposing a sort of anarchy of knowledge (Feyerabend, 2010). Moreover, the very presence of science studies would suggest that science itself is beholden to a certain scotoma of the very circuitous path wherein its knowledge becomes established as truth (Kuhn, 1962; Lacan, 1966/2006e). In itself, the absence of any meta-language, or rather no point of verification to anchor such a meta-language, lends itself to a knowledge that bears a different way in which truth is founded. Thus, then, the ethical question, as linked to truth, arises in a much more disjointed field of effects. If there is no truth about truth for this subject of science, then it will be truly as Lacan (2006e) says, "I, truth, speak" (p. 736). Oddly then, we have a method in which a subject of science is fished out of the water through the very evacuation of meaning that is attributed to science in its "objectification of the subject." But as Foucault notes more than once (as mentioned) for Lacan, science must be used differently if we are to find our bearing with respect to subjectivity and its ethics.

Lacan will take science's troubled relationship to truth (or rather truth about truth) a step further by parlaying its implications into what this unconscious knowledge must imply about how the truth of the subject must indeed operate. The truth will enter into the dialectic of analysis within speaking; it is an effect of praxis. It cannot be assimilated to any coherent (self-possessed) knowledge as that will change its status. This subject within analysis arrives as being an effect of knowledge before she encounters that knowledge. Yet that knowledge is not a meta-language; it is immanent to the dialectic of the analytic work, fragmentary and historically taken up as "where it was, I must come to be." The relationship of knowledge to truth will always exist between the time of the utterance, its literal nature, and the past, the shards of which are now re-absorbed in a new subjective position. Truth is not spelled out but sticks to an ultimately unknown:

> This lack of truth about truth – necessitating as it does all the traps that metalanguage, as sham and logic, falls into – is the rightful place of . . . primal repression, which draws towards itself all the other repressions.
>
> *(Lacan, 1966/2006e, p. 737)*

It is this division of the subject by the signifier, wherein "it" speaks of a certain subject, that renders a real, an impossible to say. It remains a question if this inaugural hieroglyphics of the subject who must slide to the next signifier rather than towards the depths renders the real of subjectivity in a manner akin to Kant's noumena. That is not answered in Lacan's (1966/2006e) essay *Science and Truth*. However, it is apparent that the subject of science/psychoanalysis is brought to account in the lack, wherein knowledge is taken to a limit through the exhaustion of its resources. This limit turns then back upon the subject. One must again note that the cut of science as an episteme – the episteme that Lacan and Foucault recognize as definitive for the subject – is easily distinguished from an ideal of science, which, like any other ideal, will have its followers, practices, and ideologies. If the long-standing debate about psychoanalysis being a hermeneutics or a science is more than a relic of history, it should perhaps consider that this intrusion of science lies at the heart of analysis (Lacan, 1966/2006d). It may be that even given its caveats on knowledge and the limits of knowledge – which an individual eventually discovers both in his own self-division and in that which can never enter the dialectic of his history – he may still claim what he has made of the non-meaning that serves as his point of departure.

The hysteric

Despite often earnestly earned disrepute among many in popular culture, falling by the wayside with church attendance, literacy, and attention span, psychoanalysis has maintained some odd foothold, if only evidenced by those who sustain it through its delegitimation (Nobus, 2016). In scholarly circles, psychoanalysis has been the recipient of many uncompromising critiques as well as generous assessments by feminists and critical race theorists (George, 2016; Mitchell, 1974; Parker, 2001; Spillers, 1996). Psychoanalysis seemingly offers a certain "logos," if you will, of the irrational (Lacan, 1957). It articulates a relationship to trauma, generation, identification, fetishization, and sexual identity. It provides a more encompassing picture of what motors the self-destructive and less comprehensible moments in human history. Given these tools, some can forgive a number of sexist as well as racist shortcomings.

In the case of feminism, psychoanalysis has configured the figure of the hysteric in a manner such that she presents a kind of feminist *avant la lettre*, who lays bare the impossible place of woman, who has been silenced, and interrogates her reproductive destiny and familial relegation (Devereux, 2014). Typically a woman and as, for the most part, the patient, the hysteric leads Freud to a new technique and manner of conceiving of treatment and thus of rendering a praxis of the unconscious. At the same time, the hysteric has been part of a feminist critique of psychoanalysis (Bernheimer & Kahane, 1985), as well as representative of its epistemological vanguard. There are many histories of hysteria; many accounts trade in a number of urban myths, such as its perennial tie to a wandering womb (Gilman, King, Porter, Rousseau, & Showalter, 1993). Yet, if one links femininity and hysteria; one can grant women diagnosed with hysteria by nineteenth and early twentieth-century medicine enormous credit for baffling Western medicine, for introducing particular epistemological questions, such as raised by conversion symptoms, and equally representing an ontological query about desire and the unconscious. If one can allow another brazen contribution, the hysteric shows that sex and sexual difference enters into the health professions and into an interrogation of science; sometimes this sexual component arises quite bluntly and more obscenely on the side of the scientist (Pickmann, 2016; Scull, 2009).

Hysteria in recent centuries was a matter of personal suffering and reflected cultural shifts, but also of challenging one form of knowledge (medicine) with other forms of knowledge – psychosomatic complaints, sexual intimations, and an impossible and inventive array of symptoms that could morph in response to a medical intervention (Gherovici, 2010). In spite of what many could easily dismiss as annoyingly anti-feminist ideas, the psychoanalytic contribution to what sort of subject is at stake in modernity is not only what has been suggested previously in terms of repression, temporality, trauma, and the place of truth. What psychoanalysis began as positing as its subject is wedded to hysteria. Now whether hysteria is linked to femininity or more fundamentally to trauma that takes on a particular form in its legacy is not a moot point. However, it can be said that the subject that stood in for this question of subjective transformation as bearing truth within those paradigms of the modern era would be the hysteric. Science in response would normalize, dismiss, or cauterize such subjective desire. Thus, hysteria in collaboration with psychoanalysis must be given credit to that which was discovered in psychoanalysis in speaking of hysteria or even of the unconscious and its tie to sexuality.

Hysteria need not be seen mostly in terms of a muffled and indirect expression of the political and social disenfranchisement of Western women. Nor is it a position that simply adds its own excesses to the regnant biopolitics of today's psy-disciplines. Rather, hysteria, as a form of address to another, forges a certain social bond in a manner that impacts the very "wordless" structures upon which such bonds are sustained as generative of a subject. The hysteric speaks but his speech generates unconscious knowledge and the truth that is so derived implicates a different ethics. It is even a more daring move to consider if hysteria's persistent if questionable relationship to women also clues one to an emergence of an ethics that may arise from the feminine position (see Soler, 2016). Keeping in mind that a clinical praxis and a social order exist along different axes, this elevation of hysteria into an ethics, beyond the cry of marginal voices, does, at least, reorient the stakes of modern philosophy. Long gone as a diagnosis (Tasca, Rapeti, Carta, & Fadda, 2012), hysteria since 1980 lives on as a way of parsing the real of the subject, of constituting social relations, of orienting knowledge towards desire, of bringing the contingency of trauma to its implications for a place of truth. While I want to avoid idealizing the place of women, it might be at least asserted that hysterics, regardless of biological sex, do wrestle with a certain problematic that is aligned with a feminine position.

Claude Noel Pickmann (2016) makes note of a common refrain about hysterics in the Lacanian clinic (e.g., Grose, 2016). They are the ones who challenge knowledge and expose shams of any discourse, including any naïve appropriation of science or modernity. She also points to the hysteric's relationship to the body. While physicians attempt to locate the symptom of the body in some organic cause, calming the "organ" or at least locating it through all sorts of apparatuses aimed to pacify the ovaries or uterus or clitoris, this comedy of remedies found in history is both laughable and horrifying when one reflects on the efforts of the medical field to cure such patients (Scull, 2009; Tasca et al., 2012). Pickmann (2016) continues with some positive implications of the hysteric's corporeal response to medicine:

> We could say that all these remedies, seen in retrospect, appear harebrained, have as their sole purpose to nullify at any expense the extravagant *jouissance* of the hysteric, a force that manifests its excessive nature through a de-regulation . . . of the organ.
>
> *(p. 38)*

I want to point to questions that arise here, related to sexuality and the body. The disjunctive position attributed to the hysteric as the one who questions the master (medical) discourse or who agitates for yet another answer when knowledge has offered its solutions is refusing both the bit of knowledge per se and the totalization of that discourse that would stop a desire that is being addressed to another. The disjuncture resides in the body, through which the hysteric may very well dramatize the suffering of himself as subject or in the formation of the knowledge that opens to the truth he is seeking – i.e., his desire deciphered in the unconscious as structured as a language. In the case of the former, Lacan comments that Freud is animated by an "order of knowledge" not aimed at harmonizing *Umwelt* and *Innenwelt*, but rather tracing the effects of surplus *jouissance* (Lacan, 1991/2007). This is entropic *jouissance*, for it is a bodily enjoyment that has circulated through the Other, meaning that this *jouissance* is mediated by the objects of exchange that are captured in object relations. At this very corporeal juncture, the body/subject is indeed this nexus of *jouissance* at the interface of inside and outside (the rim) and the disjunction resides in imposition of the Other's *jouissance* in what is now caught in the dialectic of language, love, and demand. What is a lessening of an infantile enjoyment becomes absolute in the unknown of what the Other enjoys in me. The hysterical strategy of posing as the object of the Other's desire, if only to reject that positioning ultimately, would most certainly be consonant with a proximity to the subject's mooring in *jouissance*, as a kind of perpetual vacillation between the object of the Other's *jouissance* and one's own status as a subject. On this fulcrum, sexual relations often flounder; nothing in current conservative or liberal discourses would suggest otherwise.

It may well be, as David-Ménard (1989) argues, that the conversion symptom is so fateful for psychoanalysis because it points to a privileging of the imaginary body rather than an organic one where the erotogenic exchange and the loss of *jouissance* that ties symbolization to lack is re-registered on the real of the body. The subject's repudiation of this loss (and intrusion of a surplus *jouissance*) – a loss that would have allowed a symbolized relationship to an incompletion in her being and in the Other – is instead enacted through a metonymy of erogenous sites. These sites, awry as they may seem, maintain the subject as an eroticized body (for another), but permit the subject to represent that the sexual relationship is impossible as an icon of completion. Whether one starts from David-Ménard (1989) or more closely sticks with the notions of Lacan, the body is engaged as a ciphering of enjoyment, a marking of *jouissance*, which Lacan describes as a sort of proto-signifier. Established by repetition, rather than sense, this mark, called the unary trait, scores the circuit of *jouissance*. One's departure as a subject is grounded in these repetitions of differences that reside in the domain of non-meaning. Correlatively, the loss of *jouissance* that each repetition records in entering its mark into a relationship to another instance operates to saturate what is not sustained by that series of inscriptions in giving rise to the object *a*, or remainder (Lacan, 1991/2007, p. 48).

If the hysteric is the one who brings the Other's desire forward, she also places a lost object, tied to the eroticism of the body, as in the place of truth. If the hysteric's endless desire renders her an agitator in relationship to those master signifiers and discourses that would fully denote the human subject, her truth resides beyond those discourses. Faithful to the remainder, she incarnates a certain suspicion of knowledge. If the object cause of desire may be incarnate in various semblances, in its function as lost object, it is sketched out, in unconscious formations and the slips and parapraxis through which a historical moment, once missing, reemerges as part of the field of the Other from which the subject is born. One might say that *jouissance* clings to the parasitic moments in speech that erupt to give the lie to any ongoing narrative (Soler, 2016, p. 89).

In this praxis found on the hysteric's address, one cannot be a realist about history, now conjoined in the analysis with other unconscious formations. Any piece of history that entails the subject's relationship to *jouissance* is inflected through those fantasies through which the subject has arranged a relationship of enjoyment to that unknowable remainder. Its moment as a return of the repressed is a certain coalescence between this historical moment and a given individual's fantasy, and thus with his *jouissance* as perilously excessive, itself an intrinsic trauma to one's subjectification (Mieli, 2001). History is an etching around trauma. One can never assume that such traumas do not also refer to real effects that overwhelm the subject. There is too much *jouissance* and loss of the symbolic screen through which that *jouissance* could maintain its most bearable distance. So trauma, as a matter of *jouissance*, indeed hits at the center of the subject and at what is both most real and has been necessarily barred in the advent of the signifier as definitive of a particular subject. There is thus a constitutive lack that bridges those dimensions of this subject; the excessive jouissance in the subject links to a lack in the symbolic Other. The lack in knowledge presumed in the Other becomes the degree of freedom allowable through the work of evoking unconscious knowledge. Hysteria has taken on a broader social meaning and Lacan accords it a place as a form of a social bond precisely because of its revelatory turn towards the ascendance of desire and lack in the subject. The hysteric may be no less reluctant to relinquish *jouissance* in her unconscious fantasy or symptoms, but she does recognize the absence of knowing implied by the Other's desire and her staging of that recognition disrupts the happy hum of psychological know-how, for the hysteric questions her desire (Gherovici, 2010), leading analysis down this path to the alienation inherent in language and to the insistence of *jouissance*. Still, this questioning may go to the very edge of knowledge and of being (Webster, 2015). This attribution of incaution, ascribed to hysterics, with admiration or approbation, in a sense aligns her with an epistemic question that might indicate the innovation that still marks a moment of science rather than scientism or techno-capitalism (Grose, 2016). But this possibility cannot be abstracted or idealized. As Rodriguez (2016) notes:

> It is not so much a question of praising hysteria – which is after all a neurosis – and hysterics for being neurotics, which after all requires no particular talents. But it is rather a matter of recognizing that which, in the social bond, the hysteric qua analysand creates and which testifies to the malaise of our culture [by] . . . means of expressing a human truth.
>
> *(p. 22)*

Rodriguez goes on to speak of the neurotic's reluctance to express truth because of an attachment to his complicity in enjoyment, but then again, as Rodriguez must know, he, too, is neurotic and were the knowledge not tied to repression, trauma, sexuality, or an enjoyment one repeats with more or less success, there would be no particular reluctance to encounter this truth. Rather, one follows a particular path, marked by dereliction, deviation, and missteps – and this contribution to how one might approach a locus of truth reflects the creating of psychoanalysis by hysterics. The subjectification that is being both demanded by the analysand (make this my life) and the form of the appeal to an absence that defines desire itself implies that the hysterical discourse would not be satisfied by a spa, a partner, or any great cause, even one to which she is staunchly attached. That is, despite the hysteric's clinical drama, which is related to some master signifier, cause, or ideal, the hysteric is able to sustain a question (Gherovici, 2015). Not only would Freud listen and theorize, but those hysterics who spoke would dismantle the balance of subject and object and find new grounds for truth in rendering a subjective dimension equal to the revolution of culture given by the rise of science.

References

Bernheimer, C., & Kahane, C. (Eds.). (1985). *In Dora's case: Freud-hysteria-feminism.* New York, NY: Columbia University Press.

David-Ménard, M. (1989). *Hysteria from Freud to Lacan: Body and language in psychoanalysis* (C. Porter, Trans.). Ithaca, NY: Cornell University Press.

Dean, T., & Lane, C. (Eds.). (2001). *Homosexuality and psychoanalysis.* Chicago, IL: University of Chicago Press.

Devereux, C. (2014). Hysteria, feminism, and gender revisited: The case of the second wave. *English Studies in Canada, 40*(1), 19–45.

Feyerabend, P. (2010). *Against method* (4th ed.). New York, NY: Verso Books.

Foucault, M. (1980). The confession of the flesh (C. Gordon, L. Marshall, J. Mepham, & K. Soper, Trans.). In C. Gordon (Ed.), *Power/Knowledge: Selected interviews and other writings, 1972–1977* (pp. 194–229). New York, NY: Pantheon.

Foucault, M. (1986). *The history of sexuality: Vol 3. The care of the self* (R. Hurley, Trans.) New York, NY: Pantheon.

Foucault, M. (1990). *The history of sexuality: Vol. 1. An introduction* (R. Hurley, Trans.). New York, NY: Vintage. (Original work published 1976)

Foucault, M. (1999). About the beginning of the hermeneutics of the self. In J. Carrette (Ed.), *Religion and culture* (pp. 158–181). New York, NY: Routledge.

Foucault, M. (2001). The death of Lacan. In T. Dean & C. Lane (Eds.), *Homosexuality and psychoanalysis* (pp. 57–58). Chicago, IL: University of Chicago Press.

Foucault, M. (2005). *The hermeneutics of the subject: Lectures at the Collège de France 1981–1982* (G. Burchell, Trans.). New York, NY: Picador.

Freud, S., & Breuer, J. (2004). *Studies in hysteria* (N. Luckhurst, Trans.). New York, NY: Penguin. (Original work published 1893)

George, S. (2016). *Trauma and race: A Lacanian study of African American racial identity.* Waco, TX: Baylor University Press.

Gherovici, P. (2010). *Please select your gender: From the invention of hysteria to the democratizing of transgenderism.* New York, NY: Routledge.

Gherovici, P. (2015). How to be a more perfect hysteric. *European Journal of Psychoanalysis, 3.* Retrieved from www.journal-psychoanalysis.eu/category/ejp/number-3/

Gilman, S., King, H., Porter, R., Rousseau, R., & Showalter, E. (1993). *Hysteria beyond Freud.* Berkeley: University of California Press.

Grose, A. (2016). Reclaiming hysteria. In A. Grose (Ed.), *Hysteria today* (pp. xv–xxxi). London, UK: Karnac.

Hacking, I. (1995). *Rewriting the soul: Multiple personality and the sciences of memory.* Princeton, NJ: Princeton University Press.

Kitcher, P. (1993). *The advancement of science.* New York, NY: Oxford University Press.

Kuhn, T. S. (1962). *The structure of scientific revolutions.* Chicago, IL: University of Chicago Press.

Lacan, J. (1957). Interview with Jacques Lacan (J. Braungardt, Trans.). Retrieved from http://braungardt.trialectics.com/sciences/psychoanalysis/jacques-lacan/interview-jacques-lacan/

Lacan, J. (1998). *The seminar of Jacques Lacan: Book XX. On feminine sexuality: The limits of love and knowledge, 1972–1973* (B. Fink, Trans.). New York, NY: W.W. Norton. (Original work published 1978)

Lacan, J. (2006a). Presentation on transference (B. Fink, Trans.). In *Écrits: The first complete edition in English* (pp. 176–187). New York, NY: Norton. (Original work published 1966)

Lacan, J. (2006b). The instance of the letter in the unconscious, or reason since Freud (B. Fink, Trans.). In *Écrits: The first complete edition in English* (pp. 412–441). New York, NY: Norton. (Original work published 1966)

Lacan, J. (2006c). The youth of Gide, or the letter and desire (B. Fink, Trans.). In *Écrits: The first complete edition in English* (pp. 623–644). New York, NY: Norton. (Original work published 1966)

Lacan, J. (2006d). Position of the unconscious (B. Fink, Trans.). In *Écrits: The first complete edition in English* (pp. 703–721). New York, NY: Norton. (Original work published 1966)

Lacan, J. (2006e). Science and truth (B. Fink, Trans.). In *Écrits: The first complete edition in English* (pp. 726–745). New York, NY: Norton. (Original work published 1966)

Lacan, J. (2007). *The seminar of Jacques Lacan: Book XVII. The other side of psychoanalysis* (R. Grigg, Trans.). New York, NY: Norton. (Original work published 1991)

Laudan, L. (1977). *Progress and its problems.* Berkeley: University of California Press.

Leiter, L. (1958). Queequeg's coffin. *Nineteenth Century Fiction, 13*(3), 249–254. doi: 10.2307/3044383.

Mieli, P. (2001). On trauma: A Freudian perspective. In M. Dimen & A. Harris (Eds.), *Storms in her head: Freud and the construction of hysteria* (pp. 265–280), New York, NY: The Other Press.

Milner, C. (2000). The doctrine of science. *Umbra (a), 1,* 33–34.

Milner, J. C. (1991). Lacan and the ideal of science. In A. Leupin (Ed.), *Lacan & the human science* (pp. 27–42). Lincoln: University of Nebraska Press.

Mitchell, J. (1974). *Psychoanalysis and feminism: Freud, Reich, Laing, and women.* New York, NY: Pantheon Books.

Morawski, J. G. (1994). *Practicing feminisms, reconstructing psychology: Notes on a liminal science.* Ann Arbor: University of Michigan Press.

Morel, G. (2016). Fifty shades of literary success: The vampire's appeal. In A. Grose (Ed.), *Hysteria today* (pp. 63–85). London, UK: Karnac.

Nobus, D. (2016). For a new gayza scienza of psychoanalysis. *Division/Review: A Quarterly Psychoanalytic Forum, 15,* 17–23.

Parker, E. (2001). A new history: History and hysteria in Toni Morrison's "Beloved". *Twentieth-Century Literature, 47*(1), 1–19.

Pickmann, C. N. (2016). Castration on the rocks: Hysteria in the spirit of our times. *Division/Review: A Quarterly Psychoanalytic Forum, 15,* 38–40.

Polanyi, M. (1958). *Personal knowledge: Towards a post-critical-philosophy.* Chicago, IL: University of Chicago Press.

Rodriguez, L. (2016). Hysterics today. In A. Grose (Ed.), *Hysteria today* (pp. 1–26). London, UK: Karnac.

Scull, A. (2009). *The disturbing history of hysteria*. Oxford, UK: Oxford University Press.

Soler, C. (2016). Hysteria, a hystory. In A. Grose (Ed.), *Hysteria today* (pp. 85–99). London, UK: Karnac.

Spillers, H. (1996). All the things you could be by now if Sigmund Freud's wife was your mother: Psychoanalysis and race. *Critical Inquiry, 22*, 1–24.

Tasca, C., Rapeti, M., Carta, M., & Fadda, B. (2012). Women and hysteria in the history of mental health. *Clinical, Practice and Epidemiology in Mental Health, 8*, 110–119. doi: 10.2174/17450790120801010.

Webster, J. (2015). Begin again: Hysteria as forgetting, repetition, and atonement. *European Journal of Psychoanalysis, 3*. Retrieved from www.journal-psychoanalysis.eu/category/ejp/number-3/

INDEX

Made in the USA
Las Vegas, NV
25 September 2021